The Chieu Hoi Saloon

A Novel

By

Michael Harris

authorHOUSE

1663 LIBERTY DRIVE, SUITE 200
BLOOMINGTON, INDIANA 47403
(800) 839-8640
www.authorhouse.com

First published by AuthorHouse 07/20/04

ISBN: 1-4184-3714-X (e)
ISBN: 1-4184-3713-1 (sc)
ISBN: 1-4184-3712-3 (dj)

Library of Congress Control Number: 2004093445

Printed in the United States of America
Bloomington, Indiana

This book is printed on acid-free paper.

To my wife, Takako, and my son, George;

And to Charlotte Vale Allen, Sybil Baker, Joan Campbell, Marguerite Costigan, Ezra Greenhouse, my sister Kathleen Harris, Jim Hayes, Wes Hughes, Paula Huston, Ly Thi Pfannenstiel, Gary Phillips, Myrtle Rucker, John Shannon, Marleen Wong and many others without whose help and encouragement this book couldn't have been written.

"…the dark plains of American sexual experience
where the bison still roam."

-- John Cheever

Part I

A year later, when it was Harry Hudson's blood on the floor of the Chieu Hoi Saloon, Mama Thuy remembered the first time she'd seen him – a big guy in a tweed jacket, helping Rita and Navy Swede mop somebody else's blood from around the legs of the pool table.

Rita, a barmaid who just before the fight had ducked into the ladies' room and done a line, gazed at Mama Thuy dreamily, thinking of the second after one Marine's cue had hit the other Marine on the left temple. Where the sunburned white skin was so thin you could see the veins through it. Little-boy skin. And the bones underneath were thin, too, Rita had read somewhere. Like tissue paper. The cue had made a hollow sound – though wasn't a head stuffed with brains and water and shit, without any empty space inside? But what really blew Rita's mind was that single second, when she stared at the skin where the cue had hit and saw nothing. Not a mark. Just skin. Glowing, perfectly white. Then, when the blood poured out, it seemed to spill from nowhere. *Far out*, Rita thought. She wanted to tell Mama Thuy about that, but Mama Thuy, coming in at midnight to close the place, wouldn't have the patience for it, Rita knew. *Seen enough bar fights in her time.*

So all she said, after the mess had been cleaned up, was *"Him."* Rita pointed her chin at the new guy. "Keep an eye on him. He come in here all happy, got himself a new job or somethin'. He was buyin' drinks for everybody. Then, *whoa*, all of a sudden he's cryin' and shit. Like he's a whole other person, man. Or crazy."

Or he's on something too, Rita thought.

#   #   #   #

1

At first, Mama Thuy hardly noticed the new guy. Just the blood -- threads and drops of it, and in one place a big red smear on the linoleum, mixed with suds and dirty water. She set her purse down on the bar. "What happen?"

"Couple Marines," Charlene said at the cash register. "One of 'em called the other one a faggot."

"Where they go? Take a taxi? Jesus, turn it down."

The thump of the jukebox made the base of her skull ache. She worked the remote switch herself, automatically, as she had seven nights a week for the last eight years. Hank Williams Jr., "There's a Tear in My Beer." Mama Thuy hated country music, but there was no way to get rid of it, not with her clientele. This song was one of Randy's favorites, and she checked for him down at the far end. Randy was asleep. Twenty-two years old, mental age about fifteen, sitting on his stool with one pimply cheek flat on the counter, still clutching a half-full glass.

"Wake up! Last call!" she yelled.

"Ron took 'em to St. Mary's, Mom," Rita was saying.

"Hurt bad?"

"Head wound," Navy Swede said, calm as usual. "Bled all over the place, but he'll be OK. Figured he'd better go to the emergency room, though, before he heads back to base."

"Ron was bein' an asshole again," Rita said.

"Too much water," Mama Thuy told the moppers. "You make too much work for yourself." Six years ago, in between marriages, she had lived with Ron for a month, and that mistake seemed destined to follow her forever. He hung around, looked sad, got drunk and mean, made trouble. "What they do, break another pool cue?" She sighed. "Why me?"

"B.J. was an asshole too," Charlene said.

"Tell me something new," Mama Thuy said. *"Wake up!"* she yelled again at Randy. He groaned and lifted his head, one end of his thin new mustache bent up like a spike. "Rita, you let Randy go to sleep? And Pop, too."

For nobody seemed to have noticed the grey-bearded man in the tattered black pea coat who was snoring at his table in a corner next to the shrine to the Buddha, his head tilted back against the wall. His breath through the tangled hole in his whiskers was poisonous.

Mama Thuy lit two sticks of incense. She thrust them into the forest of burned sticks on the altar, before the little fat golden statue. "Cops come in, we get another ticket," she told Rita. "All your fault."

Rita pouted. "Shit, Mom, this fight was goin' on, how'm I supposed to notice? Randy drinks too much."

"Pop, I call you a taxi, OK?" Mama Thuy said.

The old man blinked awake, coughed up phlegm, groped for the aluminum crutch beside his chair.

"Then stop serving Randy drinks, if he drinks too much," she said to Rita. "Where's your brain?"

Filipinas, she thought, not for the first time. Her friend Kim Lee, who owned a bar in San Diego, had caught a couple of her girls giving customers blow jobs in the back booths. Crazy! Like Rita. She was thirty-seven already-- the kind of girl who grew old but never grew up.

Lights on but nobody home.

"It's not my fault, Mom," Rita said.

"Then whose fault is it? They give me a ticket, they say my fault and I'm the one has to pay. You not the owner, you not the one responsible. I am."

She wondered if maybe it was time to fire Rita again. Was she back on cocaine, with her husband Walt's ship due in next month? *Heavy duty.* The trouble was, Rita brought in business. Flashed her tits a lot. Little tits, but it didn't matter. Guys liked her. Not like Charlene, who drove customers away with all her bitching.

Mama Thuy worked swiftly, automatically. She closed the Long Beach Boulevard door first, locking the folding metal screen outside and barring the door itself with a two-by-four. She wiped down the counter with a rag. She collected dirty glasses and ashtrays, filled a sink with hot water and detergent, plunged them in, washed them, set them clinking on the shelves behind the bar.

"Swede," she said. "Get me three cases of Bud, two cases of Miller, one case of Bud Light. OK, hon?"

Navy Swede, six-four and all muscle, went back into the storeroom. The new guy drifted after him.

"Pop," Mama Thuy said again. "You want a taxi?"

"Naw, I can make it," the old man said.

"You sure? I call you one."

3

Pop heaved himself slowly up, steadied himself on the edge of the table. He mumbled: "Sure as hell ain't gonna put it on my tab."

"I pay if I have to. Don't want you to get killed, Pop."

"Only three blocks," he said.

"Too many crazy people out there."

The old man hesitated. *Wants his hug,* Mama Thuy thought. She came out from behind the bar and put her arm gingerly around his waist. Pop stumbled into her--on purpose, she knew; the rubber tip of his crutch squeaked on the floor. His beard scratched like steel wool. He kneaded her shoulder, breathed crud into her face. Mama Thuy didn't flinch.

"Take care, Pop," she said. "See you tomorrow." She smiled narrowly. "Bright and early."

He left through the Anaheim Street door. The red velvet curtain flapped; traffic noise eddied in. Mama Thuy locked the screen there, too.

"OK, we closed," she said. "Everybody drink up!"

"And she would," Randy was saying, his voice shrill now that the music had stopped. "She *would* pay the taxi fare just so Pop wouldn't get mugged or run over. Even a smelly old fart like him." He said to the bar in general, belligerently: "Mom takes care of everybody. Even fuckups like me. That's why we love you, Mom. You're beautiful."

"Shut up, Randy," she said. "You think I want everybody to think I pay their taxi? No way, babe."

Swede and the new guy came back, lugging the cases of beer. Mama Thuy took each case in turn, ripped open the box, lifted the bottles out four at a time and jammed them into the ice chests under the counter. She smelled cheap perfume over the incense; Charlene was hovering behind her, waiting to talk.

"I need a ride," Charlene said sullenly. "Stanley went home."

"How come?"

"Oh, he's pissed at me, hates B.J. because he's black, and then B.J. just takes off, in *my* car...."

"You give him shit again?"

"He gives *me* shit, Mom."

Breaking open the last case, Mama Thuy could see Charlene's face without looking at it: the crooked teeth, the high forehead caked with powder, the close-set eyes rimmed with mascara that would run if she started crying.

4

"I told you, Charlene, you don't listen. When you single, don't put all your eggs on one man. Better have two or three. That's what I do." She winked at the new guy, who had sat down with his elbows on the counter, watching her.

"Stanley's just jealous. It's so fucking stupid. He's old as Pop, almost."

"B.J. got a wife in Norfolk, Virginia," Mama Thuy reminded her. "Wife or girlfriend, whatever. Got a kid." She turned to Rita. "Take off. We OK now."

"Got a party to go to," Rita said, shrugging into a new red leather coat. "*Ciao.*"

"Have a good one, huh?"

Party, Mama Thuy thought, unlocking the screen of the Anaheim Street door for her.

She switched off the outside lights, straightened the chairs by the tables and the stools along the bar. She collected the money from the cash register, the cigarette machine and the pool table and put it all in her purse. She checked Randy: nodding again but still awake.

"OK, everybody," she said. "Let's *go.*"

"I want to stay," the new guy said.

"Excuse me?"

"I--" he said and then stopped. "Here."

"You can't stay here. I lock up now. Go home."

"*In* here," he said. "I mean all night. He--" He gestured at Randy.

"I told him about the cot," Randy said.

"That was for Black Jimmy when he was caretakin'," Navy Swede said. "Or Walt when he had a few too many. Not just any stranger come wanderin' off the street."

"What your name?" Mama Thuy asked.

A simple enough question, she thought. But the new guy's plump, ruddy, sweat-shiny face suddenly went lopsided, as if a stroke had paralyzed half of it; he stared off at an angle toward a blinking Coors sign, and turned even redder. His mouth opened, but all he made was a hissing sound. Mama Thuy had to look at him, finally. It was one of the skills she had learned best over the years: how to serve a man beer, take his money, make change, even flirt with him, bend over behind the counter so he could look down the front of her blouse all the way to the navel, and never meet his eye, never let him break the bubble of concentration around her. How else could she have done it for so long? Now she *chose* to look. A big guy but soft, about forty, sandy-haired, wearing decent clothes, even a tie. A whole lot drunker than she had thought. Or sick.

Two for St. Mary's in one night?

"He said his name's Harry," Randy said.

"Hudson." It burst out gratefully, with a spray of spit. "Harry Hudson."

"I'm Thuy. I'm the owner," she said. "How can I let you stay here? Maybe you drink all my beer and wine, how do I know? I don't open up till eleven."

"I'm broke. I don't have any other p--" Harry Hudson glanced away again, as if he needed privacy to wrestle with the word. "Place."

"Hard to believe," Mama Thuy said.

"Spent it all here." He tried to grin. "I'll get paid Monday, though."

"You don't have a home? Wife and kids? You look like you married to me."

He shook his head, and she saw something else in his expression--not just shame but fear.

"Salvation Army got a shelter on Atlantic."

"He's a newspaperman," Randy said. "Gonna write an article about this bar."

"Better move along, buddy," Navy Swede said.

"Please," Harry Hudson said. His blue eyes were so naked now that it embarrassed her. "Just let me stay. I won't do anything. Believe me."

Mama Thuy studied him. Every instinct told her that he was a fool but basically harmless. Her instincts could be wrong--look at Ron!--but not often. She judged that he couldn't drink much more of her beer without passing out anyway. And somewhere in the back of her mind she was anxious. Ever since that night last spring when two Mexicans came at closing time and pointed their guns through the diamond mesh of the screen and told her sister, Phuong, to unlock it and one stuck the muzzle of his revolver right into Phuong's mouth, chipped a front tooth, while the other made Thuy hand over the money, she had wanted to get past this moment and into her car as fast as possible. Phuong wouldn't even work in the bar anymore.

Still, it surprised her a little to be telling him: "OK, but I gotta lock you in. Anything broken, you pay. You don't pay, I call the police."

Harry Hudson nodded. "You won't be sorry."

6

"I don't like it," Navy Swede said.

"We see," Mama Thuy said. Now that she had made up her mind, she didn't want to change it. "You can use the men's room," she said. "Black Jimmy leave a blanket in there, I think. Come on, Charlene." She switched off the inside lights. The many-colored beer signs died like an unplugged Christmas tree. She herded everybody out onto Anaheim Street except Harry Hudson, who stood by the pool table as if in a trance, arms hanging down. She shut the door on him and double-locked the screen.

Hope he doesn't puke in there, she thought.

"Fucking incredible," Charlene said. "You're too nice, Mom."

"No more," she said grimly. "From now on, no more Mr. Nice Guy. You watch."

Randy staggered off to the east. He lived in a garage somewhere near Orange Avenue. Swede still seemed pissed. Mama Thuy was glad to have him, though, as she and Charlene crossed the street to the parking lot of a Discount Tire Center. When Stanley or Walt was there, she had a bodyguard on either side. That was even better. The intersection stretched empty--too empty-- under the weird amber glow of the street lights. Her high heels clicked. The siren of a cop car wavered over by Atlantic. Now she felt for sure that she had made a mistake.

"Good night, hon," she told Navy Swede before he even had a chance to get any ideas. "Later, alligator."

He climbed into his four-wheel-drive Toyota pickup with lights mounted over the cab, she and Charlene into the red Porsche that her last husband, Wade, had bought her: license plate THUY 944.

#   #   #   #

That night, sleeping on the cot in the storeroom of the Chieu Hoi Saloon, Harry Hudson was spared the worst dream of all--the one in which he lay pinned to the chaise lounge by the swimming pool of the apartment complex in Garbersville, Oregon, unable to move, while his two-year-old daughter, Sally, wandered slowly but unstoppably toward the water; below the ruffles of her bathing suit (yellow with little blue flowers) were pink ovals on the backs of her thighs from lying on the hot concrete. This was only the second-worst dream--the one in which his squad waited in ambush at the edge of an old Michelin rubber plantation twenty klicks northwest of Phuoc Vinh.

7

It was December and dry, and big rusty leaves had fallen off the rubber trees, crackling when anyone moved, and it was cool enough to draw mist up out of the ground before dawn, when Harry Hudson saw a shadow materialize out of the field beyond and heard the squeak of a bicycle coming toward him. It was like a triple exposure. He knew he was dreaming this moment now, just as he knew then that he had dreamed it before, in one way or another, all his life. He opened his mouth, in Long Beach, in Vietnam, in all those other places, and nothing came out. Not a whisper. The muscles of his throat and tongue were rigid as boards. His lips numb. His cheeks and neck flushed with blood. He went out of himself then, as he often did, and came back after an indefinite time--a second? half an hour?--to panic. His mouth still frozen. In the dream the old man looked just like Ho Chi Minh, pointed straw hat, black pajamas, a wisp of white beard, though awake Harry Hudson could remember only his bony chest where the sights of the M-16 had pointed. In the dream he tried to hold the barrel down, but the rifle was flimsy, mostly plastic, lighter than air; it rose of its own will; he tried not to pull the trigger but it went off anyway, full automatic, and stitched the old man across that patch of withered brown skin and threw him off the bicycle. A calamitous noise, followed by a silence in which one wheel still spun and creaked and they suddenly realized that Charlie had been alerted for miles around, their whole night's wait wasted. Harry Hudson ran up with Sergeant Riker, whose words he had come to fear more than any words since his father's, right behind him, and saw that the old man had no gun, of course, nothing at all.

At that moment, with his entire being, Harry Hudson *chieu hoi*-ed. Gave up.

Riker looked at him for a long time, looked through him, then spat into the dust next to the old man's bare foot in its tire-tread sandal.

"Well, shit," he said.

#   #   #   #

Oct. 18, 1990

Harry,

Thank you, as usual, for the support check. (Why so much extra this time?) It couldn't have been easy for you during your job search, and I want you to know Kevin and I appreciate it.

There was a lady from Bend, Joan Pitcairn, at our Bible Fellowship last Wednesday who told how she had a near-death experience, just like in the Kübler-Ross book. She was being operated on for cancer in Portland, and she looked down and saw herself on the operating table. Then she went through a dark tunnel and came out in a meadow of beautiful wildflowers, and there was Jesus, with a brilliant light all around Him. He told her it wasn't her time yet and she had to go back to Earth, and she told us she was sorry to go, it was so peaceful and happy there.

What do you think, Harry? I used to think you had this terrible journalistic skepticism that kept you from believing, but now I think you were just too scared to reach out for anything you couldn't touch or see. Am I right? Never mind. I know near-death isn't the same as actually dying, but can't we take some comfort in this--that Sally might have gone to such a blessed place?

On second thought, don't answer that.

Still, God tells us to forgive, and I'm trying to find in my heart the strength to do that, though it's hard. When you left, to be honest, I was relieved more than anything, and when you never came to see Kevin after he was born, it only seemed appropriate. Do you blame me? But now that Kevin is Sally's age, I begin to wonder. He is your son. Shouldn't you have some kind of role in his life, besides just sending money?

Will you think about it anyway?

Seriously, Harry.

Deborah

# # # #

"Something's screwy here," the managing editor said. "This was supposed to be a one-week tryout, but you've been here ... four weeks already?"

Four weeks today, Harry Hudson wanted to say, but he thought it simpler just to nod.

"Has Steinbach said anything?"

"Not yet."

"Why the hell not, I wonder."

The managing editor's name was Robert Springer. Harry Hudson stood in front of his desk in a glass cubicle to the side of the newsroom of the Long Beach Clarion, the letter folded in his shirt pocket. It had been waiting in his temporary mail slot when he arrived for his twentieth 2-to-11 p.m. shift on the copy desk. The pain hidden in it had ambushed him. It blotted out the past two years, and for a moment he was still reaching down into that swimming pool in Garbersville where his daughter's slippery body floated beneath the surface. *Such a blessed place. Yes, please,* Harry Hudson prayed to the God his ex-wife somehow still believed in. *Make it be so. For my little girl's sake. Not for mine.*

And for that moment, when Springer called him in, he was as indifferent to authority as he had ever wished to be. Springer, neat and compact and balding, with horn-rimmed glasses, sleeves rolled up over black-haired forearms, fiddling with a rubber band, seemed far away, as if seen through a dusty window. *No older than I am,* Harry Hudson thought in mild amazement.

"Steinbach's supposed to make the call, not leave you and me hanging," Springer said. "He usually does. Why not this time?"

Because he knows, Harry Hudson thought, but he couldn't say that.

"We put you up the first week in the Queensway Hilton, right? Pretty nice digs. Where are you staying now?"

The Reef Hotel, Harry Hudson tried to say, but he managed only, "The R--." He backed up. "The R--. R--." That didn't work. He tried gliding into it. "Rrrreef Hotel." Barely. "On Elm Avenue."

"That's Skid Row, almost," Springer said. "Can't you afford any better?"

"N-not really. No."

He hoped that was enough, because it would take a long time, a lot of words, to explain why. Harry Hudson slowly woke up to danger. He wrenched himself away from Garbersville, the ache of his knees on the wet concrete, and tried to focus on Springer, but his mind skittered sideways. *That rubber band.* Wire editors used to tear stories from the teletype machines, roll them up and snap rubber bands around them. But now everything was computerized. What did they use rubber bands here for?

"It doesn't make *us* look good," Springer said.

My child support was due. Should he say that? He hated to let Springer know so much, but who could blame him for fulfilling his obligations? Nobody.

"M--," he said. Stuck again. Another glide: "Mmmmmmmm--" But he ran out of breath before the word came loose. He licked his lips. *Child support,* he tried to say, but the "Ch--" didn't budge either; no sound at all.

"Money?" Springer guessed. "You got your check?"

Harry Hudson nodded and grinned, but now his train of thought was broken. *Fine. No problem,* he wanted to say, but the "F--" was only a hiss, and how would he get back to *child support?*

"Flu?" Springer asked, frowning.

"No. I just didn't know the t--," Harry Hudson said. The first words of this new sentence came unexpectedly easily, sucked him in, then left him stranded. "T--." He wanted to say: --*town, so I picked the first place I could find.* But should he even bother with that? Should he try to say something else?

He felt his lips tremble, and sweat popped out all over his body.

"Then what's the matter?"

You know damn well, Harry Hudson thought, furious for an instant, then truly frightened. Time stretched on. He tried to imagine what he looked like to Springer--what kind of a spectacle he made. But Springer would never tell him. All his life, there had been this pact of silence that only the witless or the brutal violated. And Springer wasn't one of those.

"I-I'm fine," he finally said. "Really."

"This isn't fair to you, though," Springer said. "I'll talk to Steinbach this afternoon, OK? I guarantee you'll have an answer one way or another by the end of your shift. How's that? A deal?"

"OK," Harry Hudson said.

"When I talked to him the first week, I don't remember he had any complaints about your work, per se. Headlines, anything like that. He just said, 'This new guy, he doesn't *say* anything.'" It sounded like a joke, but Springer still frowned.

He thinks I'm a geek, Harry Hudson thought.

#   #   #   #

"Do my eyes deceive me?" Hank Steinbach, the executive news editor, had asked on the first of the twenty days, in a raucous voice that might have been cheer or jeer. He was Harry Hudson's contact on the Clarion--maybe his last chance at a decent job, after driving the length of California on the few wadded bills that were left of his savings. Steinbach knew the managing editor in Red Fork, up in the Sacramento Valley, where Harry Hudson had worked for the two years since Garbersville. The reporting slot in question had been filled, but Steinbach, almost as an afterthought, had let him take the Clarion's standardized copy editing test. Steinbach graded it at his desk, then looked up, miming surprise: "You can spell. You can punctuate. Rare abilities indeed, in this day and age." He was near retirement age, skinny and deeply danned, with wild white hair and a pockmark-ravaged face. He flashed a patently insincere

11

smile and pointed his nose at the ceiling, as if sniffing out something phony. "Let's give you a tryout on the rim, shall we?"

#   #   #   #

I had the world by the tail and never even knew it. I had *nice* things in Topeka, Kansas, a nice apartment, *real* nice furniture, a Buick Regal. Them car notes be killin' you, though. Hear what I'm sayin'? I was workin' two jobs, at Frito Lay and night shift at a nursing home, and poppin' that speed to keep up with it all. Then chillin' out smokin' weed on weekends. I never even thought of strip-dancin' or that other, goin' on the ho stroll. I had that work ethic then, just like my daddy always told me.

He had a stroke when I was sixteen. He worked for the city of Topeka, sanitation. He'd whup your ass if you got out of line, but I listened to my daddy. 'If you can't stay in school, get your G.E.D. at least,' he says. 'And don't *you* get pregnant when you're still in my house.' And I didn't. My daddy and me was close. I was the youngest girl. The baby. He was only fifty-three years old when he died, can you believe that?

But I hated that cold weather. I mean, that snow and wind and freezin' rain they get in Kansas in winter, ain't *nothin'* nice. And bein' where everbody knew my goddamn business, all my life. I got tired of it. That fool Darnell says, 'Kelly, let's go to California,' and like a bigger fool I went with him.

We first got into Hollywood in the middle of the night. I didn't know *where* we was. The motel we was stayin' in turned out to be one of them prostitution motels--short-timers goin' in and out all night right next door. Shit. We had to stay awake watchin' the U-Haul so nobody'd snatch anything. All them freakazoids goin' up and down the sidewalks all night--no tellin' *what* might be jumpin' off.

Next day we move in with Darnell's friend, I forget his name, but he had this bitch with him, twice my size, givin' me the evil eye. Tamika her name. They lived down around 77th and Hoover, *real* bad ground. This friend of Darnell's, he had the ardacity to be wantin' to put the moves on me, right in front of her. I tried to tell that Tamika, 'It ain't on *me*. He's all yours, ever greasy-ass bit of him,' but Tamika wasn't listenin', and I knew we had to get right on up out of there, or her and me was gonna get physical.

California peoples, they be *real* jealous, I believe.

12

# # # #

Harry Hudson had never worked on a big-city copy desk, but he felt strangely, immediately at home there. Maybe, he thought, fate had been steering him this way all along. He didn't have to interview anybody. He hardly had to talk. At night, with reporters and bosses gone, he and the other copy editors trimmed stories and wrote headlines undisturbed in an island of light at one end of the newsroom. No green eyeshades anymore, no pints of rye in desk drawers, but there was age-old tobacco stink in the air and cigarette burns like dark slugs on the carpet, and most of the phone calls they got were from crazies or drunks trying to settle a bet: *Hey, who had the most rebounds in an NBA game? Wilt? You're shittin' me. It's gotta be Russell.*

And almost everybody here had failed. That was clear, if surprising. Except for a couple of youngsters on the way up, the copy desk was a boneyard for newspaper people too old for reporting and judged unfit for management. Yet failure, they demonstrated, need not be the end. They lived on and joked and drew their paychecks--Spencer Lincoln, grey-templed and dignified, who owned two apartment houses in Wilmington but had been hit hard by divorce a dozen years ago and still shook his head as if trying to clear it; Andy McLachlan, a former British paratrooper who slipped across Pine Avenue to the Press Club every couple of hours for a "bracer"; Brad Pierce, who had a tramp yachtsman's windburned face and blue-water squint and still lived in a boat slip but had been beached here, apparently, for good.

And now Harry Hudson.

Rim rat.

The only trouble was Steinbach. He was legendary--a performer, a screamer. As deadline approached, he grew more and more tightly wired. Headlines and captions he might have OKd earlier in the evening he threw back at the copy editors--especially at Lincoln, who seemed to be his favorite victim--with gleeful scorn.

The worst came at the end, when they had to offer suggestions for the street edition banner: three or four words of 96-point type across the top of the front page.

"2 DIE IN GANG SLAYING," Lincoln said.

"Too long. Jesus, Spence, when you gonna learn? You have *die* and *slay* in there both."

"Well--"

"GANG HOLOCAUST," McLachlan said.

"I had an aunt die in the Holocaust. The *real* Holocaust. In Kielce, Poland, in 1944. No punk shootout deserves *that* word. Come on, Andy. Forget Fleet Street, just this once."

McLachlan flushed under his bushy eyebrows. "Damn it, Hank. If this *were* Fleet Street, I'd say, 'CRIPS CREAMED. BLOODS BLOODIED.' Something along those lines. I think I'm showing *admirable* restraint here."

"Brad?"

"2 GANG MEMBERS SLAIN?"

"Pedestrian. Jesus. What makes this different from the last two gangbangers that got banged, or the next two? How come I have to do this myself? We're running out of time."

"GANG WAR ERASES 2?" Lincoln mumbled.

"Holy shit." Steinbach bared his suspiciously perfect teeth. "The blackboard jungle, yet."

Harry Hudson's suggestions, when he made any, fared no better. Steinbach always wound up writing the banner himself. Meanwhile, Rick Holcomb, the slot man, who chain-smoked and suffered chest pains, pounded away at his terminal--the two of them working furiously, ostentatiously, while the rest could only sit. That was the most dangerous time. Harry Hudson was operating on fear alone. When he had nothing to do, the pulse of his adrenaline slowed. He got sleepy. It was a race, he knew--whether they would hire him before his lassitude became too noticeable: before he started finding himself in the men's room or the cafeteria or out in the hall without knowing how he got there, or simply scrolling through his computer the same story he had begun reading half an hour before, after which the fear would jolt him awake again.

# # # #

The Reef Hotel.

It was a block east of the Greyhound station: three stories of tan brick, with a couple of molting palms out front and no lobby at all--just a central staircase, painted battleship grey, and a desk clerk's cubbyhole to the left of the entrance. ROOMS FOR WORKING MEN, $65/WK., a classified ad in the Clarion had said.

The clerk had anchor tattoos on his arms, like a retired Navy petty officer. The sign over his shoulder said: NO DRUGS, BOOZE, WOMEN, PETS, COOKING ALLOWED. THIS MEANS YOU. Harry Hudson couldn't help but smile.

Was he still a working man? The morning before he checked in--the morning he had checked out of the Hilton--he wasn't sure. He had piled his belongings into his four-year-old Nissan hatchback, thinking he just might have to hit the road. But Payroll had cut him a check for the previous week, the computer system still let him sign on, and nobody said a word, not even Steinbach.

Harry Hudson thought of asking, but decided not to risk it. Wasn't this what he wanted, after all--to be noticed enough to get paid, but otherwise to be invisible?

On his dinner break, he drove over to the Reef and gave the dour ex-sailor a week's rent in advance. Then he felt a moment of panic. Besides the check, he had nothing left in the bank. If the Clarion cut him loose tomorrow, he would need every cent of it.

But after work, when he climbed to his third-floor room, he thought he might stay at the Reef forever. Here, as on the rim, he felt unmistakably at home. The stairs creaked, the woodwork had been painted so many times that it bubbled and flaked like rusted iron, toilets roared in the bathroom down the hall, but it wasn't Skid Row. It was clean. The faded pink bedspread had an L-shaped rip in it that somebody had mended by hand, with tiny stitches. Harry Hudson gazed at that for a long while. The room had a dresser, a lamp table, a straight-backed chair and a window that looked out past the trunk of one of the palms. A tropical touch. What better reef for flotsam like him to wash up on?

He stayed up reading a book that Holcomb had lent him:

Nov. 22, 1863

At break of day the pickets were drove in by rebel cavalry ... the companies were forming into line and getting ready for a fight. Rebels had us completely surrounded and soon began to fire volley after volley into our disorganized ranks.... Our men did well, and had there been plenty of officers and ammunition, we might have gained the day. After ten hours fighting we were obliged to surrender after having lost in killed over a hundred, and three or four times that number in wounded....

It was the diary of John L. Ransom, quartermaster sergeant, 9th Michigan Cavalry, captured in Tennessee at the age of twenty and held prisoner by the Confederates for most of the rest of the war, including several months at Andersonville, where he nearly died.

#   #   #   #

How could Holcomb have known?

The Civil War. Christ.

Sometimes kindness could scare him as much as criticism. Either way, people saw right through him and left him no place to hide. *Messengers,* he thought of them. Speaking like gods, telling him what he didn't want to hear. On the sixth shift, without any prompting, Holcomb had suddenly reached into his desk, held out the book and grinned. He had a dark mustache with a few threads of grey in it, a linebacker's body gone to fat. "You look like a reader," he said. "See what you think of this."

So Harry Hudson took it, and it sent him back to his English class at the high school in Beattie, Oregon, on the day they told him he had won the American Legion essay contest and Nancy Ishida, who should have won it, who was the best writer in school and a shoo-in for valedictorian, stared at him from across the room. The class must have been full--must have been pretty noisy, in fact--but he remembered only her sitting there, and silence. Her silhouette in the window. The cinder field outside. The pines. Beyond that, the tepee burner of the mill and the long eastern slope of the Cascades. Nancy Ishida usually favored browns and forest greens to set off her skin, but this day, Harry Hudson remembered, she wore black. A skirt and sweater to match her hair, a thin gold necklace. Her face seemed twice as pale as before, her eyes twice as dark. No girl had ever looked at him so intensely.

Angrily?

He wasn't sure. The topic had been "Our Bill of Rights: Guardian of Liberty." He had written the standard stuff. So why was he blushing and fidgeting under her gaze as if he had done something wrong?

Then, all at once, he knew. Other people's thoughts were usually as opaque to him as he imagined his to be transparent to them. But he knew, at that moment, with a thrill of certainty he had rarely felt about anything, that Nancy Ishida must have written something about her family.

They had owned land near Beattie once. A fair piece of land. They had truck-farmed and grown strawberries. Then, during World War II, they had been put in one of those internment camps, the one at Tule Lake, just over

16

the California border. They had lost the land. When the Ishidas came back, Nancy's father opened a nursery in town, and her mother substituted at the elementary school.

That was the whole story, as far as Beattie was concerned. And up until that moment, it had been the whole story for Harry Hudson, too. Hence his shame.

In the silence, he and Nancy Ishida seemed to communicate without saying a word.

Why did you all come back here? he asked.

And she answered, *Why not? It was home. Surely even you should be able to understand that.*

At the awards ceremony at the Legion Hall, he felt like a fraud. He wanted to tell the Army captain who had driven all the way from Bend that the words Nancy Ishida had written, however critical of how the Bill of Rights had been applied in her parents' case, were ten times braver and more genuine than his own. But--mercifully, for once--he couldn't speak. He smiled and nodded. He couldn't even look at the captain's face. He remembered the name tag, after all these years--BENJAMIN; the silver rifle of the Combat Infantryman's Badge; the rows of ribbons; the tailor-fit khaki dress shirt, ironed so crisply; the big hand sliding a heavy blue book into his: *Battles and Leaders of the Civil War.* That was all.

Later that night he surprised both himself and his father by asking about it.

"It was done for their own protection," his father said. "Feeling was running high then. You can't imagine it now. There could've been lynch mobs. Don't let anybody tell you different."

The fair, heavy face, much like the face Harry Hudson would eventually have, but grooved and furrowed more deeply in the kitchen's harsh light. The gleam of the oilcloth on the table. The pine boards of the company house smelling of pitch. A mosquito's whine.

Usually his father just laid down the law. But his surprise must have been great enough so that, for once, he said more.

"This Ishida girl's smart, I hear. She's got a ticket out of here no matter what. You'd think she had more sense, if you're right. There's people here--prominent people--who don't want to be reminded of how they got hold of that Ishida land. Not in the paper, in front of God and everybody, where they're gonna print your piece."

That confirmed it. An injustice *had* been done. Harry Hudson wanted to tell Nancy Ishida how sorry he was, how much he admired her. Meanwhile, he was reading his prize book: Mr. Lincoln's soldiers dying by the thousands and thousands in their great cause, to free the slaves; words that resounded with an antique valor; steel engravings of horses and flags and swords and drums.

It took nearly three months to build his courage up. Three months and a hundred missed chances, when he couldn't catch her alone long enough or his throat gulped shut or his stomach sank at the thought of even further offending Nancy Ishida, whom he had always liked, who had never made fun of his stuttering or otherwise treated him as a dork and a loser. What more could he ask of a girl? When the moment finally came, he couldn't remember when or where--indoors or out--or the expression on her face; only the thudding tumult in his own head.

"I'm s-sorry," he blurted out, with a stutterer's strange conviction that the other person, too, has kept the same thought in mind over any length of silence.

Nancy Ishida was startled.

"About wh--. Wh--." *What happened to your essay,* he wanted to say, but couldn't. "How they t--." *Treated your family,* he wanted to say. "T--" Blood buzzed in his ears. His fingertips felt heavy, swollen. He turned his face away, licked his lips ... then picked a word out of the air like his father wing-shooting a duck: "Legion."

"Oh, that," she said. "It doesn't matter. It wasn't your fault. I mean," she added with bitter edge to her voice he had never heard before, "it really *doesn't matter.*"

"But it does," Harry Hudson said. "I know what you wrote. I think--"

"Who told you? Oh, my God. It's bad enough without... They said it was confidential, but I should have known."

"It was," Harry Hudson said. "I d--." *--didn't know,* he meant to say. *I just guessed. I love you, that's why.* The blood was deafening now. This was one of the times he went clear out of himself; he came back to awareness spitting: "D--. D--."

"--laughingstock," she was saying.

"W-wrong," he managed, and relief sent him tumbling ahead, like a fall down a flight of stairs. "Wrong what they d-did to the Japs here."

"They were *citizens*," Nancy Ishida screamed. "Americans. Just like you."

She turned and hurried away, her long hair swinging. Harry Hudson stood, paralyzed, and watched her go. Fury stung his eyes--if people could see into his thoughts, he later remembered wondering, why not now? Or was it only his weak and evil thoughts they saw, and never the good ones? He knew better than to say *Jap*, and Nancy Ishida, his classmate since kindergarten, ought to know it, too. The word had slipped out, somehow ... so much confusion.

But his shame followed close behind. He *had* said *Jap*; he couldn't deny it. Had Nancy Ishida seen in him what he wanted more than anything to believe wasn't there--the prejudice that even the Grand Army of the Republic had been unable to kill?

Harry Hudson didn't know what to think. If he *was* prejudiced, he should hate Nancy Ishida for her "slanty eyes" and her "yellow skin," but her eyes were as level and clear as any other girl's, and her skin was flawless, without freckle or mole or blemish. When she brushed that hair back from her forehead or bent her slender neck over her desk to write with the concentration he so envied, pushing her sweater sleeve up to bare her wrist and forearm, her skin was as white as anybody's, if a slightly different shade, and luminous with soft blue veins. Her skin, he decided, was what he loved about her most of all.

#　#　#　#

"What do you think?" he asked Holcomb cautiously, aware that he was talking better than usual tonight, on the edge of spilling his guts. "This guy Ransom goes through stuff as bad as the twentieth century ever saw and never loses this ... purity. I don't know what other word. Decency. Optimism. Was it just the l-literary conventions of the time? Or were they really a whole d--? A whole different race of people then?"

Holcomb grunted. "A lot of it *was* convention. But this guy must have been exceptional, too, or he wouldn't have survived. And then you look at those Brady photographs, those deep, staring eyes on some of those folks, and you wonder.... Yeah, I know what you mean."

Holcomb was a transplanted Missourian, his square, bluff face half-hidden in cigarette smoke. His white shirt ballooned over his belt, stained with sweat under the armpits and dark-blue ink from a leaky pen in his pocket. He and Harry Hudson sat over coffee in the Denny's at Sixth Street and Long Beach Boulevard, long after the shift had ended.

"Nobody would write like that about Vietnam," Harry Hudson said. "N-no matter who he was. I mean--"

"You there?"

"Hell, I just drove a bus at Cam Ranh Bay."

Holcomb looked interested, if wary. He waited for more, but Harry Hudson was silent.

"Judy says it's funny about Vietnam vets," Holcomb said finally. Judy was his wife; she wrote features for the Lifestyle section. "How they don't want to talk about it, not even to each other. How they don't even *recognize* each other. But, shit, who cares anymore? We're out of fashion now. If we were ever in."

The coffee was good. The night was calm, except for panhandlers huddling in the foggy yellow light under the street lamps, which didn't illuminate much of anything but muddied all the shadow colors. Harry Hudson had never seen so many homeless people before. *Like Calcutta,* he thought. And Holcomb was so obviously a nice guy. *You look like a reader.* Harry Hudson filled his lungs with air; he decided to take a chance.

"Steinbach," he said. "What's the story?"

"What story?"

"The way he acts. *Is* it an act?"

A mistake. Holcomb frowned, all slot man again. "Partly an act, sure. But figure it. He's from the old school. A damn good newsman in his day. The way this business is changing--all flash and glitz, color graphics, *factoids,* he calls 'em, USA Today stuff--it makes him sick. I can't say as I blame him."

Harry Hudson pulled back. "I guess not."

What he had been trying to ask was: *Why won't Steinbach make up his mind?* But wasn't the answer clear enough? *He's seen every kind of journeyman, bum, fake and head case come through here in the last twenty years. He knows there's something about you, and he's waiting to see what it is.*

"Are those his real teeth?" Harry Hudson asked.

"Uh-uh. Got 'em knocked out boxing Golden Gloves as a kid in Philadelphia. So he says. Who's left to say he's a liar?"

They laughed. Holcomb lit another cigarette and looked out the window.

"Closing time," he said. "For the bars. There used to be a place called the Haven, across from the post office, not far from where you're staying. In fact, the same block as Acres of Books, where I got ol' Ransom. Best used bookstore in town. I've had months I spent two hundred dollars there. Three hundred. Judy says she wishes I was a compulsive gambler or something; it'd cost less. Got books stacked all over the place. You want any more, just holler. Anyway, the Haven was a, what do you call it, transvestite, transsexual bar. Long Beach has a big gay community, got lots of political clout--the Lambda Democratic Club and so forth--but this was what you might call the fringe. I bet you never saw anything like it in Oregon. Then again, maybe you did."

"No."

"Things are changing everywhere. Anyway, we'd come over here for coffee, and when the Haven closed they'd come up the boulevard for coffee too. Guys dressed like women, made up, with wigs and high heels, I mean *beautiful* women, some of 'em, though they all stood about six-two. Some had silicone boobs, and some had been taking female hormones, you know, to get *real* boobs. The pre-ops. And then some had gone all the way and had sex-change operations, got artificial pussies built, the works. It was fascinating, it really was. I talked to some of 'em--how all their lives they'd always felt deep down inside they were women. A whole different world."

Holcomb signaled the waitress for a refill.

"Anyway," he said, "they shut the Haven down a couple of years ago. Liquor-law violations, supposedly, but you know damn well it was the AIDS scare. Never seen any of those people again. I kind of miss 'em, you know? Judy would freak out, but they gave the city a little color. I wonder where they've all gone. I always did wonder what they'd do when they got old--even what they did in the daytime. I mean, what kind of job can a guy go to with boobs on?"

"Sounds like a s-story," Harry Hudson said.

Or a Vance Foster column, he thought.

#   #   #   #

Before Long Beach, we lived in a lot of places. Manhattan Beach for a while, but ooh wee, that was *expensive*. Lynwood. Inglewood. We figured we both could work in them convalescent hospitals, but the cost of living out here is *real* high. Darnell had a tougher time than I did findin' jobs. Then, what

21

he did make, he blew on weed or acid, or even sherm. Don't let anybody tell you makin' love on acid ain't a trip. It blow your mind. That sherm, though, that angel dust, ain't *nothin'* nice. The devil's always busy, my mama used to say, and the devil's in that sherm, you listenin' to me? Turn you into some kind of zombie. Darnell always *was* violent--he had that streak in him, just like my brother Eugene--but that sherm brought it out in him. Bad.

I liked workin' in them convalescent places if they gave me a good run, without too much heavy liftin'. Some of them old peoples, they can't turn theyselves over, even. You gotta help 'em into the shower and scrub they backs for 'em and then help 'em back into bed. And they *heavy*, sometimes. I've always been kind of petite. But them old peoples be a trip, you hear what I'm sayin'? They liked me. I could get most any of 'em to laugh if I put my mind to it. Like my mama said, someday that's gonna be *you*, Jesus willin'. So I did my best. I really did. Laughter be good for 'em, those that still got they marbles-- not them others, that's gone senile. Lord, if I ever get that way, take me out and shoot me. *That* ain't bein' alive. Like this lady I hurt my back on--three hundred pounds, she must've weighed, all floppy dead weight.

The lawyer ads, you seen 'em on TV. Mean-lookin' brother been in a car crash, sayin', *Wallace P. Kocsis got me one point eight million*, like he had a mouth full of mush. So I called him up. Sued the hospital when they wouldn't change my run, give me somethin' easier. Then, when I sued, they went and fired my ass. So Wallace P. Kocsis was gonna get me money for *that*, too, and it looked like we had a nice little settlement goin'--five or six thousand dollars, he said, maybe more--until this insurance man took a picture of me strip-dancin' at the Silver Slipper in Gardena. Shit. I thought he was just a customer. Said how in hell could I have a bad back when I'm shakin' my booty all over the stage in a G-string and pasties?

I mean, what choice did I have? I had bills to pay, you hear what I'm sayin'? And strip-dancin' paid off them bills a whole lot faster than workin' in convalescent hospitals at five bucks an hour. Darnell didn't happen to be employed at that time either. My back still pops in and out on me now and then--never been quite right since.

#   #   #   #

On the way back to the Reef, Harry Hudson stopped at the corner of Long Beach Boulevard and Third Street, where the Haven had been. A liquor and convenience store now. Still, Holcomb's talk had stirred him, brought back the taste of those furtive trips to Portland before he had married Deborah, and then again afterward. A charred taste in his mouth. A taste of danger, of the dark, of theater seats exhaling stale smoke, of the neon signs of certain bars and hotels burning in the damp air down by the riverfront.

Harry Hudson fought it, as he had fought his thirst for whiskey in the first few years after Vietnam, the first weeks after running away to Red Fork. He told himself wearily that he had no right to look at a woman, even a naked picture of one, ever again. But tonight, at last, the impulse won. He bought a sex paper called the Sun at a newsrack in front of the post office and took it up to his room.

He had read such things before, a few times, but without relating them to himself. His stays in Portland rarely even lasted overnight. It was as if he were reading about Hottentots or aliens from space. Here, though, in the L.A. Basin, these swingers, freaks, exhibitionists, whatever, were near, maybe living on the same block. He could meet them if he wanted. Big cities *were* different, he realized; they had a place for people like that. For Harry Hudson too, maybe. A place that had been waiting for him all his life, the way basic training had waited for him ever since he had been born a boy--lying in ambush for him, the way Sergeant Riker had.

Cajun spice!! She-male, honey-skinned beauty, 5-8, 125 lbs., 36-23-35, 9 1/2 hot, fully functional inches....

There were dozens of ads like this--a quick answer to Holcomb's question about what these people did for jobs. Harry Hudson shook his head. *Things are changing everywhere.* Papers like the Sun had changed, for sure. This issue had pages and pages of ads for phone-sex services, women selling photos and panties, obvious hookers, but only now and then an ad from what seemed to be an ordinary person:

Handyman will fix autos, plumbing, electrical, heating, just about anything. Payment just some sweet love making. Will go to L.A., beach cities, west San Gabriel Valley, north Orange Co. Please, women only....

And even more rarely an ad from the kind of people, he recalled, who used to dominate these pages:

Hi! We are a young straight or bi cpl. seeking horny folks that like to be video taped as we all have fun nasty sex. Cpls. or bi ladies only. No single men, fatties or weirdos. Don't be camera shy! We are trim, attrac. and disease free, U B too. Race is open. Photo and phone a must....

No single men. Harry Hudson wondered whom these folks would consider a "weirdo." But the answer to this, too, was clear: *Him.* He was a weirdo because he was alone and sitting on his bed in a place like the Reef and reading their ad. The sudden, feverish excitement ebbed out of him then; the sleepiness flowed back. Harry Hudson yawned and put the paper down. He went to the window, rubbed his stubbly cheeks, leaned on the sill and felt the blood pump into his hands. His body felt thicker than it used to be, awkward and bearlike. Past the trunk of the palm, he saw the towers of City Hall and the World Trade Center gleam through the fog. Beyond them, invisible, were the Naval Station and the harbor. Just across the street were parking lots and big old shingled bungalows that had been split up into apartments.

What was he doing here?

He tried to imagine Deborah--never a Debbie, even when she was younger--posing in a grainy photograph, legs spread, fingering her crotch for thousands of strangers to see, a wide black line hiding her eyes, but he couldn't do it--his mind stuck, the way words stuck in his throat.

To punish himself, he thought of Sally and let the guilt, always waiting, hit him and double him over with pain.

My little girl.

Harry Hudson picked up the Sun again. Did the city really have a place for him? No, he decided. Just a place for his money, what little there was of it.

Still, one ad caught his eye:
THE RABBIT HUTCH
Cocktails and Dancing
Swingers welcome Thurs., Fri., Sat. from 9 p.m.
Couples free, singles $5 cover
Rosecrans & Valley View, La Mirada
Behind Pep Boys

Then, to punish himself further, he read more of John Ransom's diary:

Richmond, Va., Dec. 20, 1863

James River frozen nearly over, and rebels say it has not been so cold for years as at the present time. There are hundreds with frozen feet, ears, hands &c., and laying all over the prison; and the suffering is terrible....

Jan. 25, 1864

Being in this place brings out a man for just what he is worth. Those whom we expect the most from in the way of braving hardships and dangers, prove to be nobody at all. And very often those whom we expect the least from prove to be heroes every inch of them....

#　#　#　#

Vance Foster.

He was the first hero Harry Hudson had ever had, not counting Sydney Carton, who had lived and died only in a book. He read *A Tale of Two Cities* in the same English class where Nancy Ishida had stared at him. The old story was his chief source of comfort in those months when he wished desperately for some way to make it up to her, to earn her forgiveness. Sydney Carton gave him hope. He could be the loner he was, it seemed, timid and voiceless; worse, he could grow up to be a drunk and a failure, and still his life had full redemption value, once he made up his mind to sacrifice it. He could win, in one moment of courage, everything he had lost or never even had the guts to try for. He wouldn't get Nancy Ishida, of course--any more than Sydney Carton had gotten *his* girl, Lucie Manette--but she would love him because he had gone to the guillotine in her husband's place. *I see her ... weeping for me on the anniversary of this day.*

Because he was also reading the book he had won in the essay contest, Harry Hudson's fantasies of the French Revolution soon got mixed up with the Civil War. The South--unfairly, it seemed to him--could claim most of the brilliance, the dashing feats of tactics. Mr. Lincoln's soldiers, he had to admit, had won largely through sheer weight of numbers. When he daydreamed, he pictured some battle so hopeless that this advantage was more than canceled out. The six assaults on Marye's Heights at Fredericksburg. Bloody Lane at Antietam. The doomed federals pinning notes with their names and addresses on their uniforms before charging at Cold Harbor.

Over time, this picture in his mind grew detailed, fixed. Harry Hudson imagined himself walking in a long line of men across a corn- or wheatfield, still gangly then, a hot sun on his back, a heavy musket in his soft modern hands that would tear and bleed if he tried to bayonet somebody, but he wouldn't have to do that; he would just have to walk, in a terrible noise and clouds of black-powder smoke, yellow stubble crackling under his feet, one foot after the other, for a few hundred yards. Couldn't he do that? Couldn't even Harry Hudson do that? Even when the minie balls whistled in on them and the men on either side of him jerked and fell? Even then? Wasn't that what boys were raised for, when you came right down to it? Wasn't that why he had joined the Scouts and played football (jayvees, anyway) and taken the NRA hunter's safety course from old Harley Stoffel, who had a brass ball joint in his shoulder, everyone said, from being shot in the woods by accident, so that his own father could roust him out at dawn during deer season? Wasn't that it? Wasn't that the reason for old men's winks, the grimness of their smiles? The not-quite secret behind everything? Any boy might have to be a soldier.

Harry Hudson practiced it, out in a stand of Ponderosa pines behind the house in Beattie where his father's anger compressed the air inside so that he could hardly breathe. He walked and dreamed. Even as a teen-ager, he was drowsy. What crackled under his tennis shoes there were pine needles; he imagined himself, if he survived the charge, telling people: "I just tried to pretend I was back home. And, you know, I swear I could smell those pine trees." Because he wouldn't be afraid. Not then. Not for the few minutes it would take him to walk those few hundred yards. Surely, that would be his reward for giving up his life: a trancelike calm when, like Sydney Carton, he would feel *the strong tide, so swift, so deep, and certain ... like a congenial friend.* Because even if he did survive, he wouldn't have expected to. Wasn't that fair?

The fantasies never quite went away. Even now, in Long Beach, at odd moments, he imagined bullets flying past him.

And in those fifteen years in Garbersville after he came home from Vietnam, if someone had caught Harry Hudson unguarded or drunk enough and asked him what he was doing, he might have answered: *Waiting for Nancy Ishida to come back.*

# # # #

Me strip-dancin' made Darnell jealous, too, even though it was his idea at first. Because the customers liked me there at that Silver Slipper, them other places. I was perky, they said. I had that perky personality. I mean, I got *good* tips. This was back before a lot of them places went to all-nude and made you do that table-dancin' shit, where you be sittin' in the customers' laps, practically, and they be tryin' to grope your ass. You hear what I'm sayin'? And you could do OK with the body the good Lord gave you, even if your tits wasn't the biggest, if they had a nice shape. Now, shit. If you ain't had a boob job done and got 44 triple-Ds on you, at least, you might as well quit.

Like I told Darnell, 'You ain't got no dog with you. Remember that, fool, the way you been treatin' me. I can turn other men's eyes just like *that* if I put my mind to it.' But it wasn't easy, dancin' in them strip clubs. It was *embarrassin'*, you hear me? Takin' my clothes off in front of a bunch of strangers. I never got used to it--not all the way. I couldn't do it, most of the time, lessen I had me a good shot of vodka and orange juice first. *Two* shots of vodka. Because it's one thing if you dance *to* somebody and do all them sexy moves--somebody you care about, I mean--but just standin' up on stage and doin' it to the whole wide world, that's somethin' else.

#   #   #   #

Vance Foster's columns pointed to a different answer--a heroism of words, here and now.

In 1965, the summer after the American Legion essay contest, the columns began appearing twice weekly in the newspaper in Garbersville, twenty miles north of Beattie and ten times the size. They ran for four or five years. Vance Foster was from Seattle, people said--retired after two decades as a political reporter at the Post-Intelligencer. He moved into an A-frame on a mountain above Garbersville and mailed in whatever he wrote about the war, about welfare people who lived out of sight in trailers in the woods, about water pollution, about Negroes and Indians and migrant apple-pickers. *About the camps for the Japanese.* About clear-cutting--which stung Harry Hudson's father, who by then was a foreman at the lumber mill in Beattie.

"He's a goddamned Red. And not like the old Reds, either, not like the Wobblies. Vance Foster doesn't give a hoot about the working man."

But isn't he right? Harry Hudson wanted to ask. *Don't you say yourself we can't keep cutting timber at this rate?*

"B--," he said and made a face, and his father read his mind.

"Even an asshole can be right once in a while. But that doesn't mean he's not still an asshole. Because, listen up. A man can be right for the wrong reasons. You understand me? Vance Foster's an outsider. He came in here and started pokin' fun at things people hold sacred, God and country, and for him it's just a game. Well, it's not. I'm as much for sustainable yield as the next man, but not if it costs me my job--and that sonofabitch would take *all* our jobs away as soon as spit."

Harry Hudson nodded, as always, and lowered his eyes. Some of what Vance Foster wrote bothered him, too. Who could believe, for instance, that the nuclear plant at Hanford, Washington, was poisoning everybody downwind and the federal government was hushing it up? That was crazy. He agreed with his father there. The line drawing above the neat blocks of type in the Garbersville Logger gave Vance Foster lean, regular features and a fedora tilted arrogantly over one eye, like The Shadow. An outsider for sure. But the Nancy Ishida business had been the first crack, the first breeze moving in that silent house stifling with the smells of pine, rubber boots, stale food, varnish, leather, wet wool and fear--the first sign that his father could be wrong. Harry Hudson began to entertain other doubts.

Then, in the fall of '65, when he had gone off to the university at Eugene and Nancy Ishida had taken her scholarship to Stanford, the columns about the Japanese-Americans' campaign for reparations ran in the Logger. Vance Foster went into the history of it. The words *Tule Lake* appeared in print, along with others Harry Hudson hadn't heard of before. *Manzanar. Heart Mountain.* Angry letters to the editor pelted in. His father mailed him clippings marked with red ink--meaning what? *You had a point after all* or *See what an asshole I told you he was?* No other comment. Harry Hudson refolded the clippings and sent them on to Nancy Ishida, though her parents must have done the same, and she thanked him politely, if coolly. "I've decided to major in journalism," he wrote in a second letter that she--perhaps sensing that this meant *I love you*--didn't answer.

\#　\#　\#　\#

"You stammer, I notice," Andy McLachlan said.

They sat in the Press Club, over the one beer Harry Hudson allowed himself each evening. A dark, cavelike place--no way to tell how dirty unless the roof were lifted off. He imagined old Clarion regulars and cockroaches alike scattering from the light.

"No need to be ashamed, lad. By God, I was twice as bad as you ever were. Couldn't make a bloody sound. Just spit in people's faces, sprayed 'em like a bloody seltzer bottle, I did. Till this sergeant I had in the Special Air Services--like your Green Berets--great brute of a chap, had us all quaking in our boots, came up to me on his first inspection--"

Like Riker, he thought.

"--and asked some question or other about the drill, you know, and all I could do was stand there and spit at him like a bloody alley cat. I thought, oh shit, I'm buggered for sure. Man truly put the fear of God in you, he did. Osborne, his name was. He thought I was having some fun with him, you see. A wise-arse. His ears turned red and he shoved his face into mine and says, 'Bugger *that* noise. What's your name?', though he knew what my name was perfectly well. It took me about ten minutes to get 'McLachlan' out, in a whisper. By then he knew what was up. 'What's that? I can't *hear* you,' he says. 'Louder.' This went on, I don't know how many times. I bloody well thought I'd die. Till I was screaming 'McLACHLAN' at the top of my lungs, and then he grinned, just a little, and says, 'That's better, lad. Now, remember this: No more whisperin'. From now on I want you to *shout*, whether it comes out or not. No fuckin' around with it.' And strange to say, that turned out to be the answer--at least for me. You'll never guess."

"What?" Harry Hudson asked.

"Osborne himself had used to be a stammerer. He told me later. Bloody awful, he said. He went at it like the old Greek, Demosthenes--put pebbles in his mouth. And shouted. Worked on it that way for years and years, he said, but there wasn't a sign of it when I knew him. So there you are."

This was kindness, Harry Hudson knew. This couldn't be easy for McLachlan--watery blue eyes, broken veins in his nose, shaggy brows nicked by frown marks as if by a hatchet. A massive, mottled forearm on the bar. Reliving old embarrassment and risking more, if Harry Hudson should choose to ask: *So how come you wound up here, soused every night? After the miracle, what went wrong?* He tried to smile, to feel the appropriate gratitude, but couldn't. He had met ex-stutterers before. A scout for the Seattle Mariners who had recited "Mary Had a Little Lamb" over and over until the blockage in his throat melted. A Garbersville city councilman who had done it by singing. Each eager to pass on the cure. Each a messenger, confirming that Harry Hudson, now and forever, was *not* cured.

He drained his beer.

"Here, lad, have another one. What's your hurry?"

"Gotta get back. I'm still on p--." *Probation,* he wanted to say.

"Oh, forget Hank. He's all bark, believe me."

"R-really." He lurched up, fumbled for coins.

"Damn it, Harry." McLachlan was angry now. "Sit back down and have another, for Chrissake."

Harry Hudson fled.

# # # #

"The psychology of it, I think, is what we want to get away from," Dr. Richardson said. "We have a behavioral orientation here, as I've told you. But just for the record, how do *you* think it started?"

An evil spirit, Harry Hudson thought.

Outside, on the campus with its hundred-year-old Douglas firs, the rain dripped--the soft, endless rain of this green, sweet-smelling, almost snowless country on the western side of the mountains.

"W-well," he said. "I don't know. M-my dad, maybe."

Click. Click.

There had been voices once, he remembered. Loud voices, sometimes affectionate, sometimes angry, but enough to fill the house in Beattie. Then, when he was seven, his mother died of cancer. Silence followed--his own and his father's. They collaborated. His father's silence came from the same source, whatever it was, that used to make him yell; he could still speak, and speak bitterly, if provoked: words that stung like the slash of his leather belt. So Harry Hudson held his breath, trying not to provoke him. He hid in books, in the woods. He *forgot how to talk*--that was how it seemed to him now.

Dr. Richardson smiled--this crew-cut youngish man with a long face, a grooved tip to his nose. "It's possible," he said gently. "But usually, a kid gets stuck at some halfway point in the speech-learning process, where *everybody* stutters, and never grows out of it. If too much attention is paid to his dysfluency, for instance...."

"B-but why d--."

Click.

Every time he stuttered, there in the university speech clinic, Dr. Richardson clicked a hand-held counter. Every time he spoke correctly, Dr. Richardson said, "Good." That was part of the therapy. Grey light from the window shone in Dr. Richardson's wire-rimmed glasses; the nail of the thumb working the counter was broad and spatulate.

"Who knows? Research is still going on. It could be hereditary in part. Some think the right and left hemispheres of your brain might be wired together differently than most people's. That looks promising, but it's way too early to say. Does it matter that much?"

Harry Hudson nodded.

"Why?"

"*W-why?* My God."

Click.

It astonished him, this question. Suppose you had an evil spirit in *you*, he wanted to ask--one that could let one word slide out easily, as if greased, and make the next word as immovable as a boulder; one that twisted your vocal cords and overrode every effort of your mind and will; one that made you seem scared and stupid even when you weren't, until you became as stupid and scared as you seemed? Wouldn't *you* want to know why?

A very rare thing: he, Harry Hudson, was angry.

"Dddon'tyyoouthiinkit'smmm," he said. "Immmp--."

This was the other part of the therapy--to slur words together slowly and rhythmically, then speed up by increments.

Click. "Don't repeat, Harry. Slow down."

"Iimmmportantffoorr*me*toknnnoww?"

"Good."

Harry Hudson glared at him. Dr. Richardson sighed.

"Speech therapists used to go into all that," he said. "The pathology of it all. They forced their clients to go up to strangers and say, 'I'm a stutterer,' to lessen their sensitivity, you know. They told them to stutter on purpose, so they wouldn't even try to hide it. I don't do that. I teach fluency, not stuttering. Think about it, Harry. Why are you here in the first place?"

To get a voice like Vance Foster's, he thought, for he had realized in Eugene that this was nothing less than the voice of the greater world. Most of his professors and many of the brighter students had it. A voice that jabbed at the powers that were and danced away to jab again; a fearless voice but also one of sophisticated mockery. A stronger voice than his father's, at last.

"How do you and your dad get along these days?" Dr. Richardson asked, gently again.

"N-not good. Heeesstillssscaresthesss--" He licked his lips.

Click.

"--ssshitooutoofmmme."

It shocked him to have said it out loud.

"Good," Dr. Richardson said.

31

# # # #

The cure half worked. It didn't kill the creature inside him but lulled it to sleep. He could talk without stuttering much if he slid ahead very carefully, as if walking on skis, and if no pressure was put on him. For about six months, he teetered and wobbled. Always before, it was the stuttering that people heard and the voice in his head, the Vance Foster voice--his *real* voice, he liked to think--that was hidden. Now, half the time, it was this slow, disappointing but passable fluency that people heard and the stuttering that lay just below the surface, ready to leap out and betray him at any moment. Life got complicated. His two selves flipped back and forth a dozen times a day.

Still, for another six months Harry Hudson kept on speaking better and better, though he didn't understand why. It was as thrilling and dubious as magic. It got good enough so that people *did* treat him differently, he noticed, even girls, despite all he had been told over the years by classmates or well-meaning adults to the effect that his speech didn't matter. That was a lie. He felt another surge of anger, even as he wondered giddily what would happen if his progress continued.

But it didn't. Dr. Richardson's method, it turned out, had a built-in trap. The better he spoke, the more he was tempted to speak automatically, the way normal people did, and that was fatal. The creature woke up, reached out an exploratory claw and touched his throat. Just an occasional word at first--he could hide it and fool the people he was talking with, even fool himself; but then more and more, and once it began to go slowly bad there was no stopping it.

Then his father died. A brain aneurysm. Harry Hudson rode the train back over the Cascades to Beattie on a muddy spring day and bought flowers for the funeral at Ishida's Garden Shop. Nancy's father said he was sorry. A short man with dirt permanently worked into his fingers; a man with sparse hair and a smooth, flat face who wore a quilted vest even indoors. "Nancy, too, of course," he said.

"Hhow is sshe?" Harry Hudson asked in his new voice. "Ddoing, I mean?"

"Oh, fine, fine," Mr. Ishida said. "Doing very well. She's so interested in these mechanical brain machines--computers. They're working on some kind of new language, they call it, with punch cards. I don't understand it, but she says it's fascinating. That's what she wants to go into."

"I ssee," Harry Hudson said. What he wanted to ask was: *Is she ever coming back?* And Mr. Ishida, like his father, seemed to read his mind.

"A lot of rich people down there. California. It's exciting, I guess. How do you get 'em back on the farm after that, eh?"

Mr. Ishida's glasses, like Dr. Richardson's, reflected light back like a barrier. His face showed nothing of what it had been like to go to that camp, just as his father's heavy face in the casket showed nothing of the tiny explosion behind it that had rent his brain. The folds of his father's flesh seemed dense as wax. A strong, repellent force pushed out from it, like an odor that only Harry Hudson could smell.

He turned away.

The lumber company would reclaim the house. He walked through it for the last time carrying a folded copy of the Garbersville Logger with the obit and Vance Foster's latest antiwar outburst. When his father was alive, there hadn't seemed to be space for them in the charged air to pass each other without brushing shoulders; now the musty rooms were echoing and huge. He wished he could feel more. His father hadn't used the belt so often, he thought. Raising a boy alone couldn't have been easy--especially a boy like him. Most of his father's savings had gone to send him to college. Harry Hudson realized that he hadn't known the man at all. He had closed his eyes years ago, as a stutterer does in a full block, when even stamping his foot won't shake the word loose and he must go deep into himself to grapple with it; when he believes--when he *must* believe--that his listener and all the rest of the universe will wait for him. Someday, he had thought, he would open his eyes and speak to his father, but now his father was gone.

#   #   #   #

Back in Eugene, he lost interest in school. It was 1967. The voice of the campus had long since decreed that the war in Vietnam was wrong, and Vance Foster's voice said, *Now is the time to stand up for what you believe, loud and clear,* but without his father's voice opposing them, he didn't know what he believed. He was alone in the world. It did no good, he discovered, to have a voice of your own if you had nothing to say. The only voice left in him was Sydney Carton's, saying, *Bad war or good, who are you to judge it? This is your chance to do a far, far better thing....* At the end of his sophomore year, Harry Hudson dropped out. He lost his student deferment, gave himself up to the draft.

#   #   #   #

Sergeant Riker.

He was twenty-two years old in the fall of '68, two years older than Harry Hudson, though it might as well have been a hundred. An Oklahoman who rolled his own cigarettes and spat sideways for punctuation; lean and stringy, in contrast with Harry Hudson's fair, smooth flesh; all sun-hardened vein and bone-end and sinew, with a brass Montagnard bracelet on one wrist and the blue tendrils of a dragon tattoo curling down the other and NAM SUCKS inked across the back of his helmet liner. A thin half-smile. A smell of sweat and tobacco and jungle rot. And a voice. A hoarse, obscene voice that, to Harry Hudson's dismay --but not to his surprise, not anymore, not after basic training and infantry school--drowned out the voice of the campus just as the voice of the campus had once drowned out his father's. What you had to say, it seemed, didn't matter--only the force of conviction behind it.

Dipshit.

They teach you to tie your shoes in that college, Hudson, or they wait for graduate school?

Move it, move it.

You call that deep enough? Keep on diggin' till I tell you.

Close it up, for Chrissake.

Strip that fuckin' rifle again, get that crap out, or next time I'll ream your ass with it. Fuckers jam enough as it is.

You awake, Hudson? I said move it.

Them claymores set right side out? They better be. I gotta go out there and check 'em, you better wish I hadn't.

What's that?

Sorry-ass motherfucker. I got news for you. There's no mommies out here and no IGs and no fuckin' Congressmen. There's just me. I'm your mommy and your daddy both. Understand?

Just keep diggin'.

What's that again, Hudson? Spit it out.

Dipshit.

34

By then it was eight months after the Tet Offensive, after the A Shau Valley campaign and Khe Sanh. The enemy was lying low, hard to find. Patrols through the forests and swamps drew, at most, sniper fire. In the single month Harry Hudson spent in the field, there was never a long line of men to be part of, nothing that could be called a charge, no moment that said: *This is it. This is what you've been waiting for.* No moment, in fact, seemed more or less dangerous than any other. Just red dust and paddy water, itch and bugs and weariness, heat that bleached the sky and rippled the tree lines in the distance, humidity that softened the wax in his ears and made him half-deaf as well as half-dumb. For all of Riker's riding him, he felt himself drift back to sleep.

The morning Harry Hudson killed the old man outside Phuoc Vinh was much like the mornings he had gone hunting with his father, when even the dawn chill and the smells of gun oil and bacon and woodsmoke weren't quite enough to wake him up out of his confusion. All he knew then was that he would see no deer, that he would anger his father by crashing too loudly through the brush, and that he would be lucky not to shoot them both crossing a barbed-wire fence, despite Harley Stoffel's instruction. It was fated. And so, too, was the way he raised the M-16 in his drowsiness and fear and pulled the trigger. All his practice in the pine grove behind the house in Beattie had been to make conscious heroism a reflex, but this reflex was mindless; it rose out of the empty place inside him where the stuttering spirit lived. After that, the last of Dr. Richardson's magic vanished. He *chieu hoi*-ed. Nothing worked. He couldn't speak at all.

Sergeant Riker had him transferred. Not, Riker claimed, because of the old man. Shit happened now and then, in the field. Tough luck. But a dude who couldn't answer a radio call, or send one, or even yell for help if his buddies' lives depended on it, sure wasn't doing to do the squad any good.

"We're givin' you a break, Hudson. A fuckin' favor with whipped cream on top. Gettin' rotated to the rear with eleven months left? Shit. I'd trade places with you myself, if I could."

It was all a blur. How had they done it? The lieutenant, the captain, maybe even higher-ups had to approve. Harry Hudson imagined that it might have been difficult, but he let it remain a blur. He loaded his gear onto a chopper and was flown to Cam Ranh Bay, where he did drive a bus for five months, between the airport, the PX and the transient barracks. Then somebody looked at his file and saw the journalism major, and he spent the last six months at the public information office, typing upbeat press releases to soldiers' hometown papers. Off duty, he stayed drunk, in a stupor of shame and relief. He waited. Here was where the voices of Sydney Carton and Vance Foster converged. Both whispered to him to wait--for a second chance he no longer expected to get, much less deserve.

Fifteen years went by. He was newly married and had a baby daughter and was working on the Logger in Garbersville where Vance Foster used to work before it occurred to him that maybe Sergeant Riker *had* done him a favor--had been trying to help him the best way he knew. That only made it worse.

Andersonville, Ga., March 16, 1864

Our mess is gradually settling down. Have picked out our ground, rolled some big logs together, and are trying to make ourselves comfortable. I am in the best of spirits, and will live with them for some time to come if they will only give me one quarter enough to eat, and they are doing it now, and am in my glory....

March 18

We have no shelter of any kind whatever. Eighteen or twenty die per day. Cold and damp nights.... Wood getting scarce.... Very poor meal....

March 19

It is going to be an awful place during the summer months here, and thousands will die no doubt.

# # # #

My mama never trusted white peoples much. Somebody on her side of the family, back before they even come to Kansas, got burned up in they own house--lynched. That was in Alabama, I think. She never told me much about it. Who it was, what they supposed to have done. But she *seen* it, when she was just a little girl. My daddy told me. How my mama saw the flames burnin' across the street and the roof cavin' in and no fire engines comin' on purpose till it was too late. So sometimes when she get that far-off look, washin' dishes, whatever, I think she be trippin' about it--though maybe it be somethin' else, like Eugene when he went in the penitentiary that first time. That be a shock to mama. All she told me was, 'Kelly, you be *real* careful.'

My daddy, though, was different, you hear me? He wanted us to go to a mixed school, learn to get along with white peoples, not be ignorant knotheads like some folks we knew. In Topeka, back then, on a Friday or Saturday night you wouldn't see no white faces down on Fifteenth Street, where them clubs are where Ike and Tina Turner got they start. They wouldn't dare. But mostly we was mixed--too small a town not to be.

Darnell was more like my mama. He had that hate and mistrust in him. Got *real* upset when I went out with some of the men be stoppin' by that Silver Slipper, and some of 'em was white.

I mean, I had admirers, you know? Strip-dancin', you get all kinds. Like Ralph. This little bitty white guy with a bald head and a pot belly--came up to my shoulder, about, when I had high heels on. Fifty-five years old. He said he didn't want nothin' sexual. Just wanted to talk, and take me out to fancy restaurants in his Cadillac Fleetwood, kind of a pearl-grey color, leather seats. *Real* nice. You wouldn't believe the places we went. French, Italian. Up in them Hollywood Hills. I mean, I looked *real* good. I didn't have half my clothes in storage then. The place I liked best was that Benihana's. The way them chefs be cookin' everthing right at your table and throwin' they knives around like they gonna cut they fingers off, but they never do.

Ol' Ralph. He never laid a hand on me.

We had us some good times. Like I say, I had the world by the tail, if I'd only known it.

But Darnell wouldn't believe me. And back in '86, I think it was, when he was out of work and smokin' that sherm, and I'd quit dancin' for a while on account of my back, and the bills was pilin' up as usual, he gets this big idea to pimp me. He'd already been beatin' on me, now and then. Now he goes to the extremities of tellin' me, if I'm gonna date white dudes, or *anybody,* the least I can do is get paid for it.

Seven years we lived together. Long enough, it felt like a marriage.

Some peoples would call it dumb-ass foolishness, I know.

Back then, I called it love.

# # # #

Behind Pep Boys?

Harry Hudson wondered if the ad in the Sun was a hoax. La Mirada didn't look like the kind of town where a place like the Rabbit Hutch would be. It was just another pastel-stucco suburb, east of the 605 Freeway and north of the 91, according to his new Thomas Guide. Valley View Avenue was flat--no sign of a valley anywhere--and so empty at 10 p.m. on a Saturday that every curb and lamppost echoed the sputter of the Nissan's engine. It needed an oil change, a tune-up. He drove through an industrial area: neat, modern factories and warehouses set back from the road behind strips of landscaping, closed for the night or the weekend, all dark. This had to be wrong.

Again he felt his fever ebb. He loosened his grip on the wheel, flexed his stiff fingers, cracked his neck. He sighed. Who but a hayseed would expect anything different? He waited for what he knew would happen, what he deserved--thoughts of Deborah and Sally to slap him to his senses, chase him home.

But then, as he neared Rosecrans Avenue, he saw a cluster of lights--a McDonald's, a couple of gas stations--and sure enough, at the northeast corner, an auto parts store topped by the faces of Manny, Moe and Jack.

The excitement surged back. The parking lot was jammed. A hundred cars, at least, though the Rabbit Hutch was the only place open in the strip mall behind the store. Next to a Veterans of Foreign Wars post with a flagpole, no less. SWINGERS WELCOME. A small stenciled sign actually said that, in the glow of the big neon sign on the roof. *Jesus,* he thought. *How can they get away with that?* He parked in the shadow of a eucalyptus tree and remembered how disoriented he had felt in Red Fork, smelling this haunting new scent. The place looked like an ordinary neighborhood bar, except for the sign. And the cars. As if some fierce energy was drawing people here--sucking them in.

He approached the door hesitantly, more aware than usual of his baggy tweed jacket, the size of his gut. *Do I need a password?* he wondered.

But the doorman, very tall and wearing a Hawaiian shirt, took his five dollars and waved him in. The Rabbit Hutch was dim and rustic, with unfinished beams and a blackened rock fireplace to the right of the entrance. To the left, he saw booths and a bar, with an aisle between them that led to the rest rooms; straight ahead, a dance floor, a deejay playing canned music, bodies jiggling in the smoky air. The Beatles were pounding through "A Hard Day's Night." Harry Hudson felt conspicuous, and a few faces did turn his way--but only, he realized, because he was blocking the line of traffic to the bar. He backed up against the fireplace, where other single men were standing.

"Want a drink?"

A waitress, in black fishnet stockings. Her face was gaunt, dead white under a spiky black wig, seeming to show only one big tooth, like a child's Halloween witch mask--so ugly that Harry Hudson thought maybe this was why she had been hired: so customers would leave her alone.

"A Bud?" he asked--not that he liked Budweiser particularly, but it was the easiest for him to say.

"Beer you can get at the bar. You want a *cocktail?*"

Gin and tonic? he thought. *Margarita?* He hardly ever had a mixed drink. The names eluded him. *Stinger?* He must have shaken his head without knowing it, for the waitress took it as a *no* and went on.

Harry Hudson got a Bud at the bar and went back to the fireplace. He wished he could be invisible until his eyes adjusted to the darkness and he could scope things out, somehow. Behind the bar was a partition, open at the top, wooden pillars strung with twinkling blue and white bulbs, that divided the room in two. At either end of the bar was a gap. The gap at his end led to the dance floor, the other to a shadowy, red-lit area of tables where the dancers sat between songs. Oldies. And the crowd, too, was mostly middle-aged, he saw with surprise. Grey hair, thick makeup, plenty of bellies like his. A few men on the dance floor wore what he might have expected--tight pants, open-necked silk shirts, gold chains; a few women flaunted a lot of cleavage. But the rest looked like a tavern crowd anywhere. In spite of the sign.

A hoax? Or did everybody know the secret here except him?

He finished his beer, left the bottle on the bar and walked down the aisle to the men's room, glancing sidelong at the booth-sitters. Garberville had folks just like these. He waited in line for the single toilet stall while other men--some of the silk-shirt guys--splashed on cologne, slicked and combed their hair. He didn't dare ask *them*. Once inside the stall, Harry Hudson pretended to squat and take a crap while he studied the graffiti on the powder-blue wall, names and phone numbers, hunting for a clue.

But it came to him only on the way back, when he looked through the second gap, to the tables. That disco singer--Donna Summer?--was gasping through that '70s song that sounded like a long string of orgasms. In the murky red light, he saw couples talking intently, intimately to each other. Even the more plainly dressed women had buttons unbuttoned, showed glimpses of thigh and breast through slits in cloth. Was that where the action was?

Blood roared in his ears.

He turned, and a heavy finger tapped his shoulder.

"Couples only. Can't you read?"

It was the doorman--the bouncer, too, evidently--looming over him. The guy had to be six-nine, at least. Harry Hudson's eyes came to a pink tropical bird on the shirt, about at collarbone level. The long jaw was blue-shaven, the expression patient but weary.

"See the sign? Singles that side only," the bouncer said, steering Harry Hudson back toward the booths. "Them's the rules here."

Sure enough. There *was* a sign over the arch, so large and legible that it was hard for Harry Hudson to believe he hadn't seen and ignored it. And clearly the man thought he had done just that.

"I'm s--. I didn't know," he said, but as usual the way he stumbled over the words sounded suspicious, even to him. "My f-first time here."

"Don't let me catch you in there alone again," the bouncer said. "You want to go in there, get a date. OK, pal?"

Harry Hudson nodded, still rankled by the opening question. *I read for a living*, he wanted to snap. But mostly he felt the old, numb curiosity. What was it like to be able to intimidate people--or, for that matter, to charm them? All he could ever do, once he opened his mouth, was throw himself at their mercy.

He went back to the fireplace and stood until his pulse slowed and, he hoped, he was invisible again. The waitress returned. "Want a drink?" she asked as if she had never seen him before. This time he did order a gin and tonic. He fished for change in his pocket to tip her, spilled coins on the floor. He apologized again.

When he finished that drink, he ordered another.

Should he leave?

He had come to satisfy himself, just once, that places like the Rabbit Hutch existed--places where the only rules were whatever horny outlaws could dream up. Satan's front parlor, they would say in Beattie. But what did they know? He was here now, and there *were* rules, it turned out--no different than the rules had been at his high school prom. Unless he had a woman of his own, he couldn't participate. He could only spend his money and watch from this side of the partition, get aroused and frustrated and tired, go home alone. A sucker. As usual.

He thought of those trips to Portland, the rain and soot, the X-rated theaters where actors who couldn't even get a hard-on half the time tried to persuade him that places like this *did* exist, after which he wandered the streets looking for someone, anyone, willing to put her arms around him, just for a moment. *Do I have to wait forever?* he remembered wondering. *Never mind what I deserve. Am I that damn repulsive?* Nobody answered--even the prostitutes he did find, who took his money impassively and lay down in the same spirit. Not that he should have expected more, he told himself. He was sinning, breaking the law. But still. He *wanted* more. Someone who would welcome him on equal terms, unlike Nancy Ishida and, later, in her different way, Deborah. Was that too much to ask? The liquor was burning in him now; he found himself angry--the anger he had promised never to feel toward Deborah again. *Chasing all over Portland like an idiot, just to pay and pay. If it wasn't for you, I wouldn't have had to.*

Bitch.

Yes, he *should* leave, he thought.

Still, if he could find somebody to dance with ... if he could walk boldly into the crowd at the tables and come out with a woman, they would pass as a couple, as far as the bouncer was concerned. That might work. Then, as they danced, he could talk to her, maybe. Learn the language. The key was to edge up right next to the dance floor--but, judging from the number of men already gathered on that side of the fireplace, once again everybody was ahead of him.

Hayseed.

Who? Harry Hudson scanned the strangers beyond the partition, recalling the dances he *had* attended at Beattie High, when he stood at the margin of the gym and rehearsed the question he was afraid to ask: *Would you like to dance?* The risk was that if he couldn't manage the "W--," he would cross the whole basketball court to where the girls waited, only to stand, face twitching, gesturing dumbly toward the floor in hope that his would-be partner would take pity on him, and pity wasn't what he had walked all that way to get. *Wwwooulddyooulliketoddaance?* He practiced it now, under his breath, over and over.

There. A woman alone, where two or three of the tables had been shoved together, as if for a picnic. Dark-haired, heavy-set, not Harry Hudson's type, but alone. He waited for a fast song to start--even here, he thought, she might resent being asked to dance slow. He set his drink down on the mantel and strode as quickly as he could through the crowd. A dozen steps, no more. The woman was putting on fresh lipstick, eyeing herself in a compact mirror. It seemed the wrong moment to ask, "Wwwould you like to dance?", but he didn't dare hesitate and break his rhythm. Then his throat tightened. She didn't seem to hear him over the music, and he doubted he could say it again.

She snapped the compact shut before she looked up. "No, thanks," she said without any change of expression, in a voice that wasn't harsh, just flat and bored.

Harry Hudson retreated to the fireplace. The bouncer, thank God, hadn't seen him. Just as in high school, he flushed with embarrassment. He drained his drink and once more tried to disappear, watching the woman resentfully. Next time he would ask one he *really* wanted to dance with. But he shouldn't push his luck. He let four songs go by--noticing uneasily how hard it was for him to wait even that long without fidgeting.

Even here, he thought. *Even these people have more self-control than I do. How come?*

Then he made a second try, slipping through the tangle as the dancers changed for the next song. A blonde with short, straight hair, in a dark miniskirt and a white blouse like a man's shirt, unbuttoned most of the way down. He had seen her dance; she was one of the younger ones. A beauty. Her slim hips had twitched, her breasts swaying in and out of sight. Her face, aloof, had floated above them. Now she sat with one of the silk-shirt guys, a man with a gold chain and a hairy chest and a mustache who resembled last night's wirephoto of Ted Turner clinching another cable TV deal--a man who looked implausibly cool and fit, out of Harry Hudson's league; but he asked her anyway, and the woman, without a smile but without hesitation either, a miracle, got up and led him to the floor.

The music started: a song Harry Hudson didn't know, an awkward in-between rhythm, neither fast nor slow. He was abruptly and brutally reminded that he had seldom danced since those months of fluency at the University of Oregon twenty years ago. His feet hopped and shuffled in the same half-learned but mysteriously remembered pattern: a ghost in his nerves. The weight of flesh shifting at his waist was new, though, and the jacket flapping against his thighs. Sweat trickled down his armpits.

"Where you from?" she asked, in a tone that suggested he should have asked *her.*

"L-long Beach."

"Oh. We're from West Covina," she said. A pause. What was he supposed to say now? He was hypnotized by the freckled skin between her breasts--an effect he had always loved. Even Deborah had freckles there. The blonde began touching him, lightly, as if by accident but too often for that: on the knee, the elbow, a teasing flick at his groin.

"Where's your lady?" she asked.

And he found, to his surprise, that he had no answer ready--just the truth.

"I'm h--," he said, and stuck. "I'm a--"

The blonde stared at him then--the only time he seemed to have her full attention.

"Let me get this straight. You don't have a lady here. You're alone."

Harry Hudson nodded and smiled his most harmless-looking smile.

The woman compressed her lips and said nothing more, but her dancing, if anything, got wilder. Her touches were fully deliberate now, though her face didn't seem to notice them: soft and continual as snowflakes, but burning. Harry Hudson wondered if something still might happen. A threesome? He didn't like the man with the mustache, he realized; he would be very uncomfortable in the same bedroom with him, but if that was the price of admission.... Was she worth it? Probably, he thought--a decision so easy to make that it shocked him. Harry Hudson began to imagine how the offer would be put to him and how he would be able to answer, with what words, when she flipped up the front of her skirt and he saw for an instant that she *had no panties on.* Then the music stopped. She turned and left the floor and didn't look back.

"Wait," he said.

But the crowd was thinning, and he had to hustle back to the safety of the fireplace. He was panting--out of shape. And trembling with anger and shame. Harry Hudson watched the blonde's head bob and disappear as she sat down. *Damn, she was good.* The waitress came by with her fright-mask face, and he bought a third gin and tonic. The sleepiness hit him then, a soft but heavy blow to the top of his skull. Now he *would* leave. Only a sullen inertia kept him standing there, the sooty rocks jagged against his back.

Time passed. Later he couldn't quite remember how the black woman came to be standing opposite him, leaning back on her elbows against the end of the bar, holding a Bloody Mary, its red a shade darker than her ballerina dress, an outlandish flurry of ruffles and lace. She had a dancer's legs, but the middle of her threatened to spill out of the gauzy cloth. She was ten years older than Harry Hudson, at least. He rubbed his eyes and blinked at her. She grinned--a friendly grin, despite sharp canines; a grin that dimpled her cheeks and showed him a glimpse of what her face used to be.

"W-would you like to dance?"

She giggled. "Dance? I *love* to dance," she said. "Just let me finish my drink here, won't you, sweetheart? Shit, I'm *dry*. And my feets is *killin'* me."

So he waited, and they went out onto the floor together. Had he ever danced with a black woman before? Harry Hudson couldn't remember. Probably not, then. But everything that had gone badly with the blonde was simple with this oddly girlish creature, who confided three measures into the song that she lived in Baldwin Park and her name was Louise. The song was "Light My Fire." A relic from Harry Hudson's youth. Even his dancing seemed easier, lubricated by heat and sweat. Louise had a whole repertoire of shimmying, finger-snapping moves, and often would seem lost in a trance, admiring herself, but then she would grin and lean close to Harry Hudson and shout in his ear. It was restful to be with her; she was willing to do almost all the talking.

"You're very brave," he found himself saying.

"Shit, Harry, you don't scare *me*."

"No, I mean ... just *being* here. In this scene. People who want something and don't ap--." He licked his lips. "Ap-pologize for it. It sure beats married folks sneaking around, don't you think? It's honest. I have a lot of r-respect for it. I really do."

"Shee-it," she said, and her giggle lost its girlishness, became a deep, throaty chuckle. *She's fifty-five if she's a day*, he thought. "There's cool people here, Harry, real freaks, but you gotta watch what you're doin', too, because, Harry"--the corners of her mouth turned down--"some of 'em are no better than *dogs*. I know."

"I bet."

"I'm just sayin' be *careful*, sweetheart. That's all."

"Thanks. I appreciate it."

The song ended. And though he was panting again, he didn't want it to end.

"How about another?" he asked.

Louise hesitated twice. First, she bent and adjusted her shoes--spike-heeled and glittering with red sequins. No wonder her feet hurt; the joint of each big toe knobbed out at an alarming angle. Bunions? Then she looked up at Harry Hudson for a long beat when she heard the next song--a slow one. He waited, shrugging, smiling that inoffensive smile, afraid to reach for her unless she reached first. Even then, he held her as chastely as he would have held Nancy Ishida: left hand well away from her body, right hand resting lightly on her quivering bare back. Louise giggled--girlish again; she slipped both arms around his neck and settled against his cheek with a sigh. Her perfume was powerful. "You smell nice," he said. Still he didn't dare tighten his grip. Over her shoulder, Harry Hudson saw the heavy-set woman he had asked first, dancing with a man whose long black curls fringed a bald spot. And the blonde. *Hoo boy.* Flattening herself against the man with the mustache and riding his knee.

"You know them?" he asked Louise.

"Who? Oh, yeah. Margot and Kevin. Sure, I know *them.* Why?"

Kevin?

Harry Hudson told her.

"Shit, Harry, that's her thing. She does it to get Kevin jealous. Don't matter *who* it is. I seen that bitch do it before. To Leroy once, that I was with. But, see, Kevin *likes* it that way. It's just a game." The giggle. "All so he'll take her home and *rape* her. And anybody else they're partyin' with."

"Oh."

"They're from out in Redondo," Louise said.

"She said W-west Covina."

"No way." She grinned. "Got a beach house that won't *quit.*"

She gave no more details. Harry Hudson kept turning Louise so he could watch the blonde, whose skirt--the dark miniskirt with nothing underneath--had started inching up her thighs. He was glad he had come to the Rabbit Hutch now; he tried to imagine what his life might have been like if he had met someone like Louise--younger and prettier, of course--a dozen years ago. It might have saved him a whole lot of grief. His mistake, he saw clearly, had been trying to be good. To be something he wasn't. When, instead, he could have been a regular at a place like this, enjoying an endless flow of adventures. So what if it wasn't a virtuous life, as people in Garbersville reckoned such things? Would it be any worse than the life he had?

"Shit, yes," Louise was saying. "That Margot, she's somethin' *else,* sweetheart, believe me."

Then this song, too, stopped. Harry Hudson was about to walk Louise back to the bar, with a defiant glance at the bouncer, when a shudder passed through the crowd. Flashlight beams stabbed in from the door. A murmur of protest circled out from the light like a ripple in disturbed water. Three sheriff's deputies in short-sleeved khaki shirts pushed onto the dance floor. They had guns and nightsticks, but they used only the flashlights, fanning out and sweeping the room. They did nothing out of line--Harry Hudson watched them closely, as he imagined Vance Foster would have done--but they were clearly taking their time, enjoying themselves. Flesh, hair, jewelry leaped out of the darkness and vanished. After that first murmur, nobody objected. People stood by, just as Harry Hudson did, with a studied air of innocence. This disappointed him.

Even here? he thought. *Shame wins even here?*

"Those vets next door," Louise said. "They been agitatin' the city council a *long* time, tryin' to shut us down.... Thanks anyway, though, Harry. You *like* to dance, don't you?"

"S-sorry. I'm not any good."

"Shit, Harry, at least you're a gentleman. Not like some of these...." She was looking beyond him, toward the tables.

"Thank *you*," he said.

You sure have rhythm, he almost added but caught himself. Once in a long while, stuttering was a blessing; it saved him from saying the wrong thing--just as now Louise saw him as shyer and more mannerly than he really was. It was the only kind of charm he could muster; it was what he supposed had worked with Deborah, in the beginning.

"Hold on, now, Harry," Louise said. "I gotta go to the ladies'."

Abandoned, Harry Hudson watched the crowd, its mood deflated, begin to head for the exit. More lights came on. It was closing time anyway, he realized. The bouncer in his bright shirt with macaws and palm fronds was nodding to acquaintances, slapping a high five. Did the help here join the customers later?

Probably, he thought. Did *hold on* mean that Louise was coming back? Probably not. *Hayseed.* He had been a fool in the first place to wear a jacket so heavy. Drying sweat stuck the shirt to his back, wisps of hair to his forehead.

Depression settled over him again. He yawned.

Outside, it was windy, the air feverish, electric. The eucalyptus leaves rattled, and the metal clip on the VFW's flag rope clinked against the pole. The deputies had left, and people seemed to recover their high spirits. Groups of four, even six--couples who must have negotiated, paired off, during those hours at the red-lit tables--clustered on the sidewalk and next to their cars, posing theatrically, kissing. Soon to drive off to one of their houses, to orgies for which all the dancing and conspiring had been only foreplay.

46

"There you are! Harry, we gotta go. I'm sorry, sweetheart, but look." Louise rummaged through her purse, a big oblong alligator one that seemed full of checkout receipts, half-peeled rolls of mints, little packets of Kleenex. "Oh, shit. I can't find a pen to write you my phone number."

Harry Hudson patted his jacket; he didn't have a pen either.

"Can't you remember it?" she said and whispered in his ear. Harry Hudson repeated the number to himself, just as he had chanted, *Would you like to dance?*--trying to ignore the big black man who came up and put an arm around her: navy-blue turtleneck, shaven skull, broad, impassive features. He nodded at her quickly, to say: Yes, he could remember.

"Later," she said.

She and the man went off to join another black couple by the side of a maroon Continental with fake wire wheels. Others milling through the parking lot hid them. Even the waitress hurried by, in her fishnet stockings. She had good legs, at least. The whole world seemed to be leaving Harry Hudson there by the flagpole, and the anger that had been building in him all night broke loose--not so much at Louise (who had been friendly, after all) as at the bouncer, at Steinbach, at the managing editor in Red Fork, Finnegan; at a long, long string of humiliations whose details he had forgotten. Then it found a focus--Margot and Kevin, with two other couples, driving out in a caravan, laughing and waving.

Follow them. Harry Hudson ran to the Nissan, strewn with dry leaves. The wind--a Santa Ana?--had blown away the eucalyptus smell, left the air sterile, like the ocean behind the breakwater in Long Beach, which had no smell either. Weird. He pulled out of the lot and followed the three sets of red taillights west on Rosecrans. Again his mind skittered sideways. Had they named the street for the Union general who might have been John Ransom's commander? *Got to check that sometime.*

The taillights wove from lane to lane, going fast. The Nissan labored to keep up. Harry Hudson clamped the wheel, clenched his teeth, fully and thrillingly awake at last, strung taut beneath the flab of the body nobody had ever wanted much. Nobody had ever done to him in earnest what the blonde, Margot, had done as a game. *She's somethin' else*, Louise had said. The street, the whole network of streets, went on forever: walled subdivisions, shopping centers, lights and lights.

They had almost reached the 605 when one of the cars suddenly swerved to the right. Then the other two. Into the lot of a closed Shell station.

What he ought to do, Harry Hudson knew, was keep on going. Look straight ahead. Pretend they had been on the same route by accident. There wasn't a chance in a thousand that these people wanted to invite him along to "party" ... but he took that chance anyway, knowing he was wrong, stupid, an asshole, because the other choice meant going back to his room at the Reef with the mended pink bedspread and the toilet noise and the palm trunk in the window--a room that all at once no longer seemed like home to him, its waiting darkness booby-trapped with Ransom's reproaches and Sally's ghost. He turned almost too late, too fast; the Nissan's left front fender clipped the curb by the entrance with a sickening screech.

He got out. The driver's door of the lead car--a white Camaro--opened too, and he had to hand it to Margot: she was the one who climbed out to face him, not any of the three men. She kept hold of the door handle. What could be more beautiful than a woman's slender wrist, with a green vein running up the thumb side? Her glossed lips shone. Her eyes were bright, hostile, steady. Trucks whooshed by on the freeway; the wind fingered her still-open blouse.

Damn, she was good.

"You *were* following us," she said. "Get lost, why don't you."

And then what else was there to do but turn around, get back in the Nissan and drive off, the bent fender scraping faintly, dangerously, against the tire?

"Creep," he heard her say to his back.

And head down the 605 to Long Beach, saying that phone number over and over to keep from having to think of anything else at all?

#   #   #   #

May 8, 1864

Awful warm and more sickly. About 3,500 have died since I came here, which is a good many, come to think of it....

May 10

New prisoners coming in every day with good clothes, blankets, &c.... These are victims for the raiders who pitch into them for plunder. Very serious fights occur.... Stones, clubs, knives, sling shots, &c., are used ... and sometimes the camp gets so stirred up that the rebels, thinking a break is intended, fire into the crowds gathered, and many are killed....

May 18

We have some good singers in camp, and strange as it may seem, a good deal of singing is indulged in.... God bless a man who can sing in this place.

May 19

Nearly twenty thousand men confined here now.... Rations very *small and* very *poor. The meal that the bread is made out of is ground, seemingly, cob and all, and scourges the men fearfully.... Hundreds of cases of dropsy. Men puff out of human shape....*

June 6

Eight months a prisoner today. A lifetime.... Enough to eat but not the right kind. Scurvy putting in its work....

June 7

Nearly all the old prisoners who were captured with me are dead. Don't know of over 50 or 60 alive out of 800.

June 15

I am sick: just able to drag around. My teeth are loose, mouth sore, with gums grown down in some places lower than the teeth and bloody.... [Prisoners] *have been trying to organize a police force, but cannot do it. Raiders are the stronger party.... Lice by the fourteen hundred thousand million infest Andersonville.... .*

June 24

I have read in my earlier years about prisoners in the revolutionary war, and other wars. It sounded noble and heroic ...; but the romance has been knocked out of the prisoner of war business, higher than a kite. It's a fraud.... All of the 'Astor House Mess' now afflicted ... with the exception of Battese [a Minnesota Indian who befriended Ransom]. *... Take exercise every morning and evening, when it is almost impossible for me to walk ... drink of Battese's medicine made of roots, keep clear of vermin, talk and even laugh, and if I do die, it will not be through neglect....*

\#   \#   \#   \#

What was it like, that first trick? You don't even want to know.

All that vodka. Shit, maybe a couple hits off the pipe, too. I was *tore up*, you hear what I'm sayin'?

Darnell had me so beaten down by then, I couldn't recognize my own self.

Later, when we'd moved to Long Beach, it got worse. That sherm had him so wired he pulled a gun on his own father when the old man come out on the bus from Kansas by surprise--come out and gave him hell about the way he was livin'. Pulled a gun right there at my kitchen table. I didn't even know he had one. After that, I told myself, 'Kelly, it's time. *Past* time you got over your fear.'

#   #   #   #

Back from Vietnam, Harry Hudson still lived in the blur. He no longer believed he could be like Vance Foster, but he had no other plan. After he was discharged from the Army, he went straight to Garbersville. He felt he was approaching the Logger as a beggar, without energy or hope, leaning against it with nothing but the slack, nerveless weight of his body, but later he saw this as one of the few truly determined moments of his life. He haunted the paper's offices for weeks until, finally, it gave in and hired him.

Vance Foster was gone--nobody was sure where. The Logger had been sold to a national chain. It had a new editor, Brent T. Owsley Jr., only eight years older than Harry Hudson, with a passion for offset presses and an eye for ad revenue and an air of bemusement about how things had been run before.

"Foster?" he said when Harry Hudson asked. "He must have been an old drinking buddy or something, to get away with all that. Family owners can be eccentric, if they like. Corporate's different. It's *not* the norm, believe me, for a paper this size. My gosh, think of the lawsuits. You know somebody shot out a window at his house, slashed his tires right here in our parking lot? More trouble than he was worth.... Why?" Owsley said--boyishly slim and freckle-faced, but more of an adult than Harry Hudson ever expected to be. "You thinking of filling his shoes?"

Harry Hudson nodded. "I always thought a n--." He licked his lips. "A name like mine was m--. More of a byline than a name anyway."

Owsley laughed.

Harry Hudson laughed along with him, sure the question would come up again, more seriously, but it never did. Maybe, he thought years later, he had blown his chance right then, trying to ingratiate himself with a joke. But there was no way to know.

He searched the files in the morgue for Vance Foster's columns. Some read as well as they ever had. Others disappointed him; glib and detached, they came uncomfortably close to justifying his father's verdict: *An outsider.*

He thumbed to duplicates of the clippings he had mailed to Nancy Ishida:

We all did it.

You did it. I did it.

We looked straight into the face of evil without recognizing what we saw.

I was a cub reporter in Seattle in 1942 when the Japanese were unloaded off ferries from the islands in Puget Sound and loaded onto trains bound east and south. Men in dark suits, women in coats and hats, children, babies, spilling out onto the dock in the rain with their suitcases and trunks, looking around, bewildered.

I saw them and I thought they looked funny. Not like "us." I felt a little sorry for them, maybe, but I never doubted that the U.S. government was justified in sending armed troops to move them along.

I didn't see any evil. I was going to be in uniform myself soon.

Of course, I was just a kid. But my editors, older and presumably wiser, didn't see any evil either--in the event I was reporting or in my callow attempts to lend it "color" and "human interest."

Here in Garbersville, many of you--my readers--participated in the eviction and internment of residents of Japanese descent, or watched it happen and didn't protest. Protesting was for pinkos, right? ACLU types. Folks of uncertain sexual orientation. Cowards and waverers, in those scary months after Pearl Harbor. Not good, upstanding citizens like you.

Some of you profited handsomely.

And this newspaper cheered you on, every step of the way.

Of course, it was just a little paper--too much a part of the community, perhaps, ever to be a truly independent voice.

But it didn't even try.

The big newspapers, in those days, were no different. The biggest and richest paper on the West Coast, the Los Angeles Times, cheered evil on even more loudly than we did.

Damning quotations followed.

The words no longer moved Harry Hudson, but they reminded him of how, in that irretrievable time before he killed the old man, they *had* moved him. They called up ghosts. Holding the yellowed, brittle paper, he remembered how Nancy Ishida's eyes had looked in that classroom in Beattie, the scent of her as he tried to apologize.

And, in spite of himself, he clung to the promise he felt Owsley had made just by asking if he wanted to be a columnist. The promise he *should* have made. Otherwise, why bring up the possibility at all?

Fifteen years later, when Harry Hudson suddenly announced that he was leaving the Logger, he cited that as a grievance. "You n-never gave me a chance," he said. "Did I ever ask f--." He licked his lips. "A raise? Did I ever turn d-down an assignment? It's th--. The least you could do."

Owsley, still slim and freckled but greying by then, stared at him.

"You don't want to do this, Harry," he said. "I can understand you're upset, God knows. Your kid and everything. You want to take some leave, fine. Take Deborah on a trip somewhere, my blessing. We can hold the fort for a couple of weeks. But my advice is, don't do anything you'll regret."

"R-regret?" Harry Hudson muttered. "Wasting half my life on this g--. This g--." *Gutless paper,* he wanted to say, and Owsley seemed to understand something of the sort. "*That's* what I regret."

"Since when am I supposed to be a mind-reader?" Owsley said, irritated now. "You never said anything. You know as well as I do, we don't need columnists here; we need reporters. Anything more, you have to *earn.* I ask you, Harry. What have you done to earn it?"

Owsley, he could see, didn't expect him to answer. And in fact it was chilling to look back on his time at the Logger as if through Owsley's eyes. It was like what he saw himself in his most depressed moments--a vision so bleak that he had to deny it outright to go on working. After the spasm of energy that had gotten him hired, he had sunk back into drowsiness. He slept twelve hours a day, sometimes fourteen. He would rather drive miles from the office than risk a phone call, and as he drove through his home country, even though it was still the only country that looked right to him--the sagebrush and pines, the clear, swift rivers, the pinkish-grey volcanic cinders, the loom of big mountains to the west--he felt separated from it by a scratching or smudging of his own sight, as if by a dirty windshield. Sometimes he would wake up on a road he knew well, by a creek he used to fish, and be unable to remember which news source he had meant to visit. He had killed the old man. He would have to park and fold his arms on the wheel, lay his face in his arms, watch the bright specks of midges weaving their circles over the green-brown water and wait for the lassitude to lift, for his thoughts to come back from wherever they had scattered.

In fifteen years, in this slow, half-tranced way, he covered City Hall, schools, cops, floods, forest fires, blizzards, lost hikers, a truck-Winnebago crash that left a whole Idaho family dead or maimed, the bulldozing of ranch land for subdivisions, the boom in ski and golf resorts and the opening of trout season. He wrote year-end roundups and man-in-the-street polls and breathless copy for the annual Lumberjack Festival. But he never wrote as much as Owsley seemed to want, and even as the clips with his byline piled up in the same drawer that held Vance Foster's, he knew that nothing he had written had made a difference in the life of the community. He hadn't dug up any of these stories; they had been given to him.

Harry Hudson was reminded of this most keenly whenever Nancy Ishida came home to visit. After the first few years, he had tapered off on the booze. He had used Dr. Richardson's exercises to recover maybe half of the speech he had lost. Even memories of the old man gradually bothered him less--though he wasn't sure if this was a relief or an even deeper shame. Beattie was part of his beat. It was easy enough to hear that she was coming, easier still to cruise down the street past the Garden Shop in the rattly red Ford pickup that preceded the Nissan. It *should* have been easy to stop and talk to her, or visit their home. But it wasn't. Each time, he became aware all over again of his softening gut, the shine of wear on his cheap polyester slacks, his grease-spotted tie. *I'm not ready,* he thought in panic. *I haven't written anything yet.*

Please wait.

And for a while it seemed that Nancy Ishida did. At any rate she stayed single. She was a computer engineer in Silicon Valley now, he heard, making probably three times his salary. The few glimpses he had through the truck window showed her to be stockier, with shorter, curlier hair and a new abruptness to her movements, but the woman Harry Hudson spoke to in his mind was always the Nancy Ishida of the classroom, her hair hair long and straight and shining, her eyes challenging him to prove his innocence. Which he could do, he thought, in only one way--the way Vance Foster had.

Wait.

Finally they left. The elder Ishidas sold the Garden Shop and retired to Palo Alto to live with Nancy--who got married, rumor had it, soon afterward. Harry Hudson heard nothing more. And what more did he deserve? he thought. A heavier depression settled over him in the studio apartment in Garbersville that was all he could afford on what Owsley paid him, given his bar bills and the fact he mostly ate out--an apartment furnished with his father's Morris chair and knotty-pine gun cabinet and a couch that unfolded into a bed and the refrigerator, stove and tubular-steel-and-formica kitchen set that came with the place, and little else. So that Deborah, when she first saw it, exclaimed, "You poor man."

Dully, he drove through Beattie, which the lumber company, having clear-cut too much of its reserves--as Vance Foster had predicted long ago--was selling off piecemeal to its remaining workers to raise cash. The Hudsons' old house was owned by a family named Rodriguez now, the board-and-batten walls sheathed in aqua-green aluminum siding, the yard littered with enough trikes and basketballs for six kids. The pine grove behind it that had served as Spotsylvania or the Wilderness had been chain-sawed to stumps, apparently for firewood.

All this time. I haven't written anything.

But in those moods when Harry Hudson saw things more or less as Owsley did, he also asked himself: *What* could *I write?* The issues Vance Foster could identify so readily as an outsider were obscured to him. He had to admit, finally, that he was too afraid of giving offense to dig very deeply, even if he knew how and where to dig. He cared too much what people thought--his schoolmates, his father's friends, people he had known all his life. And he depended on them too much. They called and mailed him information; though they thought him a little strange, he supposed, they trusted him with their stories; when he hissed or panted into the phone, they would say, "Oh, it's you, Harry," instead of hanging up.

Now Owsley warned, "Not everybody's going to carry you the way I have."

"I w-want a letter," Harry Hudson said.

"What?"

"A letter. Of r--" He licked his lips. "R--."

"Recommendation?"

Harry Hudson nodded. *You owe me that much,* he wanted to say.

"I can do that, Harry, if you insist." In the fluorescent light of the Logger's cinderblock newsroom, he saw for the first time an etching of fine lines around Owsley's eyes. "But what does Deborah say? We're worried about her, Harry. About you both. We see her every week in church and pray for her. Do you think it's the right thing, in her circumstances, to have to move?"

It was all Harry Hudson could do to stand still, his nerves screaming for flight.

"Just a l-letter," he said.

He didn't tell Owsley that Deborah wasn't coming.

#   #   #   #

Not everybody's going to carry you.

Owsley was right, as Harry Hudson discovered in Red Fork. The paper there was bigger and more enterprising--what he had always thought he wanted--but the pace was faster, too. Even at his best he might not have been able to keep up with the younger, more aggressive reporters--much less now, with Sally gone. And then he had compounded what was already an unforgivable crime--left Deborah without saying a word, just mailing her a check and driving straight away from the Logger's parking lot with Owsley's letter tucked into a pocket of the tweed jacket she had bought him shortly after the wedding. Though he may not have broken any laws, he knew he was a fugitive. He slept, in the first weeks, whenever he wasn't working or drinking; and even later he seemed to drift in slow motion through Sacramento Valley air hot enough to crackle his skin, through a blur thicker than at Cam Ranh Bay. He *had* to use the phone on the job here, and people cut him no slack. He had never realized what an advantage he had in Garbersville, knowing places and sources. Here, amid red clay, yellow grass, olive and almond orchards, suburban sprawl and a city hall filled with strangers, he was lost--as Finnegan, the managing editor, kept reminding him.

In Red Fork, Harry Hudson felt an eerie absence of restraint. Garbersville and Beattie, Nancy Ishida and Deborah, Owsley and the others at the Logger had held him in more than he knew, monitored his behavior. Which was why he had had to go all the way to Portland to sin. Now, in the wavering, smoky heat, he felt his molecules flying apart.

He thought often of Owsley. That glimpse of the tiredness in Owsley's eyes had made him see his former boss for the first time as human. He had always resented the man--his youth, his cocksureness, his shameless mingling of business sense and piety. But was it possible that Owsley, too, saw himself as a failure? Stuck in Garbersville forever, denied a chance to head one of the chain's bigger papers, only pretending to prefer country life? Was it possible that *his* bosses thought he lacked ruthlessness, keeping somebody like Harry Hudson on the payroll--only to have the ingrate walk out?

Another unlikely benefactor? Like Riker?

Harry Hudson happened to be thinking of this on the day when Finnegan--red-faced, shiny-bald and expansive, given to wearing summer-weight pastels--called him in for what he expected to be yet another ass-reaming.

It was 103 outside. The air conditioning in Finnegan's office roared. Harry Hudson's ears, as in Vietnam, were plugged with wax. He readied himself, as if it were Owsley sitting before him, to nod, smile ruefully and promise to do better. Scraping the words up in his throat, glancing sideways at a front page mounted in plexiglass (U.S. ON MOON!), he realized that he was being fired only after it had happened.

"Maybe you ought to try a bigger paper," Finnegan said, giving him Steinbach's name and a few others. "Not that I think you're ready. Let's face it: I don't think you ever will be. But what I'm saying is, we can't keep you here." Finnegan cracked his knuckles; Harry Hudson watched his thick fingers go pink with blood, then pale, as he laced and flexed them. "We think of this as a *developmental* paper. Reporters stay a couple of years, hone their skills and move on up. Or out. This isn't a place to sit back and put your feet up on the desk and make a career of it. Oh, I know we have a few old-timers, but they each fill a niche, and anyway, they've been here too long to get rid of now. You haven't. You've still got time, if you want. To find out what you *really* want to do in life."

The floor lurched out from under him. *Where can I go now?* In terror he heard himself still speaking as if to Owsley: "S-sorry I've p--. P--. Pppuut you to all this t--." He licked his lips. "All this trouble."

For once, Harry Hudson didn't mind that he was stuttering. It was Finnegan who ought to be ashamed, he thought. *Picking on a cripple.*

Finnegan shrugged. "We all make mistakes."

"T-thanks anyway. For p--. Ppp--." Even stamping his foot didn't shake this one loose. "Bearing with me. All this time."

He was begging, abjectly. For a word of praise--of encouragement, at least--in return for being such a good sport about it.

Christ. Can't he even wish me luck?

But Finnegan didn't.

Minutes later, out of the office, Harry Hudson wanted to kill him. He grew dizzy and faint with rage. He imagined picking Finnegan up bodily by the lapels of his peach-colored suit and throwing him through the window, kicking him in the balls, karate-chopping his neck, crushing his face. He thought he could do it, though Finnegan was heavier than he was and Harry Hudson hadn't been in a fight since grade school. Surely enough adrenaline was pouring through him now. He would be granted a moment of superhuman strength, just as he had once imagined that moment of calm with the bullets flying by. Surely he would have *that*, in return for ending his career ... but then he remembered what he had thought it was impossible for him ever to forget: His career had ended already. His whole life had ended that moment beside the swimming pool in Garbersville. He had no right to complain about anything, ever again. His anger vanished (though it kept coming back in surges over the next few days). Suddenly all he wanted was a drink.

# # # #

June 29, 1864

Have been reading over the diary, and find nothing but grumbling and growlings. Had best enumerate some of the better things of this life. I am able to walk around the prison, although quite lame. Have black pepper to put in our soups. Am as clean perhaps as any here, with good friends to talk cheerful to. Then, too, the raiders will let us alone until about the last, for some of them will get killed when they attack the Astor House Mess.... Will live probably two or three months yet....

June 30

A new prisoner fainted away on his entrance to Andersonville and is now crazy, a raving maniac. That is how our condition affected him....

# # # #

"--"

"Who is this?"

"H--"

A giggle. "Hey, you some kind of breather? Leroy, that you?"

"--"

"If you *ain't* Leroy, you know what you can do."

"E-excuse me," Harry Hudson said in a desperate rush.

"Who *is* this?"

"Last Saturday. I met you." Three feet to his right, Brad Pierce's terminal clicked, and Steinbach, returning from the men's room, stepped out of the shadows into the island of light and strolled around the rectangle of desks, tapping his thigh with a pica pole as if with a swagger stick. Harry Hudson hunched over the phone, trying to muffle his voice. Right now he could say anything except the one or two syllables that would tell Louise what she wanted. "At the R--." He licked his lips. "The R-rabbit Hutch."

"Wait a minute. You that white boy."

"Yeah." Now, thank God, he could say it, for whatever unfathomable reason. "Harry."

Louise giggled again. "Shit, don't *scare* me like that. You sounded like one of those breathers, you know? Or Leroy playin' a joke on me."

"Sorry," Harry Hudson said. "W-who's Leroy?"

"I introduced you all, right there at the Rabbit Hutch. I *know* I did, Harry."

"No."

"You just don't remember, Harry. Big dude. I know I introduced you. Don't argue. I told him afterwards, 'You know, Leroy, I *liked* that white boy. I really did. "Cause he likes to dance, Leroy. That's what I told him. Not like some of these *dogs*, you know what I mean, just want to stick their fingers in your pussy right out there on the dance floor. That don't turn me on at *all*."

Harry Hudson laughed nervously. Could anybody be listening in?

"Louise," he said. "You see, I remember. Y-your name."

"That's nice, Harry. I'd of remembered your name, too, sweetheart, if you hadn't kinda *spooked* me there, not talkin' and all."

"The Rabbit Hutch," Harry Hudson said. "That's quite a place."

"The Rabbit Hutch is *cool*, Harry," she said. "It's really cool. I've been goin' there for years, there and the Wide World, out in Anaheim, you know, but that's a *club*, Harry, you gotta be a member, and they check you out *very* carefully. I mean you gotta register as a couple and all. You find yourself a freak like me, Harry"--another giggle--"and I'll call Leroy and we can all get it on together. How about that?"

It was what he had hoped Louise would say--but now that she had said it, it didn't sound true. No *real* person would talk this way. It had to be an act--a persona she put on for strangers, like that ruffled dress, he thought. To hide what?

"I don't know, Louise," Harry Hudson said. "Y-you're the only girl I know."

Pierce's sun-bleached hair shifted in the corner of his vision.

"Shit, you were just there one night, Harry. Give it time. Lots of chicks hang out there at the Rabbit Hutch.... Though, like I told Leroy, if those deputies keep raidin' it like that, they might kill the whole scene. I *mean* it, Harry. It used to be, they'd come in and talk to the manager, you know, Oscar, *he's* cool, but none of this shinin' flashlights up people's skirts, see if they've got panties on. No *way*, Harry. Though if you ask me, some of these damn fools brought it on themselves, practically fuckin' right there on the dance floor, when the Rabbit Hutch is just a place to *meet* people, Harry. They all can fuck later, you know what I mean?"

Now there was no shutting Louise up. He should have called from the pay phone at the Reef, instead.

"I suppose."

"Shit, yes." Everything he said now seemed to make her giggle. "But before you go to the Wide World, sweetheart, why not try that thee-ater? That's a whole different scene, Harry. What you call down and dirty. *Funky*. That's the world. Real funky. Where I went last year when my old man and I split up, and just *freaked out*, Harry. Put my feet up on the seats in front and had seven men eat my pussy. One after the other. Seven big ol' dudes. I almost *fainted*, Harry." The deepest, bluesiest chuckle yet. "Shit, yes."

She's crazy, he thought.

Steinbach looked up from dummying a page, looked Harry Hudson's way.

"Your old man," he said. "That's not L--?"

"Leroy? No way. Leroy's just a friend of mine. Another freak. I met him at the Rabbit Hutch. We just get together to party now and then. No strings, no strings on us at *all*. Leroy's cool. But my old man, he's a *dog*. So damn tight, and got more money than he'll ever need in a million years. I told him, 'I gave you two fine, big, strappin' sons, both policemen. LAPD. Popped 'em right out and fed 'em from these two titties here.' That's why my titties kinda sag a little, Harry, from those two boys suckin' on 'em so much. But breast milk is best for babies. I really, seriously believe that. What do you think, Harry?"

He grunted.

"Shit, why ask a man that? You'll never know. But I told my old man, 'I gave you two sons, and that's enough. The least you can do after twenty-six years is give me enough to live on.' And not just *scrape by*, Harry, you know what I mean. I mean live ... like I'm used to. Live *nice*. Not have to sell my house or have a shit-ass car that keeps breakin' down. That's only fair, don't you think?"

"What happened?" Harry Hudson asked. "Did he get j-jealous? On account of the sssss--?" He didn't want to say *swinging* out loud even if he could.

"*He* got *me* into it," Louise said. "Then he got tired of it and wanted me to stop and I said, 'Hey, what's sauce for the gander,' you know? But it was *his* idea first."

"Oh."

"Hudson?" It was Steinbach. "You talking to a reporter there?"

He nodded vaguely.

"I hope so. We got a ton of stories piling up here, in case you haven't noticed."

Fear buzzed through him. "OK. Just a second."

"You at work, Harry?" Louise asked. "I didn't know. Should I hang up?"

"Yeah, sorry, I gotta go.... This theater, though, you talked about. What kind of theater? Where is it?"

"The Low Fox?" The giggle. "It's a porno thee-ater, Harry. In Gardena, some place out there. On Vermont. I *think* it's Gardena. But Vermont, yeah, that's right."

"Thanks, Louise."

"I mean it was *wild*, Harry. Not just the seven guys who were eatin' my pussy, but all the rest of 'em, standin' around us in the aisles--they'd pulled out their cocks, Harry, a dozen cocks, maybe, and they were jackin' off all around us, and they got come all over my *coat*, in my *hair*. Shit. Try to wash *that* out. I said never again, Harry, not like that."

Jesus, Harry Hudson thought.

"Weren't you scared?" he asked after a pause.

And that silenced Louise, too, at least for a moment. "Not really," she said. "I had Leroy there with me, kinda like my bodyguard, and I was just ... so damn *crazy*, pissed at my old man then.... I don't know."

"Hudson?" Steinbach said.

"The Low Fox?"

"Right, sweetheart. Tell me all about it afterwards."

#　#　#　#

What you really want to do in life, Finnegan had said.

Harry Hudson doubted he would ever come in this early for anything to do with work, but for his own obscure purposes ... here he was, at 10 a.m. on a Tuesday in the Clarion's morgue, wide awake, scrolling through microfilmed files beginning in 1942.

He found no editorial comment in the Clarion about Japanese-Americans at all. Just a brief notice on a front page--the truck farmers in Gardena and members of the fishing community on Terminal Island were supposed to report for relocation on a certain date.

Strange. Could he have missed it somehow? He ran the film back and forth for an hour before giving up.

The L.A. Times, in contrast, had plenty to say:

THE JAPS AND THEIR CIVIL LIBERTIES

A request just made to the President for a hearing looking to his rescinding of the military order for the excusion of Japanese from strategically important areas in the Pacific States appears to be characteristically ill-informed....

To assume that Gen. John L. DeWitt, the Federal Bureau of Investigation, the Army and Navy intelligence were motivated by race prejudice, greed for land, or popular hysteria, as this letter calmly does, is just silly....

The Times is not aware, nor is anybody outside official circles, of all the instances of sabotage, spying, signals from shore to ships, possession of illegal radios and the like which built up such a case against some of the Japanese residents of the Pacific Coast that the President's reluctance to sanction exclusion was overcome. But they must have been numerous....

Would the signers of this petition have cared to take the responsibility for sorting out the bad Japs from the good?

My God, Harry Hudson thought. The headlines alone:

KINDNESS TO ALIEN JAPS PROVES POOR POLICY

BLEEDING HEARTS DISCUSS THE JAP PROBLEM

REPRESENTATIVE ANSWERS PRO-JAP SENTIMENTALISM

A name caught his eye--the place where Nancy Ishida's parents had been sent:

THE STRIKE AT THE TULE LAKE SEGREGATION CENTER

The 14,000 Japanese held at the Tule Lake segregation center who have refused to harvest the crops raised there are storing up trouble for themselves and for other members of their race....

If they want to get tough they can take the consequences....

Only one of the editorials was signed--one of the worst:

By W.H. Anderson

61

Perhaps the most difficult and delicate question that confronts our powers that be is the handling--the safe and proper treatment--of our American-born Japanese, our Japanese-Americans, citizens by the accident of birth, but who are Japanese nevertheless.

A viper is nonetheless a viper wherever the egg is hatched. A leopard's spots are the same and its disposition is the same wherever it is whelped.

So a Japanese-American, born of Japanese parents, nurtured upon Japanese traditions, living in a transplanted Japanese atmosphere and thoroughly inoculated with Japanese thoughts, Japanese ideas and Japanese ideals, notwithstanding his nominal brand of accidental citizenship, almost inevitably and with the rarest of exceptions grows up to be a Japanese, not an American, in his thoughts, in his ideas and in his ideals, and is himself a potential and menacing, if not an actual, danger to our country unless properly supervised, controlled and, at is were, hamstrung.

Thus, while it might cause an injustice to a few to treat them all as potential enemies and to so limit and control their activities as to prevent the possibility of their becoming actually such, I cannot escape the conclusion--and I am by no means speaking idly or without a reasonable amount of knowledge on the subject--I cannot escape the conclusion that such treatment, as a matter of national and even personal defense, should be accorded to each and all of them while we are at war with their race.

Vance Foster had quoted from that one, adding:

I wonder who this W.H. Anderson was. And where he is now.

He was doing the job the owners of the Times, the Chandler family, paid him to do, of course, but that isn't all of it. There's a nastiness here that had to be his very own.

If W.H. Anderson is still alive, chipping golf balls around some Leisure World for the green-eyeshade set, I wonder if he knows what harm he did--and, if so, how he feels about it.

All those years in Garbersville, Harry Hudson had taken him as a model of what to avoid. If you can't be Vance Foster, he had thought, at least don't be W.H. Anderson.

But now he wondered if it mattered. Anderson had no doubt died smugly unrepentant, among people who thought as he did. His shame was buried in old, flickering microfilm that nobody looked at anymore. And Vance Foster's rebuttal, in a little paper up in Oregon that Anderson had probably never read, was buried just as deeply. Maybe he, Harry Hudson, was the only person left in the world who remembered *that*.

Where was Vance Foster? Dead as well, very likely. Long and comfortably retired, at least. Harry Hudson knew this, but that first night in the Clarion's newsroom, when he had seen Lincoln, McLachlan, Pierce and the others slumped in their swivel chairs around the copy desk, he had half expected to find Vance Foster there too, fading into the same shadows.

# # # #

It was out of the fryin' pan into the fire, you hear me? Except the fire wasn't quite so bad.

I just manage to get away from Darnell and, woop-woop-woop, here comes ol' Sidney.

Darnell. Shit. He be wantin' to get *with* me one night and I say no, I'm sick and tired of all his bullshit, and all of a sudden he starts beatin' on me right there on the sidewalk, on Atlantic across from St. Mary's. There's an empty lot there and he graps me by the neck and lifts me right up against the fence, and I'm tellin' Lynn--this white girl I'm walkin' with, used to hang out at the Black Hole too--tellin' her to call the cops, quick, but Lynn just stands there like she don't have a brain in her head. But some black dude sittin' in a coffee shop down the block--he saw what was jumpin' off and called 911 at the pay phone there, and them polices come right away in a car and got Darnell in a chokehold and pulled him off me. Shit. Like to strangled me. I had scab marks all up and down my neck. They could've put Darnell away, some serious time, too, cause he had a drug warrant on him, but I said, 'No, just detain the motherfucker long enough so I can get my clothes.'

And they say, 'You sure about this, ma'am?'

It's nice when them polices be on your side for a change.

And I say, 'Just detain his sorry ass for a day or so. Cause I am *leavin*.'

And I give Darnell a good long look where they're holdin' onto him, so he can think about all he's gonna miss.

But Darnell had the Buick--not that it even ran half the time anymore. I ain't got noplace to stay but Lynn's, and then after a while *she* be gettin' jealous, for no reason. All the places I used to hang out, I had to keep eyes in the back of my head, on account of him. Carried a knife in my purse. I got so I needed them Valiums all the time, my nerves was so bad. It wasn't *nothin'* nice.

I'm even thinkin' about callin' my mama in Kansas and havin' her wire me some money--which I swore I'd never ever do--when Sidney shows up at the Black Hole and says he's the dude called 911 and he wants to take care of me, keep Darnell from fuckin' with me. Shit. Last thing in the world I wanted was another man.

Still, I gotta admit, Sidney looked *real* good. A sharp dresser. Had them little tight curls they was wearin' then. Didn't look anywhere near forty-one.

And he could *talk*. Him and me sat there on them bar stools tellin' each other lies, and he could bullshit just as good as me. And I thought, well, at least this one ain't no dummy.

What can I say?

# # # #

The Low Fox.

It wasn't in the phone book. *Damn her anyway.* Harry Hudson looked up Vermont Avenue in his Thomas Guide. It was one of those L.A. streets that ran twenty miles or more, from the mountains to the sea. Four nights after his visit to the Rabbit Hutch, two after his call to Louise, he followed it from Gardena all the way up to Koreatown, then back south through neighborhoods so tough-looking that he kept away from the sidewalks and drove in the center lane. The Nissan still coughed. He had bent the crumpled fender away from the wheel, but sometimes, when he slowed for a red light and was aware of the idle dark men watching on corners, he imagined he still heard it scraping. Then, in a matter of blocks, everything changed. He was back in Gardena with its well-lit prosperity, sushi bars and poker clubs, Japanese signs mixed with more Korean. But nothing like what Louise had described.

A wild-goose chase.

He decided not to drive out there again, but the next night he did, and found the theater easily. Near the Rosecrans Avenue intersection--the same Rosecrans that ran by the Rabbit Hutch fifteen miles east. Not in Gardena proper, but next to it, in a narrow strip of L.A. that connected the downtown with the harbor in San Pedro. A windowless brick cube, yellow or dirty white, on a corner beyond a 7-Eleven and a couple of motels. OPEN 24 HOURS, a big sign said. A smaller sign said *Little* Fox--he must have misheard Louise. Did she have that much of an accent? He hadn't thought so. Maybe his ears really were going bad.

Harry Hudson parked under a street light and locked the car--though who would be crazy enough to steal it? He walked along the blank side wall of the theater, spray-painted with square, sharp-pointed letters that looked like another foreign language. *Was* a foreign language, to him. Once more, he teetered between excitement and fear. The air was cool now, after midnight; he was glad to hunch his shoulders into the jacket. The houses here had bars on the windows, junk cars in the yards. A big man sat in a van across the street--on guard duty for the theater, or was he a mugger?

The lobby of the Low Fox--Harry Hudson couldn't stop thinking of it as that--had an even thicker tobacco smell than the Clarion's newsroom. The porn videos and magazines looked dusty, ignored. Above a glass case of pink plastic penises and other sex aids was a hole in the wall where the projectionist, a black man with a grizzled beard, watched a re-run of "M.A.S.H." on a portable TV while moans from the film he was screening came through from the front.

"Six bucks," he said when Harry Hudson waited a beat too long.

How much of it went to the Mafia? *A real reporter would know*, Harry Hudson thought. To his left were two doorways, one blocked by a curtain, the other by a sheet of plywood. Hand-lettered signs warned against LEWD ACTS, INCLUDING MASTURBATION, saying the premises were monitored by the LAPD. A buzzer sounded, quit, then sounded again. The projectionist leaned out. Behind him Harry Hudson could see Army surgeons bent over the latest casualty, their green gowns flecked with blood.

"Go ahead, man."

Harry Hudson realized that the buzzer had unlocked the plywood door. He pushed through. A short corridor led into the darkness, where the moans grew louder. All he saw at first was the brilliant rectangle of the screen: an abstraction of fuzzy flesh tones that resolved itself into a scrotum that looked as big as a horse's, moving back and forth between a pair of straining legs.

The floor felt both gritty and sticky; the walls and ceiling were black, or nearly so. He could hear men cough and rustle in their seats as they turned--to stare at him, he supposed. To see if *he* was the LAPD. Harry Hudson stood against the rear wall until his eyes adjusted and the rows of seats came clear, scattered with watching or sleeping men. More men, he noticed, were standing along the wall like him, beyond the projector's beam of light, as if watching the others. Cops? Not likely. Black and Latino men mostly, but some whites too, in ragged windbreakers and sweat suits and jeans, with unkempt hair. No women at all. Could *this* be the place? It was scabbier even than the theaters Harry Hudson had visited in Portland. Louise had to be brave as hell to come in here.

Or nuts.

There was nothing to do but sit down, apart from anyone else, and watch the movie. It was like all the other porn flicks he had seen--a shopworn formula. Strange how it could bypass his mind and still turn him on. He got hard in no time. The women were pretty enough, Harry Hudson thought, but the men, as usual, seemed a class below them: muscular but slab-faced and vacant-looking. Except for one. He was short and brown and squat and hairy, with close-set eyes, pointed teeth and long, greasy curls. He owned up to his unattractiveness--that was the thing. He made fun of himself. He mugged lust and astonishment--an ordinary, ugly guy, a stand-in for all the losers in the theater, somehow let into paradise.

How? Harry Hudson wondered.

Before long he became aware of a pattern. Men would get up, stroll down the right-hand aisle to the rest room and disappear through a curtain. A little later, other men would follow them. Then, after a while, they would come back, one by one, with studied casualness. When he opened the curtain himself, Harry Hudson saw men standing against a beige plywood partition by the entrance to the toilets. It bore more signs: ONE AT A TIME ONLY. The men looked at him. Harry Hudson looked back. Whatever signal he was supposed to catch or return, he failed to guess it. They kept on looking, and he felt uncomfortable. Were they drug dealers or something? A toilet flushed, a man slouched out and Harry Hudson, relieved, went in. The room smelled of fresh blue-green paint, but new graffiti had sprouted already, like mildew, and he read it standing at a rust-stained urinal. An amber strip of flypaper hung from the ceiling, speckled with dead bugs. Under the paint he could smell piss and vomit and some other odor, wet and crumbling. Harry Hudson glanced up quickly: nobody was watching him. But walking out to the curtain, he felt the pressure of everyone's eyes.

As at the Rabbit Hutch, he thought: *How come everybody knows the rules here except me?*

A half-hour later, back in his seat, he had almost lost hope of any woman showing up. Then, drowsily, he heard a commotion that was louder than the usual stir that greeted a newcomer. He turned. It was a couple, picking their way down the left-hand aisle. They were black and middle-aged. The woman, bundled in an old-fashioned cloth coat, had a swollen face. The man, in a shiny Lakers jacket, held what looked like a pint of whiskey. They hesitated, then edged into a half-empty row and sat in the middle.

Another, bigger man--as big as the man outside in the van, but this one had been standing against the wall--went to the projectionist's window and muttered. Something white was passed out to him--a stack of styrofoam cups. He carried them to the row where the couple sat. He eased down next to the woman, across from her husband or boyfriend. They all seemed to know one another, Harry Hudson thought. Their voices rumbled softly. Whiskey was poured into the cups; then, as they drank, both men draped an arm over the woman's shoulders.

Silently, the men at the wall sidled down the aisles, and the seated men clustered around the couple. They leaned inward and watched. The whole theater seemed to hold its breath, the movie forgotten.

A rape? Harry Hudson thought, alarmed.

But the strange thing about it was that these ragged men seemed as disciplined as an army. There *were* rules, even here, and everyone knew them, somehow, without being told. It was a kind of ritual. An invisible line held them back, though several, just as Louise had said, unzipped their pants and took out their dicks.

The couple and their friend seemed unconcerned. Nobody else said a word.

It took quite a while. The three drank and talked. Maybe the men fondled the woman a little, but it was hard for Harry Hudson to see, even after he got up and joined the crowd in the right-hand aisle. The woman kept her coat on and bent her head. Her hair was clumpy. Finishing the drinks, they talked some more. The watchers waited patiently, stroking themselves. Cigarettes glowed in the darkness. The husband or boyfriend seemed to be exhorting the woman, who shrank into herself as the bigger man reached under her coat.

Then, suddenly, she shrugged. She took off the coat and hung it on the back of her seat, revealing flabby upper arms and a half-unbuttoned black blouse. Then she snorted, or laughed, the cords standing out in her neck, and Harry Hudson, who had been pitying her, felt his attitude change again. *No wonder she's willing,* he thought. *Outside, nobody's ever going to give her a second look. Here she's got every one of us panting. She's Queen of the Night, for Chrissake.* For that, Harry Hudson thought, public sex seemed a reasonable price to pay.

He'd do it himself, if anybody wanted.

After all, if she was queen, what did that say about *them?*

67

A pop-top fizzed; the big man held up a can of malt liquor. The woman took one long pull from it and set it on the floor. Then she bent over the lap of the man she had come with. He rested his hand on her head as it rhythmically rose and fell.

Harry Hudson imagined Louise with her feet up on the seat ahead--in those same red shoes with sequins, bent by her crippled toes.

But this woman wasn't letting herself go like that. No seven men for her; she concentrated on her partner, pausing now and then to retrieve the can and sip from it, while he chatted with the big man across her back, apparently feeling nothing. The big man had his hand down low somewhere, but she didn't react either. It wasn't sex, as Louise had described it, so much as a performance--one nobody seemed to want to come to a climax. Not the couple, enjoying all this attention focused on them; not the masturbating men, stretching out their pleasure. It was a trance, Harry Hudson thought, that they were all in together.

Still, maybe they were waiting for somebody to make a move.

Like him?

Don't be an idiot, he told himself.

Still, how would he know unless he tried? When the big man went to the rest room, leaving his seat open next to the woman, Harry Hudson saw his chance. He thought of Louise, how she would have welcomed him--of her telling him how she had *just freaked out, Harry.... Shit, yes.*

It was like at the Rabbit Hutch, slipping onto the dance floor.

No sweat.

But he had hardly stepped out of the group in the aisle and into the row when he realized it was another big mistake, like following Margot's Camaro into that Shell station. His face and ears prickled--he was blushing. He had broken the rules, just like that. Heads turned. Harry Hudson heard disapproving murmurs--not that he could stop himself now. He was still in the trance, though he could think at a great distance: *Why do I keep doing this? Over and over.* He sat down in the empty seat. The woman stiffened and looked at the screen. The reality of her, six inches away, was sobering--smells of unwashed skin and perfume and alcohol, a birthmark on one puffy cheek, or maybe a bruise. Her dull, heavy-lidded eyes. Her utter difference from Louise. Her weariness and misery. Her *fear*--for Harry Hudson saw that he had intimidated someone at last, at the worst possible time. *Oh, shit. Police?* she had to be thinking. *I'm not going to hurt you,* he tried to say, but nothing came out. He licked his lips. The woman half-turned and watched his face writhe, his spittle fly. Her expression slowly changed to surprise, then contempt. Her partner looked around her at Harry Hudson--a slick diagonal scar across the bridge of his nose, eyes with yellowish whites. "What *you* want, motherfuck?" he said.

"E-excuse me," Harry Hudson said.

More messengers.

He got up as if scalded and hurried out of the row, through a blur of faces and bodies. Nobody stopped him. He thought, in those first seconds, that he was leaving the theater, but he was afraid this would call even more attention to himself. Instead he circled back and sat as far from the couple as he could, on a seat whose vinyl had been slashed with a knife and patched with duct tape.

Harry Hudson tried to disappear--to squeeze himself into the smallest possible space, to let the darkness color him.

If only Deborah could see him now, he thought. She'd know she was better off without him.

For sure.

The big man came back and the woman and her partner talked to him, pointing in Harry Hudson's direction. The big man glared but did nothing more. He sat down. The woman resumed her blow job. But the trance was broken; she soon stopped again and put on her coat. Some of the men by the wall drifted away. She and her partner went to the rest room together, and the big man went with them, but they didn't stay long. Then all three walked up the right-hand aisle, popping another can of malt liquor, and disappeared into the tunnel that led to the curtained exit.

Harry Hudson didn't move.

They were bums here, he thought. Drunks, druggies, people who would rob you for a quarter, he supposed. Shoot or knife you if they thought they had a reason. Rape a woman in some other place. Yet once again it was he, Harry Hudson, who had failed to fit in because he lacked as much self-control as they had. They were the lowest of the low--anybody could see that--but in their eyes he was lower.

Even here!

And he thought he knew why. He had held himself separate from them--thought he was better, somehow, in spite of all he had done. They could sense it. As a new movie came on and the little brown hairy man, surprisingly, appeared again, peeking through a crack in a cabana door and rolling his eyes at naked women in a pool, Harry Hudson thought of those other men's languid patience. It was the patience of hopelessness, he thought. You took what came to you but didn't try to force any more.

Could he ever have that kind of patience? He brooded about it, sitting in the Low Fox hour after hour as some of the men, who had nowhere else to go, sprawled in sleep. At last he did seem to disappear. And, fully attuned to the darkness, he saw something he had previously missed. It wasn't just the men by the wall who had taken out their dicks when the couple came; every other seated man, too, was stroking himself somnolently, keeping some delicate balance of excitement. Once Harry Hudson saw this, he couldn't believe he hadn't seen it before. *And those theaters in Portland--what about there?*

Very late--was it dawn already?--he went to the rest room and found men still standing by that beige plywood partion, eternal sentries. Their eyes still burned with intensity. Once again Harry Hudson had no answer for them, but one very short man, squatting on the floor in a threadbare Army field jacket, dared more: He pursed his cracked lips in a kind of kiss.

And stumbling through the tunnel to the lobby, Harry Hudson bumped into two more men, one sucking the other.

"Peace," he said and raised a hand, sidled on by.

Outside, the van was gone.

#   #   #   #

July 12, 1864

Good order has prevailed since the hanging [of several "raiders" by an inmate police force, with the Confederates looking on]. *The men have settled right down to the business of dying, with no interruption.... Not less than one hundred and sixty die each twenty-four hours.... The dead are being gathered up and carried to the south gate and placed in a row inside the dead line.... They are black from pitch pine smoke and laying in the sun. Some of them lay there for twenty hours or more, and by that time are in a horrible condition. At four o'clock a four or six mule wagon comes up to the gate and twenty or thirty bodies are loaded on to the wagon and they are carted off to be put in trenches, one hundred in each trench....*

July 19

There is no such thing as delicacy here. Nine out of ten would as soon eat with a corpse for a table as any other way....

July 25

At my earnest solicitation was carried to the gate this morning, to be admitted to the hospital. Lay in the sun for some hours to be examined, and finally my turn came and I tried to stand up, but was so excited I fainted away. When I came to myself I lay along with a row of the dead on the outside. Raised up and asked a rebel for a drink of water, and he said, "Here, you Yank, if you ain't dead, get inside there!" And with his help was put inside again....

July 26

Ain't dead yet.... Can't walk a step now. Shall try for the hospital no more.

July 28

Taken a step forward toward the trenches since yesterday, and am worse. Had a wash all over this morning. Battese took me to the creek; carries me without any trouble.

\#   \#   \#   \#

Deborah.

He hadn't loved her, Harry Hudson thought later--and in Red Fork he had plenty of time to think. That was his first mistake, which had led to all the others. He had known it, too, sort of, from the beginning. The faded look of her face, without any makeup; her chapped lips, the dryness of her straight strawberry-blonde hair, the thinness of her neck and calves, the wrinkles at her wrists and the corners of her eyes--these things had bothered him, though he knew they shouldn't. He felt little desire for her. But how important should sex be? Harry Hudson tried to ask himself. It wasn't so important to *her,* judging from her plain skirts and blouses and sweaters and anoraks, her churchgoing and her dry, sensible manner. Actually, she wasn't in bad shape at all for a woman of thirty-three. And who did he think *he* was--Robert Redford? That was a laugh. If she could look at a man deeper than the skin--as she *had* to be doing in his case, Harry Hudson thought--then why couldn't he do the same to her? This was a real woman, he told himself, not a fantasy, as he was willing, finally, to admit Nancy Ishida had become--a woman who taught sixth grade at Garbersville Middle School, drove a Dodge Dart, sang in the choir at Faith Tabernacle alongside Owsley's wife; a woman who, unlike anyone else in all these years, had shown an interest.

He met Deborah one Christmas. Students of hers who were also members of the church's youth group were caroling at hospitals and nursing homes. She was escorting them around the snowy streets, waving her arms

71

and stamping the rhythm with her big grey moon boots. A trite seasonal story. Dime a dozen, even Owsley might say. But the air that particular night smelled sharply of pine and unbearably of Harry Hudson's youth and was cold enough to splinter the stars; and then he was inside a cozy church room drinking eggnog and eating home-baked cookies while Deborah leaned over the refreshments table and gave him the details, cheeks flushed, eyes bright, melting snowflakes in her hair. This was enough to corrupt him. He laid on a photog, promised the nice lady *beaucoup* column inches, wrote the hell out of it, sent her a personal copy--all so that, after a kind of dance in which he found himself following Deborah's lead--for Harry Hudson knew less about dating than the average fourteen-year-old--she stepped into his apartment and recoiled a little from the smell. *Not* a youthful smell here: something sour and closed-in, gone to seed.

"You poor man," she said.

A reclamation project--that's what she saw in him, he supposed. A desert in need of irrigation. Or a swamp to be drained.

Why did she take on such a task? He could only guess. She was divorced. She wanted children. That was clear. He was single, at least, and steadily employed. But, good God, in a town the size of Garbersville couldn't she have done better?

He should have told her. He *tried* to tell her. She was making a mistake. "Y-you j-just don't know," he said. "How w-weird I can be sometimes." But she insisted on taking this as modesty. *You're nothing like him at all,* she said of her ex-husband, Lloyd, who sold insurance and real estate in The Dalles. A glad-hander and a bully, he gathered. *You're quiet and sweet and gentle--very lovable, only it's the strangest thing: You don't know it. You really* don't *know it, Harry, do you?* He remembered these words, and clung to them, long after she had changed her tune.

He should have stopped it, right away. *He* had to, because Deborah clearly wouldn't. But if he did, he remembered thinking at the time, how soon would somebody else came along wanting to marry him?

Maybe never.

So his corruption proceeded. It was only after the wedding, after they had honeymooned, more or less, at Crater Lake, after Deborah had bought him the jacket, that he told her about killing the old man. *Now I've ruined it,* Harry Hudson thought, snug in the counter-knowledge that he probably hadn't. And, in fact, that was the night they trembled and wept together and

72

talked until daybreak, the night Deborah made love to him as she never did before or since--her skin moist and hot, her arms clutching him, her mouth sandy and loose with abandon. An abandon of the spirit more than the body, as it proved. She asked him to pray with her. And he did, awkwardly, kneeling down beside the bed, not believing but moved by her tears, her passion and his own dawning sense that he had lucked out.

Next day, though, it was different. Deborah was stiff again, embarrassed and cautious--maybe what he had confessed to her had sunk in. She felt he had made his peace with God and it was time for them both to move on. No more trembling and weeping. Whereas that was what Harry Hudson wanted never to end. Night after night, he wanted to tell her war stories and stories about his childhood and his job and have her hold him until he felt forgiven more than an hour at a time. Was that too much to ask? It seemed to be. The first note of impatience entered her voice, which turned out to have as much sting in it as Riker's:

I know you didn't have a mother, Harry, not really, but I'm not her. Remember that. You aren't one of my sixth-graders, either.

You haven't ever asked Brent Owsley for a raise? Why on earth not?

It scares me, how you don't seem to have any plans.

Watch it! What were you thinking about? Maybe I'd better drive.

You may have been satisfied to live in a fishing camp, Harry, or whatever you want to call it, but I'm not. And I work harder than you do. The least you can do is your share here at home.

Any plans, I said. Knock, knock? Anybody there?

But you can't seriously expect to rewrite 4-H press releases and shoot the breeze with desk sergeants for the rest of your life. Can you?

Harry! Did you see that car? You could have got us killed.

I'll say this for Lloyd, at least. He cared about clothes, how he looked in them.

I'm thinking about a family, Harry--our family--and all you seem to think about is yourself.

With two incomes, they were rich, it seemed. He bought the Nissan. They moved into a new apartment complex, California-style stucco, with a view of the Three Sisters on clear days. And that swimming pool.

But Deborah's voice dominated Harry Hudson's life. Like his father, like Riker, she was always right, he felt, so he never had an answer, even if he could have managed the words. He retreated into silence, which she interpreted as hostility. Which *was* hostility, he came to realize. When he asked her, please, to stop complaining, she looked at him askance. "Do you mean I can't express myself, can't be honest with you?" she would say, and he had to say, no, he didn't mean that. Later on--once, twice--he yelled at her, "Shut up! Leave me alone!", and was terrified by the thought that he had done something awful, irreparable, while Deborah, used to far worse arguments with Lloyd, was merely upset. She couldn't guess--any more than Owsley could when Harry Hudson broke his silence about wanting to be a columnist--what such an outburst cost him.

They fell, gradually, into one of those patterns that Harry Hudson had read about for years in Dear Abby and lately seen acted out in TV talk shows-- patterns that had no more to do with real people, he had always thought, than the fetishes of the deviants and perverts he had read about in those sex papers in Portland. But there they were, he and his wife. Trapped, somehow. He was the unresponsive male who goaded Deborah into a shrillness she clearly regretted at times, a shrillness that made him withdraw still more. It was stupid, ridiculous. But how to escape it?

Then there was sex. How important should it be? Not very--unless you were getting hardly any, he thought bitterly, in which case it mattered more than anything.

Yet sex, like forgiveness, was something Harry Hudson concluded he couldn't ask for, because the asking spoiled it in advance. He began to drink heavily again. And one night, coming home from a choir recital in Bend, when he nearly sideswiped a logging truck and she upbraided him as if he were one of her twelve-year-olds--though he'd *told* her, more than once, that her nitpicking rattled him, made his driving worse, if anything--he discovered the alternative to silence. He could hit her. In a cold fury, he imagined backhanding Deborah across the face or punching her with a sharp, closed fist on her upper arm, then announcing: *Every time. Every time you talk like that, I'm gonna hit you. Until you learn to keep your mouth shut.* The thought of finally, fully, getting her attention so intoxicated him that he wasn't sure why he didn't go ahead and do it. A lingering desire to be a nice guy? A sense of her innocence and frailty-- pale skin, slender bones? Or the realization that being an asshole and a tyrant took more energy than he would ever have?

Or maybe it was the *smell* of his rage, which was unsettlingly familiar. It smelled like wool blankets and smoke and mittens left too long on the stove-- like the house in Beattie when he was a little boy. Had his father hit his mother? He couldn't remember. For days afterward, Harry Hudson groped through the dimness of those years, finding in the chinks of light that opened to him a few glimpses of his mother braiding her hair, reading with him on her lap, listening to records:

Stop your ramblin', stop your gamblin'
And stayin' out late at night.
Go home to your wife and family,
And stay by the fireside bright....

That was "Goodnight, Irene," one of her favorites. And on the flip side:

So long--it's been good to know you,
But a long time since I've been home,
So I've gotta be movin' along....

But that was all. No hint of violence. Later, he worked on a story that involved interviewing a doctor in the oncology ward at Garbersville Memorial; this jarred loose the memory that his father had taken him there just before his mother died. Even then, what he recalled wasn't her face so much as the rim of grey windowlight that had outlined it.

Finally he decided that his father hadn't hit his mother, despite all their shouting, but that he had *wanted* to--wanted to badly. The tension of that wanting and not doing was what had given the air in the house that scorched smell, like an overloaded electric motor. No wonder it seemed so familiar. It had hardly changed after she was gone, except that his father *had* used the belt now and then; it was the tension Harry Hudson had breathed in every day.

Sally's birth came as a reprieve. Harry Hudson adored the baby. The love that flooded him at the sight of this tiny, helpless creature, his own, seemed just as deep, as unstoppable, as his anger, and even stronger. It justified him, he thought. At last. He would be the best father who ever was. He fed Sally, changed her diapers, spent hours gazing at her in the nursery, awash in his feelings--but by then Deborah had begun to realize she *had* made a mistake. She wasn't about to pardon any mistakes of his--and one thing was certain: he would make them.

Once, when the baby wouldn't stop crying, Harry Hudson put his face down close to hers and yelled back, insanely. Once he left her in the car while he bought a six-pack--but only for a minute, he tried to explain; it hadn't been even halfway hot.

Both times Deborah screamed at him.

And he had no answer then, either, not really. He *was* a killer, after all. Wasn't he?

75

The funeral bewildered him. It was nothing like his parents'. Deborah refused to mourn. She chanted "Hallelujah!" in chorus with a few church members--not including the Owsleys--who had lately been talking about splitting off and forming another congregation, more pure, more charismatic, more evangelical ... whatever. *A reporter would know.* She stood in the rain-- it was hammering down, and wind lashed the dark firs, and the grass was trodden into mud around the little green plastic rug that covered the grave-- and praised the Lord with an expression of joy that belied the water glistening on her face. She had become a Christian, she once told Harry Hudson, after breaking up with Lloyd. *I had to believe in it all, then, or I couldn't believe in anything.* It had made sense, in a way, when she said it. Now, he knew, she was making another leap. And as he stood beside the embarrassed Owsley, the ribs of their umbrellas rattling together, it seemed to him that this woman, his wife, was issuing one last appeal. She wanted him to leap too. Crouched beside the casket as if on the end of a diving board, hugging herself in her rain-splotched coat, hair streaming, she had become again the Deborah of that single good night together, moist and giving and unpredictable.

It awed him, but it also gave him the creeps.

The smell in his nostrils by now was different. It was the acid smell of the rubber-tree leaves, the smell of mist and mosquito repellent and gunpowder and his own clammy sweat. It told him just one thing:

Run.

# # # #

Aug. 20, 1864

Some say three hundred now die each day....

Aug. 26

Eyesight very poor and writing tires me. Battese sticks by; such disinterested friendship is rare. Prison at its worst.

Aug. 27

Have now written nearly through three large books, and still at it. The diary am confident will reach my people if I don't. There are many here who are interested and will see that it goes North.

Aug. 30

Am in no pain whatever, and no worse.

# # # #

"That place got no class," Louise said. "I told you that, Harry, didn't I?"

"What?"

"I *told* you that thee-ater wasn't nothin' but a bunch of dogs. No way *I'm* goin' back there, sweetheart. You don't know what you gonna pick up in a place like that, not these days.... You say all men there?"

"Almost."

"Shee-it." The giggle. "Maybe they're waitin' for *me*."

"Maybe so," Harry Hudson said. "You're a l-legend there, Louise. I bet they n--. Never saw anybody l-like you. Before or since."

"No lie, Harry. You got *that* right. But, seriously, I don't belong in a place like that, didn't you tell me yourself? I *know* you did, Harry. 'You got way too much class for that joint, Louise.' Those were your exact words. 'No matter how much fun it might have been just that once.' And you're right, sweetheart, you know that? A hundred percent right."

"But th--" *That isn't what I said,* Harry Hudson wanted to say. *And it wasn't what you told me at all.*

"What?"

"W-when can I s-see you?"

Over the phone--the newsroom phone again--Louise's voice dropped to a whisper, though he would have sworn she was alone.

"Not *now,* Harry. Not for a couple of months, anyway. My old man comes in and out of the house all the time. Till the settlement's final, it wouldn't look good.... *Call* me, though, Harry. Leave it on the machine."

"W-when?" Harry Hudson asked.

"*Later.*"

# # # #

Two nights later he was back, wondering why.

All the places in Southern California he had tried to feel at home--the newsroom, the Reef, the Rabbit Hutch.... Was the Low Fox, society's shithole, finally it? Maybe. All Harry Hudson knew was, on his second visit there he felt no fear. He was a regular already, it seemed. He paid the projectionist (watching Arsenio Hall this time), sat in the rear row and waited a decent interval while his eyes refocused in the dark and he breathed in what seemed to be the identical haze of smoke, two days staler. Then he took out his dick. A youngish Latino with a mustache, one row ahead and three seats to his left, noticed immediately. It was simple, Harry Hudson discovered. They needed no words. All he had to do was meet the man's gaze for a second and not look away. The Latino nodded, unsmiling, got up, circled around and sat next to him, wearing cut-off jeans and a sleeveless white sweatshirt. His legs were hairy; his muscular, tattooed shoulder gave off a spicy smell of sweat.

Harry Hudson stared straight ahead at the movie. A room in a suburban house, shag rugs, motel-type furniture, close-ups of heaving flesh. He tried to drag out the tension of the moment, to pretend he didn't know what was happening even as he felt the man's rough fingers grip and stroke him. His excitement was astonishing. It seemed to come from all around him, yet from nowhere. Harry Hudson didn't desire the Latino--he was sure of that; he didn't desire any *person* right now, even the women on the screen. But he was trembling anyway. What excited him seemed to be nothing more than the ease and the openness of it--his sense that here, at last, in this brick box, if he followed the rules, shame was banned.

Then the man began sucking him, rapidly, expertly, and Harry Hudson was surprised all over again by the force of his pleasure. He came (much too soon, he thought) and felt stickiness on his pants, the vinyl of the seat. In a daze, he saw the man raise up and smile, as if to say: *See? Just us, no sweat, man. None of that other shit.*

Harry Hudson patted the man's warm shoulder. "That was nice," he heard himself say, quite fluently and louder than he had intended. The man looked surprised, then patted him back before returning to his old seat.

A little shame returned then. Harry Hudson felt exposed, and hurried to the rest room to wipe himself off. When he came back, the Latino was gone.

Afterward, he sat in another row, spent and calm--but afraid that, once again, he had misunderstood the rules. Had the Latino had second thoughts, suspected him of being a cop? Had he expected Harry Hudson to suck *him* off? It seemed only fair, considering. At least, Harry Hudson thought, he should have stayed and talked to the young fellow, asked his name ... but as time went by and he watched a couple of similar encounters between men in the rear row, which seemed to be the designated rendezvous--no women came in that night--he saw that this was wrong. The warmth between them had been real enough, he thought, but it couldn't last longer than its own moment.

Wasn't that enough?

Take what comes. Don't hope for more. Hudson doubted that many of these men were gay. They had been plenty aroused by the couple last night--not to mention the movies. As for himself, Nancy Ishida had kept him from ever worrying too much. Bless her for that, anyway.

There were people in Beattie who would say he had just committed the worst sin of all, but he knew that wasn't true.

The life he had led had taught him that much, at least.

No, here *gay* and *straight* didn't matter. This was a fellowship of the already damned, Harry Hudson thought drowsily, beginning to be proud of his acceptance, a fragile and unlikely peace circulating through his body--this heavy, graceless body in its cooling film of sweat. Nothing mattered here. No money, no college degrees, no jobs, no pride, no expectations.

No words.

He must have dozed off. He woke up with a start, slapping at his wallet pocket, but the spell of the Low Fox held: nobody had robbed him. The theater was almost empty now. What was it--two in the morning? Harry Hudson looked around and saw two men in the rear row, where he had sat with the Latino. These men were black, both slender. One had taken off his pants entirely. He had his feet propped on the seat in front of him, as Harry Hudson had imagined Louise's; the other man, jeans down to his ankles, was fucking him. Harry Hudson watched them, rapt. They moved almost imperceptibly in the darkness below the projection beam. They made no sound he could hear.

The first man saw Harry Hudson turn and looked back, as if challenging him: *You bustin' us or what?* Harry Hudson smiled, *No,* and gave a little wave. Then he turned back to the movie, the men's slow, rhythmic movements continuing in his mind's eye. The films had gone a complete cycle, he noticed: There was same suburban room, the shag rugs, hair and skin, inane music and voices.

Amazingly, he slept again. This time when he awoke only the first man was left in the rear row, bare legs still up on the seat ahead. This time the man was watching Harry Hudson. Without the other body covering him, his spread knees and shins were outlined by the light from the screen--like the rim of light Harry Hudson had seen on his mother's face in the Garbersville hospital, only swarming with faint movement and color. The man's face was expressionless, his hair cropped very short, with zigzag razor-cut designs. He beckoned to Harry Hudson, a languorous wave of his wrist.

Come on.

# # # #

Sidney, he all right. Most of the time. It's his people I can't stand, you hear me? He was born right here in Long Beach. Got eleven brothers and sisters, ain't a one of 'em any good, and they be all *over* the place. I can't get rid of 'em. His sisters, they be heavy women, *real* heavy--can't push they way back from the table--and *real* jealous of me, except for this skinny one that's kinda the other way, you know? Likes girls. Calls me 'girlie' and 'baby doll' and all that. Shit. That ain't normal, I don't care what you say. Two cocks just don't rock. I tried to tell her, tried to be nice about it, but she don't listen. And Sidney's brothers, only one of 'em's workin', last I heard, and they all done prison time. Sellin' dope. Armed robbery. This part of Long Beach here is Crip territory. Cuzz. You wear red, like them Bloods, you better get ready to duck--they pop a cap on you soon as say good mornin'. All I know is, once them polices found out I married into the Crenshaws, they *really* be keepin' an eye on me. Ooh wee, that name Crenshaw in *all* their computers. At least nobody else on the street wants to mess with me, knowin' I'm with Sidney. That's cool. But Sidney got *his* problems. Got two kids already, by one of his old girlfriends. They been livin' here and there, with his mama, mostly. Sidney Junior, he a pistol. Nineteen, thinks he a *man* already, and Tamika, she fifteen and pregnant, thinks she a *woman*. Same name as that big bitch tried to jump me when we first come to L.A. Sidney wants me to take care of 'em. And then he wants *more?*

Shit.

Sidney's good with cars. He always tearin' somebody's engine down, makin' a few dollars that way. But he ain't got no license, you hear what I'm sayin'? Whatever them garage mechanics got. And nobody wants to hire an ex-con. His past be catchin' up with him, you know what I mean? Last time he got out of prison, they got him a job at this machine shop in Orange County, and this drill press or lathe or somethin'--some big machine there--done crushed his left hand. He had wires all up through his fingers to straighten 'em out so they wouldn't just curl up like claws. Hurt so much he still be cryin' at night, months afterward, when them doctors be pullin' the tension up another notch. Around the time I met him, Sidney got half his settlement money and bought himself a Cadillac Eldorado--an '85, but it had *real* low miles on it. The rest of the money's due, but it still ain't come. Them sorry-ass lawyers draggin' it out, same as they did with me.

The brother that's workin'--he run the maintenance on this big apartment building downtown. He in charge of *all* of it, you hear? Don't you even *try* to tell me he can't give Sidney a job too. But you think them Crenshaws would help out one of their own--somebody like Sidney who's tryin' to get serious, get his life back together? Shit, no. They be jealous--tryin' to drag him back down to *they* level.

My people in Kansas wasn't like that. At all.

What it adds up to ain't *nothin'* nice. Them bills still be comin' in, and can you believe it? I'm still on the stroll.

#   #   #   #

He had to take his turn sucking cock too, he decided. Otherwise he was only slumming.

But Harry Hudson's third visit to the Low Fox felt wrong from the start. The theater was slow to fill up, and nobody seemed to notice when he entered. He took out his dick and nobody paid attention to that either. The other men were beating their own meat or sleeping or dully watching the movie. What had happened the night before last with the Latino was an exception, he concluded reluctantly. *Just dumb luck. Which you didn't appreciate, as usual.* And the two blacks--maybe they would come in only much later, maybe never again. Who could say? Harry Hudson's disappointment surprised him, just as feeling so good had surprised him forty-eight hours before. He settled back into his seat and saw that the hairy little man with pointed teeth was back on the screen, in a different role. Obnoxious now. Sneering and gloating, slapping women's asses, inflicting his greasiness on them, clearly in charge. Why did they put up with this jerk? *Money. It has to be.* He had to be bankrolling these films. And why not, if you were an ugly guy who could afford it? But this night, for some reason, Harry Hudson wondered more about the women. They didn't all look like junkies and whores. A lot of them looked like college students, in fact. Housewives. And he had rarely seen the same face twice.

Where did they all come from?

Christ.

The idea of it--that so many seemingly ordinary women had to do that for a living--disturbed him. Harry Hudson became aware of how tired he was. He thought of getting up and leaving, but just then a man sat down two seats to the right and took out *his* dick. A fiftyish white man, beefy, wearing dark slacks and a pinstriped dress shirt. Tufts of thinning grey hair and a slack gut. Warts on his stroking hand. A thick wrist. Eyes that shone pale in the screen's reflection as he looked at Harry Hudson questioningly. The LAPD at last, bent on entrapment? Or just another poor, lonely slob like him? Harry Hudson glanced back, then quickly away. The man made no move. They played that game over again, twice. Then Harry Hudson got up and went to the rest room. It was empty. He took a piss and flushed the urinal, read the graffiti and waited. Again he couldn't block out an uneasy thought: This stinking cubicle had once been open air above one of the Japanese truck farms the notice in the Clarion had ordered people to abandon. Some of Nancy Ishida's relatives, maybe. Green lettuce, a salt breeze. What did it mean that he was standing there now? He shivered. When he was sure that nobody was following him in, Harry Hudson went back and sat in the same seat. The man gave him the same questioning look, but that was all. Cop or loser, he was leaving it up to Harry Hudson to take the risk.

He didn't want to. But wasn't that the point? he thought. If he wanted to, he would be gay, wouldn't he? This was just a matter of passing on the favor those other, nameless men had done for him.

Warts on his dick, too, probably.

But that wasn't it either, exactly. It bothered him, Harry Hudson realized, to do it with another white man. Touching dark skin was easier, more comfortable, somehow.

But why? Wasn't that just another form of prejudice?

And not against the white man, he saw clearly enough--but against those others, two nights ago. Which meant, now, he *had* to do it.

Craziness.

The man's eyes, angry and full of need, pulled at him.

Harry Hudson got up and went over and knelt on the sticky floor between the man's knees, as if it were a duty. The dick he took in his fist was huge, though still partly soft. It had a foreskin, which he pushed tentatively back. *No words.* Below the foreskin was a smooth, sectioned knob, like a dwarf apple. The man grunted and held Harry Hudson's head down. Instinctively, he pulled back. The man pushed harder, gripped Harry Hudson's hair, so that the roots stung. He seemed to have no tenderness at all. "F-first time," Harry Hudson tried to say. "Sorry," but it was as if the thing were in his mouth already, filling it up, choking him. It was like the stuttering spirit itself, and suddenly it was impossible for Harry Hudson to do what the Latino had done. His knees hurt. He tried to stand, to apologize again, but the man snarled, "Shit, you--" and wrestled him, as brutal and heedless as the man on the screen, treating him--

--like a woman, Harry Hudson thought.

That was when his fear rushed back, and with it shame and disgust. He broke away and scrambled out to the aisle. The man grabbed for him, but when Harry Hudson looked back once, he didn't seem to have moved. Heading for the exit, though, back turned, Harry Hudson heard seats creak, thought he heard footsteps--not just the white man but others, too, following him. His last glimpse of the movie had been of the hairy man, sharp-toothed, laughing. He ducked through the tunnel to the curtain, then through the lobby. Then outside. They could beat him up, rob him, steal his car. Why not? He had to walk the length of the building to where the Nissan squatted under its street light. It looked deformed, somehow--already broken into? If he ran they would chase him; if he looked back, he would see his terror confirmed. So he had to walk steadily, trying not to hear what seemed to be an echo of the scrape of his shoes on the sidewalk. They were probably just waiting for him to open the car door; then they'd pounce. Even if he got in and locked it--and Harry Hudson saw this happening, in slow motion, well before he reached the Nissan, just as he had known outside Phuoc Vinh that he had dreamed his failure, in one way or another, long before he pulled that trigger--would he have time to turn the key and shift and drive off before they shattered the window? The engine would die on him. Fucking heap. He knew it. It was the only fitting ending for a trip that had begun, he saw, back when Rick Holcomb, over coffee at Denny's, had told him about the Haven.

#   #   #   #

Sept. 6, 1864

Hurrah! Hurrah!! Hurrah!!! Can't holler except on paper. Good news. Seven detachments ordered to be ready to go at a moment's notice. LATER.--All who cannot walk must stay behind. If left behind shall die in twenty-four hours.... The greatest excitement; men wild with joy. Am worried fearful that I cannot go, but Battese says I shall.

#   #   #   #

The morning after, Harry Hudson wrote Deborah her monthly support check. It was Monday by now, his fourth week at the Clarion, and he hadn't been let go yet. He would collect another week's pay, at least--the following Monday if Steinbach kept him on; late Friday, probably, if he got the axe. Either way, Deborah would have most of it. Six hundred dollars, half again the usual amount. He dated the check ahead to Monday. That would leave him barely enough for rent if he stayed. If he didn't ... but that was the point, wasn't it? Harry Hudson thought, dizzy with fatigue, a sour, sticky film seeming to linger in his mouth.

Punishment.

#   #   #   #

"No, I can't say I have," Spencer Lincoln said over dinner on Wednesday when Harry Hudson asked if he had known any other job applicant's tryout to be dragged out so long. "Not in my time here, and that's since the Herald-Examiner strike, way back. Strange. I don't know what to tell you."

The tamales served in the cafeteria that evening surprised Harry Hudson--the genuine corn-husked kind, delicious. Lincoln's wife had been Mexican, he remembered hearing; Lincoln had lived in Mexico for a time and spoke fluent Spanish. He wrote well, too--the occasional feature or book review. A talented man, evidently. But a discouraged one, too wary now to give Harry Hudson more than a bleak half-smile, dabbing his chin with a napkin.

"It's a Guild paper, isn't it?" Harry Hudson asked.

"Our beloved Clarion? Yes, indeed."

"C-cant they c-complain? Isn't it against the c--?" He licked his lips.

"The contract? I dunno. Maybe. But we aren't exactly talking Teamsters here. The Newspaper Guild's just hanging on by its fingertips. Watch what happens the next time we negotiate, if you're still around. Management brings in all these high-powered lawyers and CPAs and media consultants, and we walk around the building with picket signs on our shoulders like they did a hundred years ago. Unions are a dying breed, believe me."

"S-so they can't help?"

The half-smile again. "I wouldn't count on it."

If we only knew you a little better, Lincoln seemed to say--*enough to care....*

Across the room, Holcomb and his wife, Judy, picked the husks from their tamales. She was pert and animated, with frizzy dishwater hair. *They seem happy, at least.* Harry Hudson felt a sudden nostalgia for this place, which he had hardly begun to know.

"You thhhink I'll still b--?" *Be around,* he wanted to say.

"Who knows?"

But Harry Hudson knew. He was losing his grip on the job now, slowing down, blurring in and out, and he suspected that everything he had done at the Rabbit Hutch and the Low Fox was tattooed on his face, plain to see.

I'm a geek, he thought.

As his interview with Springer two days later seemed to confirm.

#   #   #   #

So when Steinbach took him into Springer's vacant office around 8 p.m. on that same twentieth shift, he had already checked out of the Reef on his dinner break, loaded his car. He cringed.

"Four weeks already? My, how time flies," Steinbach said. The half-light carved deeper hollows for his eyes, made the pockmarks on his cheeks look like BB wounds. Harry Hudson dimly remembered his father's face long ago, over the kitchen table in Beattie. Steinbach's thick white hair stood almost straight up. "So what do you think?" he asked. "Does the Clarion suit you?"

This bewildered Harry Hudson. What did it matter if the Clarion suited him? Did *he* suit *them?* Was this some kind of sadistic game?

"S-sure," he said, but his vision darkened, his stomach cramped and all he could think of was what to do after the blow fell. He had eighty-three dollars, besides what was going to Deborah. That would pay for two nights, maybe three, if the motels were cheap enough. A few meals. A tank of gas. He saw himself driving the Nissan back north, as if he had a plan of some kind; sitting in a diner in Bakersfield, maybe, reading the help-wanted ads, but nothing beyond that.

He closed his eyes.

When he came back, Steinbach was saying: "...managing editor says we ought to know you well enough by now. Me, I prefer long engagements. Don't you? Elope in haste, repent in leisure, I always say."

Harry Hudson didn't understand a word.

"I've seen better work, God knows," Steinbach said. He leaned on Springer's desk in his short-sleeved white shirt and narrow '50s tie, both skinny arms crooked inward. He gazed at the ceiling.

Harry Hudson nodded.

"But I guess I've seen worse, too. So it's up to you."

"What?"

"You got the job, dummy. If you want it."

Steinbach, the calendar on the wall behind him, the rubber bands on Springer's desk suddenly wavered and flowed. Harry Hudson's eyes stung. He felt that his knees had given way and he had already curled up and gone to sleep on the floor, slept a week at least, even though, somehow, he was still standing.

"Jesus, Hudson, take it easy," Steinbach said. Now *he* seemed to be embarrassed. "It's just another lousy newspaper job, right? Nothing to get all shook up about. For Chrissakes, get ahold of yourself."

"S-sorry," Harry Hudson said, still blinking.

Steinbach grinned, his sarcasm momentarily gone. "Why don't you take the rest of the night off? It's quiet. Hell, Brad and Spence can handle things. Go out, celebrate. Least we can do under the circumstances."

"Celebrate?"

"Sure."

# # # #

'I'm a sportin' lady,' I told Harry the first time he come into the Black Hole and asked me what my profession was. *Profession.* That tickled me. I could tell he was the shy type. Big white dude, lookin' around like somebody gonna come up behind him and mug him any minute. Otherwise I would've thought *cop*, you hear what I'm sayin'? But who ever heard of a cop that stuttered?

He asks me how old I am.

'Whatever you want,' I said. 'Sweet sixteen or a good thirty-five, it's all the same to me.'

That set him back on his heels some. Got him to thinkin'. Then he asks how come I'm not in Beverly Hills somewhere, makin' about a thousand dollars a night.

'Got in with the wrong company,' I told him, thinkin' about Darnell, mostly, but Sidney too. 'Bunch of freakazoids. You don't even want to know.'

'What?' he says.

Turns out Harry never heard *freakazoids* before, and it tickles *him*. He asks me where the word come from. I don't know. I tell him I come from Kansas, how sometimes I say *cain't* and I talk real slow, California peoples say, and sometimes I talk that code, that street language, because I have to. It's all they be understandin', you know what I mean? I have to get down on they level. But I can be sophisticated, too. Like when Ralph took me to all them restaurants, I tell him.

And he says somethin' like, 'You look too good for this place. You don't fit in. You ought to be in the movies.' Or he's tryin' to. Stutterin' *real* bad then.

And I had to admit I looked pretty cute. I had my hair done up nice and my silver mini-dress out of storage. I mean, I was ready to *mess* with Long Beach. But the trouble with bein' on the stroll is, you have to do your strollin' where dudes can find you, and them polices be findin' you too. I mean, it sucks. The thing about the Saratoga--what we call the Black Hole--is, there's two other bars there, the New Yorker and the Hollywood, where Pine Avenue goes down off the bluff to where the Pike used be, roller-coasters and shit. I can circulate back and forth between 'em and not put my ass out on the street too much.

'Wanna do somethin' about it?' I ask.

And Harry says no, not this time, he ain't got the money, but it sure was nice talkin' to me.

And I say, 'Well, buy me a cold one at least. And a pack of Newports. OK?'

# # # #

Harry Hudson bought her the beer, the pack of cigarettes, then another beer. He did like talking to this girl. The prettiest he'd seen in his three weeks in Southern California, maybe. He couldn't understand why she hung out in such a dive, among winos, cripples, pensioners, a scattering of merchant seamen.

Kelly, she said her name was. She wore a silver sheath, her hair pressed in stiff curved wings beside her face, her smooth skin the color of some rich dark wood. Her fingers, tapping a cigarette on the bar, were as long as his, he noticed with surprise. Her eyebrows were plucked into perfect arches. Her smile was wide, seemingly friendly, a small gap between her front teeth. Her voice was husky.

If only he could have met her in Portland, ten years ago, before ... before.... But not now. No. Harry Hudson felt exhausted. An immense weight pinned him to his stool. He drank his own second beer as she shrugged, put the Newports in her purse and went off to talk to an older, plumper whore.

Not ever.

He walked back uptown. To avoid the Press Club, he cut east from Pine Avenue to the boulevard, then headed north again. He thought about getting his car and renting a motel room, even going back to the Reef. But the two beers had lubricated him somehow; once in motion, he didn't want to stop.

Celebrate, Steinbach had said.

So, by God, he would celebrate. He walked past the former Haven, the post office, the Plaza mall, Denny's, the YMCA. A McDonald's was still open at the corner of Seventh Street; he ducked in and had a Big Mac and coffee. Then he trudged on north, following the Blue Line tracks.

Fog was sifting in, the first hint of real autumn cold. He pulled the tweed jacket tighter around him. Under the amber lights, the neighborhood looked darker and meaner as he approached Anaheim Street; he wondered if he should turn back. But there, at the corner, was a pulsing red-and-yellow sign: CHIEU HOI SALOON.

Harry Hudson stared. He laughed.

The walls bore other signs, crudely painted:
BEER WINE POOL
BEAUTIFUL ORIENTAL GIRLS
FUN, FUN, FUN!
He went in.

#   #   #   #

Sept. 7, 1864
Hope is a good medicine and am sitting up and have been trying to stand up but can't do it; legs too crooked.... The rebels are very particular not to let any sick go. MOST

DARK.--Rebels say we go during the night.... Battese grinned when this news came and can't get his face straightened out again.

Marine Hospital, Savannah, Ga., Sept. 15

A great change has taken place since I last wrote.... Am in heaven now compared with the past. At about midnight, Sept. 7, our detachment was ordered outside at Andersonville, and Battese picked me up and carried me to the gate.... The rebel adjutant stood upon a box ... watching very close.... Pitch pine knots were burning.... As it came our turn to go Battese got me in the middle of the rank, stood me up as well as I could stand, and with himself on one side and Sergt. Rowe on the other began pushing our way through the gate. Could not help myself a particle, and was so faint that I hardly knew what was going on.... The adjutant yells out, "Here, here! hold on there, that man can't go...." and Battese crowding right along outside. The adjutant struck over the heads of the men and tried to stop us, but my noble Indian friend kept straight ahead, hallooing, "He all right, he well, he go!" And so I got outside....

#　#　#　#

Forty thousand a year, Harry Hudson marveled.

Twice what he had ever earned in Garbersville; half again more than in Red Fork.

He nursed his third and fourth beers of the evening, his elbows on the fake-woodgrain bar, in air heated by bodies, while the jukebox played "El Paso" and "Piano Man," balls clicked on chalky green felt under a pool of light, and voices--words--swirled around him. Already it was hard to remember the Low Fox, what kind of sanctuary he thought he had found there. All he felt was a lurch in his mind, as his stomach had lurched in the first throes of carsickness on mountain roads when he was a boy--a warning of its own unreliability. *Wrong again.* Would he be wrong forever? Harry Hudson asked himself, trying to cling to the thought that he was coming up in the world. At last.

He had entered the Chieu Hoi Saloon through a red velvet curtain, which whispered shut behind him. Faces turned, neither welcoming nor hostile. Faces of all colors. He saw sailors and Marines and more pensioners and an old bum in a black pea coat. It was a long, narrow room like a railroad car: orange life preservers hung high on the walls, a grimy, nubbly ceiling. A few tables. Budweiser and Miller signs. A Filipina barmaid served him, and he tried not to notice that she was braless--nipples all the more swollen-looking

89

because of her flat chest, under an off-the-shoulder white blouse. Her smile was practiced, but she had fine, even teeth. "You want a glass?" she asked.

Harry Hudson tried to smile back. "N-not here."

"I get you one, man, you want one."

"No, thanks."

It was better, he thought, in a place like this, to drink out of the bottle like everyone else. Then the Filipina asked Harry Hudson to buy *her* a drink. It turned out to be a champagne cocktail, three times the price of his beer. She clinked her glass against his, gave him another smile and moved off, deliberately, after a single sip. *More customers than just you, honey,* she seemed to say. And, in fact, Harry Hudson could see she was doing most of the work. A white woman at the far end, in a blue leotard and pink spandex pants that made her hips look squarish, leaned on the bar and stared at the pool players sullenly from under purple eyelids, ignoring everyone else.

By now he was sweating a little in his tweed, wondering what was that sweet, strangely familiar smell under the smells of cigarette smoke and piss. The Pac-Man machine behind him beeped. Two ceiling fans twirled their shadows, and a stained-glass pendant swayed by a string above his head. It had an abstract design. A peace symbol? No, by God. The V of a woman's crotch, with just a hint of thigh and belly curving.

"You like that?"

A nudge from his left. An old guy in a red T-shirt, with a crewcut and huge liver-spotted hands.

"I made that." He grinned. "Hell, I make a lot of 'em. It's my hobby. You ask Mama Thuy." He pronouced it *Twee*; Harry Hudson guessed she was talking about the bar's owner. "I made her three or four of 'em, just like that. She took 'em home, liked 'em so much she hung 'em up there. I didn't charge her." He winked. "You know, she's got more pictures of her hanging at home than she's got here."

Harry Hudson glanced behind him, at generic nudes painted on black velvet, then forward again, at the marbled glass of the mirror, the shelves of bottles and dark-blue baseball caps lettered USS PELELIU, USS PRAIRIE, USS BELLEAU WOOD. He raised an eyebrow. The old man nudged him again.

Then he saw it, on the wall down at the far end, and felt the ghost of a twitch in his nerves that once would have been surprise. A photograph maybe two feet by three, in a heavy gilt frame. A Vietnamese girl standing on a beach--in

Vietnam or stateside, he couldn't tell--with long, straight black hair and smooth tanned skin, hands on hips, squinting fearlessly, even impudently, at the sun and the camera, wearing an olive-drab fatigue shirt left unbuttoned but knotted above the navel, half-baring two of the most beautiful breasts Harry Hudson had ever seen, the cleavage between them an apparently bottomless shadow. She was the Vietnamese girl he had hunted for in the dives of Cam Ranh Bay in 1969 and had never quite found. And now, strangely, here she was. In a picture--an old picture, maybe. When it didn't matter anymore.

"How do you know?" he asked.

The old man set down his beer. "What?"

"How do you know what she's got in her house?"

A chuckle. The old man had a gut but a lot of muscle left, too. Good grandfatherly wrinkles around the eyes. "Shit, at my age," he said. "It's not like you think. She's had me over there lots of times. Dinner, whatever. Get me out of that trailer. Mama Thuy, she's got a way with her. I never seen anybody get along with just *anybody* like she can."

Then he leaned over confidentially, as if he'd been talking to Harry Hudson for years.

"You know, I've seen a lot of 'em come and go--Oriental gals, you know, marry Navy guys and whatnot--and Thuy's the only one that's got anything today. These others, they get it and then they can't hang onto it. Like there's something wrong with 'em. Something lopsided. I call 'em street people. Even when they find some nice guy, get some money, they're still street people, and it shows. You know what I mean?"

"Absolutely," Harry Hudson said.

He was one of them, probably. Could the old man tell? But it turned out the white barmaid, listening even that far away, thought it referred to *her*.

"Fuck *you*, Stanley," she said with a fury that astonished Harry Hudson. She had close-set eyes and a high forehead, caked with makeup. "You old fart. You're disgusting. Why don't you go on home, huh? You think I'm waiting around for an old fart like you?"

Stanley raised his big hands disarmingly. "Charlene, I wouldn't try to tell you a goddamn thing. You know that. You aren't gonna listen anyway."

"Just cause you hate B.J. Why don't you go on home and take your *sick* ideas with you? Huh?"

"I don't hate B.J.," Stanley said. "B.J., do I hate you? Have I ever said that? C'mon, let me buy you a drink."

91

He had the Filipina take a beer over to the pool table. B.J. shot the break and straightened up. He was young and black and handsome, in gold chains and a sleeveless Navy-issue undershirt that bared the swell of his shoulders. Harry Hudson remembered the Latino in the theater. But this B.J. seemed more than just cocky. He seemed to be relishing the feel of his own body, the sliding of the muscles, as he posed theatrically with the cue stick and drank.

"My man," he said, tipping the bottle at Stanley, his smile almost a sneer.

"Don't *drink* it, B.J.," Charlene wailed. "Don't you see what he's doing?"

"Man bought me a beer," B.J. said.

"He's tryin' to *fuck* with you, asshole." Then she rushed out from behind the bar in a flurry of tangled dyed-blonde hair and pummeled his arms and chest with fists that seemed not to make a sound or hurt him at all. She was panting, sobbing. His smile grew wider and sleepier as he held the bottle up out of reach. "He *hates* black people, can't you see? He's just a jealous, dirty old ... *sick* old ... seventy-three-year-old *honky*." She grabbed for the bottle, but B.J. ducked away and took another swig.

"I never said that," Stanley said patiently. "All I said was, there's nothing wrong with being a white gal, if that's what you happen to be. Am I right?" He nudged Harry Hudson. "Before B.J. here come along, she wanted to be Vietnamese. Took lessons from Thuy and Phuong, got so she could talk the lingo some. Thought she'd land one of those Vietnamese businessmen, get him to marry her. But no way that's going to happen. They might play around with her, but they'll marry their own kind, every time. Am I right?" The wink. "Now she wants to be black." He shook his head.

"You speak Vietnamese?" Harry Hudson asked her.

Charlene said something that sounded like it, shrill and tonal. Then, still furious: "What's it to you? Huh?"

"That's p-pretty impressive, I think. Hard language to learn. *I* never could."

"She surprised me," Stanley admitted.

"I'm gonna surprise you a lot more. Just wait," Charlene said. She glared at Harry Hudson too, but then she quieted down and went back behind the counter to fix her makeup. B.J. bent over his cue. The way everyone else failed to react, Harry Hudson figured this must happen all the time. Another set of performers, like Margot and her husband.... *Kevin*. His own son's name.

Or the couple in the Low Fox. But this time he was safe, he thought, just a spectator on his stool--yet somehow included, in a way he hadn't felt in a bar since Garbersville, at least. He beckoned to the Filipina and ordered a round for the house.

A cowbell startled him. It hung on the wall next to a NO GAMBLING sign; the Filipina was ringing it. "Big spender!" she yelled.

Everybody turned his way, raised bottles and smiled, except for Charlene, eyes brooding again at B.J.'s back. Harry Hudson flushed.

It cost more than he had figured, but what the hell. As time went by and the jukebox played old Patsy Cline songs, a warm, hazy feeling spread over him. He couldn't get Mama Thuy's picture out of his mind. Again and again, he half-turned to study it. She looked nothing like Nancy Ishida, but something about that level, fearless gaze.... It was the look Nancy Ishida had given him in that classroom in Beattie long ago. He blinked. Yes, it was. A tingle ran up his back, down the insides of his legs.

And in spite of himself, in spite of everything that had already happened, Harry Hudson began to imagine a future here, in this Chieu Hoi Saloon, getting to know this woman.

Could *this* be the place?

Why not?

He was sipping the last of his fifth beer, lost in the picture, when a voice slurred: "Hey. Were you in 'Nam?"

It was a young man--a kid, really--on the other side of him from Stanley. A bleary-eyed kid in a Dodgers cap, with pimples and a little mustache and a small, wet mouth. Drunk, from the way his head lolled on his skinny neck.

"What?"

"You understood what she said?"

"Not me," Harry Hudson said. "I'm just a d-dumb-ass newspaperman. Not a linguist."

"The Clarion? Cool," the kid said, lurching toward him. "Say, do you know how to get an article in the paper? I got one. I mean, I got the *idea*, if you can write it."

"This here's Randy," Stanley said. "He washes dishes at El Pescador. Seafood place, out at the marina." The wink. "Not bad, if you like fish. Me, I've had enough of 'em for one life."

"Who asked *you?*" Randy said, and Harry Hudson was surprised again at the hostility this harmless-looking old man provoked. "Relief cook, too--

you didn't say *that*. And I've held a goddamn job for three years straight. Not like some people in this bar. Just ask Mom."

"What kind of article?" Harry Hudson asked.

He felt he ought to listen to the kid, sloshed or not, if he was going to hang around here in the months to come. Besides, he realized, he was talking well. He had drunk just enough so that the words slid out of his throat with a mellifluous buzz, one after another. He loved hearing it so much at moments like this that it was hard for him to concentrate on what he was saying. Just the sound: that beautiful, effortless vibration.

"About fathers," Randy said. "About them that is and them that isn't, if you get my meaning." He squinted at Harry Hudson. "About some good people who took the place of *my* worthless dad, after he run off before I was even *born*."

"You could write a letter to the editor," Harry Hudson suggested.

"I'm talkin' about an *article*," Randy said stubbornly. "About what it's like growin' up as a goddamn *bastard*." Stanley, who seemed to have heard all this before, yawned and stretched, drained his beer and heaved himself up.

"Good night, all," he said. "Glad to meet you--?"

"Harry."

"Harry." He shook hands. "And you two be good," he called over to Charlene and B.J., who pointedly ignored him. He went to the men's room, came back out and shouldered his way toward the curtain, the red T-shirt stretched by his bulk, pads of fat behind his ears.

Randy was talking about some Catholic church camp--priests who had driven him and other kids up to Lake Isabella every summer in a rattletrap bus. There had been an accident this year, Harry Hudson gathered. Dozens of injuries. The program might be shut down. Randy wanted the Clarion to save it. Harry Hudson tried to listen, but the sixth beer was one too many; he felt his tongue grow thick and clumsy again. Randy's words stung, too: *Worthless dad*. And he missed Stanley--that air of solidity about the man, of having been somebody respectable once. Which must be what the others here resented.

"There must be a r-reporter on that beat," Harry Hudson said. "But I'll tell you. I sure could write an article about th--" He licked his lips. "This bar."

"That too," Randy said. "Mom's beautiful. But you gotta *know* her, like I do. What she's done for all us worthless farts. Like Stanley. You know Stanley's married?" he asked. "His old lady's a vegetable, in a nursing home, so he comes around here, sniffin' after--" he jerked his chin at Charlene--"*her*. Isn't that sick? And she screws him, don't let her tell you different. So long as he keeps on paying her. Why don't you put *that* in the paper? Ain't that the sickest thing you ever heard?"

"I don't know," Harry Hudson said mildly. "When you get to be his age, you might th--. Th--." *Think differently about it*, he wanted to say.

Randy snorted.

Harry Hudson glanced at Mama Thuy's picture again, but he could feel himself sinking now. Time hurried up, split into fragments. One moment Randy was shouting, "Ain't that right? Ain't Mom a goddamn fucking saint? Anybody wanna argue with that?" Nobody did. The next moment, Randy was looking pasty and breathing alcohol fumes at Harry Hudson, who wondered what good that church camp could possibly have done him. A couple of Marines came in and began to play eight-ball. The old bum in the pea coat shuffled with an aluminum crutch around to Stanley's stool, breathing even worse fumes through his whiskers. Harry Hudson was struck by the black grit ground into his hands. The bum caught him staring. "West Virginia," he said. "Hell fire, what'd you think? I was in them coal mines. Thirty-seven year. It don't wash out no way." Embarrassed, Harry Hudson bought him a beer. Then the bum was back at his place by the wall and a big black man had taken the stool, *his* hands scarred thickly around the knuckles as if from dozens of fistfights. Just to be safe, Harry Hudson bought him a beer too. The man thanked him profusely, gobbling his words--not a stutter, but some other dysfluency, which interested Harry Hudson for a moment before the Filipina hustled him for another champagne cocktail. "I want my cherry back," she sang, dancing away with her glass, and a big white man in a truck-company cap yelled, "Shake it but don't break it, Rita babe. But if you do break it, save a piece for me." She said: "Ron, you gonna be good tonight, OK? You want me to eighty-six you again?" He smirked: "Babe, you *know* I'm good." Then an even bigger white man came in and Rita asked him to take a look at one of the ice chests. It was on the blink. This man--she called him Swede--squatted down behind the counter. Tools clinked. More time passed--how much, Harry Hudson couldn't have said. Then B.J., who had racked his cue when the Marines started playing, loosened his shoulders, smoothed the gold chains on his chest, smiled even more widely and held out his hand to Charlene. She looked about to spit in it but instead gave him some keys.

"And put some *gas* in it, why don't you. Huh?"

"Hey," B.J. said.

"And come back *soon*, OK?"

"Soon as I do my business." Then B.J. leaned closer and kissed Charlene, bent her forward over the counter. She struggled in his arms and raked the back of his head with her red-lacquered fingernails. It seemed hardly different than when they were fighting. Harry Hudson saw that B.J. made a game of it-- always living on the edge of what other people could tolerate--and this, briefly, interested him too.

"I *mean* it, B.J.," she said. "You come back here and get me."

"Don't you worry, honeybunch," B.J. said, still smiling, turning slowly as he headed for the door, as if giving everyone a clear view of him.

"Don't *crash* it either, you hear?"

Then B.J. was gone. A car started outside, peeled rubber. "Bastard," Charlene said, reapplying her lipstick, but she looked proud, too, that she and her love affair once again had everybody's attention. Rita shrugged. Swede stood up, wiped grease from his hands with a rag. Harry Hudson kept on sinking. He went to the men's room, which smelled nearly as bad as the Low Fox's. The other black man, the one with the scarred knuckles, followed him in. The man's harsh breath echoed off the tiles, and Harry Hudson, panicked, was slow to hear in his clotted voice the sounds of embarrassment: "No sweat, man, take it easy. *Wait.* I ain't gonna do nothin'. Definitely *not.* You don't know me, man ... I *know*, I *know*, but you *will*, man, I promise you. Ask Thuy. She'll tell you. I used to work here. I'm gonna *definitely* pay you back, first thing tomorrow.... You want an IOU? I'll write you one, honest to God ... you think I like this? Hittin' on a dude I don't even know? But you look like a gentleman. That's what I told myself.... Twenty-five. That's all. Twenty-five. I wouldn't ask if I didn't need it. Shit comes *up*, man. You just don't know." The man's shadow on the ceiling bulked huge. His cheeks were shiny with sweat and round, like a chipmunk's; Harry Hudson could imagine him grinding up words inside them like nutshells. The money passed over. The man clasped Harry Hudson's hand in both of his. "You *definitely* will not regret this, my friend. Yes, you are. You are *now*. I *said* you were a gentleman.... Ask Thuy. First thing tomorrow." His grin was almost as wide as B.J.'s. He had already left the Chieu Hoi Saloon when Harry Hudson stumbled out of the men's room, uncertain whether he had been conned or robbed--knowing only that his motel money was gone, irretrievable. He found Randy asleep, face flat on the bar. Harry Hudson woke him up and asked him about the black man. "Oh, Jimmy," Randy slurred.

"Nice fella, 'cept when he's drunk. Then it's head for the high ground. Women and children first. Know how many times Mom had to eighty-six *him?*" Harry Hudson ordered another beer, resigned. Then Charlene, working her way restlessly down the bar, asked him: "Is it worth it? Bein' in love with somebody treats you like shit? What do you think?" Harry Hudson said: "M-maybe. If you f-*feel* like it's love." Close up, she wasn't really a pretty woman, though she had big, soft boobs. She had to be thirty-five, he thought. "Oh, he makes me *feel* it," she said grimly. "Once in a while. You don't think he can? Huh? What the hell do you know?" She seemed irritated with *him* again. Randy made a face at her and belched. Harry Hudson ordered a second round, blew the last of his bankroll. What did it matter now? *Celebrate.* Rita's bell rang. "Big spender!" The room began to spin very slowly. He wished he could just stay there--could go to sleep as easily as Randy, who was talking to Ron, the guy with the trucker's cap, telling the whole world that Harry Hudson was going to write an article about the bar.

"Oh, one of them *meed*-ja types," Ron drawled.

Harry Hudson discovered that he had closed his eyes. When he opened them, the bar was silent, even the jukebox. It seemed that Ron had been studying him for quite a while.

"You heard me. One of them fuckin' liars that lost us the war. Suckin' up to Jane Fonda and *her* kind while my buddies bled and died."

Harry Hudson blinked. Ron had to be kidding. Good-looking in a rugged, cowboy way, with a brown mustache like Holcomb's, only thicker and without the grey. Angry eyes, though. A man who appeared to be hell-bent on picking a fight.

Why, for God's sake?

"I w--. W--." *Wasn't even a reporter then,* he wanted to say.

"What's that, pardner? Speak up." Ron stood and leaned forward, fists on the bar, chin jutting out. "Folks here might like to know what kind of assholes helped split Thuy's family up. Left her kid over there, for one. Put her big brother in one of them *re*-education camps. Aidin' and comfortin' the enemy, ain't that it? Any way you cut it, that's treason in my book."

"Ron," Rita said.

Harry Hudson tried to grin it away. "A l-long time ago," he said.

"What?"

97

Now he couldn't repeat it. He opened his mouth and no sound came out. He could see Randy looking at him curiously. And Ron, clearly, had spotted his weakness--which, unlike Springer, he wouldn't hesitate to exploit.

"Spit it out there. Come on. Ain't it true? When did the *meed*-ja ever give Nixon or Reagan a fair shake? What makes you think you can come in here and write about *us*? Without just makin' up some cockamamie bullshit?"

"W-what did I ever d--. D--" *Do to you?* he wanted to say, but he couldn't manage that at all, even with the glide. "Ddddddd--" He licked his lips. "What did I ever ddd--" No way. His only chance was to leap into a different sentence altogether: "*In* the Army."

"What?"

"Army," Harry Hudson gasped, nauseated by the smell of his own sweat. The music started up again: "There's a Tear in My Beer." Stanley's stained-glass pendant wobbled at the edge of his vision.

"In the Army, if you was a traitor, they *shot* your ass. In the *meed*-ja, you got a fuckin' Pulitzer Prize. Ain't that right?"

"*Ron*, baby, shut up," Rita said.

There were plenty of arguments he could use--Vance Foster had used them once, eloquently. But right now Harry Hudson couldn't think of any, just as he had been unable to remember the simplest thing about first aid on that summer afternoon in Garbersville, no matter how desperately he ransacked his brain.

"You were in the Army? In 'Nam?"

Harry Hudson nodded.

"Well, glory be! Good for you there, pardner. But what made you join up with the *meed*-ja, then? It don't make sense." Ron glanced around the room, grinning now, enjoying himself. "Does it make sense to any of you? Naw. I don't think so. Maybe that's just another one of his lies."

Everybody looked at Harry Hudson

"I d-drove a bus," he said. "At Cam Ranh Bay."

He squeezed his eyes shut again. Somebody giggled. The other big guy, Swede, said softly: "Don't pay ol' Ron any mind. He's all bark." But by now Harry Hudson had given up trying to understand why Ron was attacking him, much less argue back. It didn't matter. Ron *knew*. He was a messenger, like Steinbach or Sergeant Riker. The force that pushed out from Ron's ruddy, square-cut face was the same force in Riker's voice that had negated every other voice in his head, blown him away. Twenty-two, Riker had been then. A kid, like these Marines shooting pool. Like Randy. But infinitely more grown-up than Harry Hudson was today. So what if Ron happened to be crazy and mean? He could see this too--so could anybody else who bothered to look.

And now Harry Hudson was drunk--almost too drunk to move. He hunched his back, willed himself numb, tried to close his ears as well as his eyes.

He thought of Ransom:

Oct. 4, 1864

Am now living splendid; vegetable diet is driving off the scurvy and dropsy.... Battese on his last visit to me left the first two books of my diary.... There is no doubt but he has saved my life, although he will take no credit for it.... It is said all were moved from Andersonville to different points ... but the dead stay there and will for all time. What a terrible place and what a narrow escape I had of it. Seems to me that fifteen thousand died while I was there; an army almost and as many men as inhabit a city of fifty thousand population.

Oct. 15

Am probably the happiest mortal any where hereabouts. Shall appreciate life, health and enough to eat hereafter. Am anxious for only one thing, and that is to get news home to Michigan of my safety....

Oct. 18

Now walk a trifle with the aid of crutches....

Oct. 31

Am feeling very well. Will describe my appearance.... I weigh one hundred and seventeen pounds.... You might say that I am an "honery looking cuss" and not be far out of the way. My cheeks are sunken, eyes sunken, sores and blotches both outside and inside my mouth, and my right leg the whole length of it, red, black and blue and tender of touch. My eyes, too, are very weak.... Bad as this picture is, I am a beauty and picture of health in comparison to my appearance two months ago. When taken prisoner was fleshy, weighing about one hundred and seventy or seventy-five, round faced, in fact an overgrown, ordinary, green-looking chap of twenty. Had never endured any hardships at all and was a spring chicken. As has been proven however, I had an iron constitution that has carried me though, and above all a disposition to make the best of everything no matter how bad, and considerable will power.... Believe now that no matter where we are moved to, I shall continue to improve, and get well....

Ransom was twenty-one then. Harry Hudson's age on leaving Vietnam--but he would never be able to write this about himself, he knew. Not ever.

At Andersonville, he thought, he wouldn't even have been a "raider." Not that he would have been virtuous enough to keep from stealing food and blankets from the dying. On the contrary: he would have been one of the first to *chieu hoi*, sicken and die--an anonymous straggler from history's march.

Never a hero.

Riker, too, was a better man, he told himself. He knew it. He had known it *then*, if the truth be told. But put him back in the field now and he would hate Riker all over again, as if he had learned nothing in all these years. Ron had just proved that.

Harry Hudson went on spiraling, down and down. Past the Low Fox and the Rabbit Hutch, past Steinbach and Finnegan and Owsley, even past Deborah and the old man at Phuoc Vinh. Faster and faster. He knew where he was headed but was powerless to stop. The booze was whirling him back to Garbersville, where he lay in that chaise lounge almost as drunk as he was now--where he *saw* Sally teetering from the little kids' wading pool over the concrete toward the big pool in plenty of time to save her, if only the eyes that did the seeing and the brain that calculated her rate of speed and direction and the heavy body pinned to the mesh of white plastic on the tubular aluminum frame by the weight of the sun had been wired together, not unplugged. He had to find the plug himself, fumble with it, push it in. It took a long time. It took so long that he noticed the flowers on her bathing suit and the pink ovals on the backs of her thighs and the question-mark shape of her footprint after she had stepped in a puddle, and he heard a squirrel chatter and a jay squawk in a pine tree outside the fence before he could tear himself up, as if leaving strips of his skin on the plastic, and bellow at her. Did she turn? Or did his voice only startle her, pitch her that last half-step over the edge? He wouldn't ever be sure. He had no memory of a splash. One moment she was outlined against the chain link and a white life preserver and a car passing by, and then she was gone, and there was yet another delay--maybe a quarter-second--when the brain refused to believe what the eyes had just told it before the body lurched forward as if he himself had fallen, and he ran.

He ran. And even then, even at the beginning, that contemptible voice yammered in his head: *I'm running as fast as I can. Aren't I?* Trying to justify himself to a listener who hovered just above him. Deborah? His father? Vance Foster? God? What did it matter? *Who could do any more?* Every instant he bargained with that listener to spare him his just punishment was an instant when he forgot about Sally, blotted out his little girl, whose very life, his own thundering breaths told him, could be measured in instants now. *That* was the worst sin. He skidded on the tile rim and nearly fell in, caught himself and felt a flash of incredulous joy because the pool was empty; there was nothing, all the way to the bottom, in the clear blue water with its swaying nets of reflections. *Wrong.* She was down in the deep end, hidden in a wedge of shadow. No bubbles that he could see. She had sunk like a stone and slid feet-first on the concrete slope toward the drain, her hair trailing. He jumped in, telling the listener, *Look! Clothes and all,* but the shock of the water only brought home to him how drunk he still was, how lethally clumsy. He dove and groped for her arms and they evaded him like fish or strands of seaweed; then, running out of air much too soon, he grabbed the elastic back of Sally's suit at the waist and wrenched her brutally upward above him, forgetting her for yet another instant in his panic as his lungs burned. Did her face fall into the water again after she cleared the surface, before he could catch her? He wouldn't ever be sure of that either. He wrestled her up over the side, tearing the suit, astonished at how limp and heavy she was, and then his own waterlogged jeans and shirt and shoes hung on him like lead diver's weights as he followed her, gasping.

She was lying belly down on the concrete, eyes closed, her head turned to the left and water spreading out from it--water she had swallowed? Her hair, blonde with the glints of red she had inherited from Deborah, was dark and tangled now. He knelt over her. He heard a faint human sound, a moan, thought for an instant he saw her ribs move, gleaming like pearl, felt another explosion of joy, then realized it was only his own hoarse breathing, the hammering of his heart. *Wrong.* He pressed his face against her back. The down on Sally's spine, the single mole by her right shoulder blade. His little girl. Something so real and beautiful, so soft to the touch, *had* to be alive, though the coldness of her skin terrified him. The love he felt pouring out of him seemed powerful enough to drive death out of her, like a blast of compressed air driving out the water. It was perfect love for the few seconds before he *knew* it was perfect and found himself using it to bargain again, telling the listener, stupidly, contemptibly: *Don't I deserve it? Let her live.*

He couldn't remember what the manuals said, or the answers to the first-aid Q&A's that ran in the Logger every summer. The kind of canned wire feature that he, the high-and-mighty would-be columnist, had always dismissed as filler. He pressed down on Sally's ribs below the shoulder blades, raised her arms at the elbows between strokes, aware that this was an obsolete method, long since replaced. Once, twice, half a dozen times. He was sobbing. *Hear that?*

But although he knew he was supposed to keep it up until she revived--half an hour if need be--he also knew he should call the paramedics, get somebody expert on the scene. The two thoughts wrestled each other. Every push and lift without a movement from Sally, without a sound, tipped the balance. Then he was saying, "Wait a sec, honey," not stuttering a single damned word *then*, and running toward the door of their apartment, flinging it open, feeling the shameful relief of not having to look at her anymore yet frantic at having left her alone. He pounded down the hallway to the phone and dialed 911 and heard the operator--he even knew her name: Marge Percy--heard her answer and hit a block so total it was as if he was back in Vietnam, riding that chopper to Cam Ranh Bay, communicating with hand signs and notes. *Nothing* came out. It was no time for gentle measures, prolonging, deep breathing--though Dr. Richardson would have said, *Wrong*, this was precisely the time; he smashed into the words as if beating his fists bloody on the wall: first *Hello* and then *This* and then *Help* and then *My* and then *Drowning* and then *Help* again, and the evil spirit had him so tightly gripped by the throat that he couldn't even pant loudly enough for the operator to hear and maybe guess who it was. *Harry? Is that you?* Black blobs swam in front of his eyes. Then, in terror that she would hang up, he shouted, "Wait!", and that word, that word alone, made it through.

"Hello?" Marge Percy said. "Somebody on the line?"

But then the spirit intensified its stranglehold, and he would have fainted if he hadn't thought: *The airway. Clear the airway!* He had forgotten to check Sally's tongue, and that idiotic omission gave him something else to do. He flung away the phone with a clatter and ran back outside, aware even then of how crazy and desperate he must look with his soaked clothes and hair, his right hand bleeding from some kind of cut. He hoped the neighbors would appreciate this if any had come out in the last minute and found Sally abandoned. They had become the listener. *Can't you see?* he begged them. As he reached the doorway he had another thought: Marge Percy would be able to trace the call. The paramedics still might come. He had done *something*. So for the last time he felt a surge of joy as he burst out into the courtyard into the hot, blinding sunlight and found nobody there, the husbands at work on this early September Tuesday when he had some comp time off; the wives shopping, maybe; the kids, like Deborah, beginning school this week--only Sally lying where he had left her in her torn yellow bathing suit, that damned squirrel still chattering. She looked so small. So still. Something--the booze still inside him?--shifted heavily, the way he had once seen a ton of aviation fuel swing in a rubber bag from a CH-54 helicopter. Very clearly he heard her voice say, "Daddy?" and he knew just as clearly that it was false, *wrong*, an hallucination. There was no hope. The concrete he had to cross to reach her looked impossibly wide--though he did cross it somehow, pry her mouth open and fumble for her slimy tongue, resume his pushing and lifting and, when that failed, hold her in his lap and weep. He tried to dissolve into Sally's body, to become one with his little girl forever, because he knew that if he ever separated from her again, became Harry Hudson, he would remember that even then--*even then!*--running toward her in the most perfect love he would ever feel, he had seen the Jack Daniels bottle standing in the lattice of shade under the chaise lounge and thought: *Got to get rid of that*--the evidence that he had killed her.

"Hey, pal."

It was Randy, thumping his shoulder.

Harry Hudson opened his eyes. His tears were real, he discovered, running warm down his cheeks. He wiped them with his jacket sleeve and said: "I d-don't have any place to go. I'm out of money." He licked his lips, tasted salt. "Any way I can ... j-just stay here?"

He should have stayed at that other bar, he thought. The one where he had talked to that friendly black girl. What was her name? Kelly.

All around, he could see people's expressions changing--Ron's from malice to puzzlement, Charlene's from indifference to curiosity, Swede's from pity to disgust at such an unmanly display. Then, for a second, he forgot them all. Harry Hudson finally recognized the sweet scent he had noticed when he first came in. Incense. And for that second he was back in Vietnam itself.

"Mom's got a cot in the storeroom," Randy said. "Maybe you could sleep on that. Ask her."

Harry Hudson was still working his way back to the Chieu Hoi Saloon when somebody screamed, *"Faggot!"*

Wood splintered.

One Marine had hit the other with a pool cue. Suddenly blood was everywhere, coursing down the nakedly pink side of the man's crewcut head, down the hand he had tried to shield it with, dripping rapidly on the floor, a brilliant red under the table light.

"Oh, shit," Rita said.

All the fight had gone out of the injured man at once. His face, where the blood wasn't bubbling between his fingers as he crouched and held himself, was white with shock. He moaned like a child.

"--hear what the sonofabitch called me?" the other man was saying, brandishing the stub of the cue. Tall, with badly sunburned skin and peeling lips and a cruel case of acne. Despite his aggrieved voice, he, too, looked scared and terribly young.

Rita forced the injured man's hand away from the wound long enough to stuff a bar rag against it; then she dodged away from the blood. "What'd he do to *you?*" Swede asked.

"Nothin'!"

"Then why'd you call him that?" Swede asked the injured man, who only moaned some more. "Ron, your truck's right outside, isn't it? You better take him to the hospital."

"*My* truck? What about yours?"

"No *way*," the injured man said. "Just get me back to base."

"My truck's across the street," Swede said. "You ain't gonna make it back to the goddamn base, even if the cops don't stop you. You ain't gonna die, but you're gonna need stitches. Maybe a transfusion. Don't argue. Ron?"

"Called me a *faggot*," the other man said.

"Shut up," Swede said. Then to Ron: "Mom's gonna appreciate it, big time. I'll tell her how much you helped." Then to the other man again: "Put that damn *cue* down. You're goin' with him. Hold that bandage on there. *Hard.*"

Harry Hudson watched and listened with, for once, not a trace of envy. He was exhausted. Swede could run the show. So let him. Ransom must have been like this, he thought. A quiet voice, but stronger than all Ron's scowling and complaining about bloodstains in his pickup. They draped the injured man's arm over the other Marine's shoulder and walked him out through the curtain, still moaning.

"Goddamn jarheads," Swede said.

Rita hauled some mops and a bucket out of the storeroom, beckoned to Swede, and Harry Hudson, dully, went over to help. He had lived alone; he could do *this.*

Randy put a quarter in for a song, "There's a Tear in My Beer," laid his face on the bar and fell asleep.

Then Mama Thuy came in. A smaller woman than the picture had suggested--barely five feet tall--and older, as old as Harry Hudson, maybe, in a grey jogging suit and shiny gold high-heeled sandals that clicked on the linoleum, her hair curlier, piled up on her head, circles of weariness under her eyes, but the *same person*, he could see, no question about it: her gaze--still like Nancy Ishida's!--and those magnificent breasts of hers pushing back the craziness, bringing in a wave of order along with a swirl of cool, fog-laden air. He felt like cheering. Mama Thuy had a low, straight forehead, a slightly hooked nose, a firm chin, erect posture, a wary alertness about her. She winced a little at the noise of the jukebox, stared at the blood.

And again Harry Hudson remembered riding that chopper to Cam Ranh Bay, how relief could accompany so much shame. He wasn't gay. *Not that it matters*, he said to Vance Foster, his listener now. *Not that it's anything to be ashamed of. Not these days.* But his relief was so enormous that he knew he was guilty of the very prejudice he'd thought the Low Fox had killed in him for good.

Yes. He wanted *her*.

Mama Thuy set her purse down on the bar. "What happen?"

Later, after he had helped Swede bring in some cases of beer, she even winked at him.

#　　#　　#　　#

Next morning, Mama Thuy almost forgot somebody was sleeping in her bar. She got up at eight, weeded the garden of her house on Daisy Street north of PCH (palms, cactus, bougainvillea, Vietnamese grapefruit), ate breakfast and wrapped another care package for her family. A money order for five hundred dollars, plus an equal amount in food, clothes and medicine. The Communists would take a quarter to a third of it, she knew. Like a bribe. She sighed. And her father would only complain, ask for more, call her *bad girl*, as he had ever since she got pregnant by a U.S. Air Force radio technician back when Ho Chi Minh City was still Saigon. Dwayne Cummings. Even though her father, who hadn't worked since 1975 but was still vigorous in his sixties, would spend most of it on beer and girlfriends, while her mother (shockingly shrunken in the last photos, teeth black with betel juice) would go on pretending not to know. And her eighteen-year-old son, Billy, left with her parents as a baby and stuck there ever since Saigon fell, wanted a Honda motorbike. No way to keep everybody happy, she thought.

Why me?

She gathered last night's receipts from the safe in her bedroom and drove to the bank. She took the package to the post office. Nosing the Porsche up Long Beach Boulevard, she saw the city's shifting economy like light and shadow through her sunglasses. Two tides met around Seventh Street: Rich pushing up from the tall buildings along the shore, Poor flooding down from the direction of Compton. Right now, Poor was winning. Construction on the Blue Line tracks had torn up the boulevard for a year, hurt business. The car dealers were leaving for the new mall in Signal Hill. Worst of all, the Navy might pull out in a year or two, more and more people were saying. That would sink the Chieu Hoi Saloon for sure. Mama Thuy parked in the Discount Tire Center lot, lifted a heavy plastic bag from the trunk and gazed around. The Dodge showroom just east of the bar was empty. The other blocks around the intersection held a Clinica Medica turned Scientology bookstore, cheap Mexican and Cambodian restaurants, check-cashing places, *ropa baraja* outlets, beauticians, 99-cent stores, pawnshops. Not good.

"Hey, Mama," the Tire Center manager said when she handed him one of the containers in the plastic bag. "What's this?"

"Homemade chili. Made it yesterday, heated it up." She winked. "Hope it's not too hot for you."

"Not as hot as you look, babe. Thanks." The manager was a fairly young guy--maybe half Mexican, half Korean, hard to tell. Kind of cute. Married, though. "Anything I can do for *you*, just call. I'm always here."

"Buy my bar."

"Hey, there's an idea."

"I'm serious," Mama Thuy said. "You got forty-five thousand cash, it's all yours. Beer-and-wine license, pool table, jukebox, all the tabs people owe me. I throw in the paintings of naked girls free--got them in Tijuana, cheap. Take it or leave it."

The manager laughed.

But no lease, she thought as she crossed Anaheim Street. The Chinaman who owned the building wouldn't give her one. Said it made no sense when the city might buy the place any day, knock it down for redevelopment. But nothing had happened for eight long years. She kept telling him she deserved a lease by now. Then her business would be worth more if she *did* sell. But the Chinaman wouldn't listen. As it was, it made no sense for her to spend money fixing the bar up--though it looked like shit. The blue paint of the outside walls was chipped and scrawled and smudged black up to waist level, the FUN,

FUN, FUN! signs crooked and dribbling. *Hire somebody else next time. Somebody sober.* Then that hole. Somebody--Ron, she was certain--had driven his truck into the wall near the Anaheim Street door one night, punched a three-foot-wide hole in the stucco, then backed out. She could see through bent chicken wire to the plywood patch Navy Swede had nailed in. Seven months ago, and do you think the Chinaman would get it fixed? No way.

Somebody rich like you, her father's last letter had said. *In America, the land of gold. And still so stingy to your family, your own blood. When are you going to bring us there? You promised, but the years go by....*

"Good morning, Pop. You hold this for me, please, hon?"

The old man wore the same black pea coat despite the day's heat. He smelled as if he had slept in it. He coughed, balanced on his crutch and gripped the bag while she rattled with her keys at the screen.

Then she remembered Harry Hudson.

"Hold on, Pop," she said--though what help would an eighty-year-old cripple be if the guy did something weird, rushed out at her?

Mama Thuy realized how nervous she had been by the force of her relief when she cracked the door and saw him standing quietly, much as she had seen him last, beside the pool table, blinking in the sudden glare. "Hi! How *you* doing today?" She turned on the inside lights, took the bag from Pop and set it on the bar. The beer signs buzzed and flickered. A quick glance around for damage: none that she could see.

"I'm OK, I think," Harry Hudson said. "I--."

"You sit here all day in the dark?" she teased. "Could've put on some lights here. I don't mind."

He, too, had obviously slept in his coat. His hair was askew; his face, so flushed yesterday, looked pale. He gestured vaguely at the storeroom--maybe he'd had the light on there.

"Want some coffee?" she said. "I make some in a minute."

Pop sat down at his usual table, groaning. Mama Thuy unbarred the Long Beach Boulevard door and unlocked the screen. Coming back, she got Pop his first beer from one of the ice chests. She took an orange and a pear from the bag, placed them in front of the Buddha statue, prayed briefly--*Please, nothing weird today, OK?*--and lit two sticks of incense. When she looked up, Harry Hudson still hadn't moved.

"Put up the curtain there, hon, will you? Make me happy, OK?"

He seemed to snap out of it then, more or less, lifting the red velvet gingerly from the pool table and groping to hang it in the Anaheim Street door. The bank had given Mama Thuy rolls of quarters; she took them out of her purse and broke them into the cash register. The jukebox, the pool table, the cigarette machine, even the machines in the rest rooms that sold condoms needed quarters. Mama Thuy put the coffee on. Then she took a blue plastic bucket, filled it with water and sloshed it once, twice on the dirty sidewalk.

"Thanks, babe. Have a seat," she told Harry Hudson. "Want some chili, too? How about you, Pop?"

"Hell fire, woman, what you think I'm here for? Just to look at your ass?"

"Don't be nasty, Pop. What I do to you?"

A cough. A sly grin in his beard.

"Then keep it shut, OK?"

The old man was getting harder to handle all the time. Mama Thuy put the rest of the chili containers in the microwave. She sat in *her* usual place, at the angle of the bar, where she could look through the gap in the curtain at the Porsche in the Tire Center lot. Wade's baby. Pretty, but expensive to keep up. Nice to steal, too. A van or a pickup, like Swede's, made more sense down in this neighborhood. She paid rent so she could park there and her customers could use the lot at night, and she had Randy or Stanley or Black Jimmy pick up trash in the mornings. She didn't have to bring the manager chili, too. But it wouldn't hurt. That's what Charlene and Rita never understood. *Give to get*, she kept telling them. *That's how you make it in the long run.*

Should she fire Rita? Maybe not yet. Payday at the base was coming soon, and who else could she get to work? Not Phuong.

The microwave rang. At the same moment, air brakes whooshed and a huge, cold shadow fell over the door. The Budweiser truck. As Mama Thuy ladled the chili into bowls and handed out napkins and spoons, the brewery guy, Rick, rolled a tall stack of boxes in on a dolly. He waved and, without any directions from her, steered around the pool table and into the storeroom. He came out smiling and rubbing his hands. She had a beer waiting for him. "Ten cases of Bud, six Bud Light," he said. "That's all?"

"Business slow."

"How long have I known you now--five years? To hear you talk, it's never been nothin' *but* slow." He winked at Harry Hudson. "She's got gold bars in her safe at home, I hear. Don't believe a word she says."

"*Real* slow now," Mama Thuy said.

She signed the invoice and wrote him a check. Rick glanced over his shoulder. "Jimmy stayin' back there again?"

"No, him," she said, and then, in case Harry Hudson had any other ideas: "Just one night."

"Saw the cot made up," Rick said. "Howdy do." He shook hands, introduced himself. When Harry Hudson couldn't answer, he seemed less puzzled than amused.

"Forgot your name, eh? He must've really tied one on last night."

"Heavy duty," Mama Thuy said.

"Comin' back to you now? Hair of the dog sometimes helps. Tell you what, buddy--I'll buy you one."

Harry Hudson shook his head, his face lopsided again.

"Hey, I'm just tryin' to be friendly," Rick said. "No skin off my ass."

Mama Thuy looked at Harry Hudson, staring sullenly down into his chili bowl now, and felt a surge of irritation. *Jealous,* she thought. *Only met me last night, and jealous already. Crazy.* To teach him a lesson, she leaned into Rick, pressed his arm. A nice guy. Married too, with kids, but even handsomer than Navy Swede, broad-shouldered and square-jawed, and he flirted with her the right way--nice and easy, nothing serious. A gentleman.

As Rick left with the dolly, a black woman came in. "Use the toilet?" she muttered.

"Customers only," Mama Thuy said. "Buy a beer first, then OK."

"Shit. How much a beer be?"

"Bud and Miller, dollar seventy-five. Natural Light, dollar fifty. You want Heineken, that's more."

"Shit," the woman said again. She had that crack-pipe look, unnaturally thin, her hair in ragged clumps. She swayed. "I just gotta use the goddamn toilet. Please."

"Customers only. See that sign there?"

Cords suddenly stood out in the woman's neck. She screamed, "*Fuck* you, bitch." Mama Thuy didn't blink. Then, another abrupt change in mood, the woman bent over and pleaded again, to Harry Hudson: "Buy me a beer, man, could you? I know you got money. Huh? Just one beer, so this China bitch'll let me take a crap."

"S-sorry, I'm broke," Harry Hudson said.

"You better leave," Mama Thuy said. "Stop bothering my customers."

"You hear me, bitch? I said fuck you."

"Out."

"Fuck *you*, too," the woman said to Harry Hudson, but her eyes had gone vague; she slowly turned away, thinking of somewhere else to go. Mama Thuy watched the curtain flap behind her. *Why just blacks and Mexicans?* she wondered for the hundredth time. *You never see any Asian bums. Not one.* The thought of cocaine reminded her of Rita again. *That red leather coat. Nice. Where'd she get it?*

Harry Hudson looked at her inquiringly.

"Gotta do it," she explained. "Too bad, but I let everybody go in there, they tear up the rest rooms. No kidding. They write stuff on the walls, plug up the toilets. They tear the sink out in the men's room once--left it on the floor, water all over. Cost me a bundle. So I make a rule."

"I see."

"Want another cup?"

"L-look," Harry Hudson said. "I--." His Adam's apple jerked, and it dawned on Mama Thuy that it wasn't just a matter of his being drunk yesterday and hung over today; he was one of those people who truly had trouble talking. *Nguoi noi ca lam.* "I can't pay for any of this. Not right now. Guy t-told me he'd come back this morning and pay me. T-twenty-five I lent him. Lent him l-last night. But maybe not."

"On the house," she said, giving him a measured smile. "Maybe you come back, be a good customer. Who knows?"

"I'll be back," Harry Hudson said. "I'll never forget what you d--. Ddddiid for me last night." He licked his lips. "Sure thing."

He gazed at her so heavily that it irked her all over again.

Why me?

"Who you lend money?" she asked. "Not a good idea around here. Lotta deadbeats. Right, Pop?"

The old man hawked phlegm. "Who you callin' deadbeat? I pay you ever damn dime, woman, and you know it."

Harry Hudson tried to describe the borrower; it took a while for a picture to come clear. "Oh, Black Jimmy," she said finally. "He OK. He used to work here, long time ago. Got a job with the phone company now. Make good money. He pay you back. I think."

The noon crowd began to drift in. Mama Thuy, serving beers, wiping the counter, washing glassware, had little attention to spare for Pop leaning against the wall or Harry Hudson nursing his coffee. When she relit the incense at the shrine, she remembered her father's accusing letter. It had been in the back of her mind all along. The immigration paperwork had been snarled for months now, on both sides of the Pacific. *Help me get them all here,* she prayed, *and I'll eat no meat for a month afterward. I promise.*

Black Jimmy came in, wearing blue coveralls. Shiny forehead, chipmunk cheeks, a wide grin. "Hey, Mama."

"Workin' hard or hardly workin'?"

"Workin' so hard you can't believe. Need a cold one bad." Then he noticed Harry Hudson. "Just a minute, babe. Let me talk to this gentleman here while you're settin' it up. And here. For some music." He tossed a dollar bill on the bar, scooped up four quarters in a big scarred fist.

One of the fans sluggishly stirred the air over Black Jimmy's head as he nudged a tweed-jacketed shoulder, took the next stool. Harry Hudson seemed startled, then relieved. The two men talked, though Jimmy's voice--that quick, slurring bark--was the only one she could hear over the jukebox. Snoop Doggy Dogg: a product of these very streets. Money changed hands; the two shook on it, pleased with themselves.

"See?" Mama Thuy said. "You rich again already."

PART II

"Newsroom," an unfamiliar man's voice said. "Pierce."

The line muttered with static. "Harry Hudson, please."

"He's not here."

"Will he be back soon?" Deborah tried to ask in her best schoolteacher's voice, but she heard uncertainty in it.

"He's in the hospital."

"Excuse me?"

"Got his ass shot in a bar. Can you believe that?"

Deborah felt faint. She said nothing, and this man, Pierce, seemed to realize that he might have overstepped.

"You a friend of his? Ol' Harry'll be there a while. St. Mary's. You want his room number? Hey, Rick, what's--"

She gripped the tiled counter of the kitchen in Garbersville where she stood with the phone. The light that shone through the window onto her hand--the freckled skin always dry in the winter, despite all her lotions--also lit up Kevin's hair as he made engine noises and shoved his yellow Tonka bulldozer over the floor, its rubber treads ticking. Pale, glowing hair, filaments fine as cotton candy. Like half a halo. *His* skin was smooth and sweet-smelling, just as Sally's had been. The light was kind to her son but pitiless to everything else, Deborah thought as this new anxiety mingled with the pain that never left her. It gleamed out of a pewter sky, off the snow-covered pasture out back, and exposed the nicks in the drywall, the fans of soot around the heating vents, the stained linoleum. An old house, shabbier than the apartment had been. But *safe,* she liked to think. No swimming pool, no stairs. Hardly any traffic, here on the outskirts of town away from the mountains. Just flat land, a few cows, the scrubbier pines and the sage hinting of the desert that began not too many miles east. Emptiness.

"Can I help you, ma'am?" a new voice said.

"Yes. I'm Deborah ... Harry Hudson's wife. His *ex*-wife." Thank God she didn't have to ask him directly why her check hadn't come. "Mr. Pierce says--"

"I'm Harry's supervisor, ma'am. Rick Holcomb."

"Is it true, Mr. Holcomb? He's been hurt?"

"Not too seriously, ma'am. Nothing life-threatening, anyway. But he *is* in the hospital, that's a fact. I can give you a number there, let you talk to him. Just a second."

"But how could it happen?" Deborah asked. *A bar I can imagine easily enough,* she thought. *But he wasn't the kind to get into fights.*

"A robbery, apparently. Harry tried to stop it. I guess you could say he's some kind of a hero."

The blade of the bulldozer butted her shoe. "No, he isn't," she said sharply, without thinking, looking down at her son in his miniature Oshkosh B'Gosh overalls. Kevin heard her tone, glanced up, blue eyes big.

"What?"

"He's no kind of hero."

Holcomb was silent, and Deborah realized that he probably knew nothing about Harry outside of work. Phones rang in the background. The bulldozer nudged her again, and she moved her foot.

"His child support's late. Harry's been working there a year, hasn't he? This is the first time, so naturally I was worried."

She could tell Holcomb was relieved to talk about this instead. "He had direct deposit?"

"No, he always sent me the checks himself." *And I know why,* she thought. *It made him feel big to write them out. To remind both of us of the one solitary thing he's done right.*

"He should've had direct deposit. They send the checks to you automatically then, no sweat." Holcomb paused. Through the static she could hear the bustle around him. *The city. So far from here.* "Look, Mrs.--Hudson? I'll get hold of Harry, OK? And if it's OK with him--and I can't see why not--I'll have Payroll send 'em to you direct as long as he's laid up. Would that work?"

"That would be very kind of you, Mr. Holcomb."

"No trouble at all."

The static had seemed to lift, and there was something about this man's voice, a rough Midwestern decency, that warmed her. It was like Waylon Jennings' voice when he sang:

Amanda, light of my life,
Fate should have made you a gentleman's wife....

A shaggy, rumbling voice, but it had a lyrical quality too. Oh, to have a man like *that!* Not like.... Then she caught herself. This was just another newspaperman she was talking to--an untidy bundle of bad habits, if experience had taught her anything. The only newspaperman she knew who *wasn't* like that was Brent Owsley, who was too boyish to count, wearing silly bow ties and piping his tenor in church. Besides, she had chosen the wrong man twice already. She didn't dare choose again until she had prayed and searched and located the flaw in herself that lay behind such uncannily bad judgment. *I'm a good person,* Deborah told herself. *At least I thought so. I didn't want anything out of the ordinary. So why?* Lloyd had been all glib words and hustle and self-confidence--all surface, she had discovered. Which was why Harry had appealed to her. That speech problem, his horrible taste in clothes ... the man *had* no surface, she had thought, no defenses at all. He could hide nothing from her, she had believed foolishly; she could rest safe in his gratitude. Maybe that was the flaw right there. Her arrogance. *Forgive me,* she prayed. Because Harry not only had his secrets, it turned out, he had a neediness so great that it swallowed up everything she had to offer at a gulp and disregarded it, looking for more. Always more. She had never been real to him--she knew that now. How could she ever trust herself after being so wrong? Then Sally.... She felt faint again and held onto the counter as the bulldozer bumped her, Kevin's stubborn face looking more and more like Harry's these days. "*Stop* that," she said.

"What, ma'am?"

"Not you," she told Holcomb, flushing as if he could see her.

"I have the number for you," he said, and Deborah thought: *Yes, a nice voice, whatever the rest of him's like.*

And maybe it was because Holcomb expected her to call Harry that she went ahead and did it, though she no longer had to. The check would come. She could go on paying the mortgage--not so much more than their rent had been, but still--and paying for Kevin's day care when she was teaching. It galled Deborah to be so dependent on a few hundred extra dollars a month. She liked to tell herself, *It's not that we can't get along without it if we had to; it's the principle of the thing,* but this month's scare had reminded her otherwise. She

115

thought she was holding Harry to his obligations, but he still held *her*. That was the bitter truth.

"Mommy," Kevin whined, letting the bulldozer go, pulling on her leg, trying to climb it.

She had the hospital switchboard now. This connection was clearer. But she had nothing to say to Harry, she realized--and what could he possibly say to her?

Fate should have made you a gentleman's wife.

The phone in his room rang, and somebody picked it up. She heard herself say tentatively, almost whispering: "Harry?"

"W-who?"

The sound made her shiver with loathing. It all came back to her: the way he fumbled with words, tortured them out of all recognition--the way he slowed any conversation down to *his* pace, until she could scream with impatience.

"It's me."

"D--?"

"Deborah. That's right.... I was concerned, Harry. Wondering." How should she put this? "No check came this month."

Now the noise he made sounded like gargling. Only gradually could she pick out intelligible words: "J-jesus. I f--. F-forgot all about it. Really. I got s--" Then he paused for maybe twenty seconds. "I'm sorry. I just.... T-they had a h--." Another ten seconds, while her nerves ached with strain. "A h-holdup here. In--"

"I know. Mr. Holcomb told me all about it."

"You talked to Rick?" This sentence came out perfectly. Why?

"Yes. He was very helpful. He arranged to have it sent ... direct deposit, I think he said. Automatically. So you don't have to worry about it as long as you're in the hospital. And *we* don't have to worry either."

"Yeah, Rick ... h-he's a n-nice guy."

"I think so." Deborah was tempted to say: *Unlike certain other people, who ruined my life.* How could he ever forget something as important as child support? For his own son. Even ... but she didn't know for sure how seriously Harry was hurt, and she didn't want to sound too bitchy with Kevin listening. "Anyway," she said, setting her jaw, as if facing a room full of unruly sixth-graders, "how are you doing, Harry?"

"OK, I guess. D-doc says my s--" Five seconds. "S-shoulder may always b-be stiff. The b-bullet went th--" Ten seconds, maybe fifteen. "T-through some important s-stuff. Rotator cuff? S-something like that.... Anyway, they s-say I can probably s--" A good half-minute this time, before she heard the gargling sound. "S-still *type* OK."

Kevin was tugging at her leg again. "Mommy?"

"Hush. It'll just be a minute. Harry? You still there? You say you can keep on working, then? When you get out, I mean."

He chuckled--cynically, she thought.

"Sure. R-rim-rat work's only f--" He must be trying to tell a joke, Deborah thought; he always got hung up on the punch lines. And this let it slip past her guard--the sympathy she had tried never to feel for him again. Harry's life had been hard. Sally had been his daughter, too. *Though it was his fault she died! Wasn't it?* And now he was lying all alone, in a hospital in a big, strange city, with an awful wound, after somebody had tried to kill him. *But what was he doing in that stupid bar anyway?* Deborah had wanted him punished, all right, but now that the punishment seemed to have stricken him at last, she wished instead that she could feel what she sometimes felt leading the choir at Faith Tabernacle: a healing calm, almost a trance, in which her pain and anger melted away like a soft, dying note. *Forgive me.* She closed her eyes. *Forgive him, too, for whatever made him run.* She didn't mean this, quite, but she wished she did. Finally he finished: "F-from the elbows down."

"I'll pray for you, Harry," she said. "If you want."

She braced herself for ... whatever. More cynicism?

But, amazingly, all Harry said was, "T-thanks. That'd b-be nice."

Kevin yanked harder. "*Stop* it," Deborah repeated, and then, on impulse, breaking another of the vows she had made when Harry Hudson left, she lifted the boy up to the phone and cradled him with an arm under the seat of his Oshkosh B'Goshes. "Here," she said. "Talk to your daddy."

#   #   #   #

It was Little Sidney did it, I know for a fact. He come in that night and said he had to borrow the car and get out of Long Beach for a while. He had blood on his jacket sleeve, like it'd splattered off of somebody else, you hear what I'm sayin'? He offered me some money, for the baby comin' and all. Standin' all wild-eyed there in my kitchen, his chest goin' in and out and his legs like to run the hundred-yard dash even when he's standin' still, poppin' the door of the fridge to get hold of one of my brother Eugene's beers, and this funky smell comin' off him. Not Mr. Cool settin' up there bein' a smart-ass manipulator, like he usually is. Not this time. He was *scared*, you listenin' to me? And I thought, 'Good. That's how you learn, finally. Maybe the only way.' I flashed on Darnell standin' that time in that other kitchen of mine when his old man was here, wavin' that gun. I say, 'Junior, you got a piece on you?'

He don't answer, but I don't need him to say nothin'.

'Junior,' I say, 'you ain't killed nobody, have you?'

'Naw,' he says, openin' that beer, spillin' foam on his hand. He got some scratches on him too. His Adam's apple be pumpin', hard.

We stop and listen to a siren, but it ain't headed this way.

'You sure?' I ask him.

'Pretty sure. I messed him up, though. White sucker got in my way. Dumb old honky. Wasn't any of *his* business.'

'What business was that?' I ask, though there wasn't much doubt about it-- all that money he had on him. 'You better clean off that blood,' I tell him. It pisses me off, all of a sudden, how I'd felt so sorry for him there for a minute when he let me see how scared he was. Twenty years old. Little Sidney's *grown*, but he just a kid. I be thinkin' that way, and then he decides to set up there and try to make a fool out of me, show how tough he is. Fuck *that*. Maybe I should have paid more attention to how he looked at me when he said *dumb honky*--like he wanted to let me know he knew who that dumb honky *was*. Maybe so. I'm not sure. I didn't even start trippin' on that till the day after, when I read it in the paper. Cause Harry worked there, I guess, they had a pretty big story on it. I don't know how much Junior knew about Harry--if they ever met, even. I wouldn't have told him anyway, you hear me?

Just like I never told Harry later.

'Naw, he ain't dead,' Junior says. 'Don't worry, mama, things be all right. Trust me,' he says, soundin' just like the big one. They be carbon copies sometimes. 'Just lemme have another one of these, wash up, gimme them keys, and I'm out of here.'

Sometimes Junior call me *mama* and sometimes he call me *sis*. Don't neither one of 'em sound right. I tell him to call me Kelly, but he won't. Right now I think, 'A mama's what you *used* to need, Junior, but it's past time for that. Way past. What you need now is a daddy'--but what can Sidney tell him, locked up in Chino? Or Eugene either, all *his* shit jumpin' off. I know what I ought to tell Little Sidney. I done told him enough times already--him and the big one and my brother, all three. They done heard it so many times it just spill out they ears.

But then they come back at me and say, 'What *else* we supposed to do?', and it ain't as easy to answer as you think. That's what I tried to tell Harry. What *else*? He tried to understand, but I'm not sure he ever could.

We listen to another siren. Not sure *which* way that one's goin'.

'You know what your daddy thinks about that Cadillac,' I tell him. 'That there's the apple of his eye, you hear me? So you drive careful.'

'I will, mama.'

He finished his beer, and I give him the keys.

'You keep that money, wherever you got it,' I tell him. 'Though I *need* it, you listenin' to me? Shit. I be startin' to show a little already.

Then Junior went and hugged me. Just like the big one did, goin' off to prison again after he broke parole. Junior, he kisses me on the forehead and pats me on the back like he meant it for once. Six feet tall and never had a *real* mama--just this bitch left him for Sidney's mama to raise half the time, him and his little sister. Wasn't *nothin'* nice. Now it's too late, I be thinkin' again even before he went out that door.

#   #   #   #

Harry Hudson had once seen a black youth crossing Anaheim Street in mid-block, just down from the Chieu Hoi Saloon. Tall and lean, wearing expensive high-top sneakers and a blue sleeveless T-shirt and strange, baggy rust-colored calf-length shorts. An earring. A Raiders cap set backwards on his head. One of those haircuts that, Kelly would tell Harry Hudson later, was called a "fade." A uniform. He thought about it in the cool darkness of the bar, talking to Thuy and old Stanley. About how these styles came up out of nowhere, like the slang Kelly astonished him with--like the music and the politics of the '60s, invented by people his age but nothing like him, it seemed, a tribe unlike anybody in Beattie. How did they do it? He had no clue. The pickup behind the Nissan had had giant speakers in its bed; the rap song that thumped out over the whole street seemed to be what the youth was listening to on his Walkman as he strolled languidly, rhythmically by, ignoring the screech of Harry Hudson's brakes.

"Like he was d-daring me to h--." He licked his lips. "To hit him. I mean, he looked *right at* me. He knew I was coming."

119

"Sure he did," Stanley said, and Harry Hudson could tell he was thinking about B.J. That same attitude of deliberate, mocking defiance, that testing of limits. The hot sunlight had gleamed off the mag wheels in the Discount Tire Center's window and rainbowed the grease spots on the asphalt, and a splinter of it seemed to pierce Harry Hudson's brain, already throbbing from the truck's bass beat. He hated the youth then. Hated him for *making* him hate, for exposing him in such a nakedness of rage .

He risked his life to do that, Harry Hudson marveled afterward. *I could have hit him.*

He couldn't remember the youth's face, just its studied indifference-- behind which had to be an even greater rage. What could you do with people like that?

"Too many crazies," Mama Thuy said somberly, clipping out grocery coupons on the bar. "More all the time."

#   #   #   #

The incident disturbed Harry Hudson, because in his first months at the Clarion he wanted, above all else, to stay calm. In control. He felt as if he had awakened from a nightmare, the craziness of everything he had done during the four weeks of the tryout. But then he remembered similar "awakenings" in the past--coming home from Vietnam, for instance; he remembered that they had led only to craziness of a different, if perhaps quieter, kind. After which--driving home from a night in Portland, for instance, rain beading on the windshield, the heater humming, sobriety and guilt leaking into him like the grey dawn light into the sky--he would think he was "awakening" again.

Wrong.

So he took it slowly, mistrustfully. He bought a lighter jacket and some short-sleeved shirts. He had the Nissan serviced, and it ran so well he changed his mind and decided not to trade it in. He had an Earl Scheib shop fix the dented fender, though, and paint the car a bright California orange. He rented an upscale apartment in Belmont Shore-- "on the right side of the Gimp Line," as Brad Pierce advised him.

"What?"

"The Gimp Line. Redondo Avenue, around there. East of it, everybody's in good shape, studs and babes with nice tans, nice clothes. Nobody grows old. At least nobody *looks* old. Those same bulldozers they clean the beach with, they shove all the ugly folks west of the line. It's a city ordinance. You don't believe me? All the wheelchairs and walkers, the harelips, orthopedic shoes, the really, really fat people, the ones with uncool tattoos--all west of the line. Check it out. You'll see why I park my boat where I do."

Pierce was joking, but he was right, too. There were good-looking people west of Redondo, and some good neighborhoods, but none of the crippled or deranged east of it, that Harry Hudson could see. His feelings were mixed. After the Reef, it was nice to be in such a clean, safe place, only two blocks from the ocean, even though he had nothing much to furnish it with and the bare white walls, smelling of new paint, reminded him of his and Deborah's apartment in Garbersville. But he didn't hang out in the sports bars and coffee shops of Belmont Shore, as Pierce did--as somebody with Harry Hudson's current income might have been expected to do. He went to the Chieu Hoi Saloon.

#   #   #   #

"They closed it down," Louise told Harry Hudson the next time he called her.

"What?"

"The Rabbit Hutch, sweetheart. Those vets next door did it. Shit. What are all us freaks gonna do, huh?"

"S-sorry to hear that," Harry Hudson said. Though he had his own phone in the apartment now, he still felt like whispering.

"They've been agitatin' the city for *years*, like I told you, and the city finally did what they wanted. Put a padlock on it. Ain't that a bitch? I thought it was against the law, shuttin' a place down like that when we ain't done nothin' wrong. Just dancin' is all. Am I right? I told Leroy when it happened, I said, 'That white boy, Harry, *he* ought to know.'"

"H-hard to say," Harry Hudson said, remembering that Long Beach had managed to close the Haven. "D-depends on La Mirada, what k--" *Kind of ordinances they have*, he wanted to say.

"What?"

"D-depends on wh--. Wh--"

"What?"

"--"

"Slow down, baby."

121

Harry Hudson sighed, gave up on that subject. He was sitting on his mattress, which lay directly on the hardwood floor, strewn with dirty clothes and sections of the Clarion. "That other place you t-told me about. Wh-what about that? Is it still open?"

"The thee-ater?"

"No. The W--." He licked his lips. "Something World."

"The Wide World. Sure it's open, but, Harry, I *told* you I don't hang there anymore, didn't I? I *know* I told you that."

Harry Hudson remembered nothing of the kind.

"Some of these kids there, you don't know *where* they been dippin' it. They *smell* bad. There's diseases you can get these days, no lie. I *mean* it, Harry. And with my old man on the warpath ... shit." Louise spoke at length about divorce negotiations with her husband; Harry Hudson got a crick in his neck from holding the phone. "Besides," she said, "I'm gonna have this operation on my feet. I told you *that*, didn't I?"

"What?"

"My *feet*, Harry. Gonna get them toes straightened out like I should have done a long time ago. Oh, they're gonna be so pretty, you can't believe. Gimme three, four months to get healed up, and you and me's gonna dance up a *storm*.... Too bad about the Rabbit Hutch, huh? Well, at least you got to see it once before they pulled the plug." The giggle. "In all its glory."

"I g-guess so," Harry Hudson said.

"You got *that* right. Well, gimme a ring then, OK? You and me's *way* overdue already, sweetheart, but I'll make it up to you. Just you wait and see."

#   #   #   #

He could have bought furniture, he supposed. Or even saved his money and made a down payment on a condo. He didn't have to be camping out. But he went on living as he had lived ever since coming home from the Army, except for the time with Deborah. Owning a home was for other people; Harry Hudson knew he would always be a renter. He could have cooked for himself, too, but the memory of all those meals he and his father had rustled up and eaten in silence over the oilcloth--eggs and fried Spam and oatmeal, chicken pot pies and canned beans, once in a while a venison stew--drove him out to Denny's and Norm's and Carl's Jr. and McDonald's, to a Thai place on the Boulevard and a Greek gyro place on Fourth Street, to the Clarion's cafeteria on tamale night. Twice a week, he showed up at 11 a.m. when Mama Thuy opened the bar. He paid for a Vietnamese lunch for two, which she ordered by phone, and tipped the delivery boy who brought it in plastic bags: rice, *pho* soup, salad, stir-fried shrimp.

Almost every night after work, he was back in the bar. Here, especially, he had to be careful. The problem, as he saw it, was to make Mama Thuy forget he had ever been slobbering drunk. That wouldn't be easy. It meant, at the least, behaving like a gentleman for months before he even thought about making a move. He always wore a tie and a jacket, sat quietly on his stool and had a single beer, two at the most. Lest he seem like a cheapskate, he bought Thuy and the other barmaids drinks, stood the house to an occasional round and was ready to lend a few dollars to anybody who asked. Not Black Jimmy, who greeted Harry Hudson with great friendliness and never seemed to be in need again. But Randy, several times, and even Charlene, now that the Navy had shipped B.J. back to Virginia. Money melted away. Harry Hudson had no more left at the end of each pay period than he'd had in Red Fork--especially since, having once sent Deborah a bigger check, he felt he had to keep on doing it.

He avoided Ron if he could.

Most of the time, he still slept ten hours a day, sometimes twelve.

# # # #

Soon Harry Hudson started keeping notes on Mama Thuy--as if he were really planning to write a story about the bar:

Grew up in Saigon. Several brothers and sisters--one, Phuong, also lives in Long Beach, married to Navy guy.

Thuy's father, big guy, half Chinese, insurance man of some kind, tyrannized over the family. Went shopping for ready-made switches to hit the kids with. Switches broke over their bare bottoms. Hit them harder if they squirmed or cried out. Thuy especially--"I was always bad girl."

She hates his guts, even today, but in the same breath defends Asian child-rearing methods. I tried to sympathize with her, but she says that's what a lot of American kids need: a good, old-fashioned whipping.

Hates Communists, too. A Reagan-Bush voter all the way.

She and Phuong ran away once as girls. Met at midnight on some street corner, bound for--who knows? Phuong chickened out. Thuy, typically, was ready to go through with it.

At 17, hung out with American servicemen in downtown Saigon. Got pregnant and tried to hide her condition from her father, when he spotted her in a crowded marketplace, by covering her belly with one of those pointed straw hats. Laughs now. Wasn't funny at the time.

Her family gave the boyfriend, Dwayne Cummings, Air Force guy, an ultimatum: take Thuy or the baby, Billy, but not both. He chose marriage, took Thuy to his home town, near Chickasha, Okla. (Wonder where Riker came from?) They figured on lobbying her parents, getting baby to U.S. eventually. Fall of Saigon scotched that plan.

Worries about the kid, now 19. Half-American kids often discriminated against there. Feels guilty about leaving him. Tries to make up for it by sending him stuff.

Thuy says people in Oklahoma were nice to her, but the place was really in the boondocks. Farm town. She worked in a laundry for $1.60 an hour. Left Dwayne when he seemed content to stay in Hicksville; headed for Vietnamese community in S. Calif., where Phuong was. Amicable divorce, apparently. Still close to her mother-in-law, who writes and visits.

Worked for several bars here--one in L.A., also Strollers and Honeymooners across from bus station in Long Beach. (Since torn down for Plaza Mall project.) Saved money to buy her own bar. How? Worked seven days a week, frequent double shifts. Admits she had some sugar daddies. ("I'm not ashamed," she says, giving me that direct look.) Raised maybe $50,000.

Stayed single for several years. One guy (not Ron) got her pregnant; insisted she have abortion because his family in Wisconsin didn't want him to marry an Asian. "Potatoes OK, but no rice," she says with real bitterness. Got the abortion; never saw the guy again. Was turned off on American men for some time. Dated Norwegians, Dutch, other merchant sailors. "Liked that tall and blond, blue eyes."

About the time she bought the Chieu Hoi Saloon, Thuy got married a second time, to Wade Overholtzer. Older guy, maybe 55 now. Owns German-car garage on Eastside. Well-to-do. Gave her that Porsche. "Good man." Would have stayed with him, she says, if he hadn't gotten so jealous of bar customers and pressured her to sell. Couldn't understand how important the business is to her.

Another amicable divorce. Wade comes in now and then, has a drink, shoots pool, talks to her, to the rest of us. She's right: a nice guy.

"You know what you have here?" I ask her. "A church, that's what. It just looks like a bar. We're all here to worship."

124

Mama Thuy just grins.

\#   \#   \#   \#

What the notes didn't say:

She changed age and color on him, even size. Leaning her folded arms on the counter or sitting on her favorite stool opposite the pool table, she didn't seem all that short. Standing beside Harry Hudson, though, she barely came up to his shoulder. It took him a while to realize that the shortness was in her legs, disguised by a raised walkway of duckboards behind the bar. Indoors, at night, as he usually saw her, Mama Thuy's skin was an even, dusky tan, her face smooth, except for fine laugh lines at the corners of her eyes and mouth. But outside in the 11 a.m. sun, she looked almost leathery. Her skin had the uncertain tone he had begun to notice on other people their age. Day to day, depending on how tired she was, it went pale or brown, blotchy or ashy--particularly her hands, shiny and veiny from all that scrubbing. He began to think he had arrived just in time to witness the last year or two of her beauty. He wanted to console her: *I don't care. Now that I've seen you like this, I'll never see you any other way.* Didn't he still see Nancy Ishida as she had looked in that classroom in Beattie? But he didn't say anything. On second thought, he doubted that Mama Thuy wanted to be reminded that she was growing old. And even if he could get the words out, he knew the inflection would be wrong.

Take the day she came in with a purple bruise on her neck. It looked a lot like a hickey. Harry Hudson tried to joke about it: "Hey, Thuy. Got a new boyfriend?" But the words straggled out lamely. *No jokes. Not for you.* His face stretched in a rictus that he tried to pass as a smile.

Mama Thuy didn't laugh. Though she might have, he thought, if somebody else had said it--Swede, Randy, even Pop. She spat a couple of words in Vietnamese. "Medicine," she said. "You know that." And he did remember vaguely some treatment that involved rubbing the skin--with a coin?--but not before he saw that she was seriously angry at him.

Christ. Two weeks it lasted--two weeks of even more careful behavior than usual--before she relented and talked to Harry Hudson again.

Navy Swede (real name is Carl Bjornson. I asked him why "Navy Swede," and he said there was another "Swede," worked for the Dodge agency down the block, who used to be a regular at the bar too. That's how Thuy told them apart. Just as there was another Jimmy, a white one, before Black Jimmy):

"*Thing about Mom is,*" *he says (with Stanley listening in),* "*she really doesn't give a shit if people like her or not. You know how unusual that is? I mean, it's something you almost never see. Think of that dude ... what was his name? Randall?*"

"*Wrangel,*" *Stanley says.* "*Art Wrangel.*" *He nudges Swede.* "*Boy, I tell you, when it come to lovesick fools, him and Walt sure made a pair.*"

"*Art Wrangel,*" *Swede tells me,* "*he'd been drinkin' here four, five years, regular. One day, out of nowhere, he comes up to Mom and gives her hell. Tells her he's sick and tired of waitin' for her to come across. Called her a cock-teasin' bitch. You know what she did? Tossed him out on his ass. Told him she'd thought he was a friend of hers, and friends didn't talk like that. 'My way or the highway,' she says, and by God she means it.*"

"*Ho! Talk about guys gettin' eighty-sixed--*"

What was two weeks of silence, then? Harry Hudson thought. Or a few months of trying, compared to Wrangel's years? Was that how these men would remember him, if at all--as a lovesick fool?

"*--remember that big biker?*" *Stanley asks.* "*Harry, you were here.*"

He was. He was there at 1 a.m. on a Wednesday, with the bar nearly empty. Mama Thuy wanted to close early. She'd already had a rough day. The men's toilet had backed up, and the refrigeration, despite Swede's latest repair job, was on the blink again. Also, she had gotten some bad news from Immigration, Harry Hudson guessed. A torn, official-looking envelope in her purse. Mama Thuy announced last call. She collected the money, switched off the pool-table light, locked and barred the Long Beach Boulevard door. The biker, bearded and ponytailed, in a leather vest and a rainbow-striped Navajo headband and jeans torn at the knee, ignored her. He wandered out the Anaheim Street door and back in, with a drunk's sleepy cunning; he insisted on another beer, then another. She asked him to go. He mumbled and lurched, his long arms swinging. Then, with a grin, he sat back down. She asked him again, more sharply. Suddenly enraged, he slammed his half-full bottle of Coors on the countertop, splashing her leopard-skin-print halter, and screamed at her.

"Get out! Now!" she yelled back, ran around the bar and shoved him out the Anaheim Street door with her bare hands. Just like that. Then she locked the screen.

Stanley and Harry Hudson just watched from their stools--Stanley too old and slow, despite his massive bulk; Harry Hudson plenty willing to help her, he told himself later, if she needed help. If the biker had a gun, for instance, like those Mexicans he had heard about who robbed her sister, Phuong. Stuck the barrel down her throat.... It happened too fast, though. For the biker, too. Mama Thuy's yell had just as much force as his scream--yet it wasn't a yell of panic, Harry Hudson thought; it was calculated to startle him. And if the biker had had a second to react, he would have realized that he stood a foot and a half taller than this woman, outweighed her two to one. If she'd hesitated at all ... but she hadn't. She was *in charge*. Now they could hear him rattling the screen and cursing before he drifted off. There was silence. Then he started up his Harley with a burbling roar.

Swede: *"Any man marries her's got his hands full. One tough lady."*

Stanley: *"You'd be surprised how many have asked her, though. I've lost count of how many proposals she's had. In Vegas. Right across this damn bar."*

I ask him if he'd want to marry her himself if he were single and, say, fifty years old again. Stanley shakes his head. "I dunno, Harry. I guess I'm old-fashioned. When I was married, I got used to calling the shots. Thuy there, now, she's a good friend of mine, but Jesus, she'd be orderin' me around every minute. I don't think I could take that."

Stanley is still married, of course, in a way. And Charlene is living in his trailer again, now that B.J. is gone. Which pisses Randy off no end. Randy adores Mama Thuy but wouldn't even dream of being able to sleep with her. Charlene, whom he puts down every chance he gets, is a different matter. He wants her bod, bad.

Stanley grew up in Compton when it was still a white, middle-class town. He managed an auto parts store in Long Beach for a while. Raced cars and boats. Had three kids. Then he worked for UCLA as a mechanic and all-around handyman at its marine research station on Catalina. Likes to say: "Some of those Ph.D.s would ask how come I made more money than they did. And the boss would tell 'em straight: 'I can always get more Ph.D.s, but no way I can get me another Stanley.'"

Now Stanley says, "Funny thing, Harry, my wife and I never went to bars. But we met in a bar. I ever tell you that?"

He has, more than once.

Harry Hudson exchanged a glance with Swede, wishing it were Mama Thuy winking at him instead. It was only at such a moment that he felt--that she *let* him feel, he corrected himself--that the two of them were allied against all the rest. Two sensible people smiling at barflies' foolishness.

For if the Chieu Hoi Saloon was a church, Harry Hudson thought, it was a congregation of fools, of incomplete people gathering around Mama Thuy in hope that some of her wholeness would rub off. A scruffy crew of worshippers who had long since lost the ability--if they ever had it in the first place--to control their behavior, moment by moment, well enough to pass as ·

normal citizens. While Mama Thuy, in contrast, never stopped being in charge. Never let down her guard. Never half-smiled at the umpteenth repetition of a Stanley story, or led a stumbling Pop to his table by the wall, or hugged an old friend whose ship had just come in, or shook Randy awake, or turned stony-faced when an addict came around peddling items swiped from some store (toilet-seat covers or votive candles or electric toothbrushes), or gave her opponent a concentration-shattering glimpse of her breasts as she leaned over the pool table--never did any of these things, it seemed, without being fully conscious of what she was doing. Hers was a different kind of life altogether from what they knew.

"Bullshit," says Susie (Suzy?), a prostitute who drinks in here, though Mama Thuy won't let her hustle the customers--inside, at any rate. "I've seen her cry. Just like me, when it all got to be too much. All the hassle. You're just cunt-struck, is all. She's a human being like the rest of us."

Susie is white, of uncertain age. Much the worse for wear after years of standing out on Anaheim Street and Pacific Coast Highway. Hair like straw, a badly sun-cracked face, varicose veins.

She, too, is a parishioner. Almost painfully eager to assert that she's a good person. Probably exaggerates how close she is to Mama Thuy--though Thuy did give her one of her own cat's kittens, a female, grey with white paws. Susie named her after Thuy. Reporting on the kitten's growth, what she eats, is a good excuse to stop by.

So Mama Thuy did lose her cool once in a while? Harry Hudson had never seen it.

An anecdote from Randy (dreamy look on his face, gapped teeth, that silly little mustache): "Mom, you may have noticed, don't drink much. Very, very seldom you ever see her get drunk. Almost never. I only seen her drunk once, but I'll never forget it, man. It was right after her and Wade broke up last year. She was wearin' one of those ... those little outfits of hers. You know what I mean."

I nod.

"She gets half lit and climbs right up on the pool table there and starts to dancin' to the music. All I can say is, Harry, you should've been there. She was a pro, *man. I mean, Rita used to dance out at the Body Shop, joints like that, for years, and Charlene thinks she knows how to wiggle her fat butt ... shit. Not even close to what Mom was doin'. I mean, we all just sat there with our fuckin' mouths open. Nobody said a word. She was beautiful, man." (His face even dreamier.) "Is beautiful."*

And she was. Maybe that was the only truth that mattered, despite all this talk about Mama Thuy's personality. Would anyone have cared half

128

as much for her if a biological accident hadn't given her those breasts, those shoulders, that storm of black hair (though she admitted coloring it now), those curves that flowed one into the other in a particular way? Right down to the narrowness of her wrists and the slight flattening of her skull and the hollow between the tendons at the base of her neck? Damn it, Harry Hudson thought, Mama Thuy *was* beautiful. Despite her age. If her skin had flaws, he thought, it was because the desire of thousands of men had been focused on her, as if by a burning glass, for two decades, leaving her singed and glazed. She seemed to accept this. She still wore the most revealing costumes--that leopard-skin number, black leather, purple jumpsuits, form-fitting *ao dais*, peek-a-boo things from Frederick's of Hollywood--in full confidence that customers wanted to ogle her body.

Charlene: "But classy, you know? I mean, Mom shows more skin than anybody else here--more than those hustlers over at the Dragon's Tail, even. You tell me. You're a man. How she does it without looking like a slut."

A trick Charlene knows she herself hasn't mastered.

But what could a man be expected to know about a woman's ways with clothes and makeup? The answer, as far as Harry Hudson was concerned, was both simpler and more mysterious: Mama Thuy *was* classy. But that line of reasoning led back to her personality, and he would rather stick to her body. It fascinated him. He never got tired of gazing at it. *Cunt-struck, is all.* That was true. Mama Thuy's body, he knew, was no more than a millimeter or two different, here and there, from Deborah's body, which had left him cold. Who could say why? It made no sense. Yet he was so happy to be a worshipper again--as he hadn't been in all the years since Nancy Ishida moved south--that he didn't want to question it. Besides, half the Pacific Fleet, if called upon to testify, would back him up.

Mama Thuy's personality, to tell the truth, scared him almost as much as it lured him on.

After all, Harry Hudson brooded during those months of nights, nursing his single Budweisers as the pool balls clicked, the Pac-Man beeped, the life preservers hung on the walls, Rita rang her bell, the jukebox played the same songs over and over and Stanley's stained-glass crotch twirled slowly in a cloud of incense smoke--after all, what did he have to offer her in return? He wasn't innocent, as Dwayne had been, or rich, like Wade. He wasn't good-looking and handy with tools, like Swede. He wasn't smart. All he had was his worship, his conviction that nobody had ever properly appreciated Mama

Thuy before--and what, around the Chieu Hoi Saloon, was more common than that? His happiness took on a bitter edge sometimes as he joined the little group that escorted her across the street to her car at 2 a.m. In her mind, he thought, he was just another member of her congregation of cripples. *She knew.* Of course she knew. He gave it away every time he opened his mouth. In spite of his jacket and tie and all the drinks he bought.

Something else the notes didn't say:

An anger came over him at moments like this--the same anger he had felt at the Rabbit Hutch, a frustration that seemed to reach back to high school, at least, though he couldn't remember being aware of it then. Still, he could hear the minie balls whistling past him in the pine grove in Beattie. He wished they would hit him, finally, splatter his guts out, the way his bullets had hit the old man near Phuoc Vinh. That very same old man might have been Mama Thuy's grandfather. How could he ever make *that* up to her? Harry Hudson began to hear a voice again--a voice that had never stopped speaking to him, he realized, but now, once more, whispered loud enough to hear.

Sydney Carton's voice.

You can die, it told him. *That's what you can do.*

He began to imagine scenarios: What if the biker had a knife? What if the Mexicans came back?

Swede again: "When I first hit town, I got a Dear John letter from my girl back in St. Paul. Busted me all up. It was Christmas, you know, and I was homesick as hell. Mom just patted me on the back--didn't know me from Adam then--and said, 'Things work out, hon.' Like she'd already lived a hundred years and really knew. She's done that for other guys too. Made 'em believe it in spite of themselves. Hell, a lot of Navy guys, they're just kids, and she understands that. Got a heart as big as all outdoors."

Harry Hudson was readiest to risk his life, he noticed, when he was angriest, when he loved Mama Thuy the least. That was the strange thing. To enter into the trance that was his only hope of success, he absolutely had not to care.

Rita (raised a Catholic, apparently, in the Philippines): "She killed her baby, you know that? Maybe two or three babies. I like Mama, she's OK to work for, don't get me wrong, but she's goin' to burn in Hell just the same."

#   #   #   #

Three months after hiring Harry Hudson, Hank Steinbach had a stroke. He spent weeks in the hospital and at home and appeared back in the newsroom only once, for his retirement party. Balloons bobbed over the computer terminals, and somebody--Pierce?--hired a stripper in an abbreviated nurse's uniform to dance for Steinbach. She peeled off her white garters and handed them to him, sat in his lap and kissed his cheek. She was blonde and improbably lovely. *Where do they all come from?* Harry Hudson wondered, just as he had at the Low Fox. What kind of trap was rigged out there to catch so many of the nation's pretty girls and turn them into commercial temptresses? Porn actresses, mud wrestlers, "lingerie models," the faces on the beer posters at the Chieu Hoi. Nancy Ishida had escaped it, but she'd had her scholarship. Next to this girl, Steinbach looked awful--not just skinny but shockingly cadaverous, his skin purple-blotched, his white hair askew, his cheeks eroded even deeper, his grin permanently lopsided now, if still jaunty. He kissed her back. The onlookers, even the women reporters, hooted and whistled. Then they all went across the street to the Press Club, Steinbach and people he had terrorized for years, drinking and smiling.

Then Steinbach was gone. He moved out to the desert, to Hesperia, where he wrote a monthly column on how his fellow retirees should cope with hip replacements and Social Security and coyotes in their back yards. The columns were placid, even humorous. They had nothing to do with the Steinbach whom Harry Hudson never had a chance to ask: *What did you know? Why did you let me twist in the wind for so long if you were going to hire me anyway?* That made no sense either. Steinbach, like Finnegan, had held power over him; he had been the man whom, in all the world, Harry Hudson most needed to please; yet Harry Hudson had mattered so little in return that Steinbach hadn't ever felt it necessary to explain. That was a fact. Now Holcomb was boss of the copy desk. Lincoln wrote street-edition banners that actually got into the paper, and no harm seemed to be done. Two weeks after Steinbach left the Clarion, it was as if he had never reigned there for twenty years.

How could this be?

\#   \#   \#   \#

"W-what if I come out to B--. B--. You know. Where you live. B-baldwin Park. Just to v--. Just to see you. How you're doing."

"Shit, Harry, what makes you think I live in Baldwin Park?"

131

A long pause. "Y-you said--"

"West Covina, sweetheart. I've been here sixteen years."

"I could've sworn.... Jesus. Maybe it was th-that blonde. What was her name?" Harry Hudson asked, though he knew perfectly well. He could sense the M in Margot was going to be trouble. "M–." He licked his lips. "Mmm–."

"Margot? She lives in Redondo, Harry, I *told* you that."

Which was true.

Louise giggled. "You know, she's been callin' me up, three in the morning sometimes. Talkin' so sweet. Ol' Kevin put her up to it, I bet. Wants to know how soon I'll be gettin' back in the *swing* of things, if you know what I mean."

"M-me too," Harry Hudson said.

"I *told* you, baby. Be patient. At my age, things don't always heal up quite as fast as I'd like, even these pretty new feet. But it's gonna be *cool* when I do, believe me.... Just one thing, though. Harry?"

"--"

"You listenin'? Harry?"

He managed to grunt.

"Don't you *ever* come over here lessen you give me a call first, you hear? Nothin' personal. That's just the way I do things, Harry. If it isn't cool with you, too, then forget it, OK?"

#   #   #   #

Guns ain't *nothin'* nice. You hear me? It was a gun sent Sidney back to prison this time, and it wasn't even his. It was my brother Eugene's. That old .45 our daddy had from the Army. Not one of them Glocks or Uzis or nothin'. Eugene says you can't hardly hit nothin' with it--might as well throw it at somebody, he says, as shoot the motherfucker. It wasn't even loaded--just settin' there on his suitcase in his bedroom where Eugene'd been takin' it apart and cleanin' it out in front of everbody, just to piss Sidney off. But the cops saw it. That's all they needed. 'You come right along with us, Mr. Crenshaw,' they say, woop-woop-woop, grinnin' real wide. The law say it don't matter *who* own the gun. If you on parole and you in the same house with one, that's a violation.

Course, them polices wouldn't be bustin' in here in the first place if Eugene and Sidney hadn't raised so much hell the landlord went and called 'em.

He been lookin' for some excuse to evict us ever since he first seen me bringin' tricks in here. Givin' me the evil eye, you know what I mean? He wouldn't fix that leak in the bathroom neither, that I'd been after him about ever since we moved in. Oh, he a slick one, all right. Two-faced sonofabitch. Now it was *his* turn to be grinnin', all the way back down them stairs.

It was mostly Eugene's fault, I know that. But not all of it. He was drinkin' pretty heavy there after he lost custody of them two kids to that bitch LaVonne, took 'em back to Kansas with her. He was *tore up*, you hear what I'm sayin'? He was cryin' and callin' her all kind of bitches and talkin' about goin' back there on the next Greyhound bus and killin' her. He meant it, too. Right then, anyway. Eugene *do* have a drinkin' problem. I know this. He know it too. That's one main reason LaVonne *got* them kids. My brother just don't handle alcohol like he used to back before he went in that penitentiary. But I figured he'd be OK after he slept it off. Shit. Try to tell that to Sidney. Eugene be takin' that gun out once we get him into the bedroom, all red in the eyes from that Wild Turkey the two of 'em been sluggin' down all evenin', and before I can step in between 'em, ol' Sidney's grapped onto that .45 and they be rasslin' around and screamin' and yellin' so loud I ain't even surprised when the cops come in.

'Kelly,' Sidney says just before they take him away. Just 'Kelly,' in this real soft voice.

That's what I remember. And he holds out his hand to me--his left hand, the bad one, that got hurt in the factory--just before they put the cuffs on. Like he's askin' me how the fuck *this* ever happened. 'You write me, hear?' he says. 'And come *visit*.'

I tell him I will, cross my heart.

The thing is, Sidney never told on Eugene, pissed off as he was. Eugene be on parole, too, right? And it's *his* gun. All them polices had to do was call Kansas. On their computers, whatever. But they were so damn happy to get their hooks into one of the Crenshaws again, they let Eugene go. Sidney never told, though he could've sent my brother up for a lot longer than a year in Chino.

He damn sure *wanted* to right then, I know.

But he didn't.

For *my* sake.

That's another thing I don't think Harry ever understood.

# # # #

One winter night when Harry Hudson arrived at the Chieu Hoi Saloon, Mama Thuy was already there--in fact, she was on her way out. A small crowd was leaving with her. "It's Walt," she said. "He in jail. I gotta go downtown, bail him out. Charlene, she take over the bar while I'm gone."

"Walt?"

"You know. Rita's husband. He get drunk over at the Dragon's Tail, crazy jealous, make trouble. They call the cops." She hitched her purse strap over her shoulder and sighed. "Why me?"

"Come on, Harry," Stanley said. "You don't want to miss *this*."

"Why? You all stay here and drink. I can do this myself. No need half the bar come along."

"Oh, yes we do, Mom." It was Randy, and parting the curtain just behind him--Harry Hudson saw with a buzz of panic--was Ron. "Ol' Walt'd be right there snickerin' if it was any of *us*. Turnabout's fair play."

"Hey, it's the *meed*-ja man," Ron said. "Gonna come along and tell it like it is?"

Harry Hudson looked away.

Ron grinned mirthlessly under his mustache. This time he didn't seem so drunk.

"Well, don't just stand here in the door," Mama Thuy said. "You comin', you comin', I guess. But my car only hold four. Who else gonna drive? Stanley? OK. Phuong, you come with me."

For Thuy's sister had made a rare visit to the bar. Side by side, the two women crossed the street to the Discount Tire Center lot. They were exactly the same height. They looked alike, too, in matching green camouflage-print jumpsuits sewn with patches of Navy and Marine insignia, but Phuong's face was bonier, more cynical, her stomach softer, lapping over the same wide web belt that flattered Mama Thuy's figure. Again, it was just a matter of a millimeter or two, but it made all the difference, Harry Hudson thought. As simple and as unfair as that. Phuong didn't seem to have Thuy's brains and ambition, either. She stayed at home in a shabby area of North Long Beach with a high-school-age daughter. Put bars on her windows. Seldom ventured out except to shop. Phuong hadn't so much as tried to get U.S. citizenship, Thuy had once told him scornfully--even a driver's license. Yet she was the older of the two and had been in America almost as long. *Second fiddle all her life?* Harry Hudson found himself pitying her a little as he hung back in the doorway to let Ron pass.

On the far sidewalk, the group split up. Phuong, her husband, Corbin, and then Ron--with a last-second dash--piled into the Porsche with Mama Thuy. That left Randy and Harry Hudson with all the room in Stanley's Oldsmobile.

"That Ron," Stanley said, pulling out of the lot. "Cracks me up. He don't know when to quit."

Randy in the back seat was silent, and Harry Hudson thought he knew why. Both of them would trade places with Ron if they could.

"W-where's Rita?" he asked Stanley as they trailed the Porsche down Long Beach Boulevard.

"God knows. Now she's lost *two* jobs. Thuy's gonna *have* to let her go this time, I think. And the Dragon's Tail too. Rita's been workin' there the last month or so--early shift, two nights a week." The old man nudged Harry Hudson. "Walt'd been hot on her trail ever since his ship docked. He came in and out of the Chieu Hoi today, must have been half a dozen times. Fella I know said he raised holy hell at the Dragon's Tail when he finally found her. Not that I blame Walt one bit, you understand. Except for marryin' her in the first place."

"B--." Once again everyone seemed to know the key facts except him. "W-why?"

"Why what? Why did Walt throw a chair at her, bust that big mirror they got behind the bar? That's what the fella told me. Chased her right out into the parking lot. Hell, he might have caught her, too, if she hadn't kicked off her high heels and run." Stanley shook his head. "Or why did Rita do what *she* did?"

"What d--. D--." Harry Hudson licked his lips. "She *do?*"

"I don't have all the gory details. You'll have to ask Walt," Stanley said. "But my guess is, she put that whole house of theirs up her nose."

They passed Denny's, where Holcomb sometimes still took the rim out to coffee. Then the post office where Harry Hudson had bought that issue of the Sun. Through a gap in the buildings he glimpsed the Reef's green neon sign. Then the Porsche's taillights swung west on Third Street, around the mall, and Stanley followed, his huge hand spinning the wheel with practiced ease-- maybe he *had* raced cars, in some unimaginable past.

135

"Y-you mean d-drugs?" Harry Hudson finally understood what Stanley had just said. Randy snorted.

Hayseed.

"Hell, yes," Stanley said. "You haven't noticed how spacey she gets?" Harry Hudson hadn't.

"Not half as spacey as Charlene," Randy broke in. He leaned forward and stuck his face between theirs. "What kind of drug problem *she* got, man? Don't tell me *that's* why she stays with you, huh? You her supplier or somethin'?"

"Charlene's problem," Stanley said seriously to Harry Hudson, ignoring Randy, as he doubled back east on Broadway, "is she ain't too bright. And she had a horrible family, back there in New York somewhere. Dad brought his mistress right in the house, slept with her right in front of Charlene and her mom. Can you blame her? She ran away as soon as she could. She was sixteen, seventeen. Hitched rides on trucks all the way out to Texas, and then California. Well, hell--you don't hitch rides on trucks without payin' the going rate, if you catch my drift. She was in pretty bad shape when I met her. Hell, yes, she had a drug problem.... Not like Rita, but she had one. But she don't anymore."

The jail and Long Beach police headquarters were in a glass-and-steel office building near City Hall. Across the street were converted bungalows with signs for bail bondsmen's offices and a restaurant called the Hung Jury.

"My wife, now, Denise, she might as *well* be on drugs," Stanley said. He parked behind the Porsche and unfolded to his full stature on the sidewalk. "I go there every day, Harry, and she don't know me at all. Hasn't for years. Those Filipino gals that take care of her, they feed her rice all the time and she don't care. Denise used to *hate* rice. Now they could feed her dog food and she wouldn't know the difference."

"Pretty handy for *you*, though," Randy mocked.

"Don't you believe it, Harry." He seemed to shake off Randy like an annoying small terrier at his ankles. "The way that Medicare works, you have to go broke to get on it. Sold my house, spent our savings--everything I worked for all those years--on doctors and fancy nursing homes. Then, when it was all gone and I was a fucking pauper, *then* the feds pick up the tab. Tell me that makes sense."

Mama Thuy was entering the police station already. Ron was right next to her in his blue trucker's cap. Harry Hudson felt a new flash of resentment.

"Denise and I *met* in a bar, but she never went to one afterwards," Stanley said. "I ever tell you that?"

#   #   #   #

They had to wait a long time--too long. It took forty-five minutes, maybe an hour, before Walt shuffled out through the security door into the lobby, holding his coat, a policeman's hand on his shoulder. By then the place had sobered them up. They had long since stopped laughing. *Some of them have been here before,* Harry Hudson thought, and the rest clearly felt the suction of those cells overhead. *We all look like we ought to be arrested. It was stupid to come.* They coughed and scraped their shoes. Randy cadged some change from Harry Hudson and fed the candy machines, whose humming seemed to flicker like the fluorescent lights. Phuong kept complaining to Corbin, "They got no place to sit down? Not at all? Why's that? Huh? *You* tell me." Corbin, thin and dark, paced restlessly. Stanley studied the city maps and missing-persons posters. Ron brooded at Mama Thuy's back as she stood by a thick red line on the floor, waiting for the clerks behind bulletproof glass or plastic to call her up to one of their windows.

The light here was harsh on Mama Thuy, Harry Hudson thought. She looked very small in the high-ceilinged lobby, though, as always, she stood as tall as she could. She looked work-worn, an immigrant woman out of place in that gaudy jumpsuit, taking her checkbook out of her purse, showing ID and signing papers. The clerks seemed to know her, he thought--but still, it must be an ordeal for her.

Was Walt worth it?

Would *he* be, if it ever came to that?

Joe Zuniga, the Clarion's police reporter, dropped by briefly to check the logbook. He did a double-take and looked, amused, at Harry Hudson, who tried to give him a casual shrug. Now and then a prisoner was released. Most of them went to the single pay phone on the wall and called somebody before drifting out the front door.

The last of these, just before Walt, was a woman. A black woman, pretty if unkempt, in a short silver dress that jogged Harry Hudson's memory. She had goosebumps on her arms from the chill; she shifted uneasily from one high-heeled foot to the other as she tapped buttons and listened, hung up and tried again.

"Shit, shit, shit," she said softly.

She turned to leave. Then, like Zuniga, she noticed Harry Hudson and half smiled, not sure she recognized him. He wasn't sure either. Her hairdo was bedraggled, the dress wrinkled and dirty, as if she had slept in it. But her smile--the little gap between her front teeth--brought back a pleasant feeling, a memory of having talked to her ... where? That bar on Pine Street, during his tryout. The Saratoga.

"Kelly," he said.

He was more surprised than she seemed to be that her name popped so readily into his head, slid out of his mouth. Without hesitation, she glanced back at the lobby and mimed to him: *You want a date?*

Right here in the police station? Harry Hudson was astounded. Trying to hide that he was talking to the woman at all, he edged over to the doorway and whispered, "I can't...."

"OK, OK, that's cool," Kelly said, loud enough for everyone to hear. "All I need is a *ride*, you understand what I'm sayin'? Them polices puttin' me out on the street, and nobody's home to come get me--I don't know why. Them buses stopped runnin', even if I *had* a token left. I'm gonna have to walk. Ain't that a bitch?"

"I d--. Don't h-have my car," Harry Hudson said. "I'm with *them*."

A veil came down over Kelly's eyes; her face hardened. "Fuck it, then," she said and walked out.

"W-wait," Harry Hudson cried. She halted on the steps. Every word now was a struggle. He could feel Ron staring at him, and maybe Mama Thuy as well. He was totally exposed. "Wh--. Just in case ... I mean, which w--." He stamped his foot. "Y-you going?"

"Up in North Long Beach. *Way* up." Kelly gestured vaguely, but she didn't wait any longer.

Then the security door clicked open and Walt came out--a squat man in his fifties with a dark windbreaker folded over his arm, wearing slacks and a San Diego Chargers sweatshirt. His head looked unnaturally large. He blinked in the light and shook hands with Thuy and Stanley. He had thinning hair and big pouches under his eyes and a long Irish upper lip. He tried to grin, but the heavy flesh of the rest of his face sagged down in a mask of shame.

#   #   #   #

For the ride back to the bar, Walt took Ron's place in the Porsche. Ron, disgruntled, sat next to Randy in the back seat of the Olds, directly behind Harry Hudson. "That spade chick try to hustle you?" he asked. "Or were you hustlin' *her?*"

Harry Hudson felt Ron's breath stir the hairs on his neck. He didn't answer. He was still stunned by the discovery that he had wanted to keep a secret from Mama Thuy, just as he had kept his trips to Portland secret from Deborah. He had thought things were different now. He had found a woman he truly desired--wasn't that all he needed? He had thought so. He had believed he could be faithful to her, as he had been effortlessly faithful for all those teen-age years to Nancy Ishida. But apparently not.

What had happened?

"I think I had her once," Ron said, goading him. "Not bad, either, if you like that dark meat."

Stanley, too, seemed to be in a chastened mood. Parking in the Tire Center lot, he set the brake and sat still for a moment, then turned to Harry Hudson.

"It just ain't Denise anymore," he said. "I go there every day, like I told you, and her body's there, sittin' in that chair, but she ain't in it anymore. She's gone. I know it sounds cold, Harry, but I don't feel like I'm married anymore. I've done all I could. Kid this age"--he jerked a thumb at Randy, who leered back-- "can't understand, but I bet Denise herself would say the same thing, if she could. She wouldn't begrudge me a little comfort."

#   #   #   #

In the Chieu Hoi Saloon, they tried to chase shame away. Wade was there, Mama Thuy's ex-husband, bent over his custom-made cue: a lean man with a long, shrewd face and a stringy neck, wearing a white satin Western shirt, a bolo tie. He straightened up and waved. Navy Swede was gathering his needle-nose pliers and galvanometer and rolls of tape from the counter, the ice chests rewired again, for a while. Pop sat at his place by the wall. Black Jimmy grinned. The jukebox was playing "A Boy Named Sue"; the taped audience at Folsom Prison roared and whistled for Johnny Cash, while the group just back from the Long Beach Jail called for beer to wash the taste of it out of their throats. Randy looked expectantly at Harry Hudson, who shrugged and ordered a round. Mama Thuy rang the bell. Rita wasn't there to shout, "Big spender!", though, and they all felt her absence. They looked at Walt, sitting hunched at the corner of the bar, hardly aware of the sweating bottle Charlene set before him.

"Drink up," Wade encouraged him. He came up behind Walt and slapped the sides of his shoulders in a kind of hug. Walt cringed but otherwise didn't move. "You're well rid of her, buddy. Think of it that way."

"That isn't *all* I'm rid of," Walt muttered.

"All the more reason to drink, then."

Walt still didn't move. "Drinking's what got me *into* this mess."

"That's where you're wrong, buddy. That thing between your legs, *that's* what did it. Drinking--hell, that's the cure. The *only* cure."

Randy and Black Jimmy guffawed. Mama Thuy, full-size and beautiful again behind the bar, suppressed a smile and got out more bottles.

"I confess," Swede said, sitting down next to Walt, "I didn't think you were the type. I always said to myself, 'Ol' Walt's a lover, not a fighter.' Just shows how wrong you can be about some people."

"Fuck you," Walt snarled. "All of you. Can't you mind your own business?"

"Oooh," Charlene said.

"This *is* our business," Ron said. "You ought to show us some gratitude, man. Maybe next time Thuy'll let you rot your ass off in jail instead."

"There won't *be* a next time," Walt said. He still hadn't touched his beer. Maybe, Harry Hudson thought, Walt hadn't ever been in jail before. That would explain his distress. One of an elite few, the last of the unionized merchant seamen, he made sixty thousand dollars a year shepherding container ships from L.A. to Singapore or Yokohama and back. He had always acted, like Wade, as if he was on a different level from the others. Nobody held that against him, exactly, but now that he had trashed a bar and chased his wife like any ordinary rummy, they wanted to know the details. And they would keep on pestering him until he told.

As much as Walt didn't want to talk, he seemed to realize this.

They watched him struggle--his skin a sickly yellow in the bar lights, the shadows of fan blades sliding, one after another, over his forehead. His eyes were slits. So far, Harry Hudson sensed, the others--even Rita's friends-- weren't unsympathetic to Walt, though that could change. Walt probably didn't care *what* they thought. On the other hand, he would never be the center of so much attention here as he was right now. *This is your moment*, they seemed to be telling him. *Use it.*

Mama Thuy patted the back of his hand. "Come on, Walt. We know Rita crazy. But Jesus, why you have to go crazy too?"

Walt lowered his head. Sensitized to a rare pitch of clairvoyance by his own shame, Harry Hudson could feel their pretended concern and their very real joy in scandal sucking the story out of the man, despite what Walt had to know it would cost him. He would have to admit in public that he was, in Stanley's words, a lovesick fool--no smarter than the likes of Randy or Charlene.

He would have to join the congregation.

Cross the Gimp Line for good.

Yet it's not exactly a secret anyway, is it? Harry Hudson imagined him thinking. It was so lonely being different. And here they all were, waiting for him, like that unopened beer.

Walt told.

His voice was low and raspy with embarrassment and fury, and he didn't look directly at anyone. He had married Rita five years ago. (A couple of snapshots from that time were thumbtacked in a mosaic of Polaroids on the wall above the cigarette machine. Rita, showing all those fine teeth, apparently ecstatic, snuggled up to Walt on the doorstep of their honeymoon condo in Maui. Walt looked much as he had in the police station, a ghost of a grin on his gloomy face.) They had bought a Spanish-style house in the Wrigley District. He was gone to sea half the time--

"Like me," Corbin said. "I'm not a husband, I'm a roommate. Ain't that what you always tell me, Phuong?"

"Fuckin' A," she said, nodding emphatically as she lit a cigarette. "Just a roommate. Maybe I put ad in the paper all those other months. 'Wanted: Roommate Number Two. Keep me warm while Roommate Number One gone.'" She blew smoke and brayed.

Corbin laughed as well, and Harry Hudson thought: *They get along OK.* Why had he been pitying Phuong earlier? They had a daughter, too--one who hadn't died.

--and anyway, Walt went on, he didn't expect Rita to be a hundred percent faithful, any more than she expected *him* to be, he supposed. Hell, they were grownups. At least *he* was. He didn't mind her having a boyfriend or two around when he was gone if they didn't leave any cooties behind or knock her up. (Walt lifted the corners of his mouth sourly, took his first sip of beer.) If they kept her happy for when he came home. Above all, if he didn't know anything about them. Never saw their faces. Wasn't that fair? Walt said he *knew* Rita screwed around, knew it before he married her. That was just how she was. He knew about the cocaine, too, but he thought she'd quit that--

"Rita love you," Mama Thuy said, still patting his hand. "She tell me lots of times. 'Walt, he good to me like no other guy.' I don't lie. She say that."

Walt grimaced.

--but it wasn't true, he said. Not about the cocaine. And as far as love went, that was beautiful, but then why didn't she hold up her fucking end of the bargain? Every time he came home, he'd hear all kinds of stories about her--about parties in *his own fucking house,* lines of coke on his glass coffee table, people passed out on the couch and the floor, all kinds of hanky-panky going on. Sure, she denied it. But even he could tell she was back on the stuff by then. Losing weight and all--

"Hell fire," Pop said out of nowhere.

--and then the last time his ship came in, Walt said--about the time Harry here first showed up--Rita got so wasted she forgot what day it was. He phoned her from the harbor and she didn't answer. Rang the doorbell, ditto. He let himself in the house and it was a mess, hadn't been cleaned in weeks, and there she was, in bed with a guy at ten in the morning, both of them dead to the world, loaded. He didn't have to tell Charlene, he said, who that guy might happen to be--

Everybody looked at her.

"B.J.," she hissed.

"I *told* him," Black Jimmy said in his rapid slur. "*Told* him it ain't gonna be worth it, no matter how good she be. Not just one time." He appealed to Mama Thuy. "But you think a young buck like B.J.--full of hisself, you know-- you think he's gonna listen to *me*? No way."

"What do you mean," Charlene asked Jimmy, "how good *she* is? That dumb spic."

"Charlene," Mama Thuy warned her.

Now they all looked at Walt again--with the same question in mind, Harry Hudson imagined:

How good was *Rita?*

--and he should have chucked her out on the street right then, Walt said, deliberately ignoring that question, it seemed. But maybe not. Because he still loved *her*, he insisted, had a soft spot for her--

"You mean a *hard* spot," Ron said.

They all laughed--speculating, Harry Hudson thought, about what Rita must have done to keep Walt on the hook.

--and so, Walt told them, he decided to give her one more chance, as stupid as that might sound. Well, it *was* stupid. He admitted it. Because yesterday when he came home, he found something in the mailbox that finally explained how she had been supporting her habit. It wasn't that her boyfriends were giving her money or coke, as he had once suspected. He wouldn't put it past Rita to peddle her ass once in a while, but not on a regular basis. And what she made here at the Chieu Hoi Saloon, even with tips--no offense to Mama Thuy, but that was small change. No, it had to be coming from somewhere else, and that was--

"Your house," Stanley said.

Walt froze, his punch line spoiled. Then he nodded and took a big gulp of beer. He laid his stubby hands flat on the counter and sighed.

--right on, he said. Fucking A, as Phuong would say. Rita had forged his signature and taken out tens of thousands of dollars of equity loans from one of those sleazebag lenders up in Bellflower. How many tens, he wouldn't say. But enough, the way property values were falling these days, so that a guy who bought in '88, like he did, owed more than the place was worth. He wouldn't be able to unload it for years--maybe never.

"What did I tell you?" Stanley nudged Harry Hudson. "Didn't I say she put it right up her nose?"

"And the thing is," Walt said, "she *had* to know I'd find out eventually. She couldn't hide it forever. She knew damn well I wouldn't call the law on her, whatever she did. She knew I cared about her that much. But did she care about *me?*" He drained the bottle, thumped it down. "How about *my* feelings? Christ."

"Those drugs did it," Mama Thuy said soothingly. "Not Rita. Not really."

"I didn't throw that chair *at* her," Walt said. "I aimed to miss. I didn't want to hurt her. I just wanted to get her fucking attention for once. Is that so hard to understand? I mean, I know she thinks I look like a fucking toad. I can't help that. I just...."

143

He was crying.

The others edged away from him. They had their scandal, Harry Hudson thought, and as juicy as it was, it left them unsatisfied. They had thought they wanted Walt brought down to their level, so they could laugh at him, but now they weren't so sure. The younger men had also wanted him to confirm their hopes that there was a payoff in marrying a bar girl--that the sex could be good enough to make up for all the soap opera you had to go through. But that didn't seem to be Walt's message. If he was just like them, they didn't enjoy what they saw.

Walt seemed to sense this--that his confession had done him no good. Too many of them had already known too much about what Rita had done. And they hadn't told *him*. He lowered his head again.

"Hell fire," Pop said, more softly.

There was silence--the jukebox had stopped. "Hey, drink up," Swede said.

"Another round, babe," Wade added quickly, tossing bills on the bar.

"Better be the last one," Mama Thuy said. "We about ready to close now. Gettin' late."

A cold wind flapped the curtain. Harry Hudson felt it eroding his margin of safety. All this time he had been part of the crowd; Ron, just a few feet away, had ignored him.

He thought of Kelly--still walking home in this weather, maybe, in that dress that hardly covered her.

"Roommate, you stay with me," Phuong told Corbin as they crossed Anaheim Street, her own fears returning. "You too, man," she said to Harry Hudson and exaggerated a shiver. "Everybody."

She glanced anxiously up and down the street.

If the robbers came in, Harry Hudson thought, *I would have to get up slowly, unthreateningly, move like a sleepwalker to where I could reach my empty bottle. Wrist inverted to grab the neck of it. Then, still slowly but somehow very fast, smiling softly, looking them right in the eye, without breaking the trance, I would swing.*

Mama Thuy, who had been walking ahead with Walt and Swede, stopped on the far sidewalk to let them pass and took Harry Hudson's arm.

It was the first time she had touched him.

He panicked--so sure she would ask him about the black girl that he didn't understand what she actually said until later, when he was sitting alone in his car, waiting for the windshield to unfog.

144

"My family," she told him. "Looks like they can come, finally. This year. All that paperwork I told you about? Finished. Isn't that good news?"

# # # #

North Long Beach.

Way up, Kelly had said.

It was too late by now, Harry Hudson knew. He had no chance of finding her. He should go home.

But he remembered from the giant map on the outside wall of Springer's office that the Boulevard ran straight into the heart of North Long Beach. And the Boulevard was right in front of him. He drove north on it, the Nissan's engine purring drowsily, past taco stands and car washes and vacant lots where auto dealerships had been before they moved to the new mall in Signal Hill. Tumbleweeds and trash stirred in the empty spaces. There was little traffic at this time of night. A few dark figures sat on benches at bus stops, though the buses, as Kelly had said, weren't running anymore. Homeless people? The number of them here no longer shocked Harry Hudson--yet another reason for shame, whenever he thought about it.

Now, though, he was thinking about how Mama Thuy's hand had felt on his arm: unexpectedly cold and sinewy.

And he was making up dialogue for his encounter with the robbers. *I can't let you do this, son,* he would say in a drawl that matched the sleepiness of his movements. *This lady here has worked hard for her money. You can't just walk in and take it away from her, now can you? 'Tain't hardly fair.*

An unworldly air of confidence was needed to keep both him and the robbers hypnotized.

What could you possibly buy with it? he would ask in a tone of genuine, fatherly concern. *What could be worth the risk of spending the rest of your life in prison for hurting someone who never did you any harm? Not to mention disturbing all these good folks who just wanted to come in here and have a drink in peace. Shame on you, son. Why don't you just do an about-face, right now, and go out through that curtain and get your ass home while you still have the chance?*

Meanwhile, he would be reaching for that bottle.

They've got silent alarms in these places, don't you know that? I wouldn't be surprised if the cops were on their way already.

He would cock his ear for sirens.

145

But he couldn't stutter, Harry Hudson knew. The slightest dysfluency, any facial twitch, even, would break the spell. To succeed, he thought, he would have to go clean *through* his fear. He would have to give up in advance all hope of surviving the robbers' bullets--his imagination issued them pistols now, blunt-nosed 9mm automatics. In a sense, he would have to be already dead. Only then could he enter the calm in which Sydney Carton's voice could substitute for his own.

He passed Memorial Hospital. The land rose and the neighborhood improved. Still no sign of Kelly--and he was miles from the police station already. *Give it up*, he told himself.

Beyond Spring Street, he began to look for a U-turn lane. But just as he found one--where the land dipped and rose again as the Boulevard went past a Honda dealership and under the 405 Freeway--he saw her. Limping doggedly along, her purse dangling, one of her high heels broken. At the sight of his lights, she put out her thumb, not bothering to stop.

Harry Hudson hesitated. She didn't look pretty now. In fact, if it hadn't been for the silver dress, he might not have recognized her. Her face, as the headlight glare passed over it, was blank and hostile, like Susie's sunburned face or the swollen face of the woman he had frightened at the Low Fox. He thought for an instant of going on, then braked several yards past her, halfway into the underpass.

She didn't--probably couldn't--run to meet him. He backed up a little. When he opened the passenger door, she didn't seem to recognize *him* either.

"Hey, in there. You a cop?"

Harry Hudson shook his head. *Take a load off*, he had planned to say, but her question confused him.

"C-cold out," he managed.

She just stood there, breath smoking, hugging herself, unlike the streetwalkers in Portland, who had posed seductively and called out flattering lies. Harry Hudson missed that. Those moments when women feigned lust for him, however briefly, before getting down to business had thrilled him unreasonably; after a while, the come-on had seemed the point of it all--far more than the sex that followed.

Now more shame: He wasn't trying to "date" Kelly, he reminded himself--just take her home.

"N-no cop. Really."

"Shit. It's *you*," she said. It was his stuttering, he knew, that had clued her in, as much as his shadowed face. He tried to give her that inoffensive smile. "Didn't think you'd be ... lemme get *in* here. Damn, it's cold. And my ankle ... them shoes just ain't *made* for this kind of walkin', you hear me?"

Kelly climbed in, slammed the door. She took off the broken shoe and rubbed her foot. The mass of air that poured in with her smelled faintly of perfume and strongly, despite its chill, of her sweat. The windows steamed up right away; he turned on the heater fan.

The dialogues were still running in his head: *Just how old are you anyway, son?*

"You OK?" he asked her. "You m-must be ex--. Ex--."

"Shit, I guess. *You* try to walk that far.... Where's your manners, Kelly? Thank you, *thank* you for pickin' me up." She smiled back a little, in the way he remembered. Then she looked around nervously, like Phuong. "What you waitin' for? Let's *go*."

"Where to?"

"Keep on keepin' on, straight ahead. I'll tell you where. Don't want ol' One Time to come along and get the wrong idea."

So Harry Hudson continued north on the Boulevard. They were silent for a moment, climbing into the Bixby Knolls district. Kelly was still shivering; the bare skin of her arms was ashen. He wished he had a sweater to lend her. "One Time?" he asked finally.

She seemed amused. "You ain't hip to One Time?"

"No. Is that s-something like ... that other word you told me?" He licked his lips. "F--"

"What?"

"F-reak ... something."

"Freakazoids."

"Yeah."

Kelly laughed. A wide, suddenly generous laugh that showed all her teeth and a forked vein in her neck, then drew his gaze down to her chest. "You crack me up, you know that?" She was searching for his name.

"Harry."

"Yeah, Harry.... Well, it's kind of the same thing, you understand what I'm sayin'? We call them polices One Time because they just give you *one time* to fuck up. Ain't you ever heard that?"

"B-but why--"

She turned sullen again. "Shit, they see us together out here--you white, I'm black. Them polices think just one thing, and it ain't *nothin'* nice. I just got done gettin' busted for prostitution, you hear me? Don't need any more shit jumpin' off, not tonight. They couldn't prove nothin'--just held me forty-eight hours. Then they had to turn me loose."

"I didn't know," he said. *So many things. Such marvels of language. And I thought* I *was a word person.* "T-they ll--." He licked his lips. "Llllet people out of jail so late."

"They do it all the time. Them motherfuckers--pardon my French. They do any damn thing they want."

Bixby Knolls grew steadily more affluent: glimpses of pillared mansions behind a thick, dark screen of trees. Oil money. The Virginia Country Club was around here somewhere, Harry Hudson remembered from the map. "You live *here?*" he asked Kelly.

"In my dreams," she said grimly. "Just keep on straight."

Then the Boulevard dipped again, under a railroad bridge, and almost without transition they were in another slum, as dimly lit and menacing as anything Harry Hudson had seen in his hunt for the Low Fox. Cheap motels, the abandoned hulk of Dooley's Furniture, the kind of storefront churches that seemed to spring up like weeds in decaying retail blocks: Abundance of Life Temple of Christ. United Faith Apostolic. First Samoan Assembly of God. Iglesia Evangelica. Rushing Mighty Wind. Door of Heaven. Halo Hall.... Names that reminded him of Deborah.

He had already driven farther than Kelly had walked. Still not there?

"I'm sorry," he told her, stopped for a red light at Del Amo. "I s-shouldn't have let you.... I mean, I *didn't* have my car then. But still. They h-had no right to m--" *Make you do this,* he wanted to say.

She looked at him steadily, showing neither belief nor the lack of it. Nonetheless, she took his apology as an opening.

"I know you already done helped me," she said, "and I appreciate it. You don't have to do this, I know--but could you stop at that Seven-Eleven over there and get me some B.C.s?"

"What?"

"You ain't hip to B.C.s, either? They headache powders, Harry. Only thing that works when I feel them migraines comin' on. Shit, that Excedrin and Tylenol don't do nothin'.... And could you get me a pack of Newports? The soft box. I'm havin' me a nicotine fit somethin' awful. Ran out in jail. If they

148

ever put me in there again, send me cigarette money, you hear what I'm sayin'? Twenty dollars would do fine."

Now it was Harry Hudson's turn to laugh. "OK."

"And maybe a cold one, too. One of them King Cobras?"

She insisted on limping in with him, wearing the mismatched shoes, unwilling to risk her bare feet on dogshit or broken glass in the parking lot. He let her cling to his arm. More homeless men hung around the entrance, as if warmed by the light inside. They spoke--to her, not to him--in voices as dark as their faces, almost unintelligible.

"He doin' *me* a favor this time," Kelly told them--whether protecting Harry Hudson or announcing that he was her prey alone.

He worked the ATM in the rear of the store while she leaned on the counter and bantered with the Korean cashier. The man seemed to know her, was worried at first about her disheveled appearance, frowned and asked questions, but soon she had him giggling.

"This here's my bodyguard," she told him as Harry Hudson came up. "He too big to mess with, right?"

"Right," the Korean said, his wide face shiny. "Oh, yes."

"He be the Godfather, you understand what I'm sayin'? So don't you fuck with me." This just made him grin and bob his head. "And matches--don't forget them, now."

"Oh, yes."

Back in the car, Kelly lit a cigarette, sighed luxuriously and said, "That Chinaman in there, he a *trip*. Him and his brother, too, that works days. They look just alike." In the paper bag on her lap were two King Cobras, not one. Harry Hudson had withdrawn much more money than the groceries would cost. Something had changed in him, but rather than admit it, he thought about how grateful the Korean had been to talk to her--how much a few friendly words could mean to an immigrant all-night clerk, coming from a woman who, by rights, should have been too exhausted and angry to care.

Nothing like Thuy. Yet, still, no ordinary person.

He drove on north. They were almost to the 91 Freeway and the Compton line when Kelly had him turn into an alley and park beside a two-story motel of crumbling yellow stucco, striped by the shadows of telephone lines. A cat yowled, streaked away. "Don't get any closer," she said, "or the manager'll see you. Shit, looks like Eugene's here now. The light be on up there, anyhow. But then where did he leave that Cadillac? Ain't *no* sign of that."

"W-who's Eugene?"

"That evil brother of mine. I'll tell him to step round the corner. Just wait here till I give you the sign."

He watched her limp up a metal stairway to the second floor, holding the bag by its twisted top. She knocked and a slender man opened the door. As she went in, Harry Hudson thought of leaving--this was no neighborhood to linger in, for sure. But he made no move. His change of mind was conscious now. His luck in finding her in a city this size--nobody else having picked her up--had been too extraordinary to ignore. It felt like fate. The man came out, looked once down at the Nissan, and headed for the stairway at the far end. A minute later, Kelly leaned out and waved. Harry Hudson climbed the steps, which rang and vibrated under his new Florsheim wingtips. Wind rocked him. *What am I doing here?* he thought, remembering all the other times he had thought the same thing, and this helped him feel that he was outside himself, somewhere else. The smell of eucalyptus--that was the parking lot at the Rabbit Hutch. Sharp-pointed graffiti--the wall of the Low Fox.... But then the door shut behind him. He was undeniably in the room.

With her.

"Don't even look," she said. "I know it's a mess." Like Louise, she had a second voice, Harry Hudson discovered. In Kelly's case, it was softer and more cultivated: a holdover from more prosperous times, it seemed. She was genuinely embarrassed--though who could blame her for a place like this? Still, it calmed him. "Let me take a shower first, wash this funk off of me. OK?"

"OK."

"Sit down. Open up that beer, if you want. I won't be a minute."

He rummaged in the bag. "W-where's the other one?"

"I gave it to Junior so he'd split," Kelly said from the hall. The motel had been chopped into weekly-rental apartments; there was a separate bedroom and a kitchenette. "That wasn't Eugene after all. Don't know where *he* at."

Harry Hudson sat on the sofa. He sipped a little of the malt liquor, whose bite at least cut the odor of fried food and heating vents. It was stuffy in here. Suitcases along one wall were piled with clothes on hangers. The TV and the rest of the furniture could have come from his bachelor pad in Garbersville. What caught his eye was a painting that clearly didn't belong. Kelly must have brought it with her. A picture of a little black girl in African dress, whose skull had the same elongated shape as Kelly's; the whites of her huge eyes had a bluish gleam like porcelain.

"--car done got *im*pounded, Junior tell me." Kelly's voice echoed off bathroom tile now. "All them tickets. Ain't that a bitch?" Then all he heard was the hiss of water.

She trusts me, he thought. *She knows I won't do that 'Psycho' killer thing.* This both pleased and disturbed him. *Why? She doesn't know me at all.*

Harry Hudson remembered asking Kelly at the Saratoga, long ago, why she wasn't up in Hollywood, getting rich. Already he had the answer. She was too ... human, too easygoing, not ruthless enough.

Now Kelly had become the watcher in his mind. Through her eyes, he saw himself sit quietly, set the can down, leaving most of the beer for her.

Harry Hudson picked up the broken shoe. The heel wasn't solid; under the leather or vinyl skin was only a hollow plastic tube, ground down by her walking. *Junk.* A couple of books were on the coffee table--oddly, nursing manuals of some kind.

He looked up. She was standing beside him naked, holding a towel, another towel wrapped around her head like a turban. She grinned.

"Last one out of your clothes is a dirty dog."

"B--," Harry Hudson said. "Y--." *You're already out.*

"You had *lots* of time, Harry. You ain't gettin' shy on me, are you?" She pulled teasingly at his belt, and he began to undress, folding his clothes on the table, watch and socks included, with what struck him as absurd care. Kelly spread the spare towel on the sofa--she wasn't going to use a bed, apparently. When she turned, her face no longer had any expression. With an absence of preliminaries that Harry Hudson found heartbreaking, she stretched out lengthwise, one foot on the floor, the other leg cocked up against the cushions.

I don't deserve this, he thought. For Kelly, stripped defenseless and scrubbed clean of makeup, was as beautiful as he had imagined Mama Thuy would be, though the two women looked nothing alike. Kelly was lean, not boyish but still almost hipless, with a distance runner's legs. Her buttocks were knots of muscle, her breasts almost as firm. Webs of veins--an athlete's--ran down her inner arms. Her blistered feet had band-aids on them; those long hands of hers--given the life she led, Harry Hudson thought--bore any number of little scars: cuts and burns. But her secret skin, the skin her clothes had hidden, was velvety, flawless. He wanted to stroke it, sink into it, close his eyes and sleep there forever. The word *black* did no justice to its range of burnished tones. Her nipples were still smooth--she had never had children. In her way, she, too, was perfect; and so it was obscene that he should be leaning over her, his gut hanging, putting his cold hands on her. He thought of Walt's mournful face: *I look like a fucking toad.*

"I w-want you to know, I d--," he began and hit a block so massive that he felt faint. His lips trembled; he looked off to one side, but not before he could see that he had alarmed her just when he wanted to put her at ease. "D-dddon't." Breathless now, he blocked hard on the next word, too. "Mmmm." *Mean you any harm*, he wanted to say.

"Hey, what--"

"I stutter," he told her.

Harry Hudson hardly ever confessed this, no matter how obvious it had to be. But now there was no other way out.

Relief transformed her face. For the second time that night, Kelly favored him with a smile whose friendliness astonished him. "Shit, I know *that*, Harry. I be knowin' that all along.... That all you been tryin' to tell me?"

"No. I mean, I w--." He licked his lips. "I mean, I w-won't ... won't *hurt* you."

"Shit, I know *that*, too. You think I can't tell?"

He had his doubts, as a matter of fact. She hadn't even taken him to a sink, skinned back his dick and soaped it, as the whores in Portland had.

"C'mon," Kelly said. "Let's get this show on the road, OK? I'm-a get cold again, after that shower done warmed me up."

So he bent between her knees. Eating her, he could hide himself, crouching below her as if at the lip of a mountain. He closed his eyes. Then he became only his tongue, a tiny organism exploring the vast, salty folds of a cave, bat-blind. Time stretched out. She let him do it for quite a while--let him act as if he were truly a lover, in some other place; this was, for him, the final proof of her generosity. He felt muscles twitch, heard her grunt almost inaudibly. When he opened his eyes, though, he saw her lying still, as if asleep, chin tilted at the ceiling, lips slightly parted. *Her* eyes were closed. Under that wonderful skin, he felt her rib cage slowly rise and fall. Then his thighs cramped; he shifted position. Kelly said, as if from far away: "Hey, enough of me bein' selfish here. You come on up."

I can do this all night, he wanted to say, but he knew that wasn't what *she* wanted. She wanted him to get it over with.

So he had to heave himself up, expose his pale, ungainly bulk. He glanced down in panic at what Wade had called *that thing between your legs*; it felt

152

cold and flaccid, and he was surprised to find it passably stiff. It had a mind of its own. *His* mind felt almost nothing--none of the horniness that had tormented him during the tryout. All he wanted to do with Kelly was lie beside her, talk to her, stay hidden against her skin and sometime--far in the future, after they had slept and woken again--make love to her. But there was no time. Never in Harry Hudson's life had there been the right kind of time. He had to put that numb thing into her, clutch her, kiss her breasts and neck in a frenzy, race hopelessly against himself.

"Come for me now, Harry," she said.

And he did. He cried out and fell on her. "I'm s-sorry," he said, though it was clear *she* didn't mind. Kelly slid out from under him. She gave herself a quick wipe with the towel, handed a corner of it to Harry Hudson with two fingers and went to the bathroom.

A crushing weight pinned him to the cushions--a nubbly light-brown cloth, a musty smell. Sadness. Shame. He thought of Mama Thuy, of Deborah.

Cockroaches darted in the kitchenette, at the very edge of his vision. Only the renewed sound of running water reminded him of his own wet places, turning sticky and cold. He finally gathered up his clothes and padded after her.

"H-how much d-do I owe you?" he asked.

She was sitting on the toilet, pissing, with the door open. Harry Hudson couldn't remember having seen Deborah this way. Was that possible?

"You got forty dollars?"

He nodded.

"That'll do me just fine," Kelly said. She was just getting up--while he held the folded bundle against his midsection like a shield--when somebody pounded on the front door.

Of course, Harry Hudson thought in despair. *This is when Eugene or Junior or whoever comes in and rolls me. I should have known.*

But Kelly, too, seemed alarmed--or was doing a damn good job of acting. "Oh, shit. Who that be? Mister Manager? Them India people? Here, you stay in here, get dressed. Where'd I put them jeans?"

Harry Hudson locked himself in the bathroom--little good that would do. The flimsy door rattled from the thumping. A deep voice shouted and Kelly answered: "Just *hold on* a minute, you hear me?" He fumbled with his socks and shorts, yanked on the rest of his clothes, left his tie wadded in his jacket pocket. Panting, he braced against the door and listened. The man--whoever he was--didn't come inside. He just stood on the porch and threatened her for a long time in an accent too thick for Harry Hudson to penetrate. Now and then Kelly murmured something placating. Then the latch clicked shut; footsteps clanged down the stairs.

Wrong again?

He ventured out into the hall, buckling his belt. "W-who was that?"

Kelly looked dazed. He had seen her dressed up in the Saratoga, then ragged and humiliated on the street. Then naked--the taste and scent of *that* Kelly remained with him, even now. But this fourth Kelly seemed realer than any of the others--he felt the difference with a shock, even as his fear receded. She could be somebody's little sister. Wearing faded jeans and an old wine-colored cable-knit sweater, distractedly pulling her wet hair back into a ponytail and snapping a rubber band over it. "The manager," she said. "Say he gonna evict us *right* now."

"O-on account of me?"

"Cause they didn't pay no rent when I was gone. Eugene and them. What they been thinkin' of? Shit."

The whites of her eyes were like the little girl's in the painting. Harry Hudson imagined it leaning against her suitcases, dumped out on the sidewalk. *Here's your chance,* he told himself. *To at least start deserving her.*

"H-how much you have to pay?"

"Two hundred a week. In advance. I told him I'd have it all tonight, just to get him up *off* me, you hear what I'm sayin'? But how can I?"

Eight hundred a month for this roach-ridden hole--not much less than Harry Hudson paid in Belmont Shore.

"We just done *got* evicted," Kelly said--yet another mind-reader. "Behind some more of they bullshit ... Sidney's too. This was all we could find, short notice and all." She added fiercely: "This is *not* what I been accustomed to, you hear me?" Then, suddenly, she seemed to shrink, holding her head, as if the migraine had broken through to her finally, her eyelids swollen. "Harry, what am I gonna do? Can you help me? Don't say no."

"I'd l-like to, but ... I h-haven't got *that* much on me."

Kelly just looked at him.

Harry Hudson was too exhausted by now to sort out his feelings. He wanted to comfort and hold her, even more than when she was naked. He wanted to begin the lovemaking all over again--to do it differently, somehow, do it right. He was frightened by the complications of Kelly's life, which seemed endless and threatened to suck him in for good. At the same time, he suspected strongly that he was being conned--that she had somehow staged this crisis for his benefit.

"Why me?" he said, imagining Mama Thuy shaking her head.

Hayseed.

But he couldn't say anything more.

A few blocks this side of the Seven-Eleven, he had noticed a Bank of America branch. Now he drove her there through the black wind, the scurrying trash, the baleful yellow glow of the lamps.

The lot beside the ATM was empty.

"Don't turn off the key," she said. "One of them motherfuckers come along, I'll run his ass over."

"W-who?"

"Don't you watch the news? Been a war goin' on out here, blacks and Mexicans. Them gangbangers try to sneak up on you, I'll be *your* bodyguard for a change."

Harry Hudson couldn't see anyone closer than a block away. "I guess you w-wouldn't bother s--." He licked his lips. "S-stealing *this* car."

Kelly smiled just a little through the pain in her head. "Shit, yes, I would. It run, don't it?"

"Th-then--"

"You my *friend*, Harry. You helpin' me out. I'm a good person. You just gonna have to trust me."

He looked at her. She looked back, her brown eyes unreadable. Then, hurriedly, he left the car, jogged to the bank and withdrew the two hundred, his fingers at the buttons stiff with anxiety. When he turned, the Nissan was still there, puffing pale smoke from its tailpipe, with Kelly still in the passenger seat.

"See?" she said as he slid back behind the wheel.

"T-thank you," Harry Hudson said.

"Thank *you*," she said. "For savin' my life here. You just don't know how much."

Only for a week, though, he thought. *Then what?*

"You just don't *know*," Kelly repeated.

Back at the motel, Harry Hudson waited in the car while she took the money to the office. He yawned. What was it now, four in the morning? The

155

windows were dark. She knocked and stood there in the cold for some time, as straight as Mama Thuy had stood in the police station, but infinitely lonelier, he thought. Finally a light came on. A stout woman opened the door a crack, peered past the chain. She wore a sari and had a red mark on her forehead. *India people.* Behind her the man's voice complained, as harshly as before. It was some time longer before the woman took the money.

Kelly walked slowly back to the car. Harry Hudson rolled down the driver's window. She put both of those long hands on the sill. Once more her presence, the scent of her, was powerful. He laid his right hand on hers and she didn't flinch. He had the sense that he could touch her anywhere, anywhere at all, and she would let him; but precisely because she would let him, it had no meaning. This new reality of hers made him shy.

Still, he thought, didn't he deserve at least a kiss?

"I got no right," Kelly was saying in her second voice--the quiet one. "After all you done already. Got *no* right to ask you. If you say no way, I'll understand. You hear what I'm tellin' you?"

Oh shit, Harry Hudson thought.

"It's that *im*pound. You give me enough money to get that Cadillac out, I can take the bus tomorrow and pick it up. You don't have to do nothin' more."

He exploded.

"You think ... you can just *ask* for money ... and I have to t-turn it over?"

"I *need* it, Harry."

He hated the sound he had just heard in his voice. It was the whine of many of the letters to the editor he read in the Clarion--worse letters, and more of them, than he had seen on any of his other papers. Holcomb called them Sick 'n' Tireds:

I'm sick and tired of the productive citizens of this nation having to pay to support the unproductive....

I'm sick and tired of illegals crossing our borders, taking our jobs and laying claim to public services....

Excuse me, but did the woman who wrote Feb. 16 to complain about the proposed welfare cuts stop to think about the consequences before she had her eight children?

"How much?" he asked wearily.

"Last time it ran, oh, sixty-five, I think. Around there."

"*Last* time?"

Would this night never end? He drove Kelly to the bank and back in an even greater muddle of feelings than before. Mostly, he was rigid with fury.

"You get mad, all right, Harry," she observed, "but you *cool*-mad, you hear what I'm sayin'?"

She seemed to expect an answer, but Harry Hudson said nothing. He couldn't even make up his mind about those storefront churches with their hand-lettered signs and flickering neon. Probably they were a cruel hoax on the homeless and jobless--a handout of threadbare superstition to people whose *real* needs weren't about to be met. But maybe they were a sign of the persistence, however irrational, of human hope--whatever it was that kept Kelly going.

Deborah would say so.

The lights and shadows were blurring on him now. He could hardly keep his head up, his eyes open, long enough to drive home.

\#   \#   \#   \#

'You say you're ... my *friend*,' Harry study askin' me after we knew each other a few months. 'When did you ... start thinking that, and stop thinking of me as....' He stutter, like I said. And he be embarrassed all the time, too. Come from some little town up in Oregon somewhere. *Real* shy. And he still tryin' to get a handle on that street language.

'A trick?'

'Yeah.'

'Shit, how can I remember?' I tell him. 'You get, like, *hardened* out on that stroll, *real* fast, you hear what I'm sayin'? Livin' in the 'hood like this. Hearin' them gunshots ever night. You don't trust nobody right away.'

But it might have been just the week after, when Harry shows up in broad daylight and knocks on my door like ol' Clark Kent in his tie and all, checkin' if I got enough money to stay *another* week in that shit-ass motel. That *did* surprise me. Even if Harry didn't have a clue how fuckin' dangerous this place *is*. Shit, if it'd been Eugene or Junior instead of me there when he come knockin', he could've got hisself hurt. Especially Eugene. He was so pissed off about them Mexicans messin' around with our car just after we got it out of *im*pound finally--slashin' the tires, tryin' to jimmy the lock on the trunk-- that he might have gone *off* on him, right there. Not to mention them Mexicans might have jacked him up before he even got here. Little gangbangers, fourteen, fifteen years old. Good thing Harry be the size he is.

Still, I appreciated him comin' round, you hear me? He takin' his life in his hands, even if he don't know it.

He asks me how my headache is, and I tell him it's gone. 'Them migraines is no joke, though. You just don't know.'

He nods his head and says he can imagine. Then he looks off to the side, like he does, and asks me if I got enough to pay them India people.

Now it so happens I *did* have enough saved up, but it was either the rent or gettin' four new tires, you understand what I'm sayin'? And I *know* he ain't gonna spring for no tires. Especially when them Mexicans might just come back tomorrow and slash 'em all over again. I wouldn't either, if I was him. So I tell him, 'No, we a little short again.'

'*How* short?' he asks.

I have to figure quick--how much I can ask for and not scare ol' Harry away. 'A hundred,' I say. 'That ought to hold us over.'

And I guess I got it about right. Because he kind of gulps, like he's thinkin', *I'm going to have to pay this crazy bitch's rent every week? How the hell am I going to do that?* But he don't say no.

'I suppose you be wantin' another date now,' I say.

He gets all embarrassed again. 'You don't *have* to,' he says--and he *mean* that, I can tell, even though I know he like what he see.

Ooh wee, yes.

'Last one out of your clothes,' I tell him and wink. Best thing to send him home happy. And Harry, he OK--I could tell that from the first.

But *nosy*, though, you hear what I'm sayin'? Always askin' questions, and got a memory on him like an elephant. I change my hair or get a pimple on my chin or scab up my knuckles fightin' one of my crazy-ass in-laws--that Linda, the one that like girls, I had to get *physical* with her, finally, just so she understand I ain't playin'--and Harry *notice* it. Like he takin' *notes* on me or somethin', for that newspaper he work on.

# # # #

Kelly:
28 years old.
Topeka, Kansas. Came to Calif. nine years ago.

She remembers rock fights, climbing trees, fishing off a levee, diving into dangerously shallow water, walking across a trestle and daring trains to come. Kid stuff. Nothing too bad. Stable family life, as far as I can tell. (No worse than mine, anyway.) Says she looks more like her mother but was closer to dad. Always had boys after her, but didn't date early.

Ran track at her high school. The 220-yard dash her specialty. Pride remains. "I was very graceful." Picked up a shot once on a dare and won the shot put, despite slender build. Deceptively strong. Probably could have won a college scholarship if she'd stayed in school.

Dropped out in her junior year, though later got G.E.D. Never had much use for classwork, despite obvious intelligence. Smoked pot heavily from junior high on. Occasionally came to school high on LSD. Feels little or no regret. Doesn't explain why. Resisted track coach who wanted her to train harder rather than rely just on natural ability.

Kelly loves music, has keen eye for styles of dress, knows details of local crime stories, including many that don't make the Clarion or TV.

Worked as topless dancer but had to quit because of bad back. Also has migraines, chronic heartburn ("I like them jalapeño peppers, but they don't like me"), the beginnings of arthritis in her fingers, and a fear of heights. Can't fly in a plane or even cross bridges without getting drunk beforehand.

Drinks heavily--at least when I'm around to buy.

Claims to have tried most every kind of drug without being addicted.

Worked years ago in a Frito-Lay factory. Also was an aide in nursing homes but has let her license expire. When there was a boom in federal funding for trade schools, took half a telecommunications course before dropping out--this when she and her boyfriend, Darnell, split violently and she had no permanent address, phone or car. Owes the government $6,000 (with interest penalties now about $10,000). Has no hope in hell of paying it back.

Won't talk much about how she got into prostitution. Just says, "It sucked," or "You don't want to go there."

Matter-of-fact attitude. Feels she had no choice.

Surprisingly adamant about staying off "the county"--welfare.

Has been back to Kansas a few times. Father long dead; mother still there. Three older sisters married and at least lower-middle-class. Too proud or stubborn to ask them for help, much less go back there to live. (Jesus, I would, if I were her--right now.)

Two brothers haven't done so well. The older was very sick as a newborn, suffered brain damage. In "sheltered workshop" in Topeka. Eugene, who is living with Kelly until he gets his own place, was in prison eight years. Kelly says the crime he was sentenced for--a bank robbery in which a teller and a customer got wounded--may not have been his worst.

Hints he may have killed somebody back in Kansas. Now, when not drinking, he works odd construction jobs.

Little of this violence apparent when I met Eugene. Looks a lot like Kelly. Slender, handsome, neatly dressed, just beginning to go bald. Soft-voiced. Sad-eyed. A courtly way about him. Rather likable.

I still don't know who "Junior" and "Sidney" are.

# # # #

Harry Hudson had known some black people. Mill workers in Beattie. His roommate for one term at the University of Oregon: a quiet, malt-pale boy from north Portland, an architecture major, who glued together cardboard models of buildings in their dorm room. Several in the Army. A Garbersville city councilman--the same one who had offered him a cure for stuttering. A former Black Panther, Riley Watkins, the police reporter in Red Fork, who liked to holler, "Hey, bro!" at Harry Hudson, teeth gleaming white in a thicket of beard. A scattering of news sources. Louise, of course. But not until now, in the Low Fox and the Chieu Hoi Saloon and the streets around Kelly's motel, had he encountered the much-documented "underclass"--those whom Mr. Lincoln's soldiers, sacrificed in windrows of blue, had finally failed to save. He should write about *them*, he thought in mounting excitement--though by now he ought to know better than to listen to that voice. Still, it whispered to him: If Vance Foster were still around, wasn't that what *he* would do?

# # # #

The way Kelly talked, Harry Hudson might as well be blind. He couldn't see what was going on right in front of him, she would say as they sat in the Nissan in the shade of a palm or a long-leaf pine by some rundown West Side park, drinking beers in paper bags and keeping an eye out for cops. The open-container law. Everything he did with her turned out to be at least marginally illegal. They watched the street scene, which seemed hazy and smudged even in full sunlight. Kelly told him who was a "strawberry" selling pussy, who was dealing crack, what it meant for one of the idle youths lounging on every corner to wear red or blue, his cap backwards and his baggy pants low. When an older man shuffled by aimlessly, she would say:

"He got that no-work walk."

When the shuffle had a spastic jerkiness, the man's eyes a vacant stare, she would say:

"He on that sherm. Ain't *nothin'* nice."

"S-sherm?"

PCP, she explained.

And once, when a gaunt woman, all cheekbones and collarbones, wearing a violet halter and pink shorts, approached them for change, Kelly unexpectedly asked Harry Hudson to give her a couple of dollars. Afterward she said: "You can't even recognize her *now*, but you maybe saw ol' Cynthia there in the Black Hole when you first met me. We used to hang together. Remember?"

He faintly recalled the plump whore who had been with her that night. Now the woman looked like the addict who had argued the next morning with Mama Thuy over restroom privileges.

"She so *little* now I can't believe it. Got on that pipe and just shrunk herself right up."

Harry Hudson blinked and nodded. He didn't want to say so--he knew he was the last person in the world who should judge anybody else. And it wasn't what he wanted to write. But it all seemed so stupid. Why would *anybody* live like that?

#   #   #   #

Date, rent and car impound fee: $305.

Date and rent: $100.

Medicine: $23.

Gym shorts for K.'s teen-age friend (?), Tamika, going to continuation high school with baby: $25.

Date: $40.

Toward tires for car (punctured by gang members): $70.

Bus pass: $16.

Groceries, diapers for Tamika (who lives with grandmother): $47.

Date and rent: $80.

Medicine for T.'s baby: $18.

Fee for K.'s brother Eugene to take parenting classes. He also attends AA meetings but still drinks off and on, K. says. He's challenging his ex-wife LaVonne's custody of their two children. Claims her current boyfriend in Kansas is a known child molester (!): $35.

To get K.'s watch out of pawn: $30.

Date: $40.

Late charge for storage place where K. keeps a lot of her clothes: $65.

More diapers: $12.

Car repairs (fuel pump), by guy in neighborhood: $125.

Bail (another suspicion-of-prostitution arrest): $200.

To get VCR out of pawn: $25.

Date: $40.

First and last months' rent and deposit for apartment on Molino Avenue in midcity, obtained with federal low-income housing voucher. K. and her husband Sidney--she's MARRIED--have been on list for years. Their number finally came up. Tamika and Sidney Junior are her stepchildren. As proof, handed me a phone bill with her full name on it--Kelly Crenshaw. And his. Sidney's in prison; that's why I haven't seen him. None of them breathed a word to me until the voucher came through and they needed all this money at once: $650 (!!)

Oh, yes, and the phone bill: $86.

Still paying Deborah, of course. How the hell can I save up enough to help Thuy get her family over here? Ticket for each of them--mother, father, son, another sister--will cost $950, she says, flying out of Bangkok.

# # # #

'I thought Section 8 was when they ... k-kicked you out of the Army ... b-because you were nuts,' Harry says.

'Not *this* Section 8,' I tell him. 'Our ship just done come in, and we're gettin' out of this motel for good.'

He was pissed off, I know. Learnin' all about Sidney and that, and havin' to cough up all that money at the same time. But Harry, he stay *cool*-mad, like I said. And it ain't like I had much choice. It was either grab that voucher right then or maybe miss our chance and have to wait all over again. Or maybe miss it for good. The government be cuttin' back on that program now, I hear.

Besides, livin' in that motel wasn't *nothin'* nice, you listenin' to me? Them gangbangers kept comin' back after that Cadillac. Finally Eugene went to the extremities of stayin' up all one night, lyin' in wait for 'em, and shot one of the little motherfuckers in the leg. Not with that old .45--the cops seen that one. He bought hisself a Saturday night special. A .38, I think. Them Mexicans had the ardacity to be cuttin' on them tires *again*, and Eugene got one of 'em in his sights. He got so much anger in him now on account of that LaVonne business, I don't know *what* I'm-a do with him. Shit. I'm surprised he could even shoot straight, dark as it was, and him drunk. But he said the dude fell down, and tried to get up, and then some of them other gangbangers dragged him off. Eugene only fired the one shot, and he got rid of that gun right away. Still, them India people had a good idea who done it. I didn't tell Harry, but that's another reason we had to get out of there.

'You think I *like* it, all the time askin' you for money?' I say. 'It's *embarrassin'*, you hear me? You just don't know what I been through.'

'I'd think ... y-you ought to be ... p-pretty used to it by now,' he says. Meanin' the money part. That's about as mad as Harry let hisself get.

'You just don't know,' I tell him. 'See all these greys? I'm gonna have to get my hair dyed now.'

Harry looks down at my head and says he can't see any.

'Shit,' I say. 'Don't you be tryin' no flattery on me. I'm *serious*.'

Other times, Harry act just as sweet as can be. Got hands so soft I can't believe. Like he never done any kind of physical work. 'How come you're ... s-so good to me?' he keeps askin' after we been in bed together.

''Cause you be good to *me*,' I say. What else?

The thing I can't figure out is, what's Harry's problem? I mean, he stutter, sure, but he got money, a good job. An education. He shouldn't have any problems at all, you understand what I'm sayin'? But he don't act like it, even though I keep tellin' him he in clover, he got it made.

\#   \#   \#   \#

"So *that's* what you were doing down in the cop shop that night," Joe Zuniga said.

"N-not really," Harry Hudson said. "I j-just--"

He had made a mistake right off--sitting on Zuniga's wastebasket. It was too low, and the metal cut into his buttocks; he felt ridiculous. Zuniga occupied a corner cubicle, piled with even more books and folders than most reporters'. He was about Harry Hudson's age, with a blunt Indian-looking face and coarse black hair. He wore a long-sleeved khaki shirt buttoned tightly at the wrists and neck. His hands had pale spots from some kind of skin disease. A police scanner beside his terminal hissed and crackled.

"Run it by me again," he said, "what you want to do."

Harry Hudson tried to explain: *A hooker's life from her point of view. All the daily humiliations and dangers. Police harassment. The struggles of a real, complex human being, in more detail than newspapers usually give. Against the bigger picture: poverty, discrimination.*

But the words, as usual, failed to cooperate, and Zuniga, he soon realized, wasn't nearly as receptive to the idea as Riley Watkins would have been in Red Fork.

Zuniga frowned and tapped out his cigarette.

"Three things," he said finally. He waved at the smoke in the air, and seemed to be dismissing Harry Hudson as well. "First, this paper is into *roles*, you get what I mean? If you're a desk man, you do desk work. If you're a reporter, you report shit. None of this crossin' over lines and gettin' management confused. OK?"

"W-well--"

"Second, trying to document police abuse is a very, very iffy proposition. I've been on this beat four years, and it's only now their Internal Affairs people are willing to talk to me at *all*, off the record. They're paranoid down there, man. We had a chief in here who ran sting operations on his own officers--phony bribes, hidden cameras, the works. He caught some, but Christ, he shot morale all to hell too. It wasn't worth it, *I* don't think. I mean, if I had the goods on Long Beach cops beatin' up blacks or Latinos, whoever, I'd write it--don't think I wouldn't. But you damn well better be sure you *have* the goods. If not ... your ass is grass, amigo."

"--"

Then, too, Zuniga somehow reminded Harry Hudson of the Latino in the Low Fox. The memory made him squirm. It did no good to tell himself that the experience had changed him for the better--that he felt more at ease with gay people now. The Clarion's music critic, for one: a pale, openly effeminate young man named Richard Krause, who bristled at any alteration the desk made in his copy. And the Broadway watering holes with tinted windows and names like The Mine Shaft held no mysteries for Harry Hudson anymore. But the truth was, he had caught himself more than once, even after he had gotten to know Thuy and Kelly ... not exactly flirting with the men there, but visiting under false pretenses--passing through just to feel the charge of desire in the air.

"--now, Signal Hill, that's another story," Zuniga was saying. "They had a rotten department up there for years until--when was it? '82, I think--

the wrong black guy died in custody. Ron Settles. Big football player at Long Beach State. Picked him up on a traffic violation, and he was found dead in his jail cell. They claimed he hung himself, but it didn't wash. Hell, they really cleaned house up there. Threw out the city council too. But that's just a little burg. Now, Long Beach ... you know we got *Cambodian* gangs now? They just get off the plane and they learn how to do that." He waved again. "No, Long Beach cops aren't so bad, what with all they have to deal with. No worse than the LAPD, anyway."

"I see," Harry Hudson managed to say.

Zuniga shrugged. "Your best bet, maybe, would be an Op-Ed piece."

"A c-column?"

"Yeah. Something like that."

Harry Hudson tried to rise; the wastebasket clung to him like a suction cup, and he barely caught it before it fell with a clatter. He sat back down.

"And third, I take it your source is the lady in question. I won't ask you how you met her, or what your relationship to her might be. I'm sure it's all on the up-and-up. But can you be *objective*, man? That's something you ought to think about."

# # # #

It wasn't just that he had walked, however hurriedly, through a couple of gay bars. Harry Hudson still called Louise every week, though there no longer seemed any reason for it. Habit alone--or was it sheer perversity?--prompted him to pick up the phone as he lay on his mattress in his still-empty apartment. Then, when she answered in that throaty giggle, he remembered the reason: Louise always sounded glad to hear from him.

God knew why.

Being around Kelly and Thuy ought to be more than enough for any man, Harry Hudson told himself. And, in fact, he and Louise didn't talk so much about sex anymore. Instead, the main topic was her health. The foot operation had gone OK, she said, but later there were complications. Her hip hurt. She limped. She went to another doctor, who found that her left leg was a half-inch shorter than the right. Had that always been so, or was the operation to blame? Or maybe it was because of a fall Louise had suffered the year before from a ledge in the steam room of the gym where she worked out (and where, she claimed, she had sex now and then in the Jacuzzis). She considered suing the first doctor. Then she considered suing the gym. What was the point of having pretty feet if she still couldn't dance? Harry had to remember how much she *loved* to dance. Well, they'd get together and dance again someday--and that wasn't *all* they'd do. But in the meantime ... she talked about her prospective lawsuits as she had once talked about her divorce, which had gone through, finally. Her "old man" had given her the house and an allowance. Otherwise, he rarely rated a mention anymore. For that matter, neither did Leroy, who seemed to have fallen out of favor. "He ain't got the patience to wait for me, Harry," she said. "He's selfish, that's what it is."

Harry Hudson's own patience wore thin. The medical and legal chatter bored him. He had more and more trouble remembering the Louise in the tight red dress he had met at the Rabbit Hutch. She refused to let him come to West Covina until she was "totally a hundred percent." When the hell would that be? Maybe never. Once or twice he drove out there on his own--hoping for the same kind of luck that had let him find Kelly on Long Beach Boulevard-- and came home frustrated, feeling even stupider than usual. The woman was a flake; that was certain. So what did that make *him*?

Wrong.

Still, he kept on calling her.

Which made him doubt his judgment in other matters as well. This story project, for instance, even before he talked to Zuniga.

It was a good enough idea, he thought.

Except that *he* had it. That might make all the difference.

#   #   #   #

"It's pretty, I guess," Holcomb said one night when he and Judy had Harry Hudson over for dinner. "But I grew up a farm boy. Got used to that Missouri dirt between my toes. It just doesn't seem right, livin' fourteen stories up in the air."

The Holcombs lived in a cylindrical glass condominium tower on the bluff overlooking the harbor. Harry Hudson gazed out through a curved picture window at the Queen Mary and the marina. One of the lights shimmering on the water had to be Pierce's boat. *What a view* he *must have.*

"He's thinking about leaving here again," Judy said.

Harry Hudson felt a flash of panic. What would he do at the Clarion without Holcomb around? Then he realized that this was an old topic, almost a joke between them.

"St. Looey, maybe," Holcomb mused, lighting his third cigarette since Harry Hudson had arrived. "The Post-Dispatch. Now *that* used to be a good paper. Maybe it still is."

"Snow in the winter, godawful humidity the rest of the time. No thank you," Judy said. "Besides, where would you get seafood like this?"

"No earthquakes, at least."

"Have you noticed," she asked Harry Hudson, "how those little quakes feel just like a cat scratching itself on your bed? When I feel one in the early morning, I always look to see if the cat's there."

"I--" *I don't have a cat,* he started to say, then changed his mind.

Harry Hudson turned to the table. A glitter of silver and glass. Shrimp fettucine, thin crisp green beans, rice, an avocado salad. White wine that cast trembling oval reflections on the cloth. He hadn't eaten a dinner like this since he had left Deborah. The strangeness of it, his unworthiness to be here, made his head ache and his fingers feel heavy and swollen with blood. He was grateful to see signs of disorder half-hidden behind the arch to their bedroom--piles of Holcomb's books.

"Good Lord," Judy said, grinning. "Look at the man eat! You'd think he hadn't had a decent meal in weeks."

Harry Hudson nodded and grinned back. He accepted a second glass of wine. He should leave it at that, he knew, but Zuniga's comments still stung. No single Op-Ed piece could say all he wanted to say about Kelly; he would need a series of them, or a permanent column.

"How do you like the Clarion so far?" she asked after clearing away the dishes.

And he took advantage of this to ask Holcomb what the possibilities were, though he could tell Holcomb didn't like to talk shop at home. Once more the words struggled out of his mouth; once more he had to depend on someone else's good manners. Harry Hudson remembered being stuck in Zuniga's wastebasket. He had the same queasy sensation now, in his comfortable chair, wishing he were outside the tower, in the dark and brilliant night.

"Jeez, it ain't up to me," Holcomb said. "Bob Springer's the guy you ought to talk to. But I think we got all the bases covered." He ticked off on his fingers: "Steinbach does the geezer stuff now. Charley Massengale rides around in cop cars. Jill McGonagle does the feminist angle. Tim Halevy's entertainment and humor." He raised an eyebrow.

Harry Hudson nodded. Halevy, at twenty-seven, was the most talented newspaper writer he had ever met--a better wordsmith than Vance Foster, even.

"I'd say, demographics-wise, if we *did* get another columnist, he'd have to be a Latino."

"Or a Cambodian," Judy said.

"Right. You know we have more Cambodians here in Long Beach than anyplace outside of Phnom Penh?"

Harry Hudson knew that by now. "G-gangs?" he said, remembering what Zuniga had told him.

Holcomb frowned. "Mostly a lot of regular folks who got away from Pol Pot with their skins and nothing else. Hell, we don't even have a Cambodian *reporter* yet. That's one community we could do a lot better job of covering.... Why? What brought this on?"

"J-just what I've dreamed of d--." He licked his lips. "Doing all my life."

Harry Hudson was already smiling to show them he didn't mean it literally when he remembered that other, fatal joke--the one he had made with Owsley.

More of a byline than a name anyway.

"Damned if I know why," Holcomb said, clawing a fresh cigarette from his shirt pocket and flicking his lighter. "Who gives a hoot about newspaper columnists anymore? All people pay attention to is talk shows now. Limbaugh, Howard Stern.... That's another thing. These days you have to be a fucking conservative. Demographics again. I don't suppose you fill *that* bill."

Harry Hudson shook his head.

"Coffee?" Judy asked. Her hand holding the pot was dry and freckled, uncannily like Deborah's.

"--"

She poured anyway.

"Sometimes I ask myself," Holcomb said, "whether Charley Massengale's said one interesting thing in the last ten years to earn his keep. Or broken a single story. Can you think of one?" he asked her.

Vance Foster said the Hanford nuclear plant was poisoning people, and it was, Harry Hudson thought. *It wasn't his fault nobody believed him. Even I thought he was crazy. But now they've proved it, haven't they?* Somehow, these days nothing seemed to be proven, or stay proven, the way it used to be.

Did it do any good for him to say it if nobody listened?

In any case, he knew, Vance Foster wouldn't let a few gruff words from Zuniga put him off, or joke when he was desperately serious, or plunge now into the despair that Harry Hudson felt, numb to the china cup burning his knuckles. But Vance Foster had spoken with the voice of his time. Harry Hudson could remember how powerful that voice had been. He had never imagined it could be other than everlasting. But it hadn't been. Other voices-- long since discredited, Harry Hudson had thought--had risen in their turn and outshouted it. He still loved Vance Foster's voice, but maybe he had made a terrible mistake, betting his life on it.

"Just between you and me," Holcomb said, "I'd concentrate on what's happening on on the rim. Eddie Castle's been bendin' my ear lately, saying you haven't been pullin' your weight."

Eddie Castle was one of the bright youngsters on the desk. He had taken over the slot from Holcomb when Holcomb moved into Steinbach's job.

A new jolt of panic. "C-Castle?" Harry Hudson asked.

"That boy's a comer. He's got managing editor by thirty-five written all over him. If I was you, I'd stay well out of his way."

# # # #

After that, he didn't dare talk to Springer. He had learned during those long years in Garbersville how to keep hope alive on almost nothing. The key was never to risk a direct no--at least not until he had recovered from what Zuniga and Holcomb had said.

In the meantime, habit, or perversity, kept Harry Hudson taking notes:

Kelly let slip the other day one reason why she dropped out of high school. A teacher (male) had fondled and propositioned her.

Was curious about why she reacts so negatively to lesbians, like her sister-in-law Linda. Turns out she and Cynthia--her former partner at the Black Hole, now a crack addict--used to put on little shows for customers. K. had to get "seriously drunk" to do it. Cynthia, though, was "kinda that way" (a flutter of K.'s wrist). Liked doing it--wanted to do it even when no customers around. K.'s verdict: "Two cocks don't rock."

Michael Harris

Has she ever been raped?

A slow shake of her head. No. Some dude "put a knot upside my forehead" once and nearly knocked her out, but she got away. Then there was a time, in her days with Cynthia, when five college boys had come to C.'s room on Olive Avenue. The idea was to let them in one at a time, but things got out of hand. Maybe that was a kind of rape, though nobody got badly hurt and the college boys did pay. And then in jail, when they put her in with "them big ol' butches," she had to tell them right off, as slender as she was, she was willing to fight.

She's been in a lot of fights, she claims. Brandishes her fists--no wonder they have a few scars. "I'm a bitch with my shit," she likes to say, as if she has a hair-trigger temper. But, if so, this is a side of Kelly I never see.

#   #   #   #

Harry, he a man. And a man like to hear about all that sexy stuff, I guess. But I ain't interested in livin' over my past again, you understand me? It's the *future* I'm thinkin' about.

I know that'd be news to Harry. He think I'm just livin' day to day. And it *seem* that way a lot of the time, I know. When you just tryin' to survive, day by day is about how you have to take it. But I got *plans*, you hear what I'm sayin'? I'm-a get that nursin' license renewed, even though them convalescent hospitals still ain't payin' much more than five bucks an hour. I'm-a get me a *job*. With Harry here helpin' me, that Section 8 voucher is gonna be my lifeline up out of these streets. Shit, I'm too old for the ho stroll anymore. And there's diseases out there now that ain't *nothin'* nice. Even with Sidney in Chino, I have a chance to make it, now that my rent ain't so high.

Old Miss Crenshaw, Sidney's mama, she don't miss much, not after havin' all them kids and goin' through so much hell on account of 'em. She come up the other day and told me--I mean *told* me; she wasn't doin' any askin' -- 'You been takin' money from white mens.'

Now, she *know* how I been earnin' my livin' lately, so she has to mean extra and apart from that. Somebody must have told her about Harry.

And I say, 'Yeah?' Meanin', what do she want to make out of it?

But Miss Crenshaw, she surprised me. 'Good for you,' she says. 'Sidney ain't doin' you any good, locked up where *he* at.'

170

And right then I felt like I had to defend Sidney, if even his own mama's gonna bad-mouth him. 'He talkin' *real* sweet, missin' me and all, in them cards he send.'

'They always talk sweet when they locked up,' Miss Crenshaw says. 'Just you wait.'

I can tell Harry think that way too. He be wonderin' why I stick with a man like Sidney when it cause me all this grief and there don't seem to be any advantage in it for me. I wonder that myself sometimes. But it make a difference when somebody else do the wonderin', out loud. It get on my nerves, you understand what I'm sayin'? I've had men--tricks--fall in love with me before. It go with the territory. Ain't nothin' new about it. But I never had nobody settin' up here and *studyin'* me like Harry Hudson do. I ain't prejudiced--I *ain't*. But it make it worse for me, somehow, because he work so hard bein' polite, the way some white folks do, tryin' not to say anything negative when you know damn well that's what's on they minds.

# # # #

Eddie Castle.

Watching him operate was like watching Brent Owsley before Harry Hudson had ever met him. Like Owsley, he was physically unimpressive: five-eight at most, with a cowlick and thick glasses and the small, red, moist mouth of an altar boy. He was soft-spoken and precise, a detail man. McLachlan and Lincoln and Pierce couldn't hate him the way they had hated Steinbach. But they saw--correctly, Harry Hudson felt--an even greater threat in Castle. *He wouldn't leave them alone.* That was all they asked--to be left alone for the last few years until retirement. For that, they were willing to accept Steinbach's abuse, even to see this kid promoted over their heads. But Castle wouldn't abide by this tacit bargain. He had no end of plans to shake up the department--and, God knew, maybe improve the paper too. They lacked any grounds to resist him.

In Harry Hudson's case, Castle prodded him quietly but persistently to talk to the reporters more. "You make too many changes without checking," he said. "I've told you this before. *Call* Joe if you're not sure what he meant. *Don't* dink with it on your own to make those crime stats add up."

I'm doing the best I can, Harry Hudson wanted to say. *Better than I've ever done before, as a matter of fact. If that isn't good enough, I don't know....* But Castle, he suspected, had seen through him, as Steinbach had somehow failed to do.

"D-do I have to call every t--." He licked his lips. "Every t-time I have to fix a little p--. Ppppoint of--" An inane objection, he knew as he said it.

"Style? Grammar? Of course not. *You* know what I'm talking about, Harry. I shouldn't have to tell you this."

He could feel the blur stealing over him. *When I was a kid, at the Logger, I respected the old guys on the desk. Feared them, even. It never occurred to me that if they were that old and still there, they had to be failures. But Eddie here figured that out right away. How?* Castle was leaning over him now, hands outspread on Harry Hudson's desk, still speaking with that quiet insistence. Harry Hudson's hearing faded; he grew fascinated by those plump red lips, how they moved.

"*Should* I?"

"--"

"Well?"

"N-no," Harry Hudson said.

"Am I supposed to make allowances for your speech?"

That Eddie Castle would actually say this shocked him profoundly.

"--"

"I don't think so, Harry. The job's the job, isn't it? If you want some help, Long Beach State has a clinic, I think. You might look into it."

#   #   #   #

Now that he knew about Sidney, Kelly asked Harry Hudson to drive her out to the prison whenever the Cadillac wouldn't run. The route followed the 91 Freeway east through the Santa Ana River canyon, then swung north around the base of the Chino Hills. There was a dam painted red, white and blue for the Bicentennial back in '76 and, in the flood-control basin behind it, an improbably dense, green forest islanded against yellow fields. It was summer now. The heat this far inland--as dry as Red Fork heat--made Harry Hudson appreciate Long Beach. The air, pungent with the smell of cow manure from the stockyards of Norco, was a wavering blue-grey haze that hid all the bigger mountains. It shimmered above the pavement. Bridges and embankments and undulations in the ground that Harry Hudson hardly noticed made Kelly dizzy. To numb her phobia, she insisted on drinking a beer when they set out. Then she worried all the way that the guards would smell it on her breath and refuse to admit her. This had happened before, she said. She chewed mints and peanuts fretfully.

So many things are like that with Kelly. She has to climb out of holes she digs herself. She complains that her new rent-subsidized apartment is in "the 'hood," surrounded by her in-laws, but couldn't she have used that voucher somewhere else? And she knew Sidney had a police record when she married him.

Yet she does *climb. She's as brave as Mama Thuy, in her way. Maybe braver. And nobody even halfway unintelligent could survive out there like she has.*

So how does it all add up?

The prison had been built long before subdivisions with white walls and orange tiled roofs had begun to creep over the hills. It was sprawling and low, painted a dusty beige, like the earth. It had wire fences and guard towers. Gnarled olive trees lined both sides of the drive in to the parking lot, where a lone metal trailer sat naked in the sun--for conjugal visits, Kelly said. A shed roof gave only sparse shade to the tables where a crowd of relatives were filling out visitation forms. Tattooed young women, infants in carriers, a sprinkling of old people. Almost all of them poor and ill-dressed. Minorities.

What do you say now, Joe? Harry Hudson thought, full of arguments now that it didn't count.

But it abashed and frightened him to be so close to so much pain.

Usually, he watched her line up to be searched in the guard booth--her back as straight as it had been that night in front of the motel office, her sleek dark head vivid against the sky. Babies cried, and the shuffle of the mothers' shoes in the dirt seemed to kick up gusts of sweat and perfume. He saw Kelly turn her profile, the white of her smile outlined in burgundy lipstick; then she bobbed her head, hoop earrings trembling, spread her hands, laughed--maybe even touched one officer lightly on the forearm. *She's scared stiff,* Harry Hudson thought. He could recognize that now. Somehow on the street she had learned never to show it. The only way he could tell was by how fast she talked.

If her bluff worked and they waved her on, she would pass through a turnstile and walk, more straight-backed than ever in a good dress and stockings, down a chute between two barbed-wire fences under the eyes of the guards. She would enter a waiting room where, in time, Sidney would come to her. Then they would go outside to a little fenced yard with grass and picnic tables and a couple of trees, trying to find privacy among all the other reunions. Was this the *country-club coddling* the Sick 'n' Tireds complained about? Harry Hudson wondered. But by this point, usually, he was gone. He drove back to the highway and waited in the shade of some big old farm-windbreak eucalyptus that bordered the Los Serranos golf course. He played the radio and dozed and watched men in bright shirts riding carts on the other side. A breeze rustled the leaves and the bark curling from the trunks and brought that eucalyptus scent down to him.

When visiting hours were over, Harry Hudson went back.

"You know what Sidney said them guards told him last time? They said, 'You got put in here and left that *outside? You really fucked up, man.'"*

That *meaning her. K. sounds almost proud.*

"Sidney gettin' big again," she observes, "pumpin' all that iron."

I ask her how he can fight in there, if he has to, with that bad hand.

"I done asked him that. Sidney says he use that hand just to block with, and hit with the other one."

Afterward, Kelly would need another beer. Harry Hudson would notice that the stockings had a run in them, the good dress a stain or a seam with some pulled-apart stitching.

Just once, Kelly let Harry Hudson accompany her past the guard booth. That was in July, before *her* conjugal visit. He filled out his own form, endured the pat-down search in the waiting room and shook Sidney's hand outside in the yard. All the time he thought about that trailer. It was beige, like the rest of the prison, its windows masked, an air-conditioning unit on the roof. It sat in the middle of an acre of oil-spotted gravel like an enormous joke, a mockery of love; any couple entering it would have to brave the sun's glare like the whole world's laughter before they could hide in the dark, cool interior and shut the world out. For twenty-four hours, she said.

The next day Miss Crenshaw, her mother-in-law, picked her up.

Miss Crenshaw's boyfriend (Sidney's father is long gone) drove, in his *Cadillac. I know it's stupid to complain about it--he can drive whatever he wants--but Cadillacs are such a cliche. A stereotype. If Sidney had paid the same amount for a new Honda Civic, K. wouldn't have to beg for rides.*

Sidney Junior rode with them, she said. Fresh out of--was it a CYA camp, or has he graduated to grown-up jail now?

Kelly says she could hardly walk from the guard booth to the car.

Talk about stupid. Maybe I was jealous. But I said--God knows why--something about the size of the tools some of the men I'd seen in porn movies were packing. How a woman couldn't help but be stove up.

She gave me the funniest little grin.

"Sidney," she confirmed.

I'd never seen that expression before. Her lips pursed, half sucked in, just the edges of her upper teeth visible, her eyes a little sidelong.

Later Harry Hudson decided that it must have been lust--the real thing, not feigned. And he ached to think he would never arouse it himself.

Once that summer, the guards arrested Kelly. They ran her name through their computer and found an outstanding warrant from the previous fall--a failure to appear in court--that had fluttered to life on their screen only now. Harry Hudson was about to drive back to the highway when she had them escort her over to his car. Her hair looked suddenly undone, and he could tell from the wincing V of her brow muscles that a migraine had struck. She bent to his window and touched his hand. Her fingertips were dry. "Sorry, Harry," she said. Behind her a stocky blond guard stood with his hands on his hips. He wore a black digital sports watch and sunglasses.

"W-what should I do?" he asked her.

"Nothin' you *can* do. I'll call you. Bring me some money if I'm in jail."

They took her to the Riverside jail, it turned out, and transferred her to Long Beach only after a couple of days. He brought her twenty-five dollars, standing at the same red line at police headquarters where Mama Thuy had stood. Then, after another couple of days, Kelly was released. She had already served her time.

Such a lot of trouble for nothing! I know K. does illegal things, but she's no threat to society. In fact, she's one of the most innocent people I know. So why is society devoting so much effort to hassle her? All because she went to see Sidney, who himself is in prison on a technicality, not because he'd committed a new crime. Christ. Once you get in the grip of the system, it's like it won't let go.

\#   \#   \#   \#

"You may not have realized it," Dr. Gregory said, "but that early work Alvin Richardson did with you in Oregon helped lay the foundation. Behavioral therapy was just in its infancy then. Now he's ... my God, an authority in the field. This is exciting."

Harry Hudson nodded. At the speech clinic at Long Beach State, they had tested his hearing--it *was* getting worse, apparently--and checked his brain waves by wiring electrodes to his head. Now, in a clean, bare room, he sat in a kid-size chair, no higher than Zuniga's wastebasket, his knees scraping under a kid-size table. Dr. Gregory, short and brown-bearded and bald, like a monk, handed him a paperback novel.

"Read aloud to me a little," he said.

Harry Hudson read: *The snow began to fall in St. Botolphs at four-fifteen on Christmas Eve....* He felt absurdly proud that somebody he knew was such a success. Memories crowded in on him--the rain outside the windows, the groove in Dr. Richardson's nose, the flat thumb clicking the counter, the voice saying, "Good. Good." This clinic even seemed to smell the same. Maybe, too, it was the cadences of John Cheever's prose, which seemed to pause precisely whenever he needed to take a breath. But Harry Hudson realized that he wasn't stuttering at all.

Will they throw me out, he wondered, *the way the prison threw out Kelly when they smelled booze on her breath? They'll think I don't need any help.*

He tried to summon the evil spirit from wherever it was hiding. He remembered the chopper ride to Cam Ranh Bay and those terrible moments on the phone trying to get help for Sally. His only consolation then had been that he truly *couldn't talk.* That was a fact, wasn't it? Now he panicked. Had Dr. Richardson's exercises been available to him all along? Had only his laziness and moral failure kept him from speaking then as well as he was right now?

It seemed so.

Sudden sweat stank in his armpits.

"This isn't me," he told Dr. Gregory, but even without Cheever's help he continued to hear the hum of smooth-running machinery in his throat. "It's being here ... in the clinic, I guess. Nobody cares whether I stutter or not. You suppose that's it? A conditioned reflex. This isn't how I talk at all ... out there, I mean."

Dr. Gregory looked at him calmly through heavy-lidded eyes.

"OK. Read a little more, then."

Harry Hudson had never imagined stuttering on purpose, but finally that's what he had to do.

"Don't worry," Dr. Gregory said. "We've come up with a few new gimmicks since those days. We'll get you fluent again. Just a matter of time."

#   #   #   #

Mama Thuy tried not to smile when she saw what Harry Hudson was wearing. He had a grey metal box--like a radio--clipped to his belt, with a wire that led up to a set of earphones. "What's that?" she asked when he got out of his car at her house on Daisy Avenue so she could drive him to dinner in the Porsche.

He answered in a strange new voice, like a hum--so slow that she had to ask him to repeat it.

"Ssssomething tto hhhelp mme ssspeak bbetter," he said.

"Oh, really?"

For weeks now, Mama Thuy had been secretly going out with Navy Swede. He was too good-looking to resist, finally. And *serious* for a man that young--not at all like Ron. Taking electronics courses, planning to stay in the Navy a full twenty years. A calm guy. Easygoing. Handy to have around. After all, she had tried marrying an older man, Wade, and that had its disadvantages, too. Why not go for "young and tender" again, as Phuong would say? Phuong was ten years older than *her* second husband, Corbin, and they seemed happy enough. That was why Mama Thuy didn't want Harry Hudson picking her up at the bar. It would start rumors, get Swede upset. And the fish restaurant where they were headed this evening--the Porsche had an automatic transmission, so her right hand was free to rest playfully on Harry Hudson's thigh--wasn't the one where Randy worked. This one was in San Pedro, at Ports O' Call, overlooking the ship channel.

They swooped up on the Vincent Thomas Bridge, above the Navy base and Terminal Island, so that the last of the late-September sunset glinted in on them. Mama Thuy squeezed that thick thigh just to see what he would do. Harry Hudson flinched. Then he covered her hand with his bigger, sweatier one and squeezed back. Both were silent, as if nothing had happened. It was like schoolgirl romance, she thought--two teen-age truants sitting chastely side by side in a Saigon cinema. It confirmed her suspicion that Harry Hudson, married or not, didn't have much experience.

Turning off the bridge was her excuse to take her hand away. By the time they reached Ports O' Call, fog had drifted in and softened the street lights. The parking lot was half-empty. She gave Harry Hudson his hug right then, in the car--better now than later, when he might have a couple of drinks in him and the prospect of dinner wouldn't be there to keep him in line. The emergency brake and console provided a margin of safety--she had counted on that, but not on that stupid wire. Her left-hand fingers got tangled in it. She stifled a giggle. He lurched to embrace her, his haunch squeaking on the leather seat. No matter how many times Mama Thuy had done this, it was always an

177

uncertain moment. She was trapped inside heavy, tweed-covered arms whose pressure, for an instant, felt desperate. *Like a python*, she thought. *Why always such big guys? Ron. Swede, too.* She stiffened, and he immediately let go.

"Good man," Mama Thuy murmured. Her instincts had been right again. Relieved and grateful, she brushed his cheek with her lips.

After all, some guys, you never know.

Now she knew. She wouldn't have any trouble she couldn't handle. She freshened her lipstick on the way in to the restaurant, and enjoyed the maitre d's double-take. She was wearing one of her "business suits": simple dark-grey wool, but the neckline was cut surprisingly low, if you looked from the right angle. It kept guys off balance--even bankers and accountants. Which could be useful.

"Two," she said.

Harry Hudson came stumbling after her. "I ddon't wwwant you to ffeel you *have* to hhhug me," he was saying.

"What?"

"Unless you rreally wwwant to."

"What you talking about, Harry? I always do what I want."

"I mean, it mmeans so mmuch to me ... I d--" In spite of the equipment he had on, he got stuck the way he used to do.

"Harry," she warned him. "Cool it, OK? We in public now."

The maitre d' seated them at a window table. A freighter glided into view, bound out to sea; in the lights by the channel they could see its pistachio-green hull streaked with orange rust. Chinese characters on its bow. Her father knew how to read those--thousands and thousands of them, he said. Mama Thuy turned back to Harry Hudson, who sat with his fair face flushed, a little smudge of red on his left cheek. She considered wiping it off with a napkin but decided to let it be. He looked so uncomfortable, she thought. Wearing good, new clothes that seemed to belong to somebody else. Still trying to explain:

"I'd rrather you dddidn't at all, if you ddon't mean it."

"What I tell you?" He had never challenged her quite this way before. Maybe it let a different personality out of him, talking more smoothly; she wasn't sure she liked it. "Look," she said as a cocktail waitress approached, "they have double margaritas. Big ones, two straws. You want to share one with me?"

"OK," Harry Hudson said doubtfully.

"First time we go out together. Let's enjoy it."

Why me?

But she knew why. Men liked her and wanted to give her things, and she had to let them do it or they would explode. In this case, probably some money for her family. She hadn't asked Harry Hudson directly--she didn't do that anymore, with any man. No more sugar daddies. And, in a sense, she didn't need it. Rick the Budweiser representative was right: she had a gold bar in her safe. It was worth maybe $16,000 now. She would use that if she had to, but she believed in at least one thing her father had told her: *Always keep something back for emergencies. A reserve. Never spend it. Keep it a secret. Gold is best.* He hadn't followed his own advice, and see what had happened?

So Harry Hudson wanted to help out. That was nice, Mama Thuy thought. How much? She remembered how, years ago, before marrying Rita, Walt had come into port and gotten paid off and hit the Chieu Hoi Saloon-- always a lonely guy, hanging around bar girls. "What's it take to make you smile, babe? *Really* smile. Just name it," he told her. "How about everything you got in your pocket?" she replied, honestly joking. And he pulled out the whole wad and laid it in her hand--$1,700. That was her record tip. She didn't ask, but if men gave her money, she took it. No regrets. The surprised look on her face may have been worth it for Walt, she figured. Crazy, but true. Men were like that.

Rita had a phrase for it. *It's like jackin' 'em off,* she said. *Gettin' rid of the pressure before their balls turn blue.* Mama Thuy agreed, but she also thought Rita had the wrong attitude.

Poor Walt.

"Yyyou're vvery bbbeautiful, yyou know that?" Harry Hudson was saying as their fish was served--snapper for him, calamari salad for her.

"Oh, really?"

What was she supposed to say? That she *didn't* know? Yet this was something he had obviously been working up to for a long time. Now that he had finally blurted it out, he expected a reaction from her, but it just made her feel tired.

Why can't we just be friends? Mama Thuy wanted to ask him. *No hanky-panky. It seems like whenever you go to bed with somebody*--Ron, for instance--*it always turns out bad.*

A depressing thought. Would the same thing happen with Swede?

"You shouldn't say things like that, Harry," she teased. "You married."

This always got a rise out of him--Mama Thuy wondered why. His face went lopsided, as it used to do, and his lips trembled. "Nno, I'm not."

"I think so. No b.s. *Something* going on."

Harry Hudson shook his head. They chewed for a while in silence. He used his fingers to pick bones out of bites of fish he already had in his mouth. A messy eater. She handled a knife and fork better than he did, though she had grown up with chopsticks.

"Mmust be llots of guys wwant to mmmarry *you*."

That was true, but depressing as well. She sighed, licked salt from the rim of the margarita glass, sipped on her red plastic straw and considered the inequality of love. Somebody like Charlene was starved for love. Mama Thuy, in contrast, got too much of it from the wrong people. Who was worse off?

"Sure. They see how hard I work," she said. "I own a business, don't let grass grow under the bar. That's why."

He shook his head again. "Mmmore than that."

It frustrated him, she could tell, that she didn't smile--didn't acknowledge that he had complimented her. "That ship," she tried to explain, and pointed. The stern of the freighter, receding, was still visible through their images in the dark window. "When I was single, before Wade, ship like that would come in, guys would invite all of us. All the girls from the Honeymooners. They sneak us on board, we stay all night sometimes. Party? We get so drunk we crawl around on our hands and knees, like animals. I already seen it all, hon. Believe me.That's why I stay home now, take it easy." She smiled a little now, hoping he understood. Going to bed with cute guys just because she could-- she had gotten that out of her system long ago. "We all crazy then. Young and tender."

"Thhen wwhy ddid you--" He waved his arms, suddenly agitated. *--do all that?* she knew he meant to say.

"Give you a hug? You good friend of mine, Harry. I hug all my friends, you know that."

"Bb--" He was stuck again.

"You don't want to be my friend?"

Harry Hudson's face got so pale, then so overheated, that she thought he might get up and walk right out of the restaurant, leaving her to pay-- though where could he go? It was her car. Instead, he reached into the lapel pocket of his jacket and pulled out an envelope.

"Thhere," he said, slapping it down on the table. It bulged with the money inside it. "Ddoes *thhat* pprove anything?"

"Jesus, not here," Mama Thuy said.

She was pissed. Not just because it attracted attention, here in public, but because it looked so much as if he was trying, crudely, to buy her. *No more.* Such bad manners she hadn't expected from Harry Hudson, and she thought of how little she knew about him, really. What was his life like outside the bar? Charlene claimed to have seen him riding around town with some black chick. A hooker? Then Mama Thuy remembered the night at the jail when she had bailed out Walt. *That* woman? Maybe not. Still, if he was buying sex from somebody else, maybe he had gotten into the habit of thinking he could buy anybody. For a moment, she didn't want to pick up the envelope.

But she did.

# # # #

"Oh, we have a *big* party at my house when they come, and you invited, Harry, of course. *Beaucoup* food, you see."

Driving back over the bridge, Mama Thuy gunned the Porsche's engine, heard the exhaust rasp, saw the twin needles jump on the tach and the speedometer. Suspension cables and harbor lights flashed by. To her right, Harry Hudson sat in silence, his body a despondent lump. Her irritation had mostly passed. He hadn't really meant to insult her, she decided; he *was* inexperienced, after all, and clumsy in more ways than one. Now he was trying to pretend he had never expected her to thank him, except in words. It was a poor pretense--his disappointment filled the car, like the smell of incense in the Chieu Hoi--but she appreciated the effort. And thanks of some kind were in order.

Two thousand dollars he had given her. She had counted it in the ladies' room: twenty crisp, new hundred-dollar bills, fresh from the bank.

A new record! At my age.

"Hhow come you mmarried American guys," Harry Hudson asked finally in that hum of his--just trying to make conversation, she thought--"and nnot Vvietnamese?"

"Oh, Vietnamese guys," Mama Thuy said with a dismissive wave. "If you work in a bar, they get all jealous. Think they *own* you." And even if you didn't work anywhere, she added to herself, if you stayed at home--look at her mother, all shrunken and worn down at sixty-two. "You think I stand for that? No way, Jose."

"I ssee."

"If I want a Vietnamese guy, I stay in Vietnam, right? When Dwayne ask me to marry him--God, that's a long time ago. I was seventeen, pregnant, can you believe that? *Really* young and tender--when Dwayne ask me if I want to come to the States, I say, 'Why not? Go for it.' What you got to lose? I'm not sorry."

"Ggo for it," Harry Hudson repeated dully.

"Sure."

He sounded so miserable that she couldn't help thinking: *Why not give him a thrill? Something to remember me by.* When they were off the bridge onto the flat, in the shadows of the Long Beach Naval Shipyard--tall cranes to the seaward side of the road, rocking oil pumps to the other--she squeezed his thigh again.

"Wwhat's thhis for?" he said, frightened.

This time he didn't touch her hand. Over the engine and the thump of tires on joints in the concrete, she could hear him breathing. She let her fingers wander a little. His muscles tensed; he was trying frantically to decide what to do. Then his left hand landed on *her* thigh ... not moving at first, then tentatively kneading. Then harder.

"Not *that*, Harry," Mama Thuy said.

She took his hand firmly in hers and transferred it to the slit at the neck of her suit coat. He groped as she drove, working his way down her cleavage, under her bra, hunting for a nipple. His arm was twisted at an awkward angle; his hand against her skin was stiff and cold.

Mama Thuy felt nothing except for an impulse to shiver, then to laugh. They were nearing downtown Long Beach, with its bright towers under a dome of soft, pinkish-grey glow. A spotlight pierced the sky from somewhere not far from the Chieu Hoi. Turning north onto the 710 Freeway, she pulled his hand away.

"Too bad I have my period now," she murmured.

"I ddon't ccare. It's jjust yyour bblood, isn't it? *Ppart* of you."

"Harry."

"Nno, rreally," he said earnestly.

It made Mama Thuy angry all over again that he couldn't see an obvious evasion for what it was. A way to save his face. "What if I get pregnant?" she snapped. "Huh? You think about that? You think I want a baby now? Huh? You think I want another abortion? What you gonna *do*? Jesus."

Harry Hudson sagged back in his seat, the looping shadows of the earphones on his forehead like those weird cords Jewish people wore--she had seen pictures of them; she couldn't remember where. *I'm getting too old for this,* she thought as she turned off the freeway onto PCH, then onto Daisy. By now she was more upset with herself than with him. *I used to be better at it. Or maybe I didn't see when I broke somebody's heart. Maybe I couldn't afford to then.*

She wished she were with Swede instead. *A lot more fun to go out with, that's for sure.*

Maybe it was time to get married again.

On the sidewalk in front of her house, under the street light, Harry Hudson stubbornly tried to embrace her, his wire flapping. She held him off.

"Nnot even a kkiss?" he asked in a tragic voice.

"Friends, Harry. You know that word? Don't spoil it. Please."

At least she had the money--enough for half of those air fares, at least. It was really going to happen, Mama Thuy thought, excitement seeping back into her as she entered the house, closed the door. She would be able to bring her family to the States, after all these years of hoping and praying; her father couldn't ever call her *bad girl* anymore.

# # # #

He would hit one of the robbers with the beer bottle. The gun would fall to the floor, skitter around the legs of the stools. He would dive for it. This time he imagined a revolver. Check the safety? No. *He would aim through a stampede of legs and instantly shoot the other robber's gun out of his hand.* Not because he was such a great shot. In fact, Harry Hudson had never fired a pistol. But because of the trance. After a lifetime of watching movie marksmanship, wouldn't he have the perfect groove etched in his mind, the way you could practice free throws without a basketball, sitting in a chair with your eyes closed? *No time to think; therefore no time to miss.*

He would stand up, breathing hard. A shocked silence. The robbers cowering on the floor; the smell of gunpowder like the taste of brass; Mama Thuy breathing too. Those breasts he had touched moving in and out behind ... say, that leopard-print halter. For once, his face would be as composed as hers. "You," he would say. "What you waiting for? Call the cops." She would be slow to react, seeing an entirely different Harry Hudson there. "Move your ass," he would say. *Would he backhand her across the cheek with the gun to speed her up? No. But she would know the thought had crossed his mind.*

# # # #

Harry Hudson brooded over it, though not as long as he would have done just a few months before.

He had no right ever to feel good again, he had known that afternoon by the pool in Garbersville when he fished the Jack Daniels bottle from under the chaise lounge. He shouldn't ever *want* to feel good, even. It seemed impossible then for him to pass a minute for the rest of his life without thinking of Sally. And that was proper; that was what he deserved. But it had been nearly three years now. Memory faded, as it had with the old Vietnamese man. It happened inexorably, in spite of him. Sometimes now, in Long Beach, for days at a time, he found himself almost content, despite all his life should have taught him.

Partly, it was the money, and the unexpected pleasantness of Long Beach east of the Gimp Line. Fruit trees bloomed white in February, and in May the jacarandas sprinkled purple petals over the sidewalks. The sea breeze pushed the smog off in the direction of Pasadena and Riverside, and brought a cooling morning mist in June when cities only a few miles inland sweltered. Harry Hudson grew used to the creak of oil pumps, the cries of seagulls around his apartment, the joggers and cyclists by the shore. Long Beach wouldn't ever be home for him, but he could see how it could be home for somebody else. Brownish photos from the Clarion's morgue, taken in pre-breakwater times--the '20s and '30s--showed waves scrolling up to the downtown bluffs, ballrooms on piers and people thronging the sand and the Pike amusement park. It had been a paradise of sorts--not lost so much as carelessly mislaid.

Partly, too, it was what the clinic had done for him. The grey box and the headphones sent his voice back to his ears with a slight delay, like an echo, and for reasons only Dr. Gregory knew, this seemed to help. He looked silly carrying the apparatus around, but before long, when he regained some of the fragile semi-fluency he had known at the University of Oregon, he realized all over again what a burden his stuttering had been. How could he have forgotten? Once more, every little transaction in life became easier-- ordering a "Bbbig Mmmmac," giving somebody street directions, even talking to reporters, though, like Owsley, Castle still didn't think he was doing enough. Once more--despite the shame in speaking better *now*, when it was too late--he felt like a person who had spent years in handcuffs and leg irons, unfolding his atrophied limbs in a tingle of agonized relief.

Partly, too, it was the Chieu Hoi Saloon. At the bars in Garbersville, Harry Hudson had always felt constrained, knowing that somebody from the Logger or one of his former teachers or his father's friends might step in any moment. The bars in Red Fork he could hardly remember. Now, however, he had a place where he could count on being welcomed, where Mama Thuy or Charlene would smile at him and that semi-fluency wouldn't be put to the test. He could plop down on his stool, nod hello to Black Jimmy or Swede or Stanley and be served a Budweiser without even having to ask for it.

Mostly, though, it was Kelly.

She shouldn't be different, he wrote. *Talk about clichés: A whore with a heart of gold. Who's going to believe this if it ever does get into the paper?*

But she seems to be. Why?

Maybe because she wasn't born into this life, like the ones in Portland. She's known something else--something better.

But this sounded false the moment he wrote it. Nobody was *born* to stand out on the sidewalk in the middle of the night at Pacific Coast Highway and Gardenia Avenue, next to a rock-walled motel and a laundromat, across from a pizza parlor and a body shop, and flag down passing cars. Their headlights silhouetted Kelly's legs, her high heels. Needles of glare whittled them thinner. *I still got the speed, I can outrun ol' One Time if I have to,* she liked to say--but not in those shoes; that was painfully obvious. The cops had caught her before. Harry Hudson remembered driving down dark streets in Portland, scared of the neighborhood, looking for women like Kelly, resenting their power over him, feeling that *he* was the helpless one. Here, though, it was she who stood vulnerable on those two slender legs as faceless men drove by, armored in tons of steel, their lights blinding her, their tires hissing with menace. Harry Hudson saw this himself. After work, after a beer at the Chieu Hoi, he often drove out to PCH and Gardenia, which wasn't far from her new apartment. Streetwalking was a step down for Kelly, she admitted--less chance to screen her tricks, more risk of being arrested--but she claimed she had no choice: Urban renewal had closed the Saratoga and the other lower Pine Avenue bars. On cold nights he would bring her a half-pint of brandy, let her sit in the Nissan and warm herself at the heater. She would sip and watch for unmarked police cruisers and flex her aching fingers. *Better get on gettin' on,* she would say at last. Her courage in going back out there astounded and shamed him. He wanted to protect her from the men in the cars--those men who used to be him.

"*Can't you quit?*" I ask her.

"*I be* tryin' *to, Harry, you know that. I just about got that license renewed, you listenin' to me? These things just take time, is all.*"

"*I'm sorry,*" I tell her. And I am *sorry, truly. I'm still one of those men at heart. Aren't I? It's like some mixed-up fairy tale where I'm the frog and she's the princess and I have to kiss her, not to turn into a prince--because that won't ever happen--but to break the spell that keeps her down here with the frogs.* "*I wish I could help.*"

"*You* are *helpin',*" she says. "*More than you'll ever know.*"

"*But still.*"

"*Believe me, Harry.*"

Still, what Kelly needed was more money than Harry Hudson could give her. Or no money at all, only love. Not this dribble of twenty-dollar bills he kept handing over with a mixture of guilt and tenderness and rage.

Like every other trick, he supposed, Harry Hudson wished the money and the sex could be separated somehow, but they had been joined from the beginning: a devil's bargain. The only way to separate them, it seemed, was to give her money before she asked for it, when there was no time or opportunity for sex. Then someday, he hoped, the sex might come without the money.

But why should she agree to that? Even if she's *different from the ordinary, I'm not--and she has to know this.*

She could still feel desire, he knew. Amazingly. He had seen it on her face when she talked of Sidney.

But she had also told him once, when he asked what her sexual fantasies were, that she no longer had any. *I done looked down the barrels of enough cocks by now, ain't none of 'em impress me.*

And who could blame her? Harry Hudson thought. Hundreds of men over the years, maybe thousands, had unzipped their pants and pawed Kelly, breathed smoke and liquor fumes at her, slobbered over her, bruised her, made her go down on them in parked cars, fucked her to the twanging complaint of motel-bed springs. Harry Hudson didn't want to think about those men. When he was with her, he tried to think only of the two of them, of their growing history, their relationship--again, he supposed, like every other trick.

It was miracle enough that she could love Sidney--a worthless petty crook, as far as Harry Hudson could see--and tolerate, as he referred to himself with a nervous laugh, a "hhorny honky" hanging around. By all rights, she should be numbed bone-deep, turned off on men forever.

But she wasn't.

Why?

By summer, Harry Hudson was spending more and more time with her--and not just at night, on that desolate street corner. He took her out to lunch: fried chicken, barbecued ribs, cheap Chinese. They picknicked once on a hillside on the Palos Verdes Peninsula--almost too steep for Kelly--that overlooked the ocean, spreading a blanket on the warm grass. The water was cobalt blue that day, speckled with whitecaps. Orange poppies fluttered in the breeze. He got badly sunburned. His nose peeled; she picked at it, laughing. *Black people burn too, Harry, you hear me? What? You want me to pin a ooh-wee button on you?* They drove through the miles of little stucco tract houses that stretched north and east from the Long Beach Airport, home to thousands of McDonnell Douglas aerospace workers before the recession had thinned their ranks. Those sleepily respectable neighborhoods around El Dorado Park were exotic territory for both of them. They sat in the Nissan on Signal Hill at dusk on the Fourth of July--it was like sitting on top of a wave, she said; it made her stomach drop--eating tacos and drinking vodka and orange juice, as illegal rockets shot up from the central district and exploded, one after another, green and pink and white flowers, and gunfire rattled furiously like applause.

They "kicked it," in Kelly's words. Got shitfaced. Told jokes.

"I love you in my own special way, Harry," she says. *I guess that means the same as saying she's my friend. I guess I should be satisfied.*

#   #   #   #

What *these* notes didn't say:

Kelly never flinched when he touched her, as another woman would. She accepted his hands wherever they went. That made him sad. It reminded him of all those other men whose hands had probed into the same tender places. Maybe he he had been wrong, Harry Hudson thought then. Maybe she *had* been permanently numbed--and, again, who could blame her? And later, when he had finished, in his apartment or hers, when he wished she would stay, she always sprang up out of the bed abruptly and hurried to the bathroom to wash his semen out of her. *Don't take it personal,* Harry, she said. *It just be my way.* But he blamed himself--his ignorance, his clumsiness.

In between, though, was the moment he waited for, when he could feel that generosity of hers like warmth through her skin. He didn't deserve it, but she gave it to him, the generosity, the warmth, over and over. Trick or friend, he had to pay for it, but this was the closest to a normal sex life he had ever had. He felt desire for Kelly, without any inhibition now, a strong and uncomplicated desire; and he could satisy it, over and over, without fear that it would dwindle away, as it had with Deborah. Wasn't that how people were supposed to live?

"Wwhy are you sso good to me?" he asked her, not expecting an answer.

One Sunday afternoon they went to a Travel King motel on PCH near the 710 Freeway, uncomfortably close to Mama Thuy's house. He got the key from another Indian woman in a sari. A journalistic thought came to him--*Do "India people" run all these motels? Is there a story here?*--but he let it drift away. He and Kelly had cheeseburgers and beer in a paper bag. The air conditioning rattled. A yellow light slanted through the blinds into a dimness where he could see the standard bed and chair and coffee table, the ceiling-mounted TV tilted to look down on them. Kelly was wearing a red knit mini-dress with only panties underneath. This time, instead of saying, "Last one out of your clothes," as usual, she lifted the dress off in one motion, hung it on the chair, then sat quietly on the edge of the bed, her hands in her lap. The light made the outlines of her breasts glow.

"I ain't in no hurry today, Harry," she said. "You can take advantage of me if you want."

"I ddon't wwant to take *advantage*."

"You know what I mean."

He thought he saw the curved edge of her smile, but she was looking away from him at the window, peeling the foil from a bottle of Michelob. He leaned toward her and stroked her shoulders, her hair, kissed her neck under the ear. He pressed his face against her bare back and sighed.

Harry Hudson remembered that afternoon for a long time, just as he had remembered his one good night with Deborah. This was as different as could be: sex without tears or anguish or confessions, without the exhaustion of newness. He and Kelly ate and drank and talked and made love three times. They watched soap operas and part of a Lakers game. He lay beside her and gazed at her skin, hypnotized, as he had gazed at Nancy Ishida's in that classroom in Beattie. Kelly's skin was walnut and mahogany and cinnamon. In certain lights, it was silver and volcanic ash. Her neck had fine stippled lines on it, like tree rings. The incurve of her lower back had a fuzz of coarse but almost invisible hairs that he liked to graze with his lips and chin. Her face was as smooth as a young girl's. She gave off a spicy scent.

"Hey," she said once when he seemed to be dozing off. "You lettin' time go by here."

He shook his head. "I'm fine." He kissed her mouth, feeling desire return, effortlessly, as he knew it would. "Believe me. You make me very happy."

Happy. That was what he remembered of this afternoon: for three or four hours he had forgotten everything else; he had been simply, undeservedly happy. He wasn't falling asleep, he wanted to tell her. He had woken up at last. No matter how heavy his eyes might look. *Finally I have the right kind of time,* he wanted to say. *I don't have to be climbing on you every minute if I know you're still going to be here. Talking or eating or just lying here, propped up on my elbow, looking at you, isn't time out from making love; it's part of the same thing. Don't you think so?*

# # # #

I just wish Harry wouldn't worry about the money so much. It mess with his mind. I *need* it, you understand what I'm sayin'? It's as simple as that. Otherwise I wouldn't even ask.

He think he can't turn me on sexually, which is what I can't figure out at all. All the time talkin' about how pretty *I* am, and how he just a frog. Harry done learned how to say that black-style. *Frawg.* He make me laugh. Don't he know a man who can make a woman laugh ain't got nothin' to worry about? Shit, Harry's nice-lookin', *I* think. If he ever lose a little weight, let me pick out his clothes for him, he'd look even better. Not like Sidney--but he *gentle,* you hear me? That be *real* important, if you ever lived with somebody like Darnell.

# # # #

In August, suddenly, Kelly left the streets. She took a job as an aide at a convalescent hospital on Cherry Avenue, near Fourth Street. Harry Hudson was glad for her, though the job paid so poorly that she continued to ask him for money, just as much as before. It angered him all over again that

189

there seemed to be no end to her neediness--to her quarrels with her in-laws, her complaints about Junior and Tamika and Eugene, the car trouble and the overdue bills. Harry Hudson had imagined he could back off at this point. Instead, just when he had come to think about Kelly as seriously as he thought about Mama Thuy, it was *she* who withdrew. She grew secretive, preoccupied. She was too tired, she said, to see him as often. She worked a morning shift and had to get to bed early. Her sleeping patterns were all screwed up. Her back hurt.

In September he asked: "Is it Sidney?"

"Oh, he jealous, all right, ever since he seen you out at Chino. But that ain't it. What it is, I can't even fuckin' believe, you understand what I'm sayin'? You ever see *anybody* with luck like mine?"

He shook his head, understanding nothing.

"You my *friend*, Harry. Just be patient with me, OK?"

Harry Hudson tried, but it wasn't easy. Kelly had spoiled him. He was beginning to miss her company before he had figured out why he enjoyed it so much.

It must not be love, he thought, because love, as he had always known it, was exhilaration and terror, the experience of climbing so high that he gasped for lack of oxygen. He didn't fear Kelly at all. In fact, despite all the hassle and expense, he had never felt so easy with a woman in his life.

# # # #

"What was the best sex *you* ever had?" he asked Louise.

He wanted to jolt her out of the listlessness she seemed to have settled into these days. And--no longer in hopes of visiting her, he told himself, but as an experiment, a way of measuring what he felt for Kelly--he was trying to recapture the thrill of those first talks on the phone at the Clarion.

"Oh, Harry, it's been so long I can't even remember," Louise said in the tired, slightly buzzy monotone that had come to replace the giggle.

"Ccome on, Louise. It mmust have bbeen *pretty* good, what with all you've ggot to choose from."

"You got *that* right." She seemed to perk up a little. "But it's like havin' a baby, sweetheart. Pain or pleasure, it don't stay *with* you very long--not unless you do it again right away."

He wondered about *her* two babies, those L.A. cops. What did they think of her, or did they know?

"Wwas it that time in the thheater?" Harry Hudson asked.

"What time?"

"You know. Wwhat you told me ... the sseven men."

There was a puzzled pause before she said: "Oh, *no*. No *way*, Harry. You mean those *dogs* climbin' all over me, in that low-down place? You can't be serious, Harry. I can't even believe you *said* that. No, the best time ... maybe I shouldn't tell you, though. A man might not like to hear this."

"Louise."

"Well, if you *must* know ... don't say I didn't warn you, sweetheart. It was a woman. Black like me, just a little older. She lived up above me--this was out on La Brea, in our first apartment. We hadn't been married long. I was twenty-four, twenty-five maybe. I was alone in the daytime--just a stay-at-home then--and this woman, she'd come downstairs every afternoon to visit, have some coffee. We'd talk, and she'd give me the eye. Shit, I could *feel* it, but I didn't even know what to call it then. It made me tingle, though. It didn't scare me one bit, as innocent as I was." Louise giggled at last. "I bet you don't think I was *ever* innocent, Harry, now do you? Admit it."

He grunted.

"Well, one day I was fixin' something on the stove for her and she comes right up behind me and rips my skirt down the side. Good thing it wasn't a new one. Tore it right off my ass. I mean, she was *strong*. Shee-it. Then she's kissin' on me, stickin' her tongue in my mouth, and it feels *good*--different, you know?--and all the time she's sayin'--Cherie was her name, Cherie Williams--'Don't worry, Louise. I'll buy you another one. Don't worry. Please.' Then she backs off and holds my face in her hands, and she says, all choked up, 'I been waitin' for this for the *longest*.'

"What can I say, Harry? Wasn't nothin' to be afraid of, I knew *that*. Don't ask me why. I just held out my arms and said, 'Well, here I am!'"

It worked at first. Harry Hudson was aroused on his mattress, just as he used to be, though he had no idea how much of this story--how much of anything Louise said--was true.

"I mean, a woman knows what to *do*, sweetheart, like no man ever can--even though I *like* men, you know that." The giggle again. "That Cherie, she and her friends been suckin' on each other so long they stretched their clitorises out three, four inches, like dicks. They didn't even need no strap-ons.

191

They could love you like a woman *or* a man, any which way but loose. I tell *you.*"

But his attention wandered. It bewildered him how homosexuality, or at least talk about it, had become so much a part of his life now, in contrast to the years with Deborah, when he'd never even thought of it. And that made him wonder how he was going to scrape up extra money in time for Deborah's monthly check, having given Thuy the two thousand. Not easily. He would have to send it late, without a day to spare.

"--almost made me *faint*, Harry," she was saying.

He could borrow against a credit card, if he had one. He could *get* a MasterCard or Visa now, no sweat. But he had never trusted himself with such a ready-made chute down which to slide into debt--though that wouldn't bother most people, he knew. Harry Hudson shivered. Now and then, at moments like this, he became aware of just how odd a human being he must be.

"I told my old man, he'd better let me have my fling with Cherie or he was *gone.* And he knew better than to make me choose between 'em. He wasn't *that* dumb, not in those days.... You listenin' to me, Harry? Or you all go to sleep?"

Louise's voice had gone dull again.

"Sssure," he said. "I'm listening."

"Well, you sure could have fooled *me*, sweetheart. I mean, you was *snorin'* there on the other end, I swear."

"Nno, I--"

"Forget it, Harry. Call me again, when you feel like it. But not until. OK?"

Louise had never been the one to cut a conversation short before.

#   #   #   #

Waylon Jennings and Willie Nelson were singing "Luckenbach, Texas," on the jukebox when Harry Hudson came into the bar one night in early October, almost a year after his tryout. The song reminded him of Deborah. He hadn't expected a schoolteacher to like country music, but she did. There were Wallowa Mountain ranch people in her family, on her mother's side. It occurred to him, as Phuong slid a Bud across the counter, that he hadn't thought of Deborah in a long time with so little pain. In a couple of days he could send her that check.

"Hhow ccome *you're* working?" he asked Phuong.

"B.J. back in town."

"So?"

"So Charlene disappear. Thuy got nobody tonight. So I say, 'OK, just this once.' Goodness of my heart, don't you think so?"

"Right."

"*I* think so. Goddamn nice of me, *I* think. I tell her, 'Get Rita back. Walt don't come around much anymore. Why not?' Rita crazy, but at least she don't go shack up in some hotel when she supposed to be on duty here. When some black guy snap his fingers."

Phuong snapped hers, disdainfully. Her long, curved nails were lacquered maroon, with bits of jewelry embedded in them.

"I thought Rrita lliked B.J., too," Harry Hudson said. Then, as Randy and Wade traded positions at the pool table, he noticed a full glass of beer standing on Pop's favorite table by the wall--except that Pop wasn't there. "What's that?" he asked.

"Oh, Pop. He drop dead."

"What?"

"Yesterday. Thuy try to wake him up, and he dead. Maybe eighty years old, I don't know. Yeah, just sittin' there dead. Like he asleep."

"Gee," Harry Hudson said.

"Paramedics take him away. Then Thuy put that beer there for Pop's spirit to drink. Old custom, in Vietnam. Leave it there one month."

"That's nnice of her," Harry Hudson said, surprised and moved. Where else would a bar owner do that for somebody like Pop? For a moment, he forgot all about being angry with her. "Poor old guy."

"'Poor old guy,' my ass," Phuong said, wrinkling her nose. "He *smell* bad. Old rummy, you ask me. Shit in his pants sometimes."

Harry Hudson got up and looked at the scarred wooden table, the beer and Pop's chair behind it.

"Harry! Want next game?" Randy called.

"Ain't gonna be *you* he's playin'," Wade said. Then to Harry Hudson: "Come on, hoss. Put your money down."

Harry Hudson laid two quarters on the rail. He had begun playing eight-ball, now and then, on the Chieu Hoi's threadbare felt, with its warped cues. He wasn't very good, but the game relaxed him--and it was nice to be asked, as now. He returned to his stool, still thinking of Pop.

Hell fire.

Then Phuong, wearing the same green camouflage outfit she had worn the night they bailed Walt out of jail, asked Harry Hudson if he wanted a second beer. "Why not?" he said. She had fished the bottle out of the ice and was bending to open it when her mouth gaped in astonishment, showing that tooth chipped by the Mexicans' gun barrel two years before. Harry Hudson's first thought was that Pop had just walked in alive. Or his ghost. He was starting to smile at that and listen for the squeak of Pop's crutch on the linoleum when he heard, instead, the smash of the bottle as Phuong dropped it behind the bar. He glanced her way. Phuong's jaw worked in terror but no sound came out. Harry Hudson turned and saw a young black man crouching just inside the Anaheim Street door. With a pistol. "Don't none of you motherfuckers move," he said. He wore a dark leather jacket over a navy-blue turtleneck. Sinews twitched in his lean cheeks; he was hyper-alert, eyes jumping around, and much too far away to be taken by surprise. "Empty out that till," he ordered Phuong. *"Now."* To Harry Hudson, the gun was just a round black hole.

A huge inertia held him on his stool. He had the odd sense that he had seen the robber somewhere before, and that the robber knew *him*. He noticed razor bumps on the youth's chin, a trickle of sweat at his temple. The noise of the breaking bottle seemed to linger in Harry Hudson's ears, like his voice through the wire he was wearing. *I'm not ready*, he thought in despair. After a lifetime of waiting. *Not now. Not like this.* He felt every bit of his age and his weight. And he was distracted by another hallucination: Waylon and Willie still seemed to be singing, nasally, though he knew the jukebox had stopped.

It took everything he had just to remember why he once would have wanted to get up, to say, *Listen, son*.... Not that he could hear any of the old voices or remember any names, even Mama Thuy's. All he could remember was that a thread of resolve had connected those voices and names through the years, and that pulling on this thread--trying to stand--would tear something in him, release the smell of chlorine and rubber-tree leaves. It was impossible now. Stupid. Just thinking about it drained his legs of all their strength. Harry Hudson saw this clearly, with regret, at a great distance, as if looking back on his own misguided youth.

Yet he rose up off the stool, and the black kid shot him.

\#   \#   \#   \#

At intervals, he had time to think. There was a sound he felt but never heard and a jackhammer blow that sent him sprawling to the floor all tangled up with somebody's feet, and Phuong screaming. Then he became aware of something smooth and cool against his cheek--the chromed metal leg of one of the stools. He could half-see it, a silvery blur, and breathe the dust at the base of the bar. It was quiet and peaceful there. It occurred to him that he felt no pain, and he thought: *This must be shock.* He thought of something else, too, something maddeningly elusive; it was mixed up with the acid smell of the leaves, and danced just out of reach. But then--much later, it seemed, though it had to have been just a few more seconds--somebody came up close and almost stepped over him, wearing jeans with frayed cuffs and high-top sneakers swirling with blue and black patches of leather and rubber, and Phuong made another, more strangled sound, and Harry Hudson realized that this had to be the robber, leaning over the counter to grab the money. He tried to shout. He opened his mouth, anyway, and reached up with his right arm--the whole left side of his body seemed unable to move. Something flung him down to the floor again, and this time he saw drops of blood spattering on the squares of worn grey linoleum like water dripping from a hose: brilliant red drops like those he had helped Rita and Swede mop up on that first night. *His* blood. He clapped his right hand over his left shoulder and felt the blood pulse though his fingers with frightening speed, warm and sticky, and he felt something sharp, too--splinters of bone? Then the pain may have hit him, or a nausea so overpowering that he couldn't tell the difference. He passed out. Then, when he opened his eyes, five or six men were lifting him, and a red light was pulsing through the curtain into the Chieu Hoi Saloon, like his blood. The men-- paramedics and cops--had arms so brawny that they lifted him onto a stretcher like nothing. He *felt* like nothing: totally limp and helpless. A pad was pressed to his shoulder. "What's *with* this place?" one of the paramedics said. "We were here just yesterday--some old wino checked out." Harry Hudson tried to answer, then realized that he didn't have to; he didn't have to do anything except let these fine, strong men carry him out into cooler air where the ambulance was flashing its light, and slide him in. An IV needle was pumping something into him--to replace his blood? He felt all slippery with fluids. Somebody was talking on the radio--to Sergeant Riker, he supposed.

Later he was lying on an X-ray table watching the camera track over him. Again he could smell the leaves, again he tried to pursue that maddening thought, but real, unmistakable pain had arrived now--pain that was both a throbbing heaviness and a fiery burning, pain that made him moan (he became aware of this only gradually) over and over, like a feverish child. The lights stung his eyes. "Hold still," somebody said. "We gotcha, buddy." Then he grew faint and had to abandon the effort. They must have put something else into the IV, because he awoke this time in a bed in a darkened room, where a nurse was hanging a new IV on a stand beside his right, unbandaged side. The bandages on his left shoulder and his chest were thick, unyielding. His left arm was bound to him tightly, like a splint. More time vanished. Then the nurse was gone and an elderly nun in a habit of dark blue and white was asking him if he was Catholic. *Of course. This is St. Mary's.* Harry Hudson shook his head. His neck could barely move, and when it did he could feel the pain stir, different now, half-numbed and lying deep inside him, but still there. The nun smiled faintly, as if to say: *That's OK, son. It's probably not your fault.* Then it was bright daylight in the room and another nurse was changing his dressings, cutting through the clotted gauze and tape with odd-shaped scissors. A police officer, she said, wanted to ask him questions.

Then there were shapeless days when he slept and woke and tottered to the toilet holding the IV bag aloft like the Statue of Liberty, and the pain came and went and he began slowly to remember. Pop was dead. The robber, he gathered, hadn't been caught. Was Phuong all right? He hoped so. Who had mopped the blood off the floor of the bar this time? Who was covering his shifts at the paper? What did Mama Thuy say? She *had* to be impressed now, Harry Hudson thought--at least a little--but it was hard for him to think of her in the old, desperate way. The pain, when it rose to the surface, crowded away all other thoughts; and when the morphine or Demerol or whatever it was trickled through his veins, he felt too good to care. *No wonder people take drugs. Kelly and Cynthia and the rest of them.* If he hadn't been wounded, he would never have known such bliss. He lay on the softest of sheets with every muscle unclenched and let himself try again to chase down that thought. It had seemed to him, in the split second when he rose from the stool, that he could remember, finally, why he had shot the old man outside Phuoc Vinh. Pulling the trigger of the M-16 had taken an effort on his part--a contraction of his finger--but it had also been the very opposite of effort, he saw. A giving up, a total surrender. The *chieu hoi* he had felt consciously only moments later, when Riker stood beside him in the road and said in disgust: *Well, shit.* No longer strong enough to fight it, he had let the fate he feared most carry him away. Now, at St. Mary's, with the drugs running through him, he wondered if rising from the stool had been any different. It had *seemed* so, then. Oh, yes. The effort of his will had been enormous. Yet his body, once again, may have acted for obscure reasons of its own.

# # # #

After the cops, Holcomb was the first to visit him. "I hope you don't mind my sayin', you look like shit."

You don't look so good yourself, Harry Hudson thought, raising his head from the pillow with a grunt. *Too red and mottled in the face. Those chest pains coming back?* But the words were starting to stick in his throat again. What had happened to his box and earphones?

Holcomb patted the pale-green blanket smooth and sat gingerly on the edge of Harry Hudson's bed. "How long they keepin' you? Not that *I* give a rat's ass, but Eddie Castle makes out the schedule for the rim now. He'd like to know." Holcomb grinned under his mustache. "The doc here said they might have to give you a new joint. Plastic, ceramic--some kind of space-age stuff."

"I wwanted a b--." He licked his lips. "A *bbrass* bball joint." But when Holcomb looked puzzled, he didn't feel like explaining all about Harley Stoffel.

"Does it hurt?"

"Nnot so mmuch now."

"Glad to hear it. Anyway, you've still got one operation to go, they tell me. Thank God for health insurance. Take all the time you need. But not any more--there's some kind of shakeup coming at the paper. I'm not sure *what* yet, but all I'm sayin' is, the sooner you get back the better."

Harry Hudson stared.

When Holcomb turned to leave, he stopped with his hand on the doorknob. He was still grinning. "Anybody ever tell you you're a fucking idiot?"

"Yes," Harry Hudson said.

# # # #

Zuniga came. "You got your wish, amigo. The Long Beach P.D.'s walkin' around with a broomstick up its ass, and it's all on account of you."

"What?"

"They're gonna have to name you for their Heroes' Banquet at the end of the year, even though they think privately you screwed up. But they can't *say* that. Not and keep the Clarion's good will. So you'll get to eat prime rib and stand up there and get a plaque like all the other good citizens of Long Beach who aided in the war on crime."

"I ... dddon't understand," Harry Hudson said.

"They don't *like* heroes, for one. Their advice in a robbery like that is to do exactly what the bad guys tell you, which is what you should have done. You provoked gunfire--that's another no-no. That slug could have ricocheted anywhere, whether it hit you or not. Third--"

Zuniga, he saw, was fond of lists.

"--you raised the ante on that kid's life. He *was* a kid, wasn't he?"

"P-pretty young," Harry Hudson agreed.

"Now if they catch him, he'll serve some serious time. Maybe not Pelican Bay, but serious enough. And he *knows* it. He won't come in easy."

Harry Hudson tried to remember what the black youth looked like. He had told the police what he saw. The jacket, the turtleneck, the thin, intense face. Hadn't he seen him once before, crossing Anaheim Street?

"Fourth, witnesses say you didn't have a snowball's chance of gettin' to him anyway. So it made even less sense. But, like I say, amigo, you've got the cops in a bind."

It saddened Harry Hudson to hear this now. He no longer wished to cause the police any trouble. They had helped lift him up and carry him to safety; all he wanted was for them to respect him in turn.

#　#　#　#

Mama Thuy came, carrying a plastic container of her chili.

"Bring you something to eat. Maybe hospital food not too good," she said, setting it on the table beside his bed.

At first she didn't look at him. *Strange,* he thought. That wasn't like her.

"Th--" He licked his lips, which felt stiff and cracked from disuse. "Thanks."

"Thank *you,* Harry. For trying to help my sister."

She was still avoiding his gaze--busying herself with the container, popping the top, stirring the chili with a spoon. It smelled just as good as on that first morning at the Chieu Hoi, but her obvious discomfort alarmed him. Something must have happened to Phuong. On account of him?

"D--" *Did he kill her?* Harry Hudson tried to say, but the evil spirit had hold of his throat, mocking him. "Is sh--"

Mama Thuy glanced up finally. Her eyes had those dark circles under them. "She OK. Scared shitless. No way I *ever* get her back in that bar now."

"Good," Harry Hudson said. "I mean ... ggood she's OK."

"First night workin' after that other time, and *bang!* Here they come again. Bad luck. Phuong say she have nightmares every night now."

"S-sorry."

"She ask me to say thank you, too. No, I mean it." Mama Thuy looked straight at him now, lips compressed. "But Jesus, Harry, what you do that for, anyway? Huh? Lots of crazies around here, but I never thought *you* go crazy. Get yourself shot for nothing. Killed, maybe. That guy, he only take three hundred dollars, max. I got insurance. No sweat. I mean, nobody get hurt if you just sit tight. Wade say you go apeshit all of a sudden."

She wore a beautiful dress, close-fitting, with a scoop neck, in fine patterns of red and purple, like the outfits Singapore Airlines stewardesses wore on TV. He couldn't get a fix on her. She looked small and weary, as she often did outside the bar, but there was also a vitality brimming in her, an excitement she seemed to be trying to hide. Her hair was freshly curled, dyed with a distinct auburn tinge. She wore a necklace Harry Hudson had never seen before--a gift? From whom? A gold initial T hung in her cleavage, where his hand had gone. It swung on its chain as she bent to set out napkins.

"Here, eat it," she said. "Before it get cold."

Harry Hudson ate slowly. Mama Thuy was right, he knew. It had all gone wrong; it hadn't been anything like his fantasies. Phuong's safety hadn't mattered to him at all that night. There hadn't been any benign trance; instead, he had gone ... apeshit. As good a word as any. He deserved nothing--but Thuy couldn't know that. All she could see was that he was lying here, badly wounded, having taken a bullet. For *her.* Didn't that count for something? Didn't that give him, for once, some moral leverage, some power over her?

"Mm. Good," he said.

"Too spicy?"

"No. It's f-fine. Really."

It was so weird to think that he *could* have power, even power based on a lie. He was almost ashamed to use it, though this was the time, for sure;

it would never come again ... and hadn't she bent him all out of shape on that dinner trip to San Pedro? Harry Hudson sighed, as if the pain had come back just then--and, indeed, the act of sighing did hurt a little.

Mama Thuy looked stricken--eyes even darker, mouth open. She touched his unbandaged arm. "I'm sorry."

Harry Hudson's blood leaped. *She knows after all! How I feel....*

"Y-you d-don't have to b--," he began, embarrassed at having won so easily, after all. He wouldn't force her to say what she felt for *him*. Anything like that. No. That could wait.... *Bbbe sorry*, he was trying to squeeze out of his throat when he first heard what *she* was saying:

"--gonna get married to Swede. I mean Carl. I gotta remember now. That's his name, Carl."

"What?"

"We got engaged. I'm sorry, Harry. No time to tell you. It all happen kind of sudden." She couldn't help grinning now, for an instant, and flashed the diamond on her left hand; he hadn't even noticed it. "Gonna be Mrs. Bjornson now. You invited to the wedding, if you want to come. In Vegas, around Thanksgiving, I think. Gonna have a *big* party."

The grin vanished, but Mama Thuy still faced him squarely. *One tough lady*, Swede had said ... had it been Swede? Yes. At that moment, Harry Hudson admired her more than ever, knew for sure he loved her ... even as the truth sank in, as the wall that had propped up much of his life for the last year split off and fell into rubble, waste, leaving a terrifying emptiness....

Anybody ever tell you you're a fucking idiot?

...leaving him, as always, only two choices: to be an asshole about it or say nothing.

"S-wede's a n-nice guy," he said at last.

The pain was there for real now: throbbing in his shoulder, his skull.

"You too, Harry." She touched him again. "You help with my family. I don't forget that.... But you married, I think. I don't know why, but I think so. I think if we do any hanky-panky, it's a bad thing, maybe."

Harry Hudson shook his head hopelessly.

"Come on, Harry. Eat the rest of your chili."

"Why did you n-name it that?" he asked, for no reason he could think of.

"What?"

"Chieu Hoi. The Chieu Hoi S-saloon."

"Something wrong with that?"

"It m-means s--" He licked his lips. "S-surrender, doesn't it? F-funny name for a bar."

"You say you in Vietnam, Harry. Don't you remember? Chieu Hoi mean Open Arms program. Welcome. We give Viet Cong open arms if they give up."

"I g-guess so," he said. "But still--"

She was right again, of course. How could he have forgotten *that?*

Mama Thuy grinned, more tightly this time. "Open arms for customers, but surrender for me. You ain't lyin', Harry. Bad neighborhood, crazy people, no hard-liquor license, Chinaman won't give me a lease, building about to fall down. That's not the kind of business *I* want. But it's all I can afford. You see? So that's why I name it Chieu Hoi."

She was going to leave any minute, Harry Hudson thought.

"Never used to think when I grow up, I have three husbands," Mama Thuy mused, repacking the container. "My parents, they be shocked, maybe. Think I'm a bad girl. My mother, she never dream of having three husbands. But maybe she should. What do you think, Harry?"

\# \# \# \#

Kelly didn't come.

\# \# \# \#

The phone on his bedside table rang.

"Harry?"

It was only a whisper. Harry Hudson felt a rush of hope: Was it Mama Thuy calling to say she'd changed her mind?

"W-who?" But an instant later, he knew different.

"It's me."

"D--?"

"Deborah. That's right.... I was concerned, Harry. Wondering. No check came this month."

The shock of hearing her voice was almost greater than the shock of realizing what he had done. *Not* done. "J-jesus. I f--. F-forgot all about it.

Really. I got s--" Now Dr. Gregory's magic had evaporated, too. "I'm sorry. I just.... T-they had a h--" He floundered. "A h-holdup here. In--"

"I know. Mr. Holcomb told me all about it."

"You talked to Rick?"

"Yes. He was very helpful. He arranged to have it sent ... direct deposit, I think he said. Automatically. So you don't have to worry about it as long as you're in the hospital. And *we* don't have to worry either."

"Yeah, Rick ... h-he's a n-nice guy."

Like Swede. God damn all nice guys, Harry Hudson thought.

"I think so."

He imagined her thinking: *Unlike certain other people.*

Where was Deborah calling from? He couldn't remember the day of the week. But he could hear a scuffling in the background, as if Kevin was with her. She must be at home, then. In the house she'd bought with a down payment from the insurance money for Sally's death. An old farmhouse, he gathered, out on the sagebrush flats east of Garbersville. He had never seen it, couldn't imagine what she looked like in it; all he could remember was her crouching by Sally's grave, hair streaming in the rain.

My little girl.

"Anyway," Deborah said, determined now, in her schoolteacher voice, "how are you doing, Harry?"

"OK, I guess. D-doc says my s--" Christ, he was stuttering as badly as ever. "S-shoulder may always b-be stiff. The b-bullet went th--" Just as with Mama Thuy, he found himself, idiotically, playing for sympathy. "T-through some important s-stuff. Rotator cuff? S-something like that.... Anyway, they s-say I can probably s--" He should ask Deborah how *she* was. A selfish bastard, she had always called him. "S-still *type* OK."

He thought he heard the kid's voice, then Deborah speaking to him.

"Harry? You still there? You say you can keep on working, then? When you get out, I mean."

He chuckled bitterly. *Who's selfish? She wants to know if her meal ticket's still good.*

"Sure. R-rim-rat work's only f--" It was a mistake to try a joke. This block was so bad that he had the familiar feeling that he had almost passed out, ceased to exist, in the middle of a word. "F-from the elbows down."

"I'll pray for you, Harry," she said. "If you want."

But this voice of Deborah's surprised him. It had a gentleness he hadn't heard from her in ages--had forgotten about altogether. What had happened just now?

He tried to muster his old scorn about the Faith Tabernacle--what was an educated woman doing with those Holy Rollers?--but he felt only a kind of vertigo, as if he were suspended in mid-air, looking down but not falling. Why? For three years he had tensed himself for the first time--it was bound to come-- when he would hear Deborah's voice. She would scorch him, annihilate him, for forgetting Sally even for a second. *That* was what he deserved. Instead, he found himself close to tears.

"T-thanks," he said. "That'd b-be nice."

"*Stop* it," Deborah said--it had to be to Kevin. Then Harry Hudson heard more scuffling. The phone rang a little as something hit it; she gave a grunt as if lifting a heavy weight. Then a new voice came over the line--a voice he had never heard before, a little uncertain but sounding startlingly near:

"Daddy?"

PART III

It ain't no fun when the rabbit got the gun.

My daddy used to say that, back in Kansas. And I thought about sayin' it right here in Long Beach, in my nice new apartment--though it ain't *that* nice, not in this part of town, not with them Crenshaws all around me--when I found out I was pregnant. Shit. I started feelin' sick in the morning and took one of them home tests, and then I went down to the clinic, and they both said the same thing. Positive. And I thought: *Got* to be more careful, but it was already too late. I told Sidney about it. Called him out there in Chino and said, 'Should I get an abortion or what?' And he says, 'Hell no, Kelly, this is *our* baby,' though the last I heard, it's still the woman got to go through all that pain by herself. Right? You'd think Sidney be tired of kids by now, havin' already had two of 'em and neither one turned out worth a damn. But no, he happy. *Real* happy. It cheer him right up, in that prison. And I know how he feel. I ain't got nothin' against any other woman doin' it--that's between her and the good Lord, you understand what I'm sayin'?--but as far as I'm concerned, abortion is still murder, any way you look at it.

Still, how we gonna *support* a baby with Sidney locked up and me gettin' laid off that job before I'd even got settled in yet? Me bein' pregnant would've done it sooner or later. That's how them places operate--once you start showin' and have any trouble doin' the work, woop-woop-woop, they find some excuse to let you go. But before I'd been there even two months, my back went out again. I was liftin' this old lady into bed. She wasn't even a heavy one this time--Mrs. Spivey her name, she was all shriveled up, didn't weigh hardly nothin'--but I must've got my feet set wrong under me, because I felt somethin' go *pop* in there, and *hurt*? Shit. My back hurt like a motherfucker. After that, I had to ease off some, you know what I mean? And they noticed that. I asked for a different run, some kind of desk job, maybe, but they said that wasn't what they done hired me for. See you later.

I think about Mrs. Spivey sometimes. She be one of them kind where I think: Let 'em shoot me first. Sweet little old white lady, had a good life, maybe, I don't know--but she lost all her marbles. Got that Alzheimer's, bad. Her husband come in ever day, Stanley Spivey, big old dude with a crewcut, and set by her bedside and talk to her, and she don't know who he is. I mean, what's the point of livin' like that? And the thing is, she eat good, she *young* for that place--can't be more than seventy. She could last another twenty years, and for what?

It make me wonder, with all the stress I been goin' through, if *I'm*-a be like that someday. If I live that long.

I mean, I *think* this baby Sidney's, all right, but I can't be a hundred percent sure. It could be Harry's, too. Ever since I went off the stroll, he the only other man I had sex with. I ain't used any protection with either of 'em because, shit, for years I thought I couldn't *have* kids. I went on the Pill when I was seventeen, and I kept usin' it all the time I was with Darnell--especially after I couldn't trust him no more. You hear me? Finally I come to think maybe them pills had done somethin' to my insides. Messed 'em up somehow. Because I quit takin' 'em when I got married to Sidney, and nothin' happened. *Nothin'*. And Sidney wasn't the only one in the mix. All them tricks be sniffin' around me ever day, pumpin' they sperm into me, and not plantin' any seeds. I made some of 'em use rubbers--*double* rubbers, if they looked like they dirty or something--but still. You understand what I'm sayin'? Then, when I finally go and quit that life, ooh-wee. Just like that, I'm pregnant. Do it make any sense to you?

Of course, I'm happy too. Don't get me wrong. I'm happy just to find out I *can* have a baby. And then it be nature's way, I guess--once that seed start growin' in you, nature *make* you be happy about it, just to prepare the ground right.

But sometimes I lie awake nights thinkin': What if this baby come out with blue eyes? We got all shades in my family--even got some Indian blood, on my daddy's side--and if this baby come out bright-complected, I could say it just happened through the genes. But not a *blue-eyed* baby. No way I could explain that to Sidney.

So I tell myself, it *had* to be that conjugal visit. Sidney and me, we got it *goin' on* in that trailer, you hear what I'm sayin'? Wore each other out. We done some serious work in them twenty-four hours--no shit. If any baby be comin' out of me, it ought to be on account of that. I keep tellin' myself this. But I can't be sure.

Meanwhile, Harry in the hospital, and I don't know if he recognized Junior or not. Maybe not, I come to think later on, after he got out--maybe he wasn't trippin' about that after all--but I thought if he *did*, what would he be thinkin' about *me*? Would he hold it against me, Little Sidney bein' my stepson and all? Would he think I turned Junior on to that bar, gave him the idea to rob it? Shit. I know it looked suspicious, me not goin' in to visit Harry, but I was *embarrassed*, you understand me? Didn't know *who* all else might be in that hospital seein' him. Like them other newspaper people, or the cops. Askin' too many questions. And I had that baby to worry about too, now. So I stayed away.

Even though I needed money worse than ever.

#   #   #   #

Harry Hudson hadn't been back at the Clarion more than two weeks when Andy McLachlan slipped out to the Press Club in the middle of a shift and returned weaving, red-faced, belligerently drunk. When he came into the island of light around the copy desk, sweat gleamed on his nose and jowls. Opposite Harry Hudson on the rim, another of the youngsters, Ana Chavez, looked up in alarm, then quickly back down at her terminal.

"I don't know why you even bother," Eddie Castle said.

"What?"

"You heard me," Castle said. Bent over *his* terminal, he raised neither his eyes nor his voice.

"I bloody well did *not* hear you, lad." McLachlan fell heavily into his swivel chair. He stared vacantly at his screen, then made a show of punching some keys. Where his big mottled forearm had rested on the metal of the desk was a grey smudge of moisture. "At my age, the ears aren't what they used to be. If you've something to say, I'll thank you not to mumble."

"I said I don't know why you bother to come back, in this condition. You think you're doing us any more good here than across the street on a bar stool?

"What?"

"You heard *that*," Castle said, looking at him now. "Don't play dumb."

"Why, you miserable little.... I've forgotten more about this business than you'll bloody well *ever* learn." Shame kept McLachlan's head down, too, despite the anger in his voice. "I know more about it drunk than you'll ever know sober. And do you know why?"

"Andy," Lincoln warned him.

"No, no, Spence. It's time somebody told the little bugger the truth, don't you think? He'll hear it sooner or later, and not so gently."

"Stay cool, babe," Pierce told Castle. "Just ignore him and he'll settle down."

"Why?" Castle asked, still in that quiet, even tone. "Ignoring him doesn't make the problem go away. Does it?"

"Brad, I'll thank you to mind your own goddamn business," McLachlan growled, though Pierce had only been trying to protect him. Now he reared up from behind his monitor. His face was frighteningly blurred; Harry Hudson could see Ana Chavez flinch again. "The truth.... You want to hear it, lad? Want to hear what *your* problem is?"

"Andy," Lincoln pleaded.

"Go ahead," Castle said. "Get it off your chest. If that's what we have to go through to get any work done around here."

"You *really* want to hear it?" Harry Hudson couldn't tell if McLachlan was hesitating or simply confused.

"Cool it, cool it, guys," Pierce was saying.

"He's a bloody machine, Brad, not a human being." Finally McLachlan glared straight at Castle, who sat with his light hair combed neatly back above a smooth expanse of forehead, the sleeves of his pinstriped shirt each turned up in two crisp folds, like Springer's. "Yes, you, sonny. I'm addressing *you*." McLachlan's hands gripped both sides of the monitor, as if he might wrench it off its pedestal and throw it. "We aren't *people* to you, are we? We're just rungs on the ladder of what you like to think of as your precious little career. You can climb up our backs like a bloody monkey, and flash your bloody pink arse at us from the top."

"You know better than that, Andy," Castle said. He almost smiled, still tapping keys. The others *wanted* to smile, Harry Hudson felt. Anything to break the tension. "But my shortcomings aren't the issue here, are they?"

"What?"

"The issue. How we can keep from having this kind of disruption. Keep the copy flowing. Remember copy?"

Now McLachlan *did* seem confused. He oozed body fluids, as if he might melt. Breathing loudy, he let go of the monitor and sat back down.

"Let me get him a cup of coffee," Lincoln said quickly. "Anybody else want some?"

Nobody answered, but Lincoln got up, not quite looking at McLachlan, and edged off in the direction of the vending machines. At that point, Harry Hudson still expected it to end as it usually did: a half-dozen other times in his year at the Clarion, and God knew how many times before that. McLachlan, having lurched close to the edge, would pull back in time. Life would go on.

Newspaper life.

But Castle was dissatisfied. Harry Hudson could sense this now, with the same strange clairvoyance he had felt that night at the Chieu Hoi when Walt confessed. Castle, he saw, wasn't sure he had handled this right. The youngster was living a story in his mind--as everyone did, Harry Hudson supposed, remembering his own foolish fantasies. In Castle's story, McLachlan's outbursts were the kind of test he was supposed to pass more and more easily as he grew older. But had he? *Should I have made such a fuss if I wasn't going to follow through?* Harry Hudson could almost hear Castle asking himself, pink blood visible under the translucent skin of his cheeks, his back rigid with uncertainty. *Did I let* him *manipulate* me?

Still, Harry Hudson could tell Castle was going to let McLachlan get away with it once more. And he might have, if McLachlan hadn't reared up again while Lincoln, balancing two paper cups of coffee, was only halfway back to the desk. McLachlan's eyes glittered--his confusion momentarily gone. "The Maginot Line!" he bellowed.

"What?"

This time Castle stopped typing. He let out a breath and his body relaxed, and Harry Hudson could imagine him thinking: *OK, now you've asked for it.*

"The bloody Maginot Line. Remember, Spence, when he didn't even catch it when that fool AP story said the Maginot Line was breached in World War I, instead of 1940? Can you fucking believe it? Any idiot knows the Maginot Line was a *reaction* to the Great War, not part of it. French were totally demoralized, you know...." The confusion returned; he shook his head. "Where was I? Yes. Mister Castle here *didn't know*. Incredible."

209

"Ancient history, Andy." It was Castle's last attempt at civility.

"*No*, sir. Not that bloody ancient. Not by a long shot. I might go so far as to say--do you agree, gentlemen?--that anyone capable of such ab-abysmal ignorance has *no bloody right* to run this desk."

"Andy," Lincoln said, holding out a cup.

"Go home," Castle said.

"What?"

"Go home, Andy. Now. Get the hell out of here."

"Guys," Pierce said.

"*Now.*"

"Why, you--" McLachlan flung his arms wide and jolted Lincoln so that hot drops of coffee splattered over the desk. Ana Chavez screamed. "You f--"

Then everyone saw with dread that both men had gone too far to back down. But only Harry Hudson realized that McLachlan had begun to stutter. After all these years, when it counted most, the cure had failed. And it was this added humiliation that pushed his rage, finally, out of control. Spitting, twitching his crimson face, he looked ... was this what Harry Hudson had looked like, standing in front of Finnegan's desk that last day in Red Fork? As close to murder as he had ever felt? The old paratrooper loomed over Castle, fully capable of breaking him in half.

And why not? McLachlan would be saying to himself in *his* story, Harry Hudson thought. *If I'm gone anyway, why not get back at just one of these twits, just one? Just once in my life, smash one of their fucking faces in?*

And Castle, so young, so slender, just trying to get the job done, so unfairly provoked by this ... *alcoholic* who had gotten a free ride for so long--Castle was scared, Harry Hudson saw. No way to hide it. But in his own story, Castle had to be telling himself: *If I let this asshole get the better of me, I'm finished.* Was he thinking only of Springer then, or the higher-ups? Or did Ana Chavez's neck have anything to do with it? Ana Chavez had a beautiful neck, with smooth olive skin and a prominent vein running up the side of it, under her close-cropped black hair. Harry Hudson had time to wonder what it was about women's skin that fascinated him so; he remembered the vein in Margot's wrist as she held the door handle of her Camaro in the parking lot of that Shell station west of the Rabbit Hutch. Maybe Castle was being brave for Ana Chavez, too. Harry Hudson could understand that. He even had time to think, while McLachlan was

210

teetering, hideous, on the edge of violence: *No, maybe Eddie* isn't *like that. Probably not. He isn't like me at all.*

"Go *home,* Andy," Castle said.

And to almost everyone's surprise, McLachlan left.

#　#　#　#

This bullet had been real.

Like the bullets he had fired at the old man in Vietnam--as if one of them had ricocheted back through the years and hit him, after all the imaginary bullets had missed.

It had changed Harry Hudson. If he could finally sense what other people were thinking, it was only from a great distance, through a layer of indifference whose thickness sometimes frightened him. If he thought he could hear the stories in their minds now, it was because the ceaseless babble of his own story had stopped. Sydney Carton, Vance Foster, all of it. What was left? How could a person live without a story, even a foolish one? In the silence, as he stood at the mirror in his still-empty apartment in Belmont Shore with his shirt off and fingered the ridges of scar tissue on his shoulder, the suture marks, the strange slick reddish dimple where the bullet had gone in--in that silence, he could hear only his breathing; he felt more than heard the heartbeats under the heel of his hand, going on mindlessly.

His body.

Which apparently needed no story.

The bullet had broken his body. It had pierced the skin and torn the muscle and made some godawful splintery mess of the bone. Even with the new joint, his shoulder was permanently stiff. In cool weather, it ached. He couldn't lift his left arm above the horizontal. He could still type, but it seemed impossible for him to find a comfortable position, and after a couple of hours at the computer a sharp pain branched from his shoulder up his neck and down his back and side. He knew better than to complain--Holcomb kept him posted about the Clarion's downsizing plans--but he had to take aspirin constantly.

And because his body was broken, his mind, too, was altered. He had always taken his body for granted--that awkward, heavy but serviceable mass of flesh that had gone on working independently of his mind, eaten whatever he had stuffed into it, drunk all that booze, slept wherever he had thrown it down; for all his neglect, it had never troubled him with much worse than a cold. A logger's body, after all. But that had ended. Harry Hudson was a cripple now.

He had crossed the Gimp Line for good.

And being a cripple meant more than just relative immobility and pain; it meant fear. He remembered how he had wandered through Kelly's neighborhood at night and into the Low Fox and the Chieu Hoi--a different person then. He couldn't even imagine taking such risks now. The homeless men who loomed up in the corner of his eye at gas stations, banks and supermarkets to mumble for spare change made him flinch, then duck away in panic and shame.

Only less shame than before, and more panic. *Why doesn't somebody just round them up?* Harry Hudson found himself thinking--meaning also the dark youths idling on street corners, driving the cars with boom boxes and dark windows and absurdly widened wheels. *Find some place in the Mojave and put barbed wire around it and dump them there. Why can't ordinary people just go about their business and not be bothered?*

He had become one of the Sick 'n' Tireds, he realized.

When he thought of Kelly--why hadn't she visited him, or at least called?--and the people she lived with, he couldn't help judging them more harshly than before.

Just cunt-struck, is all, that old white whore at the Chieu Hoi had said. He couldn't remember her name, but she had been right. Harry Hudson saw things differently now; he couldn't believe how obsessed with sex his other, younger self had been. *What was that all about?* he asked, and because it was part of the story that had stopped, he couldn't answer.

He doubted Kelly could possibly know the young man who had shot him, but he remembered that instant, before the hole of the pistol muzzle hypnotized him, when he had thought the face looked familiar. And it happened to be the night McLachlan came in drunk when Harry Hudson figured out why. The young man had looked a lot like Sidney--Kelly's husband--on the afternoon when Harry Hudson had followed her out of the parking lot in Chino and through the chute of barbed-wire fence under the eyes of the guards; into a reception room, where they were searched again; and then outside, where the grass and trees and picnic tables were. Sidney came up to them, in his prison blues. There was a moment, just before Sidney and Kelly embraced--a swirl of embraces all around them: perfume and sweat, tattooed shoulders, clutching fingers, smeared lipstick, a blare of salsa music--there was a moment after Kelly introduced the two men when Sidney must have felt he had to thank Harry Hudson for bringing her, had to shake hands. And he did--with a terrible reluctance. A gold tooth flashed in the left side of what was supposed to be a smile, but in Sidney's eyes there was only hate. A hate that shimmered over his blue-black face like gasoline fumes over asphalt. A hate like that other youth's--and now, in the newsroom, Harry Hudson's heart stopped: had it *been* another youth or the same one?--whom he had almost run down outside the Chieu Hoi.

McLachlan had lurched in and started arguing with Castle, but Harry Hudson hardly noticed at first.

Why not? he was asking himself. Sidney had a right to hate him. *I was banging his wife while he was locked up and couldn't do anything about it. And then I had the gall to show up in person.*

How could he have done that?

Harry Hudson had even managed to forget how Sidney's face looked-- he had pushed it right out of his memory--but the kid outside the Chieu Hoi had brought it back to him, and then the other kid with the gun--if they weren't, indeed, the same. As if they were Sidney's sons and avengers.

Another ricochet.

Then Harry Hudson saw Ana Chavez flinch; he turned his attention to what Castle and McLachlan were saying, but only on the far side of the indifference that surrounded him.

He didn't say anything. He only thought: *Too bad it's Holcomb's day off. He'd know how to keep this from happening.*

#   #   #   #

Guiltily, he followed Lincoln and Pierce into the Press Club when the shift was over. McLachlan was there. He had been drinking steadily, and by now had passed through his rage into a mood Harry Hudson had never seen in him before: somber and almost wordless. Lincoln and Pierce sat down on stools flanking him, and Harry Hudson sat on the far side of Pierce.

"Nothing's gonna happen, Andy," Pierce was saying, "as long as you sober up a little. I mean, what can they do?"

McLachlan grunted.

213

"The Guild won't *let* 'em do anything. Just get a good night's sleep and come in tomorrow and say you're sorry. Eat crow if you have to. Isn't that right, Spence?"

"I wish it was still that easy," Lincoln said, pouring his beer.

"What do you mean?"

"I should've popped the little bugger," McLachlan said suddenly. "It was right there ... but I was too bloody civilized, when it came down to it. Isn't that a laugh? I was glad here for a while--glad sweet reason won out. Wouldn't have done any bloody good, would it? Wasn't *his* fault, really. But now I don't know.... Maybe I *should* have popped him. Just on principle."

Lincoln shook his head. "Andy, that's the kind of principle that gets you thrown in jail. Even the Guild couldn't help you then."

But Harry Hudson knew that feeling, too. What had not hitting Finnegan saved him, in the end? Not his job, for sure.

"Wh--" *What are you going to do?* he wanted to say, but then he realized this was the one thing McLachlan shouldn't be asked. If the man did get fired, at his age, no paper would be likely to hire him again. And it was cruel, just by opening his mouth, for Harry Hudson to have reminded McLachlan of stuttering.

"What happened to that bloody thing they had you wearing, Harry? The Captain Marvel radio and the wires and all."

Harry Hudson shrugged. He should go to Dr. Gregory and get a new one, he knew. *Stuttering doesn't happen to you,* Dr. Gregory's favorite maxim went, *it's what you do.* And he was doing it to himself now, Harry Hudson supposed, just by not caring enough anymore how he spoke. But he thought rebelliously: *It happened to me first.*

"Besides," Pierce was joking, "how do you know he wouldn't have popped *you?* Eddie might be the Karate Kid. You can't be sure."

They all considered this surprising possibility. McLachlan was pushing sixty, with a bad liver, maybe a bad heart. Maybe, despite all his brawn and his lethal knowledge, he would have lost not just his job and the last of his self-respect but the fight as well. Which would have been worst?

"You think I'm fucking *afraid* of Eddie Castle?"

"I know you're not, Andy," Lincoln said, "but don't you think it's better this way?"

"God, I don't know, Spence." McLachlan sighed, as if suddenly exhausted beyond any hope of rest. He laid his arms on the bar and sank his face into them, up to those bushy eyebrows. "I just don't know." His shoulders rose and fell with his ragged breathing. "But the Maginot Line! Can you *imagine* someone not knowing that?"

Harry Hudson agreed with him. But he also thought: *How many stories do we run about the Maginot Line these days compared to stories about, say, microchips or hip-hop?* He shifted restlessly on the stool; his own shoulder was beginning to ache again.

"Don't worry," Pierce said. "If Eddie does try to make anything out of this, they won't back him up. The Guild would raise too much hell. Just stay cool, man, and it'll blow over. Trust me."

# # # #

Pierce was wrong. The very next day, the Clarion fired McLachlan for drinking on the job and threatening a superior. The Guild, considering the file that management had accumulated on McLachlan over the years, could muster only a feeble defense. Or so Harry Hudson heard from Holcomb, who had sat in at McLachlan's final, closed-door meeting with Springer and Castle before the shift began.

"B-but why? He d-didn't d--." Harry Hudson licked his lips. "D-do anything worse than he'd done before."

"No, but times have changed, and Andy hasn't. The company wants to cut staff anyway--older staff especially--so they pushed it this time, where maybe they wouldn't have before."

"Y-you mean Eddie Castle pushed it."

"No, he just knew which way the wind's blowing. Eddie's no dummy. And, Jeez." Holcomb sighed. "I liked Andy, we all did, but he sure could be a hell of a lot of trouble sometimes."

Harry Hudson said nothing.

"All those old, colorful guys we used to have in the newspaper business-- their time's over. The drunks, the crazy guys, the ones who never went to J-school, just picked it up on the fly. No more. The company's gonna put a buyout package together, just you watch, and get rid of everybody on the desk over fifty. Hell, I'd take it myself if I had a few more years in. Missouri's looking better every day." Holcomb squinted at Harry Hudson. "Don't worry about Andy. He's got a few shillings put away. And Social Security. He'll survive."

"I th-thought the Guild--"

"The Guild's a joke, anymore. I don't know what those guys get for their dues, you ask me." A reminder that Holcomb was, after all, management. "Company's got 'em by the short and curlies, and the quicker you realize that, the better off you are."

"I s-see," Harry Hudson said.

# # # #

McLachlan disappeared, instead of settling into retirement on a stool in the Press Club as he might have been expected to do. He must have moved out of Long Beach altogether. From shame? Soon all that remained of his twenty years at the Clarion was his name, in big angular red letters, on one of the dictionaries the copy desk used. McLACHLAN. To Harry Hudson, the word was a shout, as that drill sergeant long ago in England had demanded: *That's better, lad. No more whisperin'. From now on, I want you to shout.* It echoed in his head as he watched Eddie Castle run the desk in the weeks that followed. Was Castle trying extra hard to seem calm, or was he genuinely unconcerned by what he had done? Harry Hudson couldn't decide. Most observers, after all, would say Castle had been in the right. Harry Hudson couldn't argue otherwise. But to him, only one thing mattered:

McLachlan had once tried to be kind to him.

# # # #

Daddy? the voice on the phone had said.

# # # #

The buyout offer came toward the end of the year. Lincoln took it and left. Those apartment houses in Wilmington would support him nicely. Pierce, who had less time in at the Clarion and whose lump-sum payment would have been smaller, wavered, then decided to stay. As did Harry Hudson, whose "package" would have been little more than ordinary severance pay.

This is unfamiliar territory, Hank Steinbach wrote in one of his columns from the desert. *The Cold War over; real estate values going down after two generations of Californians had come to believe that, by divine mandate, they always had to go up.*

And our corporate leaders, I think, have panicked. Their cost-cutting mania betrays that they see only the short term, that their faith in California's economy was never more than platitude-deep.

He didn't dare mention any corporate leaders in particular, Harry Hudson noticed.

Me? I think things are going to get better. Call it the perspective of geezerhood. I remember the Great Depression, a hole so deep it seemed we never could dig out of it, but we did. For Americans in my lifetime, the only sensible bet has been on things getting better, and richer, than we ever could have dreamed.

I'd still bet that way. Whether it's Pacific Rim trade or computers or Hollywood, something's going to haul the sun back up, make it morning again in Long Beach.

This is clearer to me now than it ever was when I was in the middle of the action. In 30 years of working late shifts, I never saw the sun rise--or set, for that matter.

This morning, though, in my back yard in Hesperia, I saw it come up over the mountains in a peach-colored glow. Against it, the black fronds of the Joshua trees looked like the spiky feathers of roosters about to crow. Real birds were hopping on the frost-covered ground.

When full light came, it was dazzling....

He went on and on in this vein, this new, strange Steinbach--an old city boy discovering nature.

\#   \#   \#   \#

Daddy?

\#   \#   \#   \#

"Now you know, Harry, I ain't got anything against black folks, no matter what Charlene'll try to tell you. Right? I try to treat everybody fair, as an individual. Even B.J., who doesn't even halfway deserve it. Ain't that right, Thuy? You ask anybody."

Mama Thuy, clipping her coupons, waiting for the Miller man, nodded.

"But some of 'em's nothin' but *niggers*, like that one that come in here and held up the place and shot you, Harry." Stanley nudged his sore shoulder. "Sorry. I keep forgettin' that's the one.... But just between you and me, do I have to apologize for usin' that word? Some of 'em call *themselves* niggers, you

217

know that? You ever listen to 'em? I wouldn't use that word around Jimmy, anybody like that, but hell...."

Stanley drained his beer.

What was Harry Hudson doing back in the Chieu Hoi Saloon? The stool he sat on might have been the same one his blood had stained--blood wiped off the plastic with one of Mama Thuy's rags. Down by his feet were the squares of beige linoleum, the dust and lint he had breathed in the peace of shock, gum wrappers and pennies. Nothing had changed. The orange life preservers on the walls, the velvet nudes, Stanley's dangling ornaments, the photo of Thuy at the beach, the smell of incense. Wade clattering pool balls into the rack. Randy pushing in through the curtain, the bill of his Clippers cap bent up like his former mustache, his walk a sort of shy swagger, a goofy grin on his face. *Something's up, and he wants us to know.* And Thuy's seemingly total lack of surprise. "Where *you* been, Harry?" she had asked.

"Wh--" He could only spread his hands.

"Take a load off. Let me get you a beer. On the house."

He sat.

"Bud, right? Then let me show you wedding pictures. From Vegas. Why didn't you come, Harry? You missed a *good* party, no lie. Why you want to hurt my feelings?"

What confused Harry Hudson most was the absence of fear. He should be nervous--and probably still would be, in the dark. But it was daylight now. And Mama Thuy, he had to admit, looked good. Tanned even at this season, wearing a new version of the leopard-skin outfit. She seemed genuinely glad to see him, and who else, these days, would even pretend? He had been lonely, he realized--so lonely that he let this woman, whom he should hate, maybe, slide glossy snapshots of her and Swede across the bar, smiling as Rita and Walt had smiled in *their* wedding pictures. He sipped his beer; the icy tingle of the first one was as satisfying as ever.

Isn't this good enough? Just a place to sit and drink and talk to somebody once in a while?

"H-how is it?" Harry Hudson asked. "Mmmm--." He licked his lips. "M-married life?"

Mama Thuy slapped him lightly on the good shoulder, then slid an eye toward Wade. "Shame on you, Harry. You want to make trouble?" Then, lower, she said: "Swede a good man. You know that. But we argue sometimes. He want kids, and I say, 'You crazy? I'm too old. Had a kid already.'" She sighed. "No way to keep everybody happy, Harry. And my family coming, too."

If he didn't know better, Harry Hudson thought, he would feel hopeful. Maybe the thing with Swede wouldn't last too long. Hints like this were Mama Thuy's way of keeping them all on the hook. No wonder Wade still hung around. Harry Hudson almost felt sorry for Swede. In a way, the lucky man who won her for a while was in the most vulnerable position of all.

Then the red curtain billowed, just as it had when the black kid came in with the gun. *There* was the fear ... but it was only Randy.

"Harry, you old sonofagun!" he shouted. "How you been?"

Shaken, Harry Hudson bought him a beer. Then he bought Stanley one, and Thuy a champagne cocktail. Just like old times. Randy, in the cap and new jeans and a stiff new lumberjack shirt, his neck and wrists spindly as a child's, squirmed with the pressure of the news inside him.

"What's up?" Mama Thuy asked.

"Oh, nothin' much. Nooothin' much." He drew it out, gloating--and Stanley, Harry Hudson saw, was the target. "Just spendin' a little time with my woman, is all."

"Wh-who's your w--?"

"You know her, Harry. Best-lookin' woman around here. Not countin' Mom, of course."

"*Thank* you," she murmured.

"Y-you still live--?" Didn't Randy live in a garage somewhere?

"Shit, no. Got my own apartment now. You're behind the times, man. Been with El Pescador *five* years now, and the fuckers finally gave me a raise. And then my no-good dad, that asshole that ran off before I was even *born*--I told you about him, didn't I?"

Harry Hudson nodded.

"Well, he *dies*, up in Delano somewhere, and left me some money. Just a month ago. Not much--it ain't like winnin' the lottery--but, shit, it's better than a kick in the ass, right? First thing I did was come right in here and pay my tab. Two hundred and forty-three bucks. Didn't I, Mom? First fuckin' thing. Don't think I forget who my friends are.... And Charlene, she needed a little help." Even on his stool he swaggered. "Well, I could give her some."

"Ch-charlene?"

"She get her teeth fixed," Mama Thuy said. "Braces. They cost a lot. And she lose weight, too. You be surprised, Harry. Charlene no spring chicken. She know it time for her to get serious. Find a husband."

"She's got *me* now," Randy said. "No need to look any farther."

Harry Hudson raised an eyebrow; Mama Thuy shook her head. The old collusion between them, once more.

"I thought she'd given up on those rich Vietnamese guys," Stanley said. "Thought she had *that* much sense at least."

"Who knows?" Mama Thuy teased. "Maybe B.J. get a divorce, finally. Come back and get her."

"No way," Randy said, wiping foam from his upper lip. "My woman never had anybody care for her like I do. Never in her whole fuckin' life. You think she's gonna give *that* up for somebody did nothin' but shit on her? Or somebody old enough to be her *grand*father? Hell, no."

"Have it your way," Stanley said, huge and imperturbable as ever.

Randy wanted to stay there, enthroned on the stool, and drink and brag some more, Harry Hudson could tell, but he was too excited to sit still. Soon he wandered back outside. The rest of them had wanted to squash the kid, dumb and obnoxious as he was, but they had been gentle with him, too. Randy was happy--it was the happiness they all wanted. It would end soon enough, probably. *Leave him alone.* Meanwhile, the mention of B.J. had gotten Stanley started on "niggers."

"Now take Compton," he said. "You're too young to remember what it used to be, even if you'd been here. But when *I* was young, Compton was a nice, middle-class town. My dad had a hardware store there. Nice as any place. But once the blacks came in, it just went to hell. You can say it wasn't their fault--not *all* of 'em anyway--but the fact remains, Compton's a shithole now. The city council's nothin' but crooks. The state pours money into the schools there, and the schools are shitty. Roofs leakin', classrooms haven't got any books. Where did all that money go, Harry, except into somebody's pocket? If it ain't their fault, whose fault is it?"

"M-maybe the wh--" Harry Hudson licked his lips. "Wh-white people who left."

"Can you blame 'em? I know people still live there, widow ladies I went to school with. Their property values went down so fast they couldn't sell, and now they're livin' behind bars, like they're in jail. Tremblin' like rabbits. Afraid to go out on the street where all the muggers and crack dealers are. What did stayin' put do for *them*? They should've run when they had the chance."

Maybe if more had stayed, Harry Hudson wanted to say. It was strange. Stanley was only saying what he himself believed now, but to hear Stanley say it made it suspect all over again. "Wh-what about the J--?"

"What?"

"Jjjjjjjj." Harry Hudson could feel his face distort itself in all the old ways; he looked off to the side, lips quivering. "J-japanese."

"What about 'em?"

"In the old days. Y-you had some l-living there?"

Stanley looked surprised.

"Sure we did. Over Gardena way. Truck farmers and whatnot. I remember they'd come into my dad's store--couldn't speak English, some of 'em, just laid down their money and took their change and never said a word. But if anybody tried to cheat 'em, they'd never do business with you again. It went though the grapevine. They stuck together, kept to themselves, mostly. Worked hard. Now look at 'em."

"Th-then they g-got r--. Rounded up."

Stanley wagged his head patiently. "That's another thing, Harry, that people these days just don't realize. It was for their own good. We were in a *war*, for Chrissake. A war that had hit *home* on us, not way off somewhere around the world. It was the only thing we could've done. Believe me."

Stanley said this with conviction, just as Harry Hudson's father had said it over the kitchen table in Beattie. But that very memory made Harry Hudson realize that he had been testing the old man, and that Stanley had failed the test. If you could be wrong about Nancy Ishida, how could you be right about Kelly and all the rest of them?

Afterward, Mama Thuy said: "You come again." She extended a cool hand across the bar. "And come to my party, Harry, when my family get here. You promise?"

She named a date that sounded familiar to Harry Hudson, but in his distracted state he couldn't remember why.

"OK," he said. "I g-guess so."

# # # #

221

The next time he was in the Chieu Hoi Saloon, the TV was showing, for the dozenth or hundredth time, the videotape of LAPD officers beating Rodney King. It had happened back in March, but now, with a trial approaching, it was on the air again. In grainy black and white, the nightsticks rose and fell; the man on the pavement writhed. Harry Hudson knew how those cops felt. Put the kid with the gun in King's place, and he would be right in there among them, hammering, kicking. His good arm tensed. His throat went dry. Somebody behind him at the bar--Ron, maybe--hooted. But later, in his apartment, Harry Hudson tasted a thin, sour bile of shame. That was a mystery. Where did it come from? he wondered. What in his childhood had made him, in that pine grove in Beattie, pretend to be a Union soldier instead of a Confederate? What had made him instinctively try to take Kelly's side?

Some memory of his mother's gentleness, he supposed. But the only other answer came as a surprise.

His father.

The old man would come home from a day at the mill and sit across their greasy plates on the oilcloth and talk about the workers. The few blacks he judged with particular care. So-and-so *isn't pulling his own weight*, he would say. So-and-so else *might do all right, if he keeps it up*. Grudging praise, at best. A scrutiny sharper than he ever aimed at white workers, or even Mexicans. But also a feud with another foreman--what was his name? Hodges? Harry Hudson wished he had listened to more of those dinnertime stories, instead of trying to retreat into the silence that his father's voice had broken--an ex-South Carolinian *who won't even admit Negroes are human beings. Says they're some kind of ape, or a missing link between the apes and us. Have you ever heard such crap? I told him: You ain't back home anymore, Earl. This is Oregon. This is 1961, for Chrissake.*

So.

It's true. I never really knew him at all.

Harry Hudson missed Beattie. Mountains free of smog. Rivers that didn't run in concrete. Air damp enough to carry the scent of pine. You could live quietly back there, out of harm's way. He shouldn't ever have left.

And for the first time in more than twenty years, he missed his father.

#   #   #   #

Daddy?

The voice on the phone had shattered something in his mind, as thoroughly as the bullet had broken his body. He knew he had a son. *Kevin.* Didn't he always flinch when he heard that name? Weren't the checks he sent every month to Deborah intended for the boy's upkeep? These were all things he thought he knew thoroughly, knew better than he'd ever wanted to--but it seemed he hadn't known them at all before he heard that voice.

Daddy?

Such a small voice, over all that distance. Hesitant. Hell, the kid was only three. Probably had only a vague idea of who his daddy was. But eager to talk to him. That was the worst of it.

You don't want to talk to me, Harry Hudson thought. *Not if I could forget you exist--not really forget, but you know what I mean.* He had to rely on Deborah, and a little of the old bitterness came back: *She'll clue the kid in on what an asshole I am. Just wait.*

But even Deborah, in that first letter to Long Beach--hadn't she asked him to get more involved in Kevin's life?

Time after time, Harry Hudson nearly got up the nerve to call them. What stopped him wasn't just pain and weakness, the grey layer of indifference around him. He could have struggled through that. What stopped him was the memory of the moment when he burst out the door of the apartment complex in Garbersville after trying to phone 911 and saw Sally's body lying across the sunstruck patio and thought he heard her crying out to him:

Daddy?

Kevin's voice in his ear had sounded exactly the same--*exactly*--as if it, too, was an hallucination, a torment. He couldn't stand to hear it again.

Still, where the voice had entered his mind, cracks radiated out from it, like the cracks around a bullet hole in a windshield, crazed and glittering.

Had Deborah been hinting that she wanted him back?

If so, would Owsley rehire him?

Just like that, it seemed, he had a story again.

#   #   #   #

When the phone rang in Belmont Shore one Saturday morning, his first notion was that it had to be Deborah. That was odd, Harry Hudson thought later. The most likely possibility would have been someone from the paper--or even Kelly. *Her* phone had been shut off, the last he knew. He hadn't tried more than a couple of times to find her since--her neighborhood scared him too much. But sooner or later, he figured, she would call. She would need money. And he would be glad enough to give her some, just to hang out with her again, hear that husky voice, laugh at her jokes.

He wouldn't touch her, he vowed. Not that he felt like it. Not that Kelly would want him to now, in the shape he was in. He would remember Sidney locked up in Chino.

But couldn't they be friends? Hadn't she said, *You my friend, Harry,* more than once?

So what the hell had happened?

Still, Harry Hudson was certain this was a call from Garbersville. As he knelt to the phone on the bare floorboards, he tried to prepare himself to hear either voice--Deborah's or the boy's.

Fear thudded so loud in his ears that the voice he heard, though familiar, puzzled him at first:

"Harry, is that you?"

"--"

"This the right number? You the *newspaper* Harry Hudson, sweetheart?"

"L-louise?"

"That's right, baby. Long time no see, ain't that the truth?"

"You s-sound so d--." Harry Hudson licked his lips. "D-different."

Her voice had lost all its energy. Compared to the old Louise, she spoke in slow motion, slurring the words, as if half asleep or under some powerful medication.

"I ain't gonna lie, Harry. I ain't been doin' so good lately. My car's in the shop, out there at Aamco. Transmission's shot. I need somebody to give me a ride."

"--"

"*Today,* sweetheart. That's what I'm tryin' to say. I need a ride *today.*"

She waited.

"OK," Harry Hudson said cautiously. "W-where to?"

"The hospital."

"Gee. Sure. If there's n-nobody else. Is it an em--" He licked his lips. "Em-mergency? What happened to--" He couldn't remember the name of the big man at the Rabbit Hutch.

"Who?"

"Y-your friend."

"Leroy? Shit, I ain't heard from him in the *longest*." From the dullness of her tone, she no longer seemed to care. "Ain't heard from *anybody*, Harry, no lie. Even you. How come?"

"S-sorry," Harry Hudson said. "I've b-been sick, too. Sort of."

"That's too bad, baby." Her voice faded out, then back. "Anyhow, I thought if I got hold of directory assistance, maybe I could find you." Finally a ghost of the old giggle. "I said to myself, 'Louise, maybe that nice ol' white boy down in Long Beach ... the one liked to dance so much ... maybe he'd be willing to help a lady out.'"

And he would do it, Harry Hudson knew--God knew why.

"You live in ... W-west Covina, right?"

"No, baby. Baldwin Park."

"B-but you said--"

"Never *mind* what I said, Harry. I can't be tellin' people my true home address till I get to know 'em better. I'd've told you sooner or later, for sure, if only things hadn't got so fucked up.... Baldwin Park. That's it."

#   #   #   #

Driving north on the 605, he saw necklaces of razor wire on the poles of freeway signs, meant to keep kids from shinnying up and spraying graffiti on them. The last time Harry Hudson had seen this much razor wire was in Vietnam. It made the scene of stalled cars and roadside trash and oil-spotted pavement and bright, wintry sun look like a war zone. And it hadn't even worked. The kids had somehow climbed up there anyway, risking their damn fool necks to ruin perfectly good signs that commuters needed to know where they were going. *Why?* The perversity of it maddened him. Like the gun at the Chieu Hoi, it seemed aimed directly at him, a threat. Spidery scrawls. CHAKA in big black letters. *Round 'em all up*, he found himself thinking again. *Ship 'em out to the desert and forget where you put 'em. Then maybe....*

This time, though, Harry Hudson's fury had no staying power. He knew he was mostly upset at himself for letting Louise talk him into this--on the day of Mama Thuy's party and, later, of that police banquet he desperately wished he could skip.

He could hardly remember what Louise looked like. Just the red dress and that story about the Low Fox.

Too many crazies, Mama Thuy would say.

And he was one of them still, apparently. He felt more uneasy the farther he drove. He recognized, like an old, familiar taste or smell, the out-of-control sensation he'd had driving from Garbersville to Portland, sneaking across the dance floor at the Rabbit Hutch, sidestepping down the aisle toward the swollen-faced woman at the Low Fox, rising off that stool. How could it happen again so soon, after what should have been the last "awakening" he or any other man would ever need? Harry Hudson tried to think of Deborah and Kevin, but the sun flashing off glass and chrome distracted him. He felt totally alien from his broad, pale hands on the wheel. Meat. Beyond them, for once, the San Gabriel Mountains were green and clear.

# # # #

A dog growled behind the door--a big dog, it seemed. "Rex! Damn it, go in the back." Even shouting, Louise's voice sounded tired. Claws scrabbled; a heavy body thumped against furniture. "Shit. Rex! I *know.* You want to take *care* of me, sweetheart, but it's just ol' Harry. You never met Harry, did you, Rex? I don't think so. Just a *minute*, Harry." More scratching and bumping. "Damn it, go on *in!*" Waiting, Harry Hudson had a moment to look around.

This part of Baldwin Park was well-to-do but gone a little to seed. Sixties ranch houses in Swiss-chalet style with jigsawed eaves and birdholes under the roof peaks. Big houses on big lots, but several had peeling paint, loose roof shakes, the lawns either rank clumps or scrubby, dormant Bermuda. A satellite dish rose behind Louise's house, but her garage door was badly warped. The tangerine-colored door in front of Harry Hudson was scored with the dog's claw marks and dented farther down, as if somebody had tried to kick it in.

All this, in the unforgiving light of a sky that today had real distance in it, summits and clouds.

Crows cawed.

When the door opened, the gaunt, grey-haired woman he saw, wearing shapeless blue sweats, leaning on an aluminum crutch, couldn't be Louise. Her mother? Harry Hudson looked past her, though the living room to a glass patio door against which the dog silently leaped, bushy and white. A husky? God help him in the summers here. But the *voice* was Louise's; it pulled his gaze back. "Harry?" The woman squinted up, as if he was just as hard to recognize.

"W-who else?"

"You look *different*, somehow ... without that sport coat on. Only time I ever saw you, sweetheart, you had that coat."

"Yeah, well." The bullet hole, the bloodstain: he'd had to throw Deborah's tweed jacket away. "C-can't fit in it anymore," he said and grinned. Which would have been true too. His gut had expanded alarmingly, now that he didn't move around so much.

He felt he should reach out, give this pitiful remnant of Louise a hug, but she turned away. "I'm about done packin', Harry; just rest a minute. Shee-it. Don't want to forget all they told me to bring, have to go *back* for it." Her crutch squeaked on the tile of the entryway, and Harry Hudson wondered where he had heard that sound before. *Old Pop, in the Chieu Hoi.*

"You want a cup of coffee, Harry? I got some instant in here."

"No, thanks."

"You sure, baby? Wouldn't be any trouble."

He suspected it would, though, and declined again. Harry Hudson sat gingerly on Louise's couch, unsure of where to put those hands of his, the fingertips heavy with blood. His haunches sank into soft brown leather; the carpet under his shoes was thick, champagne-colored; he saw a big-screen TV and mirrors and decorative lights and stiff dried plants, like cattails, in tall vases. All carefully arranged, dim and opulent. A hidden luxury here. *A love nest.* "N-nice place," he said as the dog on the patio circled, then lay down, its wide white head on its paws, still watchful.

"Why, *thank* you, sweetheart." Louise was in some other room now. Was he expected to follow? He imagined velvet drapes, a waterbed. "I really think I could've gone into that field, Harry, if I'd had a mind to. Shit, yes. I mean *professionally*. Interior decoratin'. I always had that *eye*, you know--what goes with what--even when I was a girl. My friends are always sayin', 'Louise, what you do helpin' us out for free, you could make a *fortune* at if you went into business.' What do you think?"

"Maybe so," Harry Hudson said.

"Shit, yes." She came back out with a blue canvas tote bag, a white dog's head, like Rex's, embroidered on it. She glanced around. "Is that *everything*? Did I turn off that damn furnace, I wonder?" The real Rex jumped up, eager to be let back in. "I *know* I told that boy to come feed you, baby, don't worry."

The crutch left dents in the carpet. The patio light deepened the hollows over Louise's collarbones, which reminded him of ... who? *That friend of Kelly's, the one who went on the pipe.* Harry Hudson felt ashamed even to have thought of going into the bedroom with her. Still, the way Louise used to talk on the phone ... and when they had first met, at the Rabbit Hutch. Who could blame him? Some of the anger he had felt on the freeway trickled back. What *did* Louise do for a living? Maybe nothing. Probably just lived off gullible men.

What else could you expect?

It was a racist thought, and he knew it.

Harry Hudson wondered where Louise's ex-husband was. Ran an import-export business, she had told him once. After the divorce, she had gotten $1,500 a month alimony. Plus the house. Maybe that was all, though, he reflected. It would explain the shabby exterior, the car in the shop.

Louise cracked the patio door, knelt and reached her arms through. Those long dancer's hands were the only part of her that seemed unchanged. She hugged Rex, nuzzled the fur of his neck, let him lick her, rocked and crooned to him. Then, reluctantly, she snicked the door shut. She groaned as she straightened up, regaining the crutch and bag. "Well, I guess that's it, Harry," she said, as if this were going to be more than a hospital visit--as if she were never coming back.

"You w-want ... any help?"

"Just hold the door, sweetheart. I'll be OK."

Outside, the light half blinded him, even as it exposed the tiniest details. The grain and speckle of the concrete walk over which her crutch scraped. The way the web of her hand swelled as she pushed down on the grip of it. Little crevices he had never noticed before in her cheeks and forehead. Ashy patches on her skin. As he opened the car door for her, the crows in the bare trees resumed yelling.

"You know where the hospital is, don't you, Harry?"

He stared.

"Shee-it, what am I *sayin?* You ain't never *been* here before, have you, sweetheart?" Louise sighed, as if this were another unexpected, unfair burden. When she failed to move, he reached to hold the bag for her, but she gripped it tightly.

"Ain't too slick a ride you got there, Harry, do you?" she said. "Thought for sure you'd have one of them Beemers--man wore a jacket and tie like that. Wouldn't you think so? Don't they *pay* you all at that newspaper?"

"S-sorry," Harry Hudson said, irritated again.

"No, *I'm* sorry, baby. At least you came." Louise struggled in, resting the crutch at a diagonal against the seat back, cradling the bag in her lap. "Just wait a minute, Harry. Never *could* get them seat belts right, any car except mine. Wait, wait.... *There.*"

Harry Hudson sat behind the wheel. "Which way?"

"Turn left at the corner down there, then keep on goin' straight. I'll tell you where to turn next."

So he drove. Nothing had happened the way he'd imagined it would when he and Louise finally got together again. Red lights, perfume, music, a squirming pile of bodies. Cries of abandon. He had pictured it often enough, sitting by the phone in Belmont Shore, jacking off in the bathroom, back in that other story. Now he groped to say something that fit the way she was now. Something kind, if belated:

"H-how have you been, Louise? Really."

She didn't turn her head, or answer for half a block.

"Well, you can *see* me, can't you, baby? What's it look like?"

"I don't know. I mean--" He licked his lips. "Is it that h--"

"What?"

"That h-hip thing. You said you fell in a gym?"

"Shee-it, Harry, that was just the *beginning.* You know I sued that doctor? Sued his lyin' ass."

"Y-you told me."

"Them hospital lawyers called me in, Harry. Heavyweights, no lie. They sat me down at this big, shiny desk and they all lined up behind it and gave me the evil eye, Harry, I shit you not. Said they weren't gonna *tolerate* any friv ... frivolous lawsuits from the likes of me, and if I wanted to press it, they had more money than I did, and they'd drain me *dry.* That's their exact words, Harry. I know *you* never saw me cry, not in a million years, but them lawyers had me so scared right then ... and they wouldn't even give me a *hankie,* Harry, to wipe my eyes with. Just sat there like big ol' granite rocks up on Mt. Wilson there. They said they *knew* about me. They'd been checkin'. And they'd let everybody know what the *real* cause of my illnesses was, lessen I settled-- signed my name on a piece of paper right there."

"My God," Harry Hudson said. "B-but--" *What real cause?* "Isn't ... what they did. Can they *do* that? Legally?"

She shook her head.

"I dunno, Harry. I just signed it. They made me feel so bad."

"Sure, but Jeez.... What about your sons? The t-two cops? Couldn't you ask them?"

"Just one, Harry," Louise said sharply. "I never told you two."

Hadn't she? He could have sworn.... *Two fine, big, strappin' sons, both policemen, LAPD. Popped 'em right out and fed 'em from these two titties here. That's why my titties sag a little, Harry, from those two boys suckin' on 'em....*

"LAPD?" he asked cautiously.

"That's right, Harry. But he lives way out in Culver City. Works in that Rampart Divison. I couldn't ask *him*. He don't know anything about this part of my life. The partyin' and all."

"Still--" *That's no farther away than Long Beach,* Harry Hudson thought. Nothing quite made sense.

He reached into his shirt pocket for loose aspirin, swallowed two.

"Keep you from gettin' heart attacks, sweetheart," Louise said. "My old man used to take 'em the same way ... *There!* Turn right. Damn, Harry, you almost missed it." He had almost hit a beige Jeep Cherokee turning left--his tires screeching, only air under his outside wheels.

"Wh--" *Why didn't you tell me sooner?*

"Shee-it, Harry. You like to give *me* a heart attack. If I ain't got enough problems already."

Light-headed with fear, he drove slowly into a poorer part of town: laundromats, *carnicerias*, a Travel King motel like the one he and Kelly had stayed in on PCH. *I shouldn't have come.* His shoulder hurt from the wrench he had just given it. *Christ.* He wasn't up for all this emotional turmoil, either-- trying to figure out what, if anything, Louise said was believable; whether he should feel sorry for her or not.

It seemed impossible that the elderly woman beside him, hugging her bag, was the same one who had told him: *They'd pulled out their cocks, Harry, a dozen cocks, maybe, and they were jackin' off all around us, and they got come all over my* coat, *in my* hair....

Had he dreamed that up? No. But maybe Louise had--or wished she had.

"W-what about y-your old man?" Harry Hudson asked. "H-he knew. You said he g-got you into it."

"'Scuse me, Harry. Got me into what?"

"The partying." It saddened him a little that she seemed to be ashamed of that now. Somebody in the world should be free of shame, Harry Hudson thought. No matter what it costs. At least one person absolutely should not give a damn. *And I thought it was you.*

"Oh, yeah, he knows," Louise said. "But he's got his own life now. He don't want to hear from me, not like this. Not till it's time. Oh, no…. There *will* be a time, though, sweetheart. Can't be puttin' it off forever."

"M-maybe if you called him now." *Or your son.* "M-maybe you've got 'em all wrong. If you--"

"…*none* of 'em," she was saying. "None of my good-time friends so much as drop by. Leroy. Felicia. Kevin and Margot … they all think I got *cooties* or somethin'." At last, the giggle. "Shit. Only one cares about ol' Louise now is Rex. My baby. Let me tell you, Harry: No human being'll love you like a dog can. That's the gospel truth."

Harry Hudson nodded. "He s-seems to be a nice dog."

"He *is*, Harry. Ol' Rex is my sweet, sweet baby. Never cops an attitude. If I ever start feelin' down, he's right there to cheer me up."

"You'd b-better be careful. People m-might start t-talking about you two."

"What?"

"You know." He had meant it as a joke, he thought, but maybe he was probing for the old Louise underneath. "Woman and a b--" He licked his lips. "A b-big dog. You know."

Louise turned to him, genuinely shocked.

"Oh, *no*. I can't *believe* you said that, Harry…. Me and Rex?"

He tried to wave it off.

"Oh, *no*, Harry. I thought you was a gentleman. I used to tell Leroy, 'That white boy down in Long Beach, he's a *gentleman*.' But no. No *way*. You nothin' but a *dog*." Louise was crying, suddenly. Her face rubbery, shapeless. The tears rolled down her cheeks and she made no attempt to wipe them. "Sayin' something like that, when all I tried to do was *protect* you. Shit, I got HIV. Found that out just after the Rabbit Hutch shut down. That's what them lawyers was talkin' about, Harry. That's why I never had you on up here."

"My God." Stunned, Harry Hudson reached out through thickened air to pat her shoulder, but Louise flinched away.

"Tijuana shit like that.... I thought I *knew* you, Harry, after all this time. But I guess I was wrong. You just let me out here, anywhere. I'll call me a taxi."

"For P-pete's sake," he said. "I'm *sorry.*"

"I was tryin' to look *out* for you, Harry ... and you said you *liked* to talk to me on the phone."

"I d-did."

"Well, then, why you go and say something *mean* like that, to someone who ain't never hurt you? Not one time."

Because it once would have made you laugh, he thought.

They rode on in silence. Louise's tears dried, but she still didn't touch her face. She squeezed the bag so hard that her knuckles were yellow.

"Isn't that it?" he said.

This hospital wasn't a high-rise like St. Mary's; it was a long one-story building across from a park, with a facade of white stucco arches and a Spanish tile roof. There was room for his car right in front.

"You can just let me out here," she said again.

"C'mon, Louise," Harry Hudson said. "I *said* I'm sorry. Let me walk you in. B-been a long time ... haven't s-seen you."

He got out, went around the car and opened her door. It occurred to him that maybe his premonition back at her house had been right; maybe she wouldn't ever be returning home. Rex would wait forever. And that meant ... he didn't exactly think of her dying; what struck him was that none of his questions about her would ever be answered.

Louise still refused to let Harry Hudson take the bag. Empty-handed, he followed as she limped up to the hospital entrance, glass panels that parted with a whoosh.

"Can I c-call you here?" he asked.

"Ain't stayin' here any longer than I *have* to, sweetheart, you can bet on that."

She crossed the lobby, leaned her crutch against the counter, bent with that same soft groan and wrote on a clipboard. Her script was large and rounded, like a schoolgirl's. A receptionist glanced at it. "Mrs. Way?"

It was the first time Harry Hudson had heard Louise's last name.

Time was running out, he thought desperately. He should hug her now ... do *something* to make it up to her, to take back those few hurtful words that had spoiled a year's worth of what could have been friendship; that had slipped out, as such words always did, too fast to be retrieved.

Like saying *Jap*.

\#   \#   \#   \#

Driving back to Long Beach--to Mama Thuy's party, and then to the police banquet--Harry Hudson no longer noticed the rumble of traffic or the slant of the afternoon light. Voices sniped at him from all directions. His own and Louise's, saying the same sorry things they had said, over and over. Then other voices, too. Like Randy's:

Asshole that ran off before I was even born.

How could he have fucked up again? In spite of a warning. He had felt things beginning to go wrong, driving up this same stretch of freeway. And still....

His head throbbed, and he swallowed more aspirin.

A new idea had begun to take shape inside him--or an idea so old he had forgotten it long ago. Maybe, he thought, heroism wasn't a matter of going places, doing things, after all. Not walking in a line of soldiers or rising off a bar stool. Maybe it was just staying put. Doing your duty. As his father had, and Randy's hadn't.

Or Louise's friends.

Or me.

Maybe he should go back to Oregon, be with his kid, no matter how hard Deborah made it for him.

An idea so stark and simple, Harry Hudson thought, had to be true.

\#   \#   \#   \#

I *told* Junior to bring that Cadillac back, soon as he had a chance to. He hid out a few weeks with some of his homies up in Lynwood, but after a while it didn't look like them polices was huntin' him in particular, you know what I'm sayin'? And he starts showin' up in Long Beach again. I told him, I need that car *real* bad. As big as I'm gettin', it ain't no joke ridin' them buses cross town to get my prenatal care, or even buy groceries. You hear me? But instead he lets Miss Crenshaw borrow it first, when her boyfriend's back in Texas seein' *his* people, and Miss Crenshaw lets my sister-in-law Brenda drive 'em both out drinkin', sluggin' that Jose Cuervo right out of the bottle. Ain't *nothin'* nice. And they total it. Sidney's car. My sister-in-law ... this was one of the heavy ones, not the one that likes girls. That's Linda. Them paramedics got Brenda to the ER alive, but that's all. She died there about a half-hour later.

It's a wonder Miss Crenshaw didn't die too. The good Lord was watchin' out for *her*, you understand what I'm sayin'? I mean, she didn't even have her seat belt on, and that's why she got thrown free. They was crossin' that bridge over the L.A. River on Anaheim Street, and went through the railing and fell all the way down. Hit that cement. Not in the river--not *that* far--but where the bridge just start goin' up. Right next to that *im*pound lot where we done had that car towed I don't know how many times. Shit. That Cadillac landed upside down, on its roof, and just squashed itself flat. It's a wonder Brenda even *got* to the ER. And Miss Crenshaw ... some angel must've flown down in there and caught hold of her in mid-air and let her down nice and easy, because all she did was break three ribs and an ankle. Broke it bad--she got screws and plates in it, probably won't ever walk normal again--but it's still a miracle, you hear me? I told Sidney that, out in Chino. Tried to make him feel better--tried to picture Sidney there, how he looked, holdin' that phone. Bad news don't do *anybody* good in prison. He be so broke up about Brenda, he hardly even heard me when I told him about the car.

But *I* think about it, ever day. That's evil of me, I know. I never did like Brenda, and she ain't never had much use for me neither, but she *gone*, you understand what I'm sayin'? Let her rest with the Lord. But I couldn't help thinkin' about it all through that funeral. Miss Crenshaw's boyfriend come back, and I had to ride alongside of her, in *his* Cadillac, and all the time I'm cussin' out Junior and Brenda both, under my breath, for wreckin' *ours*. I hate funerals. Ever since the one when they buried my daddy, back in Topeka. And this time it was rainin'--just a drizzle, but we all had to squeeze under them umbrellas, *way* too close for comfort. I'm out to here, and ain't got a thing nice to wear. You listenin' to me? Little Sidney, he standin' over there on the far side of the preacher, with his homies. Scared to get too close to me. Well, he got *that* right. Pregnant or not, I'd whup his ass.

I wished I could have got drunk. But I had to quit that, cause of the baby.

Then, after we done looked at the casket--no way they'd open it, kind of shape Brenda must've been in--that's when Tamika come up to me. Taller than I am now. Got *hips* on her. Carryin' *her* little baby, Ebony, and wantin' to feel me and see if mine kickin'. Which it have been, quite a while now.

'Auntie Kelly,' she says, 'can I stay with you now?'

And I remember it's Brenda she been stayin' with lately, back and forth with her grandmama, either way till she wear out her welcome. That back-and-forth all their lives been what fucked up her and Junior both, I believe.

She done caught me in a weak moment. You hear me? Tamika look a lot like her daddy--like Brenda, too. And she got no business bringin' that baby out in weather like this. It need better care. I can see this. And Tamika says, what with her county check *and* mine....

What can I say?

#   #   #   #

"Thank you for coming, Harry," Mama Thuy said. "To be with my family when we all so happy now."

She smiled warmly at Harry Hudson, framed by her front door. She had put on a dress for the occasion--not an *ao dai* but another Singapore Airlines-style outfit, this one maroon. Her hair was upswept; the tanned skin of her cheeks and throat glowed. She took his hand in both of hers. Squeezed it hard. What had he done to deserve such a welcome? She pulled him into the parlor. Harry Hudson felt too weary to resist. His headache hadn't gone away. Nor had the voices stilled: *I got HIV ... you nothin' but a dog.* He just wanted to sit down in a corner and eat something--he could smell roasting pork--sip a beer, distract himself from shame by checking out the dark, carved furniture Mama Thuy had bought in Hong Kong, screens, calligraphy, the big studio photos of her that Stanley had told him about. Plenty of skin but in soft focus, tasteful. A world carefully kept apart from the hookers and dope dealers on PCH just a half-block away.

But Mama Thuy had hold of his elbow, steering him into the crowd. He glimpsed Jimmy and Charlene and Ron and, through a kitchen window, Swede manning a barbecue out back. Then Phuong pushed through toward him, leading a thinner woman in black silk pajamas who looked like her and Thuy both.

"My other sister, Loan," Mama Thuy said.

Loan, too, clasped his hand with unexpected fervor. Her smile, almost a grimace, made the cords of her neck stand out. Behind her was a boy of eight or nine, carrying a puppy--the kind of dog Harry Hudson remembered from Vietnam, its tail curled up over its back.

"She thank you very, very much for helping our family," Mama Thuy said. "This boy"--who half hid behind his mother when Harry Hudson smiled at him-- "he her son. Her husband dead, years ago, in a camp. The Communists."

Hadn't somebody told him that? He tried to recall. He had been drunk, maybe. Ron?

"H-how old is he?" Harry Hudson asked. An oval face, big dark eyes. *So young to be starting life in a whole new country.*

Mama Thuy looked a little puzzled, then conferred with Loan. "Twelve."

"I hope he g-gets into a g--" He licked his lips. *Good school,* he wanted to say, but Mama Thuy didn't seem to feel the boy was worth so much of his attention. She pulled him into the kitchen--as brightly American as the parlor had been Asian: pale yellow, with daisy-patterned wallpaper. More people sat at the table, around a boom box whining a Vietnamese song, and stood by the stove. Harry Hudson could hear somebody outside chipping ice. Pungent smoke drifted in from the patio.

"*My* son," Mama Thuy said. "Billy."

He had her small features, isolated in the middle of a bigger, rounder face. A plump young man--what was he supposed to be, twenty?-- who gave Harry Hudson an indolent, appraising look.

"Mr. Hudson," she said in English. "He the one who helped us, gave money for your plane tickets."

Billy, with slicked-back hair, wearing a Hawaiian shirt, held a beer in one hand, a heaping paper plate of meat and salad in the other. He shrugged, meaning he couldn't shake Harry Hudson's.

"Billy," Mama Thuy repeated.

Billy smiled--a quick, facile smile--and ducked his head. "Oh, we thank you," he said. "Yes, sir. We *very* happy, come to America."

"Th-that's OK," Harry Hudson said. He saw Billy's eyes flicker shrewdly--noting that there was something wrong with this big blond man's speech; filing it away, like everything else he was learning here. "D-don't m-mention it."

Mama Thuy frowned. "You got to meet my *father*, Harry. He back here somewhere. I just ... there he is."

Phuong was bringing him, saying something in his ear that he seemed to ignore. A tall man for a Vietnamese, still sturdy for his age, wearing a khaki shirt and shorts and rubber sandals. A gleam of wire-rimmed glasses, a mirthless smile. *The child-beater?* The hand Harry Hudson shook was as sinewy and cold as Thuy's.

Like Phuong, Mama Thuy spoke to him in Vietnamese.

The man nodded slowly, looked Harry Hudson up and down. "You speak French? *Parlez francais?*"

Harry Hudson shook his head.

"My father want to speak French with somebody," Mama Thuy explained. "Not so good with English."

"S-sorry," Harry Hudson started to say, but the man had already lost interest; with deliberate rudeness, he turned and walked back outside, his bare calves bowed, rubber soles flapping on the concrete.

"He speak real good French," she sighed. "No chance here."

"Don't mind him," Phuong said. "He always that way. We tell him all about what you done, Harry. He thank you."

What had he done?

It dawned on Harry Hudson that, to these women at least, he *was* a hero of sorts. The two thousand dollars he had given Mama Thuy had meant something after all. Last fall, he had wanted badly for it to mean something--to Thuy. But now, he thought in embarrassment--now, to these people, it meant far too much. He wasn't a benefactor, as they seemed to think; he was hardly a human being at all. *Ask Louise.* He was almost grateful to Billy for having an attitude. *He knows, maybe.* And Thuy's old man, for sure. *Knows I just wanted to get in her pants. Like all the other barflies here.*

The puppy squirmed out of the little boy's grasp, darted between people's legs, barking, picked up a scrap of meat on the patio and ran. The boy chased after it. Harry Hudson tried to catch his eye.

Swede called from the grill: "Better come and get some, Harry. It's goin' fast."

In mid-stride, the boy seemed to flick a glance his way. If anyone could forgive him, Harry Hudson thought crazily, it would have to be this child.

But Mama Thuy was approaching him again. "My mother," she said.

Her mother was one of the smallest women Harry Hudson had ever seen. She bowed and opened a mouth that at first seemed to be toothless--but her teeth were black. The top of her head with its grey-streaked hair, pulled back with a rubber band, reached barely above his waist. Her body, inside black pajamas like Loan's, was like withered brown twigs. Like the body of the old man he had shot, in the damp dust of the road, that bicycle wheel spinning. Only her hands were huge. They seized Harry Hudson's with more strength than he would have thought possible; then--unbearably--she fell against his thighs and wept.

# # # #

When we all so happy.

It had been that way too, Mama Thuy thought. For days and days. She had planned for her parents to live in the guest house out back. She had paid Jimmy and Walt to help Swede fix it up. New paint, new plumbing. But for those first nights no one could bear to be separated again. They lay on her living-room floor on sleeping bags and futons--all of them, side by side--and talked. The sea breeze blew in the curtains, and they marveled at the air: so cool, so dry. The air of America. Just another in the chain of amazements that had begun with landing at LAX, their trip on the freeway in her Porsche and Swede's truck, her house full of appliances, closets full of clothes, the safe with the gold bar in it.

Even her father had seemed to approve.

So much to talk about! They hardly had time to sleep, those nights. Nearly twenty years. Their life in Vietnam, her and Phuong's life here--they had to catch up on it all. And it seemed inexhaustible: the talk, their joy in one another. Both flowed like the air. It had never been like this in the old days, that she could remember. Before she met Dwayne and all that trouble started. Maybe America had changed her family. *Or maybe we all just grew up*, Mama Thuy thought. And for once she let down her guard when people could see her--not alone after work, with the door locked and the night's receipts in the safe and no one to care if she cried over some silly old Vietnamese movie on TV about a girl forced to marry an ugly and evil landlord to pay off her parents' debts. She had paid off everything, she thought now, crying and laughing both. They were all safe.

No more *bad girl*, ever.

So what had gone wrong? She looked back on those first weeks and saw no single big thing--just a lot of little ones. Her mother walked out to PCH one morning and ran back breathless and trembling; a ragged, crazy man had shouted at her. *Maybe a homeless guy,* Mama Thuy told her. *A lot of them out there. They won't hurt you.* But her mother wouldn't be reassured. *If they're crazy, why doesn't the government help them? Or lock them up? One or the other. A rich country like this.* Mama Thuy had no answer.

Then her father went out and saw the streetwalkers and drug dealers. He knew what they were. He came back and demanded to know why she had moved her family into a place like this. *Because I live here. It's close to my work.* And this seemed to remind him that she owned a bar, stayed out late, wore revealing clothes. As if he had charitably forgotten it. *Work?* he asked. Couldn't she have found some other job? *Something less....* The corners of his mouth curved down in a sneer; his glasses had that old, frightening gleam; she suddenly felt like a child again. She wanted to ask: *Less like the places you went to in Saigon, playing around, while my mother stayed at home?* But somehow--and it shocked her profoundly, after all these years of independence--she couldn't say that aloud, not when her father was there. He was boss again. Still. Ordering her to keep him supplied with cases of beer, cartons of cigarettes.

You think I went to college? She did say that. *What else could I do? Keep on working in that laundry in Oklahoma for $1.60 an hour? It's the only way I could bring you here. The only way I could buy a house anywhere.*

But her house, in his eyes, no longer reflected credit on her. He looked slowly around, at the Hong Kong furniture, the studio portraits, the safe. *Oh, yes, I see. You had a good time here, all those years we suffered.*

Her father didn't want to move into the guest house. He wanted her and Swede to move there. Swede, easygoing as he was, wouldn't agree to that, she knew. Fortunately, her mother understood. But her father, after they did move, made his unhappiness clear. There was a cold snap--even a Southern California winter was a surprise to them--and he complained bitterly. He ran the gas full blast day and night, left streaks of soot around all the vents, over Swede's paint job. *What do you expect?* he asked her. *You put us out here like poor relations. Like dogs.*

Now, watching Swede lay fresh meat on the grill, Mama Thuy saw a dog trot by, onto the lawn Randy had mowed for her yesterday. It stopped, spread its hind legs, trembled and shat right under her Vietnamese grapefruit tree. She yelled, but it didn't run off until it had finished. She had to go to the garage for a shovel and carry the stinking stuff back to her compost pile. She brandished the shovel at the dog--the puppy Phuong had found for Loan's boy, to replace one he had left in Saigon. That was nice of her. But the damn mutt had taken over the house. It chewed everything. Chased Mama Thuy's cat, old and fat now, not used to such treatment.

And Swede, she thought, was like the cat--unexpectedly put on the defensive. *I know it's your family,* he would tell her, nodding, rubbing his chin. *I know it's a different culture. They need time to get used to things over here.* Trying so hard to be understanding, when he didn't understand a thing. As big and strong as Swede was, he wasn't half as tough as her father--not in the ways that counted--or half as tricky. Her father would take over, too, sooner or later.

I know it's their language, Swede had grumbled already, once or twice. *It isn't fair to ask 'em to speak English. But when you're all goin' on and on like that, I don't know ... I feel kind of left out, here in my own living room.*

And once or twice, already, Mama Thuy had lost her temper: *Then learn Vietnamese. How come I'm the only one can speak both? Why nobody else?*

Her father's daughter, after all.

Now she went over to the grill in full view of everyone and put her arm around Swede's back. "How's it goin', hon?"

"Startin' to run out. That everybody, you think?"

"I think so. When this get done, why don't you stop, eat some yourself? Have a beer."

"Maybe I'll just do that."

Randy hadn't come. *I'll do your yard, Mom,* he had told her, his mouth a grim line, *but I ain't gonna show up if that ... I ain't even gonna say her name. That bitch is there.* Meaning Charlene. Who was talking now under the bougainvillea arbor with her new boyfriend. *Excuse me,* Mama Thuy thought. *Her fiancee.* A guy Charlene had met in Las Vegas, named Les, who had bushy red sideburns and worked for a company that installed air conditioning in the casinos. *Better hurry,* Mama Thuy thought, *before you gain that weight back.* Charlene was all dressed up--nylons, high heels, a nice beige suit--but the waist of it seemed a little tight. And she never could keep a wisp of hair from escaping somewhere. Her long face was flushed. Even with the new teeth, her smile looked uneasy. Gas? Suddenly Mama Thuy found herself thinking: *My God, is she pregnant? Wouldn't that be something?*

She laughed out loud.

By who, then?

"You're in a good mood," Swede said.

"Why not, babe? It's my party."

Randy? She had never quite believed that, despite all his bragging. Charlene must have promised him some, but no way.... Though with Charlene, who could know for sure? *Probably Les.* But just before Charlene met him, hadn't B.J. been back in town?

No wonder she's moving so fast.

Mama Thuy had tried to explain things to Randy yesterday as she pointed out what needed to be done--which bushes to clip, which to leave alone.

She think this is her chance. She don't want to miss it. This Les, he have a good, steady job. Vegas, they always need air conditioning.

I got a steady job, too, Randy had said stubbornly. *Don't I, Mom? And this guy don't even know her. How long, three weeks? How can he love her more than I do?*

I don't say he love her more. All I say is, he got more money.

I gave her money. All my fuckin' dad left me.

Well, that's why.

Why what? If she needed more, I'd go get some, Mom. You think I can't? You think I'm too stupid or somethin', like Ron and Stanley and the rest of them think? Well, you're wrong.

I don't say that either, Randy. She put a hand on his thin arm. *But I try to tell you how Charlene think. She have a hard life, long time now. She don't want to be poor no more. I don't know if she love Les or not. He nice enough guy, I guess. I don't know. Not my type, OK? But if you really love Charlene, then you gotta try to be happy for her.*

We were *happy, I thought. Shit, how much money she need? With both of us workin'....*

Who knows what make people happy? Mama Thuy sighed.

In the end, she hadn't been able to make Randy feel better. Instead, he seemed to blame her for ... what? Telling him the truth? Not warning him earlier about what everyone else had known was certain to happen? She had never dreamed she might lose Randy as a customer, but ever since Charlene dumped him, people said, he had been drinking half the time at Max's Steiner, a mile east on Anaheim Street.

Why me?

She took a deep breath, smelled incense and honeysuckle, pork fat and charcoal. She went around the yard picking up empty plates and beer cans. She smiled at Stanley, who sat in a lawn chair between Harry and Walt. Stanley still acted calm, but he had changed almost overnight as soon as he knew Charlene was going to leave town for good. He had always been such a strong old man.

241

Now he was just old. *Like Pop,* Mama Thuy thought, and then: *What's Charlene got, anyway, they go so crazy over her? Rita I could understand.* Stanley's crewcut had lost its last few dark hairs, and his skin couldn't hold any color anymore. He reminded her of a pig she had seen as a little girl, sleeping by the side of a country road; the layer of mud on it had dried and bleached almost white, so that until the animal suddenly, frighteningly moved she thought it was a stone.

Swede offered her a plate. "Hungry yet?"

She waved him off. "Later, hon. I tell you before. Anytime I give a party, no time to eat till afterwards."

And Harry. *He* should be feeling better, with everybody appreciating him at last. Eating good food. But he looked just as gloomy as Stanley and Walt. *Slugging down those beers, too. How come?*

A scream from the kitchen.

Mama Thuy rushed inside, into a fog of smoke, saw flames leaping on the stove, her mother's and Loan's scared faces. She grabbed a wide metal pot cover and dropped it with a clang over the wok they had been cooking in. Under it, oil sizzled fiercely. She turned off the burner.

"What happened?" she asked in Vietnamese, waving her hands.

Phew! What a mess.

Her mother opened her mouth, showed those betel-stained teeth as if the smoke had darkened them. "It just ... caught fire."

"She can't see that high," Loan said. "The counter either. I have to watch her every minute."

"Where's your stool?" Thuy asked her mother. Somebody must have taken it outside. The boy? "I'll get it."

"She shouldn't try to cook on these things," Loan said.

"I can't eat all that meat," her mother was explaining. "I just want a little something to put on my rice."

"Swede made nice barbecue," Thuy said, but she knew nothing could keep her mother from spending half the day in the kitchen, not after all these years. It was cruel and useless to try.

"Without rice," her mother said, "I just don't feel I've eaten, somehow."

"It's OK. We can clean it up. I'll get your stool." She turned to Loan. "Why don't you go outside? Meet somebody."

"Who?" Loan asked.

"Who knows?"

"That big black man, he scares me a little."

"Jimmy? Don't worry about him."

Mama Thuy had a moment's misgiving. In those first weeks, she had joked with her sister about finding a new husband, but the way Loan threw herself at every American guy she met--and not gracefully, either, but as if she were getting old and running out of time, like Charlene--maybe she ought to stay in the kitchen.

Lights on but nobody home?

Mama Thuy found the footstool. Corbin, squatting on the back stoop, had set his plate on it. She picked scorched pieces of chicken out of the wok with a pair of long cooking chopsticks. The oil was full of black flakes. She pulled on quilted gloves and carried the wok gingerly out behind the guest house to dump it, hoping nothing spilled on her dress.

Coming back, she saw her father sidle up to Harry, embrace him roughly, grin and offer him a beer. *The old actor.* He must have realized he'd been a little too rude to Harry--and now Harry grinned back, more grateful than if her father had been nice from the beginning.

Slick.

Her father was a bad man in many ways, Mama Thuy thought. So how come, next to him, nobody else seemed quite like a man at all?

Charlene had changed everything except that perfume. Mama Thuy could smell it beside her now. "What do you think?" Charlene asked.

"Think about what?"

"Les."

"Go for it," Mama Thuy said. "What you got to lose? Like when I came to the States, eighteen years old. I said, 'Why not?'"

Charlene squeezed her arm. "Thanks, Mom."

"What I got to do with it? It's your life."

"Still."

Still what?

Mama Thuy drifted away. It occurred to her that she hadn't seen Billy for a while. Then, as if on signal, something popped like gunfire behind the garage. She ran around the corner in alarm and found Billy and Loan's boy there whooping and setting off firecrackers. Gunpowder smoke, scraps of red paper, black burst marks on the concrete.

"You crazy?" she yelled. "Police come any minute." They gaped at her and she realized that she was speaking English. "This is dry country," she said in Vietnamese. "They're afraid you'll start a fire."

The boy seemed properly scared, but Billy didn't. "Look. No fire here," he said.

"Still, it's the law in Long Beach."

"No police, either." He gestured languidly, as if the yard belonged to him and he was showing it off. "See?" Then she realized that *he* was speaking English, in deliberate mockery: "Lighten up, man."

Where had Billy learned to talk like that? The way he looked at her, he knew she was asking herself this question--and finding the answer: *Those guys on the street.* Right at the start, she had taken him aside and told him: *You'll see guys here in America who don't seem to work, and they have cars, guns, cell phones, pagers. Girlfriends. Yes, Vietnamese guys too, like you. But they're just headed for trouble. I want you to get a job. It doesn't matter what kind, as long as it's honest. Go to school. They teach English as a second language at City College, right there on PCH. Believe me. I've lived here a long time. The slow way is the best way.*

But the fast way, it seemed, was the only way Billy knew.

A long time you left me in Vietnam, he had said then.

It was natural, Mama Thuy supposed, for Billy to resent her for that. As his grandfather did. She was a stranger to him now, just as she found it hard to connect this large, arrogant young man with the baby she had held and suckled. Still, it hurt her worse than anything else to hear him say it.

Saigon fell, she said. *I had no choice.*

You think I had a choice?

Once Mama Thuy had overheard him saying to Loan: *She doesn't even look like my mother. Like anybody's mother. I mean, she looks so young. Like a movie star, almost. I feel like I ought to ask her out.*

Now her father came up behind her and laid a heavy hand on her shoulder. "What's wrong?"

"Firecrackers. They'll get us all in trouble."

"What trouble?" her father said. "A man was selling them out of the trunk of his car there yesterday." He pointed to PCH. "Cheap, too. And I knew you were having a party. So I got some."

"It's against the law here," Mama Thuy insisted.

"So? They aren't doing any harm. If you're a boy, it isn't a real party unless you have some firecrackers. Right, boys?"

Billy grinned, and even Loan's son nodded cautiously.

"You spoil them," she said. *So they'll grow up and become like you,* she wanted to add, but couldn't. Instead, she asked, "Why is it just the boys you spoil?" Implying: *And the girls you beat.*

Even that went too far. Her father's eyes got cold behind the lenses, and the hand on her shoulder tightened. "I said *no trouble.* Do I have to repeat myself? Don't you have enough to do in the kitchen?"

Mama Thuy refused to answer. She turned before she could see Billy's grin widen--as she knew it would--and strode away, hot and stiff with humiliation. Swede had bent over the grill, scooping out ashes. He wore a white T-shirt; under it a ridge of muscle ran down the side of his back. Swede was a beautiful man, she told herself. A good man. Here in this house she had bought, this yard she had dug and planted out of nothing. So why couldn't she be as happy as that dimwit Charlene?

She nuzzled Swede's flank, felt that muscle with her cheek, knowing her father, watching, would disapprove.

"Hey," Swede said.

"You think you can get a transfer?" The idea had come to her all at once. "Hawaii, maybe?"

"What brought this on?"

"Just thinking, hon," Mama Thuy said, but then she saw past Swede's ear to where Loan was talking with Ron. The sun was about to set--it happened fast at this time of year--and the air had cooled. The two were against the shadow side of the house. It struck Mama Thuy as dangerously intimate. Ron was leaning toward Loan, his right hand braced on the stucco above her head, his left hand gesturing with a beer. Loan was leaning back at exactly the same angle, smiling up at him. The age-old dance. *Like she wants him to fuck her right there,* Mama Thuy thought.

How to warn her? Ron was a good-looking guy, still. And he could be charming, she remembered--at first.

"Probably could, eventually," Swede was saying in his calm and steady way. "It'd take a while, but I could put in for one. Pearl Harbor. Why not? But what would *you* do? Your folks just got here. And you sure as hell couldn't pack up the bar and take *that.*"

"Crazy, huh? Forget it, then."

But she wouldn't forget, Mama Thuy knew. It was like the day when she first decided to leave Dwayne and Oklahoma and $1.60 an hour. She didn't know quite how, but she was sure that this time, too, she would figure out a way. Swede might not realize it, but this was their only chance to stay together, probably. Leave her family the house--sad as that was. Take what she could get for the bar before the Navy pulled out of Long Beach. Move on.

Mama Thuy took another deep breath. She tried to think it all through, but more firecrackers began snapping behind her. Something fizzed--a rocket? Then Harry Hudson got up from his lawn chair. He came toward her, wavering--the drunkest she had seen him since that first night, a year and a half ago.

"C--." She had seen it before--how he blushed, looked off to the side, wrestled with himself as if his tongue were suddenly as big as a cow's. She knew he couldn't help it. But this time she could feel herself showing impatience, and saw panic in his blue eyes.

"P-phone," Harry Hudson said. "C-can I--" Then he seemed to get stuck for good. He gestured with his hands--dialing, holding a receiver to his ear.

"Local call?" Mama Thuy asked.

Harry Hudson nodded.

"OK, go ahead. In the kitchen."

When she looked their way again, Loan and Ron were gone.

#   #   #   #

Christ, I'm drunk, Harry Hudson thought.

He didn't exactly see double, standing in Mama Thuy's kitchen, but the edges between things were vague. She had taped a list of phone numbers to the wall, and the beautiful script, the European barred sevens, made him imagine her as a pupil in a Saigon classroom, learning penmanship from a French-trained teacher. Wooden desks. Ceiling fans. Her hair long and straight, as in that photo on the beach--but he couldn't help seeing her adult breasts too, under the *ao dai* or the starched white blouse.

The shine of the yellow wall hurt his eyes. Why couldn't somebody turn down that radio? He found a phone book, dialed the Police Department's non-emergency number, afraid they would have one of those voice-mail systems that depended on him to say some particular, unavoidable word, like the name of the city when he called directory assistance. He couldn't cope with that. The sound of a live voice--a woman's--came as a relief. But then it seemed to him to be the voice of Marge Percy, the dispatcher in Garbersville. How had she gotten transferred to L.A.?

"Marge?" Harry Hudson said, amazed. "It's m-me."

Thank God, he thought. He could talk to her this time.

"I said, can I *help* you, sir?" the woman said, and he realized in horror that it wasn't Marge Percy. Of course not.

An image from the worst dream--Sally's bare pink legs below the bathing suit--flashed through his mind. He could lie right down and sleep now, under Mama Thuy's table. Never mind the boom box.

How could he start all over and say what he had called to say? Each word was immensely heavy; it had to be dredged up from sea-bottom mud, hauled dripping to the surface. One by one.

"Excuse me, sir, a banquet?"

"Hhhh--" Harry Hudson licked his lips. "H-heroes. I'm a hero." Saying this so baldly to another human being shocked him back into incoherence. "S-supposed to b--. To b-be there."

"Sir?"

"C-can't come," he managed to say. He wanted to add: *Because it isn't true. Ask Louise. Besides, I already had my banquet today.*

The woman began to sound concerned. "Are you feeling all right, sir? You don't seem--"

Gratefully, Harry Hudson said: "No. N-not good. Sick today. Please tell 'em, OK? Sorry."

"Well, we're sorry too. I don't have anything to do with it--you know, the people who are putting it on. It's another department. But I think ... can I have your name, sir? I'll try to pass the word along in time."

Giving his name, of course, meant dredging up the two heaviest stones of all.

As he hung up, awash in sweat, Harry Hudson felt as if he were falling toward the mattress in Belmont Shore. The slow-motion plunge seemed, strangely, to be a momentum he could use. *Call Deborah,* he thought, *before I crash. Now or never.*

#   #   #   #

Daddy?

# # # #

Pregnant, you think about all kinds of shit. I mean, it slow you down, make you feel so bloated and heavy, and you always be listenin' inside yourself. You understand what I'm sayin'? Listenin' for the baby, for what all your body be doin'. And then you start hearin' your *mind*, too, all them little wheels goin' round. Like I hadn't had time to hear 'em, all those years I was in that fast zone. Ain't *nothin'* nice.

I thought about one time I got busted for prostitution, and the court commissioner was a black man. He looked down at me from where he was sittin'--me in my jail suit, my hair all funky--and said, 'Don't you feel ashamed, young lady, dragging your race down like this?'

And all I wanted to say was 'Fuck you.' You hear me? What did he know about my life, all the shit I been through? What's race got to do with it? All kinds and colors been datin' me. Always have. And *him*, settin' up there like a schoolteacher--he looked like that social studies teacher back in Topeka tried to put the moves on me when I was sixteen years old. Had that same kind of jaw, same little mustache. 'Bet *you* got somethin' goin' on the side too,' I wanted to tell him.

But livin' with Tamika made me think about him again. Shit. All Tamika wanted was for me to baby-sit Ebony while she hung out on the corner with her friends. Didn't hardly lift a finger around the house. And as far as her county check went, I never saw none of it. You listenin' to me? She smokin' that sherm, just like Darnell used to. And that's what be wrong with her baby, I think. Ebony slow. She big enough to crawl now, but she don't. She ain't like them crack babies, all skinny and twitchin' and shit, but she *slow*. I told Tamika, 'This baby ain't normal. You better go see the doctor, have 'em check her out,' but Tamika don't want to. She afraid they'll take Ebony away. I tell her, 'They damn sure *will* take her away, lessen you get her some help.'

That was when she was still talkin' to me, not tryin' to get physical. When she was still callin' me Auntie Kelly instead of all kinds of bitches.

I thought about Harry, too. Because he used to *listen* to me, at least, like that court commissioner wasn't about to. No way. I be talkin' to Harry in my mind sometimes, settin' here in my apartment when Tamika done left Ebony and gone out somewhere, up to no good. I be tellin' him things I couldn't tell Sidney or Eugene, or even my mama. Because he'd never answer me back. Not ol' Harry. He'd just set there with his tie on and smile and nod, like he takin' notes in *his* head.

On the story of my life.

Because I'll tell you straight out: I *am* ashamed.

I'm angry as fuck, too, don't get me wrong. Better not *any* man so much as look at me sideways right now. But I'm ashamed like I never was before.

What I be tellin' Harry is, *Look at Tamika and then look at me. What's the difference?*

Oh, I tell *her* there's a difference, all right. You better believe it. I get on her *ass* about leavin' that baby.

'I'm only sixteen,' she say. 'Can't I have any fun anymore?'

And I say, 'You done *had* your fun. Now Ebony need you. *You* the mama'--soundin' just like *my* mama when I hear myself. And maybe I was just as much a knothead as Tamika, when I was sixteen. Should've stayed in school, like my mama said, grab-ass teacher or no.

'But I didn't get knocked up,' I tell her. 'I got my G.E.D., girl. I had that work ethic. Got *two* jobs, Frito Lay and that nursin' home.'

'Ain't no jobs like that here, Auntie Kelly,' she say.

'They's nursin'-home jobs, I know that for a fact.'

But they don't pay shit, and she ain't got the trainin' anyway, and she roll her eyes and look at me ... it remind me of somethin' Harry said once. He asked me how some folks can be so street-smart and so damn helpless at the same time. *Those* people, Harry said. Bein' careful he didn't say *you* people, and piss me off. Ol' Harry tickled me sometimes. But I know what he mean. Put Tamika out on the street--hell, put her ass in jail--and she survive OK. Don't ask me how. But make her go job-lookin', fill out applications and shit, and she don't know *what* to do.

At least I had hope at her age. You understand what I'm sayin'? Tamika ain't got any hope. How come?

She start cryin', and say, 'Just one mistake, Auntie Kelly. How come just one mistake and my life's fucked up forever?'

And I tell her, 'You made more mistakes than just one, girl,' which is the same thing I tell Harry, in my mind. But still, it seem harder here these days than it was in Topeka, for kids like her. It's like that night Little Sidney come in after he held up that bar, with Harry's blood on him. He knew he'd fucked up, same as I did. Whether he admitted it or not. Wasn't *nothin'* nice. But what was he supposed to do?

249

One night, though, my patience run out. Tamika be smokin' that sherm, and she brought some old dude in to turn a trick. Right in front of her own baby, even if Ebony sleepin'. I sent *him* packin', you hear me? And I told Tamika, 'From now on, you live in my house, you abide by my rules'---right *straight* out of my mama's mouth.

And Tamika went off on me. Like I say, she grown now. And that sherm make peoples so strong, you can't believe. I couldn't walk much better than Miss Crenshaw anymore, my ankles was so swoled up. Shit. All I could do was just defend myself, keep her from hittin' my stomach.

And all the time she callin' me bitches and sayin', 'You think you're better'n me? You ain't got high? You ain't never turned tricks?'

And I say, 'Shit, yes, I'm better'n you.' Soundin' just like that court commissioner now, while she kickin' and scratchin' and tryin' to yank out ever last bit of my hair.

Well, she left, finally. Praise the Lord.

And left me with Ebony again. Left me all scabby and bruised up and thinkin', *If I'm better than her, how come none of it show? We both got babies, both on the county, and neither one got a man that can help us out. We sisters under the skin,* I tell Harry--because it's him I'm talkin' to again, in my mind.

Ain't that reason to be ashamed?

That's when I decide I better *call* Harry. Now or never.

Junior, he stayin' up with his homies in Lynwood again, so Harry ain't gonna see him, even if he done figured out who Junior is. Which I kind of doubt now. Because if Harry did, seems to me, there'd have been a whole lot more heat after Junior way back then, you know what I mean? Eugene, he workin' on some kind of hustle to get money to go back to Kansas, fight in court for *his* kids. I don't hardly see him no more. And Sidney--well, what he don't know won't hurt him.

I *know* this Sidney's baby. I tell myself this ever day.

When it get born--if it *is* Sidney's--that's when I'll call my mama. The way she feel about white peoples, she won't be too happy about any blue-eyed grandbabies neither. But any other kind of grandbaby--it'd be her heart, I know. I been thinkin' like her so much these days, I can feel it. You hear me? It *past* time. We two done been apart long enough.

But it *could* be Harry's. There's always that chance. He got a right to know, don't you think? That's only fair. And I got a right to ask him for assistance, long as I'm broke, got no car anymore and got Ebony to feed too.

#   #   #   #

Deborah had been thinking about Harry lately, for an odd reason. Some groups in Oregon, including the breakaway faction of her church, had begun campaigning for a state initiative measure to deny "special preferences" to homosexuals. Petitions were being circulated in Garbersville. Deborah refused to sign. People asked her why, and she couldn't say. It had something to do with her embarrassment over the spectacle she had made of herself at Sally's funeral. The spirit of God had filled her then--she wouldn't ever deny that--but she had also been half-crazed with grief, she saw now. Her true self was a slenderer vessel; the spirit properly ran though her in a smooth, steady stream, like the voices of her choir, not in violent splashes. She hadn't joined that faction after all. She had stayed in the old Faith Tabernacle with the Owsleys. What homosexuals did--*whatever* they did--appalled her to think about, but she also couldn't stop thinking of the faces of her sixth-graders, especially the boys. That was the age. Puberty. Nowadays, the state education office in Salem sent out a lot of information. Teachers were advised to watch for kids who might be emerging as gay or lesbian, counsel them if necessary, keep them from being hazed. And she thought she could see the signs, with one or two in every class. Boys and girls whose eyes expressed more than the usual pre-teen shyness or bewilderment. The ballot measure, she felt, however well-intentioned, would only do them harm. Stigmatize them. *Her* kids. The state office was right, no matter what the words in Leviticus said. But who could she say this to? Nobody she knew, outside the school. So she found herself talking to Harry, in her mind.

He would agree, Deborah was sure. *Don't they have enough to do?* he would ask. *Why can't they just leave people alone?* Part of it was Harry's sluggishness, his passivity, which used to frustrate and irritate her so. No way he would ever find the energy to do something public-spirited. But he saw clearly enough that the energetic folks who did most of the good in society also did most of the harm. *They think Jesus told them to be assholes?*

He drove the money-changers out of the Temple, she would have said.

So? What's that got to do with it?

And he might have quoted something by that long-gone columnist for the Logger--Vance Foster--he admired so much. A wild man, an old Sixties radical, as unlike Harry himself as could be. The quotation would badly

251

overstate the case, but it would make her think. And pray. This surely was an issue to be prayed over, and when Harry called her out of the blue, late one Saturday night, she thought for a moment that it might be an answer.

A hope that faded almost as soon as she heard his wet, clotted voice. He had been drinking.

"D-don't hang up. I gotta t--" He made an ugly sound. "Talk to you."

"Now?" Deborah said. Meaning not just *Now, after three-plus years?* but *Now, when it's late and I'm tired and about to turn in?* Even on weekends, she usually followed a school-day schedule: up before six, in bed by nine. She had stayed up this late only so she could listen to part of the Fauré Requiem on a CD player she had borrowed from the church, turned down low so as not to wake Kevin. She wished she could get the choir to tackle something like this--so serene and otherworldly--but its simplicity, she knew, was deceptive. She lacked the musical training to bring it off; she was no more than an enthusiastic amateur. Should she go back to school? That might be possible, summers, she had been thinking just before Harry called--a new thought, and a surprising one. It wouldn't be easy, but nothing truly stood in her way.

"T-talk to Kevin, too," Harry was saying.

"What? I'm not going to wake a three-year-old child for--"

"*Listen.*"

And something--the liquor in his voice or the darkness outside the farmhouse--triggered a memory: of driving back from choir practice in the rain. They had nearly hit a logging truck. She had upbraided Harry, and he had ... done nothing, exactly, but the air in the car had grown cold and dense as iron. *He's going to hit me,* she had thought, and although he hadn't, the memory made her flinch as if he had. She had never felt that kind of fear with Lloyd--but Harry was bigger, after all.

Fate should have made you a gentleman's wife.

"L-let me come back," Harry was saying now.

"What?"

"I was w--" The ugly sound again, grating on her spine. "W-wrong. All wrong. How many t--" She waited ten seconds. "--times you want me to say it?"

Harry wanted to come back? The idea had taken this long to sink in, and now that it had, Deborah realized that she didn't want him to. It made her ... not afraid, but uncomfortable, somehow, to be talking to him at night, even on the phone. It reminded her of how lonely the house was. It brought the darkness inside; it made *her* feel alone, and she had thought she'd gotten over that by now. She had never wanted Harry back, she realized. She had thought she had, for a while, but she hadn't.

Forgive me, she prayed.

"You said I should t--" Twenty seconds. She could see him clearly in her mind: turning his face sideways, licking his lips. "--take more of a r--" Five seconds. "B-be with Kevin more."

"You can have *visitation,* Harry," she said. "Have I ever said you couldn't? Have I ever put any obstacles in your way? It was you who ran off, remember?"

The music stopped. Deborah would have to play it again tomorrow. In the silence she could hear the tapping of a pine bough on the window of the laundry room out back, the creak of the floor as she shifted her feet. Was Harry sulking? She hadn't always been sure that his stuttering wasn't partly an act; he could use silence so well.

"It's good you want to *discuss* it, anyway," she said. "I can't fault you for that. But good Lord, Harry--now? I don't know what to say."

"Sssssss--" he said, exactly like a teakettle hissing. "I'm s-sorry about the w--" Twenty seconds. "W-way I got pissed off about sss--" Ten seconds. "S-sex." Ten more, as if saying this had shocked *him.* "W-wasn't you. It was me. I'm just n-no good. N-never was.... But you didn't c--"

Didn't what? Deborah remembered how much she hated the way Harry made her wait, whether what he was trying to say was important or not. Especially, as now, when the sentence she was trying to keep straight in her mind wasn't the one he ended up finishing.

"Y-you were always g-good to me."

"What *about* sex?" she asked, genuinely puzzled.

"--"

"Harry?"

"I'll c-come right up there, honey. Soon as I can get things ... together down here. It'll be d-different. I promise. If Brent'll hire me again--"

"Are you *insane?*" Even then, Deborah noticed that her voice had no hysterical pitch to it. It was low and calm. Her head was still ringing faintly, like a tuning fork, with new knowledge: Harry was behind her now. He had been part of her life and now he wasn't. That simple. She carried the phone over to an easy chair and sat down, leaned her neck against the nubbled upholstery, closed her eyes. She thought she could hear Kevin's soft breathing behind the wall. "Brent Owsley's *hired* new people, Harry, way back. I don't know if.... You shouldn't give up the job you have now, just...." She braced herself against the chair. "I don't *want* you back, Harry. That's the truth."

"--"

"I'm sorry, Harry, but I think it's best for me to look ahead now. You too. Don't you?"

"--"

She wished he could help her out now, a little at least, but it didn't matter. Harry had been a mistake. Not a bad person--not really--but a mistake. She should have known it the day she first saw his apartment and exclaimed, *You poor man.* The life he had been leading then wasn't something she could save him from, she saw now; it was his real life.

"S-sally," he was saying. "I didn't.... I *loved* her. I didn't..."

"I know, Harry." She could give him that. The anger was gone, now that she was free of him, now that she could see him growing smaller and smaller as he receded into the past. She could feel some compassion now; she didn't have to force it. *Thank God.* Was this how prayers were answered-- behind a person's back, after hope seemed lost? "I know you loved her. It was as hard for you as it's been for me. We'll never get over it, not really."

She heard a whisper of a sound--Kevin turning over in bed.

"--"

Deborah wondered if that nice boss of Harry's, Mr. Holcomb, was still around and could advise him. Harry *needed* help of some kind. Another new thought came to her: the stream of advisories from the state office included information about learning disabilities and mental illness. Attention deficit, dyslexia, hyperactivity, depression, bipolar disorder. Things nobody had known about when she was a kid. Things maybe nobody'd *had* until scientists named them. Even now, she hadn't often thought about mental illness in terms of adults. Some people were crazy, of course. Insane. But grown-ups whose lives were simply grey and bitter and confused--all they needed, she had always thought, was Jesus Christ. He would heal them. She had told Harry *that* often enough. But maybe he needed something else first, to prepare him. "Have you thought of seeing anyone?" she would have asked. "Professionally, I mean. They have these pills now. I'm not saying they'd be right for *you*, but you could see...." But Harry had hung up. Even then, tired as Deborah was--emotionally exhausted, in fact--she thought of calling him back.

#   #   #   #

The last phone call of the day jerked Harry Hudson out of sodden sleep. As with the first call, he knew it had to be from Deborah. Reconsidering. Giving him another chance after all. If only he could pick up the receiver in time. He flung himself across the mattress and knocked over an empty beer can, which rolled wobbly, dented, across the floorboards. He listened as the rattle of aluminum on wood receded in the darkness, and had a second or two to regret that Deborah was saving him. He needed to be saved, he knew that; it had been terrible when she wouldn't take him back--*Are you insane?*--but he had to admit it had been a little bit of a relief, too.

Instead, the voice he heard was Kelly's.

"You woke, Harry?" she said. "Good. Well, set down and grab hold of something, you understand what I'm sayin'? Because I got a story to tell *you*."

#   #   #   #

Shit, I should've called him a long time ago. Harry don't know *nothin'* about Junior, it seem like. He come right over the next mornin' and give me money, brought some of that take-out Chinese food like we used to eat. That fried rice and spareribs ain't much to my taste now that I'm pregnant--too greasy. But it's the thought that counts, you hear me?

Harry say he glad to see me again, and he sound like he mean it, too-- though he look like he done seen a ghost. Maybe that's how bein' a daddy affect some mens. I dunno. I *told* him it probably Sidney's baby, but he don't hardly seem to listen to that.

What can I say? Harry *serious* about it, right from the get-go.

When he saw I had Ebony to take care of too, he went back out to Sav-On and got me diapers and formula. Damn near bought out the store. That shit *expensive*, you hear me? But Harry ain't trippin' about money like he used to. He *different*. I can't quite put my finger on how or why. It ain't Junior--I know that now. And it ain't just that he got hisself shot and move kind of stiff, you know, on account of his shoulder. He *act* different. Harry all the time fussin' over me now, askin' if I'm OK. He notice ever bruise on me, ever place Tamika done got me with her fingernails. I tried to put makeup on 'em, but it ain't *nothin'* nice.

'You want me to take a blood test?' he says. Stutterin' *real* bad. Worse than he used to.

255

'Don't even go there,' I tell him.

Harry look kind of puzzled.

'I told you. I'm pretty sure it Sidney's baby. And even if it ain't, it gonna have to *be* Sidney's baby, you hear what I'm sayin'? No point in findin' out shit you wish you never knew in the first place.'

'But--' He can't hardly get the words out. 'If it's mine--' And he shakes his head, like he can't even believe what he's hearin' himself sayin'. 'Maybe we ought to ... I don't know. Get married or something.'

'I done already got *one* husband,' I tell him, 'and two would be just about enough to put me in the crazy house. No thanks.'

'I mean--'

'You want to do somethin' useful? Go take one of them AIDS tests,' I tell him, and he look like he seen that ghost all over again. Shit, I was just jokin'. Messin' with his mind a little. I went and took me that test when I first found out I was pregnant, and it turned out negative. Thank you, Jesus. All them years on the stroll, and I was still OK. Harry be about the last man I'd worry about that way, you understand what I'm sayin'? But you sure wouldn't know it, to look at his face.

#　#　#　#

On Monday, Joe Zuniga stopped him on his way through the newsroom. "They aren't happy, you missed that banquet."

"I was s-sick," Harry Hudson said.

"But couldn't you have let 'em know ahead of time? That's just good manners, man. I was there. They said you flat didn't show."

"I d-did," Harry Hudson protested. "I called."

"Yeah?"

"Yeah." He tried to remember what he had said Saturday night to the woman whose voice sounded like Marge Percy's. She had promised to pass the word along, but maybe she was humoring him. He had stuttered so badly, maybe she had written him off as crazy or drunk.

"Must not've got the message, then," Zuniga said. "It pissed off the honchos here, too. Springer. The Man in the Blue Suit, even." That was what everyone called the publisher, a well-tailored man-about-town who rarely appeared in the newsroom. Zuniga's flat, pitted Aztec face gave no sign of which way his own sympathies lay. "They liked the idea of all that good PR with the cops, I guess."

"D-does it m--" Harry Hudson licked his lips. "Mmm--" *Matter?* he wanted to say. He marveled that anyone could still care about such things. *They'll mail me the damn plaque.*

But then he saw Castle sitting with Springer in the managing editor's glass cubicle, and both gestured to him.

It was like that interview with Springer a year and a half ago, when he'd had Deborah's letter in his shirt pocket. Again he saw things as if through a dirty window. The two men's lips moved--they were saying pretty much what Zuniga had said--but he understood them without quite hearing the words. Harry Hudson was back in the blur. The gap between him and them--normal people for whom PR counted, managerial types who felt fully qualified to call him in and lecture him on "appropriate behavior"--was too wide to cross. And Springer and Castle seemed to sense this, too, the longer he stood there slack-mouthed without answering. He wasn't normal anymore, if he ever had been. Springer's forearms, he noticed, were as hairy as ever. A barber had shaved a perfectly clean line down the side of Castle's neck. The rubber bands on the desk were gone, though. How come?

"Appropriate behavior"? *My God,* Harry Hudson thought. Didn't they know he was a murderer?

# # # #

The blur.

That's how he had always thought of it, after he had somehow passed through it into a calmer, more forgetful mood. But whenever he was in it, he realized all over again that things weren't blurred at all. They were clear. The truth was simple--just impossible for him to face at any other time.

He had no right to live.

Maybe he'd never had that right, Harry Hudson thought now, even as a kid, weak and useless and twisted as he was. But surely he had forfeited it the moment he shot the old man in Vietnam. His life should have ended right then, on that road through the rubber trees. He had known this clearly enough, riding that chopper to Cam Ranh Bay as the green, bomb-pocked land slid by below the open door and the hot wind rippled his fatigues, wondering why he didn't jump. He *should* have jumped, he thought. Then he wouldn't have had to drag himself on through the fifteen years in Garbersville. He wouldn't have met Deborah and screwed up her life; he wouldn't have had a chance to kill Sally. He had known the truth again, even more clearly, weeping beside his little girl's body on the wet concrete, picking that bottle of Jack Daniels out from under the chaise lounge. *You should die.* And not in some noble, sacrificial way, as he had let Sydney Carton's voice trick him into believing. But just to rid the world of his presence.

Twice he'd known the truth. *Twice.* Wasn't that enough?

But no, he had gone on living, dragging his trail of misery behind him. And for what? So he could kill Kelly, the woman in Long Beach he'd liked best, and kill a baby even more innocent than Sally, if that was possible--a baby not even born yet.

#   #   #   #

He had remembered the good-looking Latino guy at the Low Fox. But how had he managed to forget the black man who had beckoned to him, patterns of light from the screen--Harry Hudson's own mother's light-- flickering over his hands and face?

#   #   #   #

She fucked the world, he thought of Kelly. *She could have gotten it from anybody.*

And he tried to tell himself: *What are the odds I could have gotten it, just those couple of times?*

But he knew it was his fault. Knew it in a way that had nothing to do with logic. He had gotten away with murder before, and now, at last, his punishment had come.

Only why couldn't it have been just *his* punishment? Why did Kelly and the baby have to suffer too?

#   #   #   #

Harry look into the crib where I got Ebony sleepin', the crib I done got for *my* baby. Ebony kind of light-complected, in spite of her name, and maybe he think she look like our baby gonna be, if it *is* ours. I know it ain't, but

Harry be trippin', and it kind of spook *me* out, the way he stand there leanin' over that crib, lookin' and not sayin' a word. Like if he look long enough and hard enough, it gonna *be* our baby. When Ebony wake up, he let her grab hold of his finger, the way babies do, and he hum to her. Harry don't stutter when he hum. He say people who stutter don't do it when they sing, neither. I ask him, *Why don't you sing all the time? Then you'd be all right.* But just to think of Harry singin' all the time made me smile.

# # # #

When Kelly's stepdaughter's baby slept, her eyelids seemed glued shut; she seemed to sleep with all her might. Kelly had told him the baby was "slow," but when she awoke, she cried and sucked her bottle with the same fierce energy. When Harry Hudson put his finger down to where she lay in the amber light from the window shade, she grasped it. Squeezed it in her fist. Could viruses swarm in the blood of a child just like her, strong enough to destroy so much life? He couldn't imagine such a thing. But he had seen the pearly skin over Sally's wet shoulder blades without any life in it, and that had been impossible, too.

# # # #

How could he *ever* have forgotten that? Yet he must have.

# # # #

Mid-May the baby be due, the doctor say. Here it only startin' to be April, but I feel so swoled up and heavy now, it tire me out to have to take care of Ebony. Too bad Miss Crenshaw still in no shape to help out. How *she* did it--all them kids she had--I don't even *want* to know.

Last time I called Sidney out in Chino, he say Tamika been bad-mouthin' me, sayin' I stole Ebony from her. Shit. She can *have* the baby, if she get off that sherm and have a decent place to live in. But she ain't livin' here. I told Sidney this. 'I ain't lettin' that bitch in this house again. Not after the way she went off on me.' You understand what I'm sayin'?

I ask Sidney: 'What about her mama? You all still stay in touch, I know that,' I tell him. His old girlfriend, name Jean, she live in Cypress. Ebony be her grandbaby more than mine. How come *she* ain't steppin' in?

Or the rest of my no-good sister-in-laws. Even Linda. 'I don't care if she like pussy more than cock,' I tell Sidney. 'She had two kids of her own, you hear me? She can feed a baby, wipe her behind, just like anyone else.'

#   #   #   #

What the blur did was bring forgotten things back, mix one time of his life with another. No time separated the moment outside Phuoc Vinh from the moment by the swimming pool or from the moment he lived in now. The truth was timeless. Everything else--every one of the stories he had made up for himself during the intervals in between--was exposed as blatant and pitiful self-deception. The cautious contentment he had begun to feel last summer, even the seemingly final indifference and fear he had felt since being shot-- both were lies.

He was evil. He, Harry Hudson, from Beattie, Oregon. Only an evil person could forget what he had forgotten. *That* was the truth, and the only truth. No wonder his stuttering had proven to be incurable; the squirrel-sized spirit he had imagined tangling his vocal cords was nothing less than his entire self, seamlessly corrupt. No wonder the messengers had come to him, one after another, and cried out in anger or alarm: his father, Sergeant Riker, Ron, Louise. What was wrong with him couldn't be hidden.

Simple.

Now, once more, he slept fourteen hours a day, but he was never quite asleep. At night, the truth seemed to be an anvil, as broad as the earth, millions of tons of steel hanging a yard above his head, poised to crush. *What's it waiting for?* In the daytime, he was never quite awake. The truth then was a dense and sticky medium through which he pushed his way slowly, like a diver in a weighted suit. It was the smoke from latrine fires at Cam Ranh Bay and the heat pressing him down on the chaise lounge's white plastic webbing in Garbersville and the haze of burning rice fields south of Red Fork, all at once. In the newsroom, the words on his terminal screen flickered, changed shape and meaning. His mistakes multiplied. In his car, he could hear bullets flying past him again: *zip, zip, zip.*

He told the watcher (for he had a watcher again): *Go ahead. See if I
care.*

And the watcher seemed to say: *What about your kid?*

It took him a second to realize that the kid being referred to was
Kevin.

See? You forget. Over and over, you forget.

But I can't stand any more, Harry Hudson said.

So?

#　#　#　#

Eugene drop by. He been workin' construction up in Vernon, Cudahy,
some place like that. Got hisself a car--an '83 Chevy. Piece of shit, he says, but
it ought to get him back to Kansas for that court date. I tell him if he don't
leave till after the baby come, I might not have to ask Harry for a ride.

'Sooner than that, probably,' he say, and shake his head. 'Sorry, Sis, but
I didn't set that date. Or the date the baby's comin', neither.'

'Shit,' I tell him, 'it's like I count on Harry more'n anybody in my own
family. If you can call them Crenshaws family.'

Eugene look at me. 'Go get him, girl, if you want.'

'You ain't *nothin'* nice,' I tell him.

And he grin. 'Naw, we evil, both of us, that's a fact. But ain't a whole
lot of good Sidney gonna be doin' you locked up, or even after.'

I stop that kind of talk right away, you hear me? After what he done to
get Sidney locked up--and Sidney keepin' quiet about it--my brother ain't got no
right to diss him. You understand what I'm sayin'? Still, he had a point.

#　#　#　#

Harry Hudson began fading in and out, as he had during the weeks of
his tryout.

One day, in the apartment in Belmont Shore, he took a bath and came
to himself an hour later, with the water nearly drained out of the tub and cold
around his heels and buttocks. He saw his body as if for the first time in years.
The dent from the bullet in his shoulder was purple. His spread-out belly had
a scattering of long, dark hairs on it that never used to be there. Other tufts
of this hair had grown on his elbows. His toenails were yellow and rotten with

261

fungus. His penis was wizened. He shuddered at the ugliness of it--this body that he had dared to lay against Kelly's, and had wanted to lay against Mama Thuy's, too.

# # # #

Finally, Linda say she'll take Ebony before my time come. Thank you, Jesus. Pin a ooh-wee button on me. She say Tamika back stayin' with her old boyfriend, the one knocked her up in the first place. He just be usin' her, I believe. Livin' off what she make on the street. Linda think so too. Course, Linda don't think *any* man up to much good. She say Miss Crenshaw been gettin' phone calls from Junior lately, and that the last thing *she* need. Only way he able to hang out up there in Lynwood so long is if he sellin' drugs or shit. And Miss Crenshaw know this. She ain't stupid. At least she gettin' back on her feet, finally. I can tell Sidney that.

# # # #

He should tell Kelly the truth. Any decent person would.

If he told her, she would hate him. Despise him. That was OK, Harry Hudson tried to convince himself; he deserved that. But if he told her, it also seemed to him, their deaths would pass over the line from possible to certain. Whereas if he kept his mouth shut, maybe nothing would happen. *That* was possible, too.

# # # #

What's *wrong* with Harry, anyway? Used to be, we made each other laugh. Shit. Not no more. He Mister Moody *all* the time.

# # # #

Even in the blur, he could face the truth, like the sun, only in flashes that made him wince and left dead spots in his vision. Now, when he visited Kelly's neighborhood, Harry Hudson told himself that he had no reason to fear the homeless, even if they jumped him and took every dollar he had. They had a better right to it. Didn't they? And of course he wasn't attacked.

The coins and bills he held out were taken by hands that, though crusted with filth, had a human warmth. The voices startled him, they sounded so sane and ordinary. "God bless," many of these derelict men and women said. Was it Deborah's God they believed in? He should ask. He should stop and talk to them, hear their stories as penance for having forgotten--*wrong!*--that they were his brothers and sisters. But he couldn't. He flinched away almost as quickly as before, hurried on.

Why?

Kelly, in her apartment, pulled up her blue maternity blouse, pulled out the elastic waistband of her jeans. "See? My belly button done turned inside out."

It had, he saw--just as Deborah's had done.

"Feel, Harry. There. He startin' to kick now. No, *there.*"

But Deborah had looked strained and awkward in pregnancy. Kelly had lost none of her beauty, he thought, though every detail of it had changed and the marks of her fight with Tamika hadn't healed yet. Her face was rounder than before, her breasts full, her ankles swollen; her stomach, when he touched it, was warm and as taut as a drum, its brown against the blue even richer, grained and luminous like the wood of a violin. If he rapped it, he thought, it would give off a musical sound. But the rapping instead came silently from within. From the baby.

"Or *she* be," Kelly went on. "Lots of women say they *know* which one it gonna be. But I can't tell for the life of me. What do you think, Harry?"

It doesn't matter much, he should answer, very gently. *It probably won't live very long.* But the thought of what that would do to her face made him hold his pale hand against her belly instead, absorbing the blows. Feet, elbows-- who could tell that either? Like Ebony, this child had a powerful charge of life in it. That charge passed right up through his fingertips. It astonished Harry Hudson for a moment, how much tenderness he felt for them both, how weak and happy this made him.

He had been wrong, back in the summer: It *had* been love, all along.

And for the length of that moment Harry Hudson believed that his fears were groundless. The baby and Kelly would live.

Just because Louise has it, he told the watcher, *and I had a chance to get it, it doesn't mean....*

Oh, yeah?

Yeah.

Wouldn't you like to think so? the watcher said, and then, savagely: *Wouldn't you have liked to think so when you let Sally die? Christ. What does it take to make you remember?*

Then the moment was over, the dead spot faded away. Harry Hudson saw only the truth again, and understood that love was another emotion he had no right to feel anymore.

Wrong again.

"It's s-soft," he said aloud.

"What?"

"Your skin." He took his hand away. For it seemed to him that, too late, he knew what women's skin was for, after all. Hadn't Nancy Ishida taught him that long ago? It was for love. Which meant it was forbidden now, no matter how much he wished he could lay his cheek against it, close his eyes.

"Been rubbin' that cocoa butter on ever day," Kelly said. "No way *I'm* gettin' them stretch marks, you hear me?"

Then she heard a sound from the the bedroom. She excused herself and went in for Ebony. Harry Hudson stayed put. This apartment had no more furniture than the motel in North Long Beach, but it was clean. The painting of the big-eyed African child hung on a wall now. The nursing texts stood alone on a shelf. Kelly had bought or made ruffled curtains for the kitchen window. Such a long, hard way she would have had to go, he thought, even if he hadn't ... but what a long way she'd already come, from PCH and Gardenia! *I could have lived with this woman,* he found himself thinking as she came back with the baby. *Don't we look like a family?*

Kelly held Ebony in the crook of her left arm, against her shoulder. Her left hand held an empty bottle. With her right hand she patted the baby's back. Burping it. Gestures he knew in the fiber of his own nerves and muscles, from having held Sally.

"Heard this tomcat yowlin' out there in the alley," Kelly said. "Wantin' to climb up here and *belong* to us, I reckon."

"T-that would be nice," Harry Hudson said.

Her indignation startled him. "You crazy? You think I'd let some cat get near this baby?"

"Why not?"

"Shit, you probably think it some old wives' tale, but them cats, they be smotherin' the *life* out of a baby if you let 'em. Don't laugh, Harry. They suck the breath right out they mouths. You understand what I'm sayin'? That one out there--big ol' *grey* tomcat--he got the ardacity to do it, too. I seen it in his eyes."

At first Harry Hudson did want to smile, but then he pitied Kelly in a way he never had before. What chance had she ever had, really? Set loose in the world with only scraps of an education. Believing such stuff. Once he had imagined he could save her, but now the watcher set him straight: *You bought her, man. You're no different from any Southern cracker slipping across the tracks for a little fun, any slaveowner swaggering down to the cabins. Admit it. You're an asshole.* And the secret he was keeping from her--struggling like her baby to be born--was the proof. Harry Hudson flushed and broke out all over in sweat. Suddenly the pressure to tell her, inflating in his chest, was unbearable. "I'm s-sorry," he began.

But somebody was knocking on the front door, and Kelly had gone to open it. In came a skinny woman with orange-dyed hair, three diamond studs in her ear, a denim shirt with the tail out and skin-tight, patterned pants. "Might as well pick her up now," she said. "Happened to be passin' though. Hey, there, pookie-pookie," she said to Ebony, and to Kelly again: "She look fat. You been feedin' her good, I can tell. But it's time you got a *rest.*"

"Ain't no hurry," Kelly said. She held Ebony tighter. "You all can take your time, let me know a little in *advance,* you hear what I'm sayin'? We doin' all right."

"Shit, girl, we here now. No point in makin' another trip."

"Who all's *we?*" Kelly's eyes widened. "Oh, no. *You* ain't comin' in this house."

The skinny woman, Harry Hudson guessed, had to be Linda, the sister-in-law, but Kelly was looking past her, out the doorway to the landing where a second, younger woman had just climbed the stairs.

"She this baby's mama," Linda said. "She got a right--"

"Got *no* right. You see what she done to me?"

"Give Ebony here," said the other woman--only a teen-ager, Harry Hudson saw, but tall and full-figured, wearing a white T-shirt with ragged black lettering: NO FEAR. Beaded braids swung from her head.

"You get *out* this house, bitch," Kelly said. "Let Linda take her."

"She *mine.*"

It was the violence Kelly had always told him about, that he hadn't believed in and had never seen in her before. She and Tamika screamed at each other. Their fists clenched and the cords stood out on their necks. They screamed louder and louder, as if from a lifetime of desperately trying to be heard over other voices. The baby cried. Linda at first tried to make peace, but then she yelled at Kelly and Tamika both. They seemed to ignore Harry Hudson, though maybe his presence, and the baby's, was what kept them from actually hitting one another. Tamika's face glowered just as her father's had in the prison yard in Chino. *I paid for this girl's gym shorts once,* Harry Hudson thought. He swallowed an aspirin. He felt a sticky sensation--tears drying on his cheeks. He hadn't known he had been weeping. When the two women had left, taking Ebony with them, and Kelly had sat down heavily, her breath rasping and her eyes red, the pressure to tell her was gone. Had he really been about to do it?

# # # #

Damn. That's the *last* thing I need, eight months gone. Gettin' all worked up like that. Got me one of them migraines afterwards, had to lie down, and even then I could feel this poundin', you know what I mean? All over me. My blood pressure was *real* high. The doctor done warned me about that. Ain't good for the baby, he say. *Or* me. And it's all behind that bitch Tamika. *She* the one.

At least Ebony gonna be stayin' with Linda, so even if Tamika come in and out, that child'll study get some care.

But Harry. Shit. It freaked him out, seein' what life be like in the 'hood for real. You hear me? I thought he was gonna shit--like he thought Tamika was Junior comin' up them stairs, comin' to shoot him again.

# # # #

Things at the paper were the way they used to be. Harry Hudson had no idea what other people were thinking anymore, and he was transparent to them. Every mistake he made now was noticed. Three times in a single April week, guessing what a reporter meant to say instead of calling to confirm it, he introduced error into a story, forcing the Clarion to print a retraction. Each time it had seemed a logical guess, but it went awry with a dreamlike certainty. Jose Arballo, 9, wasn't the son of Raul and Lourdes Arballo--all three photographed feeding ducks at a pond in El Dorado Park--but the son of Raul's brother, Raymundo. The MicroTec Co., involved in a lawsuit over land subsidence in the oil fields, wasn't the same firm as Micro Tech, whose warehouse had burned in a naphtha pipeline explosion on the West Side last year. Alice DeMaestri, a former licensed vocational nurse at Harbor-UCLA Medical Center, had allegedly strangled four old women and gone on shopping sprees with their credit cards, but deep in the story it said authorities were charging her in only three slayings. Harry Hudson's headline said four.

Wrong.

Finally, Eddie Castle called him in.

"How can I put it?" That faint flush was under Castle's skin again. "There's an allowable rate of screwing up on this desk. Nobody's perfect. Certainly not me. But I think you have to agree you've exceeded that rate. You follow?"

Harry Hudson nodded.

"Consider yourself on probation from now on. Tighten it up or else."

By now it shouldn't have astounded him to hear another, younger person talk to him this way. But, as always, it did.

#   #   #   #

Worse, he couldn't help whining to Holcomb in the cafeteria that night. "He's still pissed about that p--" He licked his lips. "P-police banquet." How could he explain that he had been too embarrassed to go? *They carried me out, in those strong arms. They saved my life. How could they have known?*

Holcomb didn't look at all well these days: heavier, blotchier, his chest pains more frequent. Fleetingly, Harry Hudson realized that the older man might need as much sympathy as he did right now. But he couldn't stop.

Holcomb grunted, shoved pieces of meat loaf around his plate in a pool of brown gravy. "What is it with you and Eddie?" he said. "Why can't you get along? Christ, he's just a kid. He ain't that tough. Shouldn't take a whole lot of smarts to stay out of his way."

"B-but you t-told me," Harry Hudson said. *To watch out. He'd be managing editor by thirty-five.*

"Be that as it may. I'm tellin' you *now*, Eddie Castle's gonna be the last of your problems once those Singletary people buy this paper."

Harry Hudson stared.

"This isn't official now, mind, so keep it under your hat. But it's a done deal, *I* think. The Man in the Blue Suit got tired of makin' ten percent a year off us when his daddy made twenty, twenty-five. And he doesn't care that much *where* his money comes from--the paper or something else. Unlike his daddy. That's what happens to a lot of these newspaper families. They lose interest. So the chains move in. Trouble is, the Clarion ain't all that much of a prize anymore. Long Beach has stopped growin', and there's no room outside to expand. They missed their chance to go into Orange County when the Register was just a pissant Nazi rag. No more. So who'd want to buy 'em out? Only some outfit like the Singletarys, that'll come in and gut the place, squeeze costs down to the bone. You think your Guild contract's gonna stand up then? Shit, no. They got lawyers up the wazoo. They'll say it's an asset sale or some such. I've seen this happen before, in Missouri. There's laws they can use to ... hell, they can renegotiate *everything*."

Harry Hudson still stared.

"Like I say, I've seen it before. Paper Judy worked on just before we got married. Old Singletary himself came in just once, made a speech. He had armed guards with him, I shit you not. Said he didn't want any *sabotage*, people destroyin' the presses, takin' home pencils and paper clips and such. Said it like he was jokin'. With a smile. He told everybody not to worry, he wasn't layin' off a single soul. Lied through his fuckin' teeth. He got rid of a third of the staff the first week, gave the rest a pay cut. Sent his new executive editor in to do the dirty work. The people who stayed, like Judy--they got handed a sheet of paper with their new salary on it and told to sign it right then, or else. Anybody who hesitated, asked any questions, they were gone. *Bam.* You don't believe it? You don't think this could happen in the U.S. of A. in the last gasp of the twentieth century? Shit, yes, it can."

Holcomb gulped meat loaf, dripped gravy on his shirt.

"*Real* reason he had the armed guards ... guy told me this saw it himself. This was down in Texas, when Singletary was just startin' out. He wasn't so good at lyin' then. He stood up there in the newsroom and made his speech and *told* 'em they were gettin' canned, and they threw beer bottles at him. Bounced a couple longnecks off his head. After that he didn't take any chances."

For the first time, Holcomb grinned a little.

"I wish they had video cameras then, and somebody had shot it, like this Rodney King thing. That would've been something to see. Throwin' beer bottles. He ran like a spooked rabbit, the guy told me. There's people in this business would pay a pretty penny to have a copy of *that*."

#   #   #   #

The AIDS clinic.

Thanks to the Clarion's classifieds, he knew where it was. It was a pink, square building on Fourth Street, next to the Art Theatre (showing the "Rocky Horror Picture Show") and across from a Unocal station. Foggy morning light shone through the window on a few people scattered among rows of folding chairs, filling out forms on clipboards. Medical history, sexual history. Harry Hudson felt conspicuous; they were mostly street people. The woman in front of him had a grimed, deeply wrinkled, sunburned neck. He thought of the hooker at the Chieu Hoi, whom he hadn't seen in months--the one to whom Mama Thuy had given a kitten. Then she half-turned, and he saw that it was somebody else. But the name came back to him. Susie. Suzy?

One by one, as their names were called, they filed down an echoing corridor and had their blood drawn. The nurse said he would get the results by mail in a week.

Surely that was all. Harry Hudson, cotton taped to his arm, was eager to leave. But there was one more step, the nurse said. They were going to be counseled. He was directed to a cubicle, and sitting there behind a desk, looking subdued and businesslike, with her freckles and her frizzy dishwater hair, was Judy Holcomb.

"Harry?" she said--a flicker of surprise.

"_-"

"I thought it was just ... somebody with the same name. Would you rather talk to another of our--"

Harry Hudson shook his head, wondering if he hadn't heard a rumor that she was volunteering here. "Dddd--" *Doesn't matter now,* he wanted to say.

"You seem so *worried,* Harry. Rick says you always seem to be ... well, not worried, exactly. Like you're always somewhere else, he says. But from your form here ... I can't see much risk, to tell you the truth. You don't use intravenous drugs."

He hadn't mentioned the Low Fox.

"And you certainly needn't worry about *this.* Your being here, anything you say, is totally confidential."

She was kind, as he would have expected Judy to be. Nothing in the world was more important than kindness. But when he didn't deserve it, nothing was harder to stand there and bear.

269

# # # #

'Get one of them answerin' machines for your phone,' I told Harry. 'Just in case.' Ever since Tamika went to the extremities again, I been feelin' funny. Like the baby been stirred up, somehow--like it ain't gonna wait full term. And it *scare* me, bein' alone like this. Maybe Eugene stop by at the right time, or maybe Miss Crenshaw's boyfriend come back soon from Texas, or maybe Linda and them ... but I can't be sure of a ride if it happen all of a sudden. You hear me?

'So hook up that machine,' I tell Harry, 'so even if you ain't home right that very minute, I can leave you a message.'

And he promise me he will.

# # # #

"H-how soon?"

"June, maybe," Holcomb said. "That's when they'll announce it. Then a couple more months to do the deed."

Judy Holcomb made a face over her coffee. True to her word, she had given no sign of seeing Harry Hudson at the clinic.

"God, to think after all those years, the same goons could be *here*," she said. "With their sickening macho shit. And their little pieces of paper. They're like one of those movie slashers--when you kill them, they just won't stay dead."

Harry Hudson felt distanced from such worries. Long before the Singletary chain took over--if indeed it did--the baby would be born. He himself might be showing symptoms. He shouldn't even care that it was tamale night at the cafeteria, or that the tamales still tasted good.

"We're at a weird time in history," Holcomb mused. "First time in a hundred and fifty years there's no alternative to capitalism. None whatsoever. Nobody arguin' on the other side to keep the bastards honest. Most everything the working man ever got, from the eight-hour day on down, came because the Reds were agitatin' for it, and they gave the working man that much to keep the Reds out. Maybe so. But what now? There ain't any more Reds. Good riddance--overseas. But what about here? Only people I see anymore inveighin' against worship of the almighty dollar are the Pope and Pat Buchanan. Ain't that a hell of a note?"

"Rick always wishes he'd been a Red," Judy said. "It's his deepest secret, so don't tell anyone."

Holcomb snorted.

"S-steinbach likes it," Harry Hudson ventured, remembering that column from Hesperia.

"What?"

"T-the almighty dollar."

"What the hell does *he* know?" Holcomb peeled the husk off a fresh tamale; steam rose. "He was a desk man, for Chrissake. Not an economist. He thinks the business end doesn't know what it's doin', layin' people off, but they do. And Singletary knows even better. If it's makin' money you care about, that's their *field*, man. They're pros. Don't tell me any different."

But Steinbach sounded so sure, Harry Hudson thought. When would he ever be able to resist a confident-sounding voice?

"... all ass-backwards," Holcomb was saying. "Used to be liberals and conservatives; you could tell 'em apart. Shit, nowadays the most radical force on the planet is your conservative businessman, and the most hidebound, head-in-the sand defender of the status quo you can find is a labor union. Just tryin' to hang onto a few good-payin' jobs, keep 'em from disappearin' south of the border. No greater vision. How'd that happen?"

"S-spence," Harry Hudson said.

"What?"

"He once said s--" He licked his lips. "Something like that." On a night much like this one. Tamales. The same sense that he would be leaving all this soon.

"What's *he* know about it either?" Holcomb said. "Ol' Spence was a dilettante, workin' here. He didn't need the money."

Then why had Lincoln done it, Harry Hudson thought--taken so much of Steinbach's abuse? It must have meant more to him than that.

"My dinosaur," Judy said proudly.

But when Holcomb had gone to the men's room, she whispered: "I'm worried about him, Harry. He's *got* to slow down. I keep telling him that. But he doesn't know how. And he's afraid if he does, Singletary'll let him go."

# # # #

271

On the last Wednesday of the month, Harry Hudson faded out, and when he faded in again he was at the library, a concrete bunker near City Hall with a garden on top. He was looking for John Ransom's diary. He didn't expect to find a copy there, but in fact found two, with an introduction by Bruce Catton and engravings like those in his old *Battles and Leaders*. So it wasn't as obscure a book as he'd thought, not so exclusively his. This bothered him, somehow.

Sept. 27, 1864

Have prided myself all during the imprisonment on keeping a stiff upper lip while I saw big strong men crying like children; cruelty and privations would never make me cry-- always so mad, but now it is different and weaken a little sometimes all to myself....

Oct. 3

The (Savannah) hospital is crowded now with sick; about thirty die now each day. Men who walked away from Andersonville, and come to get treatment, are too far gone to rally.... Battese here, will stay all day and go back tonight. Says he is going with marines to be exchanged.... Says he will come to see me after I get home to Michigan.

Oct. 28

Am feeling splendid, and legs most straight. Getting fat fast....

Camp Lawton, Millen, Ga., Nov. 2

All who want to can take the oath of allegiance to the Confederacy and be released; am happy to say that out of all here, but two or three has done so, and they are men who are a detriment to any army.....

I was a detriment to any army, Harry Hudson thought.

He read on: Confederate officers at Camp Lawton, discovering Ransom to be literate, plied him with a good meal and offered him a job helping them write dispatches. Ransom refused.

Nov. 13

And so I am still loyal to the Stars and Stripes and shall have no fears at looking my friends in the face when I do go home.

After all he'd been through, I would have accepted in a minute, Harry Hudson thought.

Soon word came that Ransom and other Union prisoners would be moved by rail to extreme southern Georgia.

Nov. 19

Believe I shall try and escape on the journey, although in no condition to rough it. Am going to engineer this thing to suit myself and have a little fun....

Have edged up to another comrade, and we bunk together.... While he is no great guns, seems quite a sensible chap....

Fun? Harry Hudson thought.

Nov. 20

Had a falling out with my companion ... and am again alone in walking about the prison with my coverlid on my shoulders. Am determined that this covering protects none but thoroughly good and square fellows....

At his reading table, Harry Hudson felt a heat, a heaviness, on his back. He looked up. A bar of sunlight had angled down from one of the high windows. He imagined it to be Ransom--a scarecrow with crippled legs, a ragged blanket; touching him with a buoyant but shrewd gaze, knowing at first glance that he wasn't a good and square fellow.

Nov. 21

Men are very restless and reckless, uncertainty making them so. Try my very best not to have any words or trouble with them, but occasionally get drawn into it, as I did this morning. Came out solid however. Is pretty well understood that I can take care of myself....

The heat grew more uncomfortable, but Harry Hudson didn't shift his chair. It was part of the punishment. Every word he read shamed him, as he had known it would. Had he ever in his life "come out solid"?

Nov. 22

And now my turn has come (to leave Camp Lawton).... *A nice cool day with sun shining brightly--a fit one for an adventure and am just the boy to have one...*

In the woods near Doctortown Station, No. 5, Ga., Nov. 23

At about three o'clock this a.m., ... I went through the open door like a flash and rolled down a high embankment. Almost broke my neck, but not quite. Guard fired a shot at me.... Expected the cars to stop, but they did not..... Am happy and hungry and considerably bruised.... Sun is now up.... All nature smiles--why should not I?--and I do.... Not over sixty rods from where I lay is a path evidently travelled more or less by negroes going from one plantation to another. My hope of food lays by that road.... LATER: Have broken off spruce boughs and made a soft bed.... Hope the pesky alligators will let me alone.... Thus closes my first day of freedom and it is grand. Only hope they will be many, though I can hardly hope to escape to our lines, not being in a condition to travel.

Nov. 24

Found an old negro fixing up a dilapidated post and rail fence.... Seemed scared at the apparition that appeared to him.... Was very timid and afraid, but finally said he would divide his dinner as soon as it should be sent to him.... Boy set down the pail, and the old darkey told him to scamper off home--which he did. Then we had dinner of rice, cold yams and fried bacon. It was a glorious repast.... Is very fearful of helping me as his master is a strong Secesh., and he says would whip him within an inch of his life....

The slave passed Ransom on to the next plantation, where he was hidden in one of the cabins.

Nov. 25

The negro man (who lived in the cabin) *goes early in the morning, together with all the male darky population, to work on fortifications at Fort McAllister. Says the whole country is wild at the news of approaching Yankee army.... Children perfectly awe struck at the sight of a Yankee. Negroes very kind but afraid. Criminal to assist me....*

Harry Hudson, sweating now, was surprised to feel something else besides shame. Something he hadn't noticed when he read this section before. Ransom had put these people in danger for "fun," for an "adventure," not a serious escape attempt. Could that be justified? He tried to imagine himself in Ransom's place, roaming the pinewoods--he pictured the woods around Beattie--in an exhilaration of freedom. Who could be blamed for that? It was a miracle that the man, after Andersonville, could enjoy such high spirits again. And Ransom had risked his own life, jumping off that train. Still, it disturbed Harry Hudson a little.

The slaves, as it turned out, couldn't keep Ransom long. He wandered for a few days, got hungry and finally chanced going to a white woman's house.

She pretended to believe his story, then sent out a black child to bring back a posse with guns and bloodhounds.

Nov. 30

The woman began to cry. Told her I understood the whole thing and she need not make a scene over it.... (Ransom accepted a shirt from her.) *And so my adventure has ended and have enjoyed it hugely....* (Back in Doctortown, he was held for the next prisoner train.) *LATER--Have seen a Savannah paper which says Sherman and his hosts are marching toward that city....*

Blackshear, Ga., Dec. 2

On the train were two more Yanks named David and Eli S. Buck, who are Michigan men. They were runaways who were out in the woods nearly three months and were in sight of our gunboats when recaptured. .. We have mutually agreed to get away the first chance.....

In the woods, Dec. 13

How does that sound for a location to date from? ... When near Savannah, not more than a mile this side, David Buck jumped off the cars and rolled down the bank. I jumped next and Eli Buck came right after me.... My cap was knocked off by a bullet.... Eli Buck was also singed by a bullet..... Train did not stop, and we ran until tired out. Knew that we were within a line of forts that encircle Savannah ... only twenty rods or so apart.... It was very dark.... All at once Dave stopped and whispered to us to keep still, which you may be sure we did. Had come within ten feet of a person who was going directly in the opposite direction.... Dave Buck says, "Who comes there?" A negro woman says "it's me." and he walked up close to her and asked where she was going. She says: "Oh! I knows you; you are Yankees and has jumped off de cars." ... Owned up that such was the case. She said we were her friends, and would not tell of us. Also said that not twenty rods ahead there was a rebel picket, and we were going right into them. I think if I ever wanted to kiss a woman, it was that poor, black, negro wench....

Black and *negro, and a wench besides,* Harry Hudson thought. Had Ransom, in his young life, ever kissed anyone? Nowhere in the diary had he mentioned it, one way or the other.

The woman took them to a safe place in the woods. Her brother came with food. Plans were made to sneak the Yankees through the line of forts.

Were very smart colored people, knowing more than the ordinary run of their race.

It was the only false note in the diary--if indeed it *was* false and not just Harry Hudson's inflamed imagination. But it seemed to him that, even to Ransom, the slaves weren't real human beings. Not quite. And that explained why the Civil War hadn't been won then, or even today. Because Ransom was the best that white America had to offer--truly a man in a thousand. And even he carried a germ of Harry Hudson's own disease.

The slaves would lead Ransom and the Bucks through a dilapidated fort that the Confederates had yet to repair. The Yankees would be passed on to the isolated farm of a Union sympathizer. There they would experience a Huck Finn-like idyll--camping out in a canebrake, swimming and hunting wild pig--until Sherman's army arrived. But Harry Hudson didn't want to read any more. He sighed and closed the book, stood up, got the sun off his back at last. He flexed his stiffening shoulder. The wall clock said he was late for work.

# # # #

Around midafternoon he was scrolling through a long, dull story about solid-waste recycling when he noticed that Springer had come out of his office to join a group clustered around the TV set. Holcomb was there too, and Castle. There was a stillness that had nothing to do with the shrilling of phones and the hisses and yelps of Zuniga's police scanner. Then, abruptly, it ended. The editors broke apart, shaking their heads; they seemed to wander, dazed, without any clear idea of what to do next. Each seemed to carry a fragment of their conversation with him: "Simi Valley ... *all* counts ... can you fuckin' believe it?"

"What's g-going on?" Harry Hudson asked Pierce.

"It's the King verdict. The cops walk."

Harry Hudson couldn't understand. After the videotape, how could that happen?

"That's cop country up there," Pierce said. "Half the LAPD *lives* in Simi, I heard."

"The revenge of the Sick 'n' Tireds," Holcomb said, sitting down at his terminal with a grunt. "Only thing now is, what happens? Nothing? Or do we get Watts all over again?"

# # # #

Florence and Normandie.

Rioting. Fires.

A white truck driver--a Long Beach guy?--pulled right out of his cab by an angry mob and stomped.

Korean grocery stores in flames. Appliance stores looted. People of all races running through the streets with VCRs, packs of diapers, food.

Firefighters getting shot at. Few or no police to be seen. Chief Gates off at a fund-raiser--in Brentwood? Check.

All South Central a war zone as darkness came on.

It was the biggest story of the year--of their whole working lives, maybe-- but for those in the Clarion's newsroom it was frustratingly out of reach, still fifteen or twenty miles away, an amorphous blob they could imagine spreading over the map taped to the side of Springer's office. Reporters and photographers left, came back, dashed out again, but how much would they be able to get before deadline? Nobody knew. Meanwhile, every story previously budgeted for Thursday was killed or shoved to the back pages. Making room for the blob, which so far consisted of a few names, hardly any verifiable facts and no *reasons*, except for the verdict itself. Most of what the editors did know came from the despised TV. Newscasters in helicopters, babbling. Paid to keep talking even when they had nothing to say. But TV, at least, showed what the blob looked like: buildings and cars ablaze, towers of smoke, crowds eddying away from the outmanned LAPD, then surging back. As Harry Hudson watched, the scene--somewhere in Compton--tilted on edge and a woman newscaster squealed; they were being shot at from the ground.

"Holy shit," Pierce said. "Let's go look."

"What?"

"Up on the roof."

Pierce left, and Ana Chavez followed him. After a few minutes, Harry Hudson went too. He rode the elevator up past the executive suite, to a shack like the cupola on a railroad caboose. It opened out onto the flat, tarred roof. Pierce and Ana were leaning against the parapet. No skyscrapers blocked the view to the north. Beyond the roofs and trees and telephone poles, the night sky glowed with more than the city lights. It was orange and wavered with shadows that seemed to stretch for miles. Ana, bare-armed, shivered and leaned closer to Pierce. The sea breeze at their backs was chilly, but another, stronger wind seemed to blow against their faces, carrying--maybe they only imagined it--heat, particles of ash, faint sirens and shots. The air truly was filled with bullets now, Harry Hudson thought. *Zip, zip, zip.* They heard helicopters for sure--news crews or the sheriff's patrol? It was like Vietnam--not the terror of that moment in the rubber trees, but flares and rockets seen from base camp: the danger too diffuse to be frightening. He felt fresh and alert for the first time in weeks. Pierce and Ana, too, looked happy. They went back to the newsroom reluctantly.

The TV was still on. The blob was still spreading--not confined to one area, like Watts, but throwing off embers like a brushfire in the mountains during Santa Ana season, igniting new blazes everywhere.

Parker Center, the police headquarters in downtown L.A., under siege. A line of cops holding off the mob.

Chunks of pavement shattering the ground-floor windows at the Times.

Harry Hudson was thinking about Ransom's diary again when the phone call came:

"Harry? You gotta get over here *now.*"

"You all r-right? You know what's h--" He licked his lips. "H-happening out there?"

"Shit, yes, I know. Shit jumpin' off *everwhere.* That's why I need you, Harry. Come quick."

"But, jeez, we're b-busy here. I mean--"

"Please, Harry, *now.* You promised."

Christ. The baby, he thought.

Harry Hudson looked up. Springer and Castle were at the TV; Holcomb, head down, was hammering at his terminal. None of them would let him go if he asked, but it might just be possible to sneak out with nobody noticing, like McLachlan in the old days heading across Pine Avenue for a "bracer." With luck, he could get back in an hour. Forty-five minutes. He could say he been in the men's room, doubled over with diarrhea--for they *would* notice. Of course they would.

# # # #

I knew Harry'd be pissed when I told him it wasn't the baby comin'. Not yet. But I had no choice, you hear me? Eugene called and said he was stuck out at Rosecrans and Atlantic--Lynwood or Compton, he wasn't sure. On the border there. Said his car done burned up. Today was his last day of workin' construction before he went back to Kansas, and he said he stopped off to have a cold one and shoot a little pool. Then shit started happenin', and he stayed inside this bar for a while, and when he stuck his head out, this dry-cleanin' place where he'd parked was on fire, and the fire had done spread to his car and the two cars either side of it. The whole front wall come down on 'em, he said. Wasn't nothin' he could do. Couldn't save nothin' in it. His '83 Chevy. He was callin' from a phone booth--lucky he found *that*. Said he had to get the fuck out of there before he got busted or shot by accident. Either one. Said he felt naked, nothin' but glass around him and the fires lightin' him up like a target in a shootin' gallery. I could *hear* shit jumpin' off around him--people yellin', some kind of crash. He said he couldn't talk long. Told me to *hurry*.

'What can *I* do?' I ask him.

'Get me a ride,' he says. 'I don't care who. Get me to a bus station somewhere. What about your mother-in-law? Ain't her boyfriend back from Texas yet?'

And I tell him no.

'Shit,' he say, and then I don't hear him for a moment. I hear more yellin' and what *could* be shots--I can't tell. Then Eugene say, 'You my last chance, sis. If I don't get to Kansas, I be losin' them kids for good. And if I get busted *here*, same thing. LaVonne gonna get 'em.'

'Hold on,' I tell him. 'I'm-a get *somebody*.... Wait a minute. How this person gonna find you?'

'Just *get* here,' he say. 'Rosecrans and Atlantic.' Did he say somethin' about Junior just before he hung up? I couldn't tell for sure.

So I called Harry.

And Harry came right away, and now he pissed, like I said. He have to hurry on back to work, he say. Don't I know this is a hell of a big story--they be firin' his ass if he desert his post, all that?

'A big story to *you*,' I tell him, 'but Eugene ain't no story. He my brother.'

What can I say?

Harry don't say much of anything then. He just look at me there, in my bathrobe, with my hair a mess and my stomach stickin' out--just look at me with his tie all crooked and his face gone wild. He pissed, but at least he don't seem to be scared, like he was when Tamika come in. Thank the good Lord for that.

Then he gone.

\#   \#   \#   \#

The northbound 710 ran at ground level, or dipped below it, so he couldn't see more than the orange glow. Traffic, strangely, seemed almost normal. Holcomb had told him once that the L.A. freeways had been built to let people drive through or over South Central and never see it, never have any contact with that world. Maybe so. People were driving into the smoke and driving out of it as if parts of the city--its blood vessels or nerves--could go on functioning while the rest died. But this surely couldn't last. The smoke grew thicker--not what he could see of it in the darkness but the smell: a throat-scraping stink. Harry Hudson drove as fast as he could. It wasn't far to the Rosecrans interchange: a point about halfway, east and west, between the Rabbit Hutch and the Low Fox. Eight or ten miles. Like most L.A. distances: nothing to drive, an interminable walk. He remembered Kelly trudging with her broken shoe along Long Beach Boulevard. Then he thought of Rosecrans again. He had never found out whether this street he kept ending up on was named after the narrow victor at Stones River, the loser at Chickamauga. So when the off-ramp came, he nearly missed it. He had to swerve right across two lanes in front of a honking semi, then up and back left over the freeway.

He could glimpse fires now, north *and* south. Then the road fell back to ground level, and he wasn't ready, just as he hadn't been ready when it was time to rise off that bar stool. Going up on the roof of the Clarion had awakened him. He was angry at Kelly still, and feverish to get back to the office. So it wasn't how he had thought it would be, driving into the zone where the bullets were. He had thought he would welcome it. Those people had a right to kill him, just as the homeless had a right to his money. Why shouldn't they punish him for the sins of his ancestors? Nothing that happened to *their* ancestors had been fair, either, he had told himself. The bullets would blow all the evil out of his skull. *Zip, zip.* Blow it away at last. Good riddance. But instead, starting west on Rosecrans, Harry Hudson was afraid. He remembered the kid with the gun and the hammer-blow of the bullet knocking him off the stool and the pulsing of his blood, like the chopper blades overhead: *whup, whup, whup.* The fear in his body was stronger than anything his mind said. He glanced around. Nothing told him what to do. Trees. On the left a produce stand. Whaley Middle School. On the right a neatly lettered sign: CITIZENS OF ZION

MISSIONARY BAPTIST CHURCH. Up ahead, Shell and Unocal stations, a 7-Eleven, Chief Auto Parts, a couple of taco stands. An ordinary intersection. No crowds or fires here. Maybe Eugene had called from blocks away.

The signal was green, but sirens halted him. A police car went screaming north on Atlantic, flashing red and blue lights, and a fire truck came after it--a small one, paramedics. Then a wall of smoke rolled across in the opposite direction. Harry Hudson blinked and coughed. Something *was* burning up to the north. He squinted to see it, and then saw two men, black men, moving closer to him on the right, past the Shell pumps. One was bent over, half-carrying, half-dragging a big black suitcase. The other waved at Harry Hudson, then pulled his arm down, as if uncertain. Harry Hudson wasn't sure he had seen Eugene often enough for them to recognize each other. He hesitated too. Then the man grinned--he had Kelly's grin, the little gap between the front teeth. Harry Hudson waved back, pulled to the curb and cracked the passenger-side door. Eugene was shouting over his shoulder at the second man: "*Leave* that motherfucker. How many times I gotta say it?" •

"Shit no, I ain't. He got room in there."

It wasn't a suitcase at all, Harry Hudson saw, but a TV set. A Sony. Maybe a 27-incher.

"I haven't got time," he said.

"Open up that back there. Just slide her in."

"Fool. *Leave* it," Eugene said.

But it seemed to Harry Hudson that they would get out quickest by doing what the other man wanted. He flicked the latch for the hatchback, and the two raised it and slid the TV into the rear. He could feel the little car settle. Then Eugene climbed into the front and the other man behind him. Harry Hudson looked up and down Atlantic--flames visible half a mile off, but no more police cars--and swung a U back east toward the freeway.

"Anybody stop us and see that, they think we been lootin'," Eugene said.

"Shit, *ever*body lootin'." The breath in Harry Hudson's ear smelled sweetly of whiskey. "This the *up*risin', man. Ain't lootin'. We just gettin' back our own."

"You a fool, Junior," Eugene repeated. "What you gonna do with that thing? You ain't even got a place to put it."

"It's worth big money, man."

"Not now, it ain't."

"W-where to?" Harry Hudson asked. "Long Beach?"

To his surprise, Eugene didn't answer at first. He frowned and finally said: "I dunno. Wish I could get clear *out* this city, find me a bus station. Then I could get to Kansas."

"*I* ain't goin' to Kansas, man."

"I don't give a fuck *what* you do, Junior," Eugene said. "Just cause I happen to run into you down here, that don't mean I got to change my plans to suit you. And that Long Beach bus station just ain't gonna do it. There be cops watchin' *ever*body go out. "

Harry Hudson wondered if that was true, but the next moment, as he turned up onto the southbound 710, the thought was wiped out of his head. The face of the second man--Junior, Kelly's stepson--slid to the dead center of the rear-view mirror, shaded by a blue baseball cap. Then it slid away again as Harry Hudson straightened the wheel, but it had been Sidney's face in the prison yard and the face of the kid who had shot him. Both. And the kid he had nearly run over outside the Chieu Hoi. *The same one.* And Tamika. Harry Hudson realized that he had known this in some sense ever since the two men got in. He just hadn't wanted to admit it.

Now, just as surely as if words had been spoken, Junior *knew* he knew.

"Riverside," Eugene said suddenly. "How 'bout that way?"

They were already at the 91 interchange, and a ramp labeled Riverside led up to the right, over the freeway and to the east. Harry Hudson had no thoughts in that instant, only panic. He turned.

"Where you goin' *now?*" Junior yelled.

"R-riverside," Harry Hudson said. "Like the man said."

"Turn around."

"... don't have to go *that* far," Eugene was saying. "Just--"

"Turn *around.*"

Harry Hudson kept driving. All he could think was: *If I go fast enough, they won't dare.*

"He the one," Junior said.

"What you talkin' 'bout now?"

"The honky I done capped. At that bar. The one been messin' around with Mama all this time."

"That so?" Eugene said.

There was silence. Harry Hudson imagined that he heard the roaring of the fires behind them, though maybe it was just a roaring in his ears. The tires thumped on joints in the concrete. The TV in the rear rattled. He glanced sideways and saw the yellowish whites of Eugene's eyes looking back at him curiously. Then he glanced at the mirror again. Junior was pulling something out of his jacket pocket. *The same gun.*

"Look at that!" he squealed--just like the lady newscaster.

"What?"

"Him," he told Eugene.

"Junior, put that fuckin' piece away," Eugene said, but he seemed to share none of Harry Hudson's urgency.

"Shit, no. He--"

"Do it. Please. That thing make me nervous," Eugene said, but Little Sidney only lowered the muzzle slightly. Eugene didn't try to push him further. He turned back to Harry Hudson: "That true? You been messin' with my sister?"

They were crossing the 605 now, into Cerritos. No fires here, just ordinary street lights, a darkness of houses and trees.

"N-not anymore," Harry Hudson said. Every part of his insides squirmed. It wasn't just the gun--it was the gun in Junior's hand, which had pulled the trigger before and would do it again, he knew. Any moment.

"You was just ... dippin' it once in a while, then." Eugene sounded almost amused. "When the fancy took you. Am I right?"

Harry Hudson felt faint. "N-no." He licked his lips. He saw Eugene's face lean closer. *Didn't he know Kelly was a hooker? Of course he did. Then--* "W-we were f--. Friends."

"Friends," Eugene said.

"Bull*shit.* Behind my daddy's back, and him in Chino."

"No, she say that too. Say this white man--what's your name? Harry? Say ol' Harry here been helpin' her out, with money and all. Tell me to watch out for him, see he don't get hurt."

"Fuck the money. He--"

Eugene grinned. "Shit, Junior, I didn't know better, I'd say you was jealous on account of *you.* Not your daddy."

"What?"

"You ain't so slick. She catch you lookin' at her sometimes."

Junior's face in the mirror twisted with rage, just as it had that day on Anaheim Street, and Harry Hudson's fear surged again. "I should cap you too, motherfuck."

Eugene's grin didn't fade. He raised his hands. "Like I said, if I didn't know better. Shit, man, you paranoid."

"*Your* fault my daddy in there anyway."

For some reason, this bothered Eugene more than the threat, Harry Hudson saw. The man sobered all of a sudden; the passing lights showed him looking older: his balding temple, the razor bumps on his jaw.

"You right about that, Junior. I don't like your daddy all that much-- you know that. But I owe him one."

"You got *that* right."

"But it ain't gonna help your daddy none to waste ol' Harry here. You see what I'm sayin'? You might as well just sit back and enjoy the ride."

"Where we *goin'?*"

"Riverside. Right, Harry?"

Harry Hudson nodded.

"Right. We goin' to Riverside. Then ol' Harry here can bring you back, if you want. Meantime ... you got a bottle there, don't you, Junior? You ain't drunk *all* of it, have you? Then pass it on up here."

It was Jack Daniels. A nearly full pint. Eugene tilted it back and took a deep swallow, his adam's apple pumping, then offered it to Harry Hudson, who waved it away. Eugene shrugged and passed the bottle back to Junior.

"Just as well, you drivin' and all," he said.

Passing through Fullerton, the freeway narrowed from four lanes to two; then other freeways--the 5, the 57--branched off. There were construction projects: piles of fill, concrete barriers, temporary lanes laid diagonally to the original ones, a confusion of lines and reflective dots and broken asphalt. The TV set banged. It helped Harry Hudson a little, having to concentrate on the road so hard. The bottle was handed back and forth a couple of times; the gun lay quietly now in Junior's lap.

That smell. It was the smell of the bars in Cam Ranh Bay and Garbersville and Red Fork, but mostly it was the smell of that other bottle of Jack Daniels, standing open and half empty under the chaise lounge. Harry Hudson had never drunk that brand since. It was like a dream, having Jack Daniels, of all the brands of whiskey there were, turn up in Junior's jacket pocket now--and this helped him too, strangely enough. Maybe he would wake up any moment and be back in the newroom, writing headlines. KING VERDICT SPARKS RIOTS. Maybe....

"Shit, *we* could drive," Junior said.

Eugene, drinking, said nothing.

"We don't *need* this honky, no way. Just his ride."

"What you suggestin'?" Eugene seemed amused again. "Drop the man off and go on to Riverside--just us? You *know* Riverside?" No answer. "I didn't think so. How 'bout you, Harry? You been there?"

Harry Hudson nodded--a lie: he had never gone past the turnoff for Chino.

"Fuck the *bus*," Junior said. His voice had thickened. "Keep the motherfuckin' *car*. Go to Kansas in that."

Eugene's grin widened. "How 'bout *you*, then? I thought you didn't--"

"Shit, I never been to Kansas. It ain't so cold there now, is it? Get out from under them warrants here. No tellin' what gonna happen now."

"No offense to you, Harry," Eugene said, "but I don't think this little ol' car be *sturdy* enough."

Absurdly, Harry Hudson felt insulted, but it seemed to make some sense to Junior. There was another silence as they passed the exit for the 55 and entered the Santa Ana River canyon. The freeway had widened again: four white lanes poured toward their headlights. The traffic had thinned.

Did I make a mistake, leaving the city? Anything could happen out here.

Anaheim Hills. Yorba Linda. The river, behind a dark line of cottonwoods, was to the left. On either side mountains closed in, and though Harry Hudson knew they were covered only with brush and grass they looked, at night, as thickly forested as the mountains of Oregon. The road zigzagged; he speeded up, trying to stay in contact with the few red taillights that remained. Trying to outrun the thought he knew was on the edge of Junior's mind.

"Hey, you don't gotta prove nothin'," Eugene said.

"*Fuck* lettin' him go," Junior said at the same instant.

"What?"

"He the one saw me. The one I capped. Ain't no way he gonna let *us* go."

"How 'bout that, Harry?" Eugene said. He paused for an answer, still grinning. "Young man's got a point here. Hate to say it, but he do."

"--"

"You gonna drop us off. Then you run straight to the phone and get Junior here busted 'fore that bus ever pulls out. Or have 'em waitin' for us the next stop down the line. That's what you thinkin'. Right, Junior?"

"Yeah," Junior said.

"I know you gonna deny it, man. Say you never had no such thought in your head. But how can he believe you? Right? Same dude he put a bullet into. No way *I* could trust you, if it was me."

"--"

"Man, I been *tryin'* to save your ass, like Kelly want me to. But this makin' it hard. C'mon, Harry. How you gonna solve Junior's problem here?"

There was no way, Harry Hudson saw. Junior was right. The facts were plain. If he somehow survived this, he would call the police for sure. How could he have driven the last ten miles or so with his guard down, with such an idiotic feeling of safety? *Wrong.* He should have been planning, calculating, every second. Now it was too late. He was really going to die now, and he knew *where:* in the narrowest, darkest part of the canyon, with a mountain rising straight up on the right and an empty golf course on the left, across the river. Green River. That was the name of the exit. He would die there, at Green River. Junior would kill him. His life would end, *bang.* Harry Hudson struggled in vain to put his mind to it, to think as clearly and seriously as the situation deserved, but his body didn't have to be told: He was pouring sweat, drowning in a funk that blended with the smell of the whiskey and Eugene's and Junior's sweat, as if the three of them had only one body.

The freeway tilted to the left at Green River, toward the river, as it made a sweeping curve. He remembered this from driving Kelly to the prison. To see Junior's dad. If he could get that far, he would yank the wheel and swerve across the westbound lanes and into the gorge. A long drop onto jagged rocks. High water, too, at this time of year. Take the bastards with him. With any luck, the car would blow up.

"I g-got a kid," he told Eugene. "Up in Oregon. Three years old. I gotta get b--" He licked his lips. Soon. "Y-you have kids, don't you? That's w-why you're g--. Going back."

Surprisingly, this sobered Eugene for a second time. *He's drunk,* Harry Hudson noted in some distant part of his mind. *They both are.* Their moods, like McLachlan's--like Harry Hudson's own when he was drinking--could change in a flash.

"You makin' me cry, man," Junior said.

Harry Hudson drove on. Then, all at once, they were there, at the Green River curve, and he still wasn't ready to die, after preparing all his life. *Why not?* He tightened his grip on the wheel, measured the oncoming lights, saw clearly where he ought to turn, but he had forgotten the concrete barrier *between* the eastbound and westbound lanes; he would have to smash through that first, and then--if the car held together--the wood-and-metal railing on the far shoulder. But the concrete looked strong. He wouldn't hit it head-on but at a shallow angle, showering sparks, and bounce off. That still might do the job, but it left doubt in his mind, as did Eugene's grave face, so much like Kelly's at that moment. It seemed, even as Harry Hudson jerked the wheel, that the idea was a stupid one, that somebody else had dreamed it up, and he jerked the wheel back. The Nissan fishtailed. A passing van shrieked.

Junior yelled. The tires, the TV set, the gun thudding on the floor--Harry Hudson heard them all.

"Mother*fuck!* Watch where you goin'! Now look what you done."

Eugene had managed to hold onto the whiskey. Junior scrambled for the gun, came up with it.

And now the chance was gone--their chance and his too, Harry Hudson thought. Because they had left the canyon, passed the Chino turnoff and the dam, and come out onto a plateau where the city of Corona lit up a long slope to the right. A golden glitter. Miles of streets. It felt safer here, but the smell of the Jack Daniels nauseated him. What did it mean that he was still alive? He shouldn't be.

Eugene was talking to him--had been, for a while.

"...take *care* of them kids," he was saying. "Keisha, now, she six, and how do I know somethin' ain't been jumpin' off already with that ... that *pervert* LaVonne with? You *know* he a pervert, don't you, Harry? Kelly done told you, I know. So that's why I gotta get back there. And Little Gene, he four. What happened to *him* last year I wouldn't wish on nobody."

"What you *sayin'* now?" Junior protested.

"Harry here be right, too, Junior."

"Bull*shit.*"

"Thank you for remindin' me, Harry, what's the *main* thing I gotta do. Shit, I know I'm drunk. That whiskey done tore me up. Always do.... But Little Gene, now. You know what happened? He done fell out of a second-story window when LaVonne, that *bitch,* wasn't watchin' him." Eugene looked so angry for a moment that Harry Hudson wondered if this mood, too, would break. But it didn't. "Little feller landed on his head. Been cement, it'd killed him, probably. But it was just dirt. Still, that boy ain't been right since. He need all kinds of special care that he ain't been gettin', probably. And I wasn't *there.*" Eugene slammed his fist on the dash. "That's what's worst about it."

"What about *me*, man?" Junior wailed, and for the first time Harry Hudson felt something for him besides fear.

"You ain't a daddy yet," Eugene said. "You don't understand what it's like. But Harry do."

"They gonna bust *you*, showin' up in that court," Junior said. "If you *do* get back to Kansas. You'll see."

Eugene didn't reply. He just shook his head and took a last pull from the bottle. He was a fugitive of some kind, Harry Hudson knew. He was a heavy drinker, maybe an alcoholic, an ex-con who had no regular job, and he had lost custody once. What chance did he have of getting those children back and--even if he did--of taking better care of them than his ex-wife had? Not much. Yet he was risking his freedom to try. Harry Hudson thought about this as his sweat cooled and they crossed Interstate 15. Turnoffs to San Diego and Barstow. The stockyard smell of Norco seeped into the car, adding to his nausea; he reached slowly into his shirt pocket and swallowed a pill. "Aspirin," he told Eugene. It was part of the strangeness of life after death that he felt so close to this man now. They still had one body. And Eugene, it was clear, had some of Kelly's goodness in him.

"You're doing the r-right thing," Harry Hudson said.

"I know, but it be hard sometimes," Eugene said, setting the bottle on the floor. "Main thing, Junior, is I don't want you goin' to no penitentiary. I *been* there. Seven years. And it ain't *nothin'* nice. I know you think you tough shit, and maybe so. You'd survive. OK. But just survivin' don't mean that much, once you get back out." The moisture on his face still shone. "That's one thing I *can* do for your daddy--keep your ass out of there. And my sis, too. She care 'bout you, fool, even if you don't."

"But he turnin' us *in*, lessen I.... You said so yourself."

"We just gonna have to trust ol' Harry here. If he Kelly's *friend*, like he say, he don't want nothin' to happen to her stepson, right? Even if you *did* cap him one time by mistake."

"He ain't gonna--"

"And Harry, you gonna have to trust *us*, just a little bit, and not go runnin' for some phone. OK?"

Harry Hudson nodded.

They had passed the Riverside city limits some time back, an amusement park, a shopping center, but nothing that looked like a downtown. The air had grown murky. Was it smog, or were fires burning here, too? They went ten more miles, and Harry Hudson began to be afraid again. How long would the mood hold?

The headlights picked out some naked, rocky hills, tumbleweeds on the shoulder, and he thought: *Christ, we're in the desert already. I must have missed it,* but then the road turned and dipped under a railroad bridge and rose again, and he saw tall buildings to the left and DOWNTOWN signs.

"Take that University Avenue there," Eugene said. "I think that be right."

So he knew after all. Harry Hudson almost giggled out loud, though it scared him all over again to slow down. The protection of noise and speed was gone. They went down the off-ramp, stopped completely, then turned left in the darkness under the freeway. He was clenching his teeth so hard that his jaw ached. On the far side, the smog, smoke, whatever it was, swirled around the courthouses and office blocks, lines of palm trees, glimpses of ornate older buildings: bell towers, tile mosaics. Were those sirens he heard? Eugene told him to turn a block north, then left again. Junior had been quiet too long. What was he doing with the gun now? Harry Hudson couldn't see.

"*There* she be. The Greyhound," Eugene said with satisfaction. It was still a few blocks ahead. "Now, Harry, you gonna have to find yourself a bank here. Guess it don't matter *which* one. They all take them ATM cards, right?"

Harry Hudson looked a question.

"I got *my* fare with me, but Junior here don't. It be a long way to Kansas, and a growin' boy like this need to eat, too."

It was like that night on Long Beach Boulevard when he had gotten money for Kelly. Out in the chilly air, fumbling with the card, watching the Nissan at his back. He withdrew the daily limit: three hundred.

Yes, sirens, out west across the river, maybe. Eugene took the money, riffled it, pursed his lips. "That'll do."

"Fuck. I'm *really* goin' to Kansas? Right now?"

"You'll thank me some day," Eugene said. "Ol' Harry here, too." He handed some of the money--not all of it--to Junior. "This way, Harry payin' your way and all, he be involved too. He be an accessory after the fact, you gettin' away. Am I right?" He looked at Harry Hudson. "Not tryin' to scare you none. I'm just tryin' to ease Junior's mind a little."

Harry Hudson nodded.

"That TV, Junior, gonna have to stay here. Sorry."

The station looked like an old railroad depot that had been upgraded with ornamental concrete block and beams. The inside, though, was dreary. A sallow light emphasized every stain and scuff mark on the off-white walls, and the usual ill-dressed passengers sat or paced, their footsteps echoing. No cops. Maybe they were all too busy right now. Big black slotboards held the schedules. "Barstow, Vegas, St. George, Utah," Eugene said. "Palm Springs, Phoenix. Which you want to try, Junior?"

"Fuck if I know," Junior mumbled. He seemed shrunken in the light, more like a kid than Harry Hudson had ever seen him. He had put the gun away.

"Never been to Palm Springs before," Eugene said. "I come in that other way. So why don't we try it?"

They stood in line, Harry Hudson too.

Junior glanced around uneasily. He heard the sirens too. Eugene, so much like him, it seemed now--slender, graceful build, black leather jacket, fancy tennis shoes--was studying an Army recruiting poster on the wall.

"You in 'Nam, Harry?" he asked. "You *old* enough."

Harry Hudson shook his head. "Hell, I j-just drove a bus. In Cam Ranh Bay."

"You a bus man too, hey? That's cool. Well, Harry, I hope you get it together again. With *your* kid."

Gratitude, the memory of that closeness in the car, kept him standing here beside Eugene, even as his nerves screamed to go. It was true: Kevin had saved him. He had babbled about his son just to win a little time there at Green River, he had thought, but maybe not.

Daddy?

"Good luck," he told Eugene and meant it, shook his hand.

"You too, man," Eugene said, and mouthed silently: *Get the fuck out of here before he change his mind.*

# # # #

The sirens came closer. A police car swept past the alley into which Harry Hudson had turned to unload the TV set--but not before he had wrestled it up against his chest and shoved it into a hedge of oleanders. He bent and lifted the Jack Daniels bottle out of the front of the car and fired it into the night as hard as he could. He heard it smash. Then he started trembling, his legs went weak; he leaned against the door of the car and threw up on the ground beside the right front tire.

# # # #

On the return trip, he stopped for coffee at an all-night McDonald's in Corona and took more aspirin. If any rioting was going on in that city, he didn't notice. He drove past the spot near Green River where the freeway tilted toward the gorge, and it barely registered. His mind had been blasted clean. The car seemed to drive itself; the distance to cover in this direction was nothing--just a few minutes, it seemed, zigzagging west through the canyon toward the orange glow.

He might have taken the 605 back to Long Beach--he couldn't have said *where* he was going--but he let the car pull him on, up to a roadblock the Highway Patrol had set up to divert traffic south on the 710. Barriers of cones and red fusees on the 91 funneled down to two police cars parked in a shallow V across the pavement, flashing their roof lights. When Harry Hudson got to the head of the line, he rolled down his window, left his seat belt buckled and waited. One of the officers walked up to him slowly.

"Sir, where you think *you're* headed this time of night?"

The officer's face, under the crescent shadow of his hat brim, was lean and stringy, sinew and tendon. *Sergeant Riker.* No, too young to be Riker now, but the resemblance comforted Harry Hudson; it was part of the benign trance he found himself in at last. Junior hadn't killed him; what could the cops do, except pick him up in their strong arms again and carry him away? He took out his wallet, handed the officer his Clarion ID and sat relaxed. If he opened his mouth, he knew, he would be lost. He would sound uncertain, or drunk. But for once he was able to wait.

The officer squinted at the laminated card, even shook it twice. Then he walked slowly back to his car and showed it to his partner. Harry Hudson could hear the mutter of their voices mixed with the radio without understanding a word. Then the officer walked to the Nissan, slower than ever, and returned the card, bending so that the shadow covered almost his whole face.

"Wouldn't advise it, sir. Not at all. But it's your funeral."

Dipshit.

Where were they when I needed them? Harry Hudson thought, and then, startled: *They must hate newspaper people.* He smiled and nodded, though, and drove carefully around the roadblock. Ahead of him the freeway was empty. A

291

*free*way--the word finally made sense. Once the police had disappeared behind him, he speeded up to ninety miles an hour, then slowed to ten, then wove back and forth across all four lanes. He sang, hoarsely, his mother's song:

Good night, Irene, good night, Irene,
I'll see you in my dreams....

On either side of the 91, now, but mostly to the north, he could see the fires. Six or eight of them. They had grown bigger, and this time he was facing them, awed. They rose straight up through the dark, windless sky; and though he could hear a roaring again, and sirens and choppers, each pillar of flame seemed to burn in a universe of its own, as privately as his car rolled down the broad, smooth concrete. The words of Deborah's Bible came to him: *A pillar of cloud by day ... a pillar of fire by night.* But these blazes, he thought, weren't beacons to light a people to freedom. There was too much darkness in between them where the refugees could lose their way. L.A. was too big. The city had always taken Harry Hudson, kid from Beattie, beyond awe; it was beyond comprehension how human beings like him could have built it, mile on mile, laid these ribbons of highway, brought water across the desert, drilled for oil, launched ships and space shuttles. Now he thought: *They weren't like me. Or them*--meaning the rioters. They belonged to a different species, the people who built and owned and ran the city; and he, disqualified by weakness, could understand the rage of those left out through no fault of their own. Why not destroy what couldn't ever belong to you? He was on their side, he realized--he had to be, since he had helped Eugene and Junior escape. *Go ahead. Burn it down,* Harry Hudson thought, though he knew it wasn't about to happen, no matter how hard they tried. L.A. was too big, and those who had made a muddle of solving the city's problems would be efficient enough at cracking down.

#   #   #   #

The trance held until the Low Fox--for that, he saw, was where he had been going all along. The air smelled of charcoal and fried rubber, the 7-Eleven at the corner had been broken into, and shadowy people ducked between the cars, but he drove on, undisturbed. Only when he had parked beside the cinderblock cube did he wonder if it was still open.

It was. The smoke he smelled inside was the old tobacco stink. The magazines on the side wall and the dildoes and vibrators and jars of gel in the glass case below the projectionist's booth looked dusty, as if none had been sold since Harry Hudson's last visit. Only one change: Next to a faded MAKE LOVE, NOT WAR poster from the Sixties, with a pretty hippie girl getting it on, somebody had hung an inflatable plastic sex doll up near the ceiling and stuck dildoes in every orifice. The contrast--deliberate, it seemed--was truly obscene. The projectionist was the same bearded black man as before, watching another "M.A.S.H." rerun. Harry Hudson gave him six dollars.

"Seven now, man."

He forked over the extra dollar. The buzzer sounded; the plywood door unlocked. Inside, in the darkness, with the sound track moaning, the uproar on the streets might as well not exist. He let weariness guide him to a seat. The cracked, taped vinyl and the sticky floor felt familiar. Once his head leaned back on the cushion, he didn't think he had the strength to raise it. Was this home, after all? Was there a level *below* the underclass, where people would sit and watch people screw on a movie screen until the building caught fire-- where even the *uprising*, as Junior called it, didn't touch them?

This movie was strange, Harry Hudson noticed even as he dozed off. It had been shot in black and white, apparently by a crew of amateurs, as if the Low Fox had decided it didn't matter *what* ran. A man as gloomy-looking as Walt was seducing high school girls, played by obviously older women with their hair tied back in pigtails. His first victim had become an accomplice. She lured her friends to the man's apartment and cheered him on as he deflowered them, then took them anally. "Yeah! Spread her *out*. Fuck her in the *ass*," she would cry, mugging at the camera so blatantly--all teeth, as if shot through a fisheye lens--that she seemed a teen-ager after all.

Harry Hudson awoke. He must not have slept long. The same film was running, the gloomy man grunting and straining, the girl-woman chanting, "Yeah! Fuck her in the *ass!*" This time he didn't start or slap his pockets. He felt no fear--he, who had once run out of this place in panic, and was now the only white man here on the night L.A. blew up.

No, not the only one. Another man, older, with an ascetic, Scandinavian face, wearing a silvery nylon raincoat, sat two rows down and four seats to the left. Harry Hudson's eyes had adjusted now. He could see the dark men all around with their cocks out, stroking them with a rhythm that seemed to be joined, seat to seat--although he knew it was as private for each man as the heart of each separate fire he had seen.

The shift was over at the Clarion, he thought suddenly. Gone.

He studied the other white man in drowsy fascination. High cheekbones that the light from the screen turned as silver as the raincoat. Black hollows under them. It was a proud, even arrogant face, as if the man had come here on this night, of all nights, to bait the people at the Low Fox, to flaunt his superiority and dare them to do anything about it. Hair short enough to show the planes of the skull, a long jaw, a thin, high-arched nose. W.H. Anderson must have looked like that, Harry Hudson thought, writing his Times editorials about the "Japs" back in the days of green eyeshades and black telephones. Gazing out of the bottoms of his eyes at his typewriter, sneering a little, as he tapped out those cruel sentences. The fantasy took hold of Harry Hudson: Anderson's ghost had come back to gloat over the destruction of South Central as the living man had gloated over the emptying of Little Tokyo in 1942. *Look at this. Don't they deserve it?* Anderson's profile seemed to say. So it surprised Harry Hudson, jolted him sharp awake, when the man turned to reveal his own cock out, his own hand pumping. His face, seen straight on, was as ravaged by loneliness and desire as any man's there. And the man he was looking at was Harry Hudson.

# # # #

When he woke up in Belmont Shore, it was nearly noon, but he woke all at once, rigid with fright. He heard a faint, regular beep: the answering machine. Its red dot of a light was on. Three messages. It must have been beeping all night. He crawled over the floorboards and pressed the replay button.

The first was from Holcomb: "Harry? You there? Where the hell'd you go, anyway? We're up to our--" Then somebody else shouted and Holcomb hung up.

The second, two hours later, was from Castle: "Harry, wherever you are, when you *do* get in, we deserve an explanation. You know how short-handed we are? After what's happened to Rick.... I don't care what the reason is. Just disappearing without a word to anyone. That goes beyond ... beyond the *pale*, as far as I'm concerned."

What happened to Rick? Harry Hudson wondered.

The third was from Kelly, at three in the morning, when he must have been driving back from the Low Fox: "You OK, Harry? Eugene say you picked him up. Said to say thank you. He done called from the bus station in Palm

Springs. Stoppin' over on the way to Kansas." She paused. "He say Junior with him. Little Sidney." Another pause--a longer one. "Ain't *nothin'* nice, I know. But I ain't had nothin' to do with it. So help me God. If you only knew ... but Harry? You still study gotta be *with* me. That baby comin' any day now. For *real.* Harry?"

He went into the bathroom, showered and shaved. His face in the mirror looked no different from before. Again he thought: How could that be?

# # # #

The Chieu Hoi Saloon was closed. Some of the Cambodian shops east on Anaheim Street had been gutted overnight, and a fresh fire spewed black smoke to the north along Atlantic. But there were few people out now, and little traffic on PCH, and he reached Mama Thuy's house easily. Swede had a CB radio, and the family at the kitchen table huddled around it, listening to the same sirens and voices that must be coming over Zuniga's scanner. Thuy's mother came up and pressed his hand in gratitude--for what? Her father sat silently and smoked. "If they try to bust in here, we're ready for 'em," Swede said, but there seemed no real danger. Harry Hudson told Thuy that her bar was untouched. She shook her head. "They think we all Korean, maybe," she said. "Vietnamese, Chinese. All Oriental people look the same. What I ever do to them? Not just black people. Mexicans, too. Everybody go crazy. Why me?" There was no sign of Loan or her boy or the puppy, and Harry Hudson, after a few minutes, grew restless. He wished them good luck and left.

# # # #

"Oh, I don't look for men in bars," Rita said. The Dragon's Tail was open, and she sat on the stool next to Harry Hudson's, reflected in the mirror that Walt had broken last year. She wore tight white pants and a burnt-orange halter. He had bought her a glass of Hennessy cognac for ten dollars--half of which went to the house, she said--and she absently kneaded his bad shoulder. It felt better than he wanted it to feel. Rita's touch, like Margot's, had no kindness in it, but it was a skilled touch. "Not anymore. Not after Walt."

"You s-see him?"

"No way, Harry." She closed her lips over those beautiful teeth. "It'd be too easy. I could have him back like *that* if I wanted. But I don't want. Too much sadness, you know? You know how Walt is."

Harry Hudson nodded. "I j-just s--" He licked his own lips. "Saw Thuy."

"Mom? How she doin'?"

"OK."

"Shit. Mom. All those *old* days. I gotta give her a call," Rita said, but that seemed to be all. They watched the TV. The images on the screen were no different from yesterday's: the parking lot of a Kmart somewhere; people running to and from the store, smashing windows, pushing shopping carts piled high with anything they could grab; cops appearing in the lower right-hand corner; the looters rushing away and to the left like iron filings pulled by a magnet; the cops charging them, less than platoon strength; more people circling in behind, as if the magnet's polarity had reversed. Then the whole scene tilting as the helicopter banked.

Harry Hudson had bought a street edition of the Clarion. SOUTHLAND AFLAME, the banner said. Who had written that? Now he spread the paper on the bar and set his beer on it. Rita's fingers kept working. A fine-looking woman in spite of it all. He read what the reporters had written and the desk had edited, and he tried to match it with what he saw on the screen. He couldn't help being impressed. The stories marched down the columns, one after another; they had names and numbers in them, and Tim Halevy's color stuff, in particular, was very good. *That could have been mine,* he thought, and then: *No, it couldn't.* The words didn't match the drama of the TV, but the photos were good and the names and numbers were probably mostly right. They looked solid in print. He believed them in spite of what he knew about how they must have been gathered last night by young people running around the city with cameras and tape recorders, ignorant and scared and jazzed out of their minds, and shaped into some illusion of coherence by Holcomb and Castle. The people he had abandoned. It was strange to think about: All histories of this time and this place would have to begin with the few half-assed facts the Clarion had put together. The paper had done a job-- Singletarys coming or no.

"You go back to work soon?" Rita asked.

"M-maybe I can c-come back t--. Tonight."

"No, they gonna close early. Gonna be a what-you-call-it. A curfew. Dusk to dawn, they said. You buy me another one?"

So he bought Rita another cognac, and she began to tell him about her life. She came from the hills above the city of Roxas on the island of Mindoro. Her family had a rice farm. Terraces. Stooping all day in the sun. She had wanted to leave as long as she could remember. When she was sixteen and finished with school, she talked to her cousin, a sailor on an inter-island cargo boat, and he let her stow away the next time they went to Manila. She couldn't say goodbye to her parents. That made her sad now, to think of it. But she wasn't sad then, hiding among the big logs--teak and mahogany--in the hold. She had a bed of gunnysacks there and the logs smelled good and the trembling of the steel ship was like her own heart. And the best thing--

Harry Hudson had no reason to listen to her, but he did.

--the best thing was how the sailors treated her. Of course her cousin was there. But a girl, a pretty girl, all alone on a boat--it amazed her now, to think she'd been crazy enough to put herself at such risk. They could have done anything to her. All those men. Fifteen or twenty of them. Young guys, too, and young guys--Filipino *or* American--were usually animals. But no. They were good to her. Brought her food from the galley. Treated her like a little sister. It was the best adventure of her life, though of course she didn't know that then. When she got to Manila, she found a job as a waitress in a barbecue restaurant where American Navy guys sometimes came to eat, and one day a guy came, an older guy, a chief petty officer, with lots of stripes on his sleeve. He joked with her and gave her a big tip, and she told another waitress, "I want to have his baby." The other waitress laughed, but as it turned out--

"You h-have a kid?" Harry Hudson asked.

"A daughter. Same age as Phuong's daughter. You know Phuong? They go to the same school."

"N-never saw her," Harry Hudson said.

"You think I bring her around these bars? No way, man." She kept massaging his shoulders and back, as if rubbing in the scent of her perfume.

--as it turned out, she hadn't been married a year before he died. Some weird kind of skin cancer that suddenly went inside him, and the doctors couldn't stop it. She went to live with his parents in Idaho. Did Harry Hudson know Idaho? Terribly cold. Like his parents. They belonged to some church-- no, not the Mormons, something else--but they didn't treat her like Christians at all. They didn't like her being Catholic. They didn't like her hair or her skin, and especially they didn't like her being so young and pretty. And they didn't like the baby inside her, even though it was *his* baby, too. So strange. They thought she'd married him just to come to the States. A "little mercenary," they called her. They thought she must have been a bar girl. A whore. But maybe they were just so sad about him dying, she thought now. They were *really* old people, and he was their only child. And she didn't speak enough English then to explain things to them. But she knew she had to get the hell out of there, so one day--

"That's too bad," Harry Hudson said, and discovered that he meant it.

--one day she got on a bus and came to Southern California, where lots of other Filipinos were. And she thought to herself: If they want me to be a bar girl, I'll *be* one. Make money that way. And she did. Harry Hudson had been around bars enough to know every bar girl had a sad story. Husbands who had cheated on them or beat them. But her story hadn't been sad; it had been--

"Look at *that,*" cried the middle-aged woman behind the counter. "Here come the Army!"

The TV showed a staggered double column of Humvees rolling down Long Beach Boulevard, not four blocks from the Dragon's Tail.

"Wasn't that this morning?" Rita asked.

"No, man, right now. Right here in Long Beach."

Harry Hudson watched the olive-drab convoy come, bristling with guns and radio antennas. Kids waved at it from under a MARISCOS sign; the soldiers waved back. Meanwhile, Rita's fingers never stopped.

--anyway, what Harry Hudson had to understand, her story had been true love. Maybe because it had ended so soon. No time to go bad. But it *was* true love. Her first husband had held her against his hairy chest--he was very hairy--and made her cry out, *ah! ah! ah!,* it felt so good. Like nobody else. Maybe when she met Walt--

Harry Hudson tried to think of Walt's face, confessing that night. He tried to watch the soldiers. But Rita's hands were wandering now, pinching his nipples, sliding down his flanks.

--when she met Walt, she was trying to make the same thing happen. With another older man. But Harry Hudson knew Walt--

He nodded.

--and there was no way it could work. Maybe that sounded like a romantic thing for her to say--that true love came only once. But to her it was only practical. She supposed Harry Hudson thought Mama Thuy was practical.

He nodded again, his face flushed.

"But that's not true," Rita said. "She's more romantic than me. Nobody gets married three times unless they're romantic. It means you don't give up hope. *I* think it's stupid."

She hadn't said anything about boyfriends or cocaine, or about where her daughter had been living.

"I know what you're thinking," Rita said. "You're like all these other guys. You think you're the answer for my troubles. Like God sent you. You think if I let you into my bed, you'll make me go *ah! ah! ah!* just like he did. Don't you, Harry?" Her fingers had reached his thighs, and now she made a grab for his dick, which, he discovered, was painfully stiff. "See? You all want pussy. All pussy-crazy, even when they're burnin' half of L.A. down."

He was trembling so much that beer slopped on the newspaper. Rita was right. He had thought he would never feel this way again, but for this moment, once more, he believed that nothing in life could be more important than making love to a woman like this, with her smooth face and mocking eyes, her nipples standing out under the burnt-orange cloth. Walt had no choice but to go for her. None at all. He reached out, and she backed away.

"Buy me another one?"

#   #   #   #

Arriving at the Clarion building, Harry Hudson was still shaken. Nothing he had felt since last night--since he had discovered he wanted to live--seemed the right thing to feel. This rush of desire ... not for Kelly or for Thuy but for Rita, whom he didn't even like very much. It made no sense. Nor had he paid proper attention, driving down the Boulevard, to the Army he had once been a detriment to. The 270th MP Company, California National Guard.

#   #   #   #

299

"Langston was in this morning," Joe Zuniga said at the next urinal in the men's room. "Flew up from Cabo soon as he got the news. He was askin' me if I'd heard anything about blacks *stockpiling weapons* before the verdict. I told him no. What's he thinkin'? Gangbangers just *got* guns. They aren't thinkin' about doin' any D-Day thing, invadin' Bixby Knolls. Or Beverly Hills. It all just happened. But he tells me to check on it. Says some of his *associates* heard something. Where? In the locker room at the Virginia Country Club?"

Langston was the publisher, the Man in the Blue Suit. Zuniga looked as if he hadn't slept all night, but even his snort of disgust was cheerful.

Harry Hudson glanced sidelong at him zipping up his pants. No, no desire here. Not a trace. Only at the Dragon's Tail.

Pussy-crazy.

Just cunt-struck, is all.

But then what had happened to him last night? Again?

"W-what h--" Harry Hudson licked his lips. "Hhhappened to R--" This took a stamp of his foot, a whole series of contortions. "R-rick?"

"He had a heart attack." Zuniga looked up, wiping his hands on a paper towel. "You were here, weren't you, amigo? I thought they called in everybody, day off or no."

Zuniga, he saw, had been too busy to notice whether he'd left or not.

"I mean, h-how b--. Bad is he?"

"Not *too* bad. For a heart attack. Man, he just keeled right over there at his terminal. Face looked like ... like a piece of liver, man. Scared the shit out of us. Little Eddie really had to take charge, and he did. I'll give him that. Stepped right in there and ramrodded."

"H-he's OK?"

"Who?"

"Rick."

"He's in the hospital. You know those chest pains he kept gettin'? Well, it finally caught up with him. Not *too* bad, though, they say." Zuniga seemed to try his best to look concerned, but the happy adrenaline was still pouring through him. "Man, what a night." He started to leave, then turned in the doorway. "You still got that story idea of yours? This would be the time, maybe. If there ever *was* a time. Why don't you talk to the man?"

# # # #

Fear seized him as he entered the newsroom, but he saw that the meeting in Springer's office that preceded every night shift was going on longer than usual. Springer and Castle were still in there with the elderly editor-in-chief, the sports and business and features editors and the Man in the Blue Suit. Castle, the youngest, seemed to be doing much of the talking.

Harry Hudson turned on his computer. He couldn't focus on any of the stories waiting to be edited, but he couldn't sit still and do nothing either. So he called directory assistance for the hospital in Baldwin Park.

"Mrs. Way is no longer with us," the nursing supervisor said.

"Y-you mean--"

"She's been released. Gone home."

But when he called Louise's house, he got only beeps and a recording: the number was no longer in service.

He was absorbing this fact--that he might not ever be able to get in touch with Louise again--when he saw Castle spot him through the office's glass wall, and his stomach filled with dread. Then the Man in the Blue Suit stepped between them. *Langston,* Harry Hudson corrected himself. James V. Langston. The publisher wore an actual navy-blue suit and his dark hair was offensively sleek, but again Harry Hudson couldn't quite feel what he wanted to. The silver-dollar-sized patch of tanned scalp on the back of Langston's head made it impossible to ridicule or hate him. It made him mortal, like the rest of them; made his sudden cameraderie with the staff seem a pitiful fawning. Did he regret planning to sell the paper now?

Harry Hudson called Riley Watkins, the police reporter in Red Fork.

"That you, bro? Hey, that's right, you're down in the *middle* of that shit. What's happenin'?"

You know as much about it as I do, Harry Hudson thought, and maybe he said it aloud, too, because Watkins said:

"Yeah, but you're *there*. And I'm stuck up here in Hicksville."

The envy in his voice struck Harry Hudson. It was true: Watkins, if anyone, was the man to be here. He told him what Zuniga had said about the weapons-stockpiling rumor.

Watkins' chuckle buzzed in the receiver, then stopped. "Man, that's rich. I wish they *had* got organized, like the Panthers did. Now they gonna get the worst of both worlds, I'm afraid. Scared people shitless without makin' any use of it. You think George Bush is gonna look more kindly on the brothers and sisters now?"

Harry Hudson grunted.

"Wasn't it Long Beach ... yeah, sure it was. Where that cat, what's his name, Jackson, got himself stopped in traffic and gave the cops lip with a video rollin', see how far they'd overreact, and they shoved him through a plate-glass window? Those ol' boys got off too, I recall."

Harry Hudson remembered hearing about that. Why hadn't he brought it up in his argument with Zuniga? *No worse than the LAPD.* As if that meant anything now.

"Look, bro, I'll call you right back, OK? Got another line here."

Watkins hung up. The meeting was ending. Castle leaned over to Springer and said something, and Springer looked Harry Hudson's way, his mouth grim. *Go talk to the man.* The editor-in-chief blocked the door, waving his hands. His frail, suspendered body was all that held them back. Then he stepped aside, chopping the air for emphasis, and Castle started forward just as Harry Hudson's phone rang. He knew who it was. Not Watkins again--not so soon.

"Harry? My water done broke. You gotta get here *now.*"

"OK. H-hang on."

It was like the moment last night when he had yanked the wheel and turned up off the 710 onto the 91 and headed for Riverside. No thought at all. He stood up without switching off the computer and made for the door. "Harry," Castle said, and Springer shouted, "Hudson," but he didn't pause or look back. He half-ran the length of the hall and clattered down the stairs. No waiting for the elevator. Ana Chavez was climbing up--to tone her calves, stay in shape? A lovely woman, he thought. As lovely as Rita. Harry Hudson stopped short just above her, gasping for breath, his face working, and said, "I'm s-sorry for l--" *Looking at your neck,* he wanted to say. *It's beautiful, but I had no right.* It seemed vitally important to confess this now, because his life was nearly over. "For l--," he tried again. Ana--amused, thank God--looked over her shoulder. Brad Pierce had come up behind her, bent to hear and slipped a hand around her waist. Harry Hudson remembered how they had leaned together up on the roof last night. How happy they had looked. *I'll be damned.* "Way to go," he told Pierce and hurried on. He wanted to bless them both but had no other words except *goodbye.*

He reached the bottom of the stairs at the same instant Castle burst out of the elevator. "Harry." Castle was almost pleading. "Give us a *clue*, Harry. What's going on here? You can't--" Castle trotted after Harry Hudson, grabbed his sleeve, which only infuriated him. "You owe us an explanation, Harry." Harry Hudson jerked his arm away. Even now that he had given up everything--*even now!*--the man wouldn't leave him alone.

Run.

# # # #

"Keep hold of me now, Harry," she said as they went down the stairs to his car.

For a moment, nearly losing her balance, carrying her stomach out in front of her with both hands, she looked like Little Sidney wrestling with that TV set.

Kelly seemed to read his mind. "Peoples got shit all up they apartments there. Stuff they done looted. Hidin' it."

"They n-never had much," Harry Hudson offered.

"Ain't no excuse for *this* shit. Not when I'm havin' a baby."

He wanted to tell her about Junior, about leaving the Clarion, but there was no time. The Nissan sputtered--had he pushed it too hard last night? As he turned the first corner, a jet of flame shot up to the northeast, on Anaheim Street. More Cambodian shops? *First Pol Pot and now this.* At least the eruption of smoke drew the sirens away from where they were going, to St. Mary's on 10th Street. Would his ID work anymore, he wondered, if the cops stopped him and called the paper?

All the while Kelly held herself, fingers spread wide. "Hope I ain't gettin' nothin' on your seat there," she said in a small voice. Sweat shone on her upper lip. "Just bear *with* me now, Harry. You mens don't have to go through this. Ain't *nothin'* nice. You just don't know."

# # # #

Kelly's labor lasted seventeen hours. She was a first-timer and narrow down there, the nurses said, and the baby, though three weeks premature, was big. Her contractions began in earnest at seven Thursday evening, and the baby was born at noon Friday. Harry Hudson, except for a few trips to the vending machines and the men's room, stayed with her the whole time. It was nothing like how it had been when Sally was born. In Garbersville he had had to wait outside, and Deborah had delivered quickly. Here the nurses let him sit beside Kelly's bed and hold her hand and watch the monitor that had been hooked up to her. A green line registered the baby's heartbeat. "Doing fine," they said. "Baby's doing fine."

He had decided to live, on the road to Riverside, and now his life was over. Both these things were true. But as long as he held Kelly's hand they seemed to cancel each other out, to hang in a balance like a supersaturated solution in one of his high school science experiments in Beattie, the solid stuff kept by pressure alone from precipitating out of the water. The pressure now came from her strong athlete's hand, those fingers as long as his. Clutching, relaxing, clutching again. It kept him focused on the peaks and flats of the green line, the hum of the monitor, the muted voices and footsteps in the hall, the squeak of passing gurneys and, above all, the current of Kelly's pain, which ran from her fingers into his--the same fingers that had once felt the current of the baby's life. Each time a contraction came, she squeezed so hard that he winced in sympathy. "Just stay with me, Harry," she said over and over. His neck stiffened and his shoulder ached, but he was glad of *his* pain: It seemed to him that she must have had a reason besides money for not calling a taxi. If you could even *get* a taxi to come to her neighborhood now. She must have wanted him, Harry Hudson, to drive her. That was a fact, and it made him happy. He was the father, maybe, after all. When this thought came too close to where he couldn't let it go, his mind flinched, skittered, and he noticed how, strangely, what she was going through was like making love. Her eyes shut, her mouth opened, her body arched; even her cries were choked back, as if she were still afraid of being heard through a flimsy motel wall. He wanted to tell her not to worry. All the shame was his, he tried to say by way of their fingers, by smiling and wiping the sweat off her forehead with a tissue. But this, too, came too close.

They gave her Demerol--the same blessed stuff they had given him when he was shot. "Baby's doing fine," they chanted. Now she could smile back.

"Drugs," he teased.

"This ain't no drug," Kelly said. "This just *feel* good."

Her hand in his, slippery, was calm now.

"Why don't you go now, Harry? I be OK. Don't you have to get back to work?"

He pretended to check his watch. "N-not much time left, anyway."

"Go on, then."

Harry Hudson shook his head.

"Somethin' ain't right," Kelly said before the drug took her away again. It shamed him that even now she could spare part of her attention for him; and shame, if he let it, would bring back the truth.

"Go get you somethin' to eat, at least," she said. "I'm *serious*. I be OK. For a little while."

He went to get coffee and a candy bar and stretch his legs. The hospital was dark now. He saw nuns disappear around corners and wondered which was the old one who had asked him if he was Catholic. The way their habits flicked and vanished was like an hallucination; even the coffee--as bad as Clarion coffee--couldn't clear his head. He was exhausted. Last night and today had caught up with him all at once. When he sat down beside Kelly again, he seemed to dream without actually falling asleep. He could feel her hand even as he was driving down the 91 again, through Compton, and the pressure of her fingers was also the fury that gripped him, stronger than it had ever since that time in Finnegan's office. He was ready to kill someone. He had a weapon--his father's old deer rifle, which he had driven all the way to Garbersville to get; no other would do. It lay in the back with Junior's TV. Rattling. The pillars of fire burned on either side, and the concrete stretched smooth and empty in front of him. All the time in the world, it seemed, but in truth he was hurrying. His anger would burn out soon, like the flames; and weariness, like the dark, take over. He had to do it quickly, but who should he kill? Finnegan? Castle? The Man in the Blue Suit? Singletary, whom he had never seen? The true villain seemed beyond all of them, hidden. He imagined the rioters on the streets below hunting along with him, likewise baffled and running out of time. The man who had caused all their pain would have an estate so big, so well gated and tripwired with alarms that at best he, Harry Hudson, would get only a glimpse of him from far-off shrubbery, though a lighted window. Tomorrow the man would fly away. Florida. Zurich. The figure in Harry Hudson's sights--if it *was* the right man--would be gone forever once he crossed the room. But other people's bodies interposed, and the gun wavered. Uncleaned for twenty years, would it even shoot? Then somebody grabbed his arm. The police?

"Harry. You *get* 'em now. Them nurses."

"What?"

"Get me that spinal. That ep--"

"--"

It made her laugh, in spite of the pain, that neither one of them could say *epidural*.

"That blocker thing. Please, Harry. Get 'em *now*."

When the nurses had come with an anesthesiologist and the thing had been done and he thought she had dozed off herself, she laughed again.

"You know, you was cussin' when you was asleep there. You hear me, Harry? You a *trip*."

How could he ever have doubted that he loved her? He had been right to stay with her, even though his shoulder hurt worse now, his eyelids were gummy, his mouth was coated with mucus, his armpits and feet stank and his heart felt scalded by the anger of his dream. Harry Hudson vowed not to fall asleep again, and half succeeded. Instead of going back out on the 91, he remained in the hospital room; he just wasn't always sure that the room wasn't in Garbersville and that the suffering woman beside him wasn't Deborah and that he hadn't gotten home in time to see Kevin born after all. He heard janitors swishing mops and watched the green line blip onward steadily and heard the nurses say out of an endless reservoir of calm, "Baby's doing fine," and maybe he did sleep a little, because the next he knew, a tinge of natural light had leaked through the curtains and washed in from the hall, where the janitors were buffing the floor now, and then--it must have been midmorning already, though dawn, he thought, had just come--they put Kelly on a gurney and rolled her into the delivery room and told her to push. Here the outside light shone straight through the window, and Harry Hudson--still allowed to stay with her and hold her hand--felt it searching him out. There was no place to hide. He tried to burrow back into sleep, but the walls were too white, the chrome instruments gleamed; a doctor had come in now, with new nurses-- a big blonde one and a middle-aged Filipina--and their voices were like the splinters of light, sharp as knives, forcing his eyes open.

"Here, make yourself useful," the doctor told him. "Hold her shoulders up there. That's right."

He braced himself against Kelly, his left cheek against the smooth muscles between her shoulder blades, the groove of her spine, and now, whether his eyes were open or closed, Harry Hudson felt safe again for a while: aware of nothing but the heat and sweat of that wonderful skin, the force of her contractions battering him. He remembered crouching below her in the motel in North Long Beach that first time, exploring her pussy with his tongue--the same sense of being at once hidden from her and totally intimate.

He was closer to her now than he had been to anyone since he tried to hide in Sally's limp body, weeping beside the pool in Garbersville. Closer than he had been to Kelly when they made love in that Travel King; closer even than to Eugene and Junior in the car. When she pushed, strong as she was, she nearly broke his neck. *Good,* he thought. He wished it would never end. He would hold her forever. It was only later--when it dawned on him that things had gone on too long already, that the doctor was frustrated and that Kelly's cries were ragged with exhaustion--that the truth, like the light, filtered back to him and he heard the watcher again. Was something wrong with the baby? *Maybe it's better if it does die,* he found himself thinking for a second, horrified at himself, and the watcher said: *Maybe it's better if* you *do. Except that wouldn't solve the problem, would it?*

After that, his safety was gone. Harry Hudson had no strength anymore; it was all he could do to keep Kelly from falling backward. Time passed--five minutes or another hour? Then the doctor's youngish, sallow face, jaw black with five o'clock shadow, bent down intently, and the Filipina nurse uttered what might have been a prayer in Tagalog. It moved Harry Hudson--words he couldn't understand but whose benign meaning seemed clear. Was the wetness on his cheek from Kelly's back or his own tears?

See? he tried to tell the watcher.

You see, dipshit. Now.

A final convulsion, then a cry. The baby's cry. The doctor held it up. "A girl," he announced, grinning. "A *big* girl." Harry Hudson looked up past the rim of Kelly's shoulder and saw a simple groove between the baby's legs, like Sally's. Wet black hair stuck to her head--a surprising amount. Eyes shut tight, skin a dark, mottled violet. Arms and legs jerking. A face bruised by the suction cup they had used to pull her out, so that she resembled nobody--not even any baby--Harry Hudson had ever known.

What struck him, though, was the umbilical cord. It ran from the baby's stomach to the part of Kelly he still couldn't see; it was shiny and grey with darker speckles on it, like a kind of Japanese food--he couldn't remember its name--that Nancy Ishida's mother had brought to school one day for a potluck. Food that looked like rubber, or plastic. It was still uncut, this thick, strong, snakelike cord--still pumping blood into the baby even after she had been born, pumping his poison into her.

307

"Sidney," Kelly said, and she *was* crying; her face was as wet as her back. Harry Hudson, grief-stricken, was slow to realize that she was crying with joy. "She got Sidney's face. Thank you, Jesus."

#　#　#　#

Melissa Marie Crenshaw. Sidney and me had it picked out.

Eight pounds, seven ounces.

They give her to Harry to hold while the afterbirth come out of me and they sewed me up where they done cut me a little to get her out. At least it ain't one of them Caesarians, you hear me?

Harry look at her while he's holdin' her, like he wish it was his baby after all. He look sad. I know he want to know how *I* know it ain't. Shit, I just *know*. I be the mama. Don't ask me why.

Then they give her back to me and I thank 'em all--them nurses and the doctor both--and I scoot her up on my chest and lay back a little. It feel so good to hold her--so good not to be pushin' anymore--that damn if I don't just about fall asleep right then. You understand what I'm sayin'? I'm so tired, it be like fallin' backwards down a long, deep tunnel. Ever part of my body feel like somebody done beat me with an axe-handle. Even my hand that Harry been holdin'--like he squeezed the arthritis right out them fingers.

Melissa Marie. She my heart.

No more, though. I'm *serious*. Women always say that, I know, but I ain't *never* goin' through this again.

#　#　#　#

Konnyaku.

The word for that Japanese food came to Harry Hudson as he rushed after the doctor.

The baby, wrapped in a soft white cloth, had felt solid, even heavy, and an old fear came back to him: that he might drop it. The nurses and the doctor were working on Kelly. Then, out of nowhere, this thing, the placenta, slid out of her into a basin, ribbed with veins like a leaf of purple cabbage, flapping like a fish, only bigger and bloodier. He had never seen one before. *My God*, he thought, *what women have to go through*. Then they took the baby from him and laid it on Kelly's chest while they bent and sewed her up. She looked completely wasted. He patted her shoulder and she didn't even turn her head his way; it was all she could do to hold the baby. And without the baby's weight in his arms, he, too, swayed as if about to fall.

Any minute, they would find out. Wouldn't they? They would test any newborn's blood. Maybe they knew already and were keeping quiet about it while the nurses cleaned up, took the baby to the nursery and wheeled Kelly to the recovery room; while the doctor....

Where had he gone?

Harry Hudson glanced out into the hall, then left at the nurses' station. Nothing. He ran in the other direction, rounded a corner.

There was the doctor, tired too, walking away slowly, splay-footed. He was tall and lanky, a little stooped; only the loose skin of his elbows hinted that he wasn't as young as he seemed.

Konnyaku. That's what the cord had looked like. Pumping death.

The doctor heard him come up from behind, and turned.

"--"

Harry Hudson, out of breath, could only gape. The floor the janitors had polished this morning was already scuffed. The doctor's green scrubs had flecks of blood on them. Like in "M.A.S.H."

"What?"

"The b--" Harry Hudson said. He didn't dare look at the doctor's face. "Is s-she all right?"

"Mrs. Crenshaw's fine," the doctor said. "Took her own sweet time about it, but no complications. None at all. Really. If you'll excuse me--"

The doctor waved his hands. He had taken off the translucent gloves, and he must be going to wash up--a habit so deeply ingrained, he couldn't wait.

"The b-*baby*," Harry Hudson finally gasped.

"What about her? She's fine, too." The doctor smiled--his face couldn't be avoided now. Yellow, horsy teeth, that black-shaven jaw. He must be used to having to reassure husbands and boyfriends. But his hands still fluttered.

"--"

Harry Hudson didn't know how to start. *Is there any way she could have HIV?* he wanted to ask, but he was stuck at *Is,* and even if he got past that, somehow, no way he could hurdle all the other words in between.

HIV, he tried to say straight out, but *H* was the same jinxed breath-sound that began his name.

"What?" the doctor said, frowning now.

"--"

The doctor waited, shrugged, scraped his shoes as if to leave, and how could Harry Hudson follow? He was back in that other hallway, in Garbersville, dissolving by the phone. Able to tell Marge Percy only, *Wait!*

Now he couldn't even say that.

The doctor, turning, displayed a row of pens in his breast pocket, and Harry Hudson, beyond all shame, snatched at one....

"*Hey*, there--"

... pushed up his sleeve, blocked the man's path and wrote on the inside of his left forearm in blue block letters: ANY CHANCE OF AIDS?

The doctor stared at him, took the pen back and deliberately replaced it in his pocket.

It was over. The next thing, Harry Hudson figured, would be a call for security. Then the police.

"The baby?"

Harry Hudson nodded.

It was so strange, when he stole a glance at the doctor at last, to find *him* embarrassed.

"No chance of that." The deep voice was mild, if puzzled. "Mrs. Crenshaw had her tests. Part of our prenatal care program these days, especially for the at-risk population. Your baby's fine, believe me."

"And K--." Harry Hudson licked his lips. "Her?"

"Mrs. Crenshaw?"

Another nod.

"I just told you." Harry Hudson had a sense that the doctor--if his hands hadn't been unwashed--might have reached out and touched his arm where it still stung from the ballpoint. "You aren't the father, are you?" It was as if, after all these hours, the doctor was seeing him for the first time--his slept-in clothes, his bleary eyes. The whiteness of the skin around the blue ink. "I see. Do you mind telling me what your relationship is?"

"J-just a f-friend," Harry Hudson said.

"Well, friend, don't lose any more sleep about *that.*"

"S-sure?"

"Sure."

The doctor left. Harry Hudson, stunned, wandered out the entrance of the hospital, onto its front porch on Atlantic Avenue. He was too full of incredulous relief to think yet about what it meant--that the doctor had assumed he was Kelly's ... lover, without question. Until now. For at least half of those seventeen hours, he, too, had forgotten what colors he and she were. Or even that there *were* colors. It truly hadn't mattered. Only later would he be able to reflect on it, appreciate it: how for all those hours of holding her hand he hadn't even thought of judging Kelly; hadn't, even in his head, taken any goddamned *notes.*

\#   \#   \#   \#

Joy.

Dec. 23, 1864
Dave ran out of the woods swinging his arms and yelling like mad, and pretty soon Eli and myself appeared, whooping and yelling. The 80th Ohio was just going by....

The sun was warm on his shoulders, and the sky would have been blue, except for a silky, greasy film of smoke. A Humvee was parked a block north, at Anaheim Street. Long Beach seemed quieter this afternoon--choppers in the air, but no sirens, no shots. An ambulance with lights flashing but no noise turned into the driveway to the emergency room. Harry Hudson could feel the sun trying to break through the film, like his joy trying to break through the kind of truth the watcher, any minute now, would remind him of. The warmth swelled. It burnished the dirty brass of the sky; it grew in him even though he knew perfectly well it was only dumb luck that he *hadn't* killed Kelly and the baby--and himself. And he had fucked things up all over again by going back to the Low Fox.

\#   \#   \#   \#

Even restroom soap couldn't get all the ink off. Here and there he had punctured the skin--tattooed himself. Rolling down his sleeve, he thought of all the reasons not to do what he was going to do.

He wasn't just evil. Maybe worse, he was a fool.

He had lied to Kelly, over and over, and had no right to ask her.

It wasn't even his baby.

\#   \#   \#   \#

Harry come when I still be in the recovery room--*wiped out,* you know what I'm sayin'? Damn near asleep. I can't even raise my head, hardly, when he talk to me, and I don't understand right off what he tellin' me. How he want to *live* with me, woop-woop-woop. Take care of me and Melissa, and his own kid, too. Who *that* be? Harry never told me he had no kid.

'I can get *some* kind of job,' he tell me, so that mean I guessed right. He must've lost his job at the newspaper.

I tell him I'm sorry about that. I know it had *somethin'* to do with me.

No, no, he says, it would've happened anyway. He lyin'--just tryin' to make me feel better.

'For *real,* Harry,' I tell him.

No, no, he says, me and the baby was more important. He just have to find somethin' else.

'Just one newspaper in Long Beach, far as I know,' I say. 'What else you can do? Teach school? I can't see you gettin' your hands too dirty.'

Harry tell me he ain't jokin', he *serious.* And I know this. I *do.* But *he* ought to know, any woman just had a baby ain't in no condition to talk about heavy shit like this.

Now I have to. So I tell him straight out, as few words as I can: I'm still married to Sidney, and he gettin' out soon, on good behavior. And it wasn't Sidney's fault he got put *in,* this time. And Melissa his baby, no doubt about it. Sidney be gettin' some kind of work placement when he get out of Chino, he tell me. Next month. So I feel like this might be our chance. I'm-a stay with him, I tell Harry. Do my best to make this marriage work, no matter what evil thoughts ol' Eugene be puttin' in my ear. Do that sound ungrateful? I don't mean it to be. Shit, no. 'You saved my ass I don't know *how* many times,' I tell Harry. 'I wouldn't have made it if it wasn't for you. You my friend.'

Harry look at me, but he don't argue. He don't say nothin', and I feel myself slippin' back down that tunnel. Fadin' away.

'Besides,' I tell him, 'you ain't stayin' around long, are you?'

#　#　#　#

Until Kelly said that, Harry Hudson hadn't realized that he was going to leave Long Beach. With or without her. Soon.

# # # #

He found Holcomb's room on an upper floor.

"J-jeez, Rick."

"What the hell are *you* doing here?" Holcomb said. His body seemed thinner under the pale-green blanket, and his forehead was very pale.

"Y-you all right?"

"Fair. Judy was just here. Told me to shut up and take it easy." Harry Hudson started to grin, but an angry undercurrent in Holcomb's voice stopped him. "No bypass. Just bed rest."

"That's good."

"Yeah, I guess. I just wish it was some other time."

Harry Hudson found himself with nothing more to say. He didn't want to get close to Holcomb in this mood, yet he couldn't just turn and leave.

"B-brad," he said finally. "I s-saw him w--" He licked his lips. "With Ana."

"Didn't you know about that?" *A real reporter would.* "She's been living on his boat for the last week. Sooner or later she'll wise up, but until then...." Holcomb tried to shrug, but even that seemed too much of an exertion. More grey threads had appeared in his mustache overnight.

"W-what's wrong with it?" Harry Hudson had liked the idea of their being in love.

Holcomb didn't answer that. "At least she'll clean up his boat for him before she goes. He'll get that out of it." He slowly turned his head away, as if he could see through the window all the way to the marina. "Damn. Story like this, and then the ticker had to go. I guess I'd better go back to Missouri for real. Not much point in hangin' around here. But there *could* have been." His voice rose, and he turned back to Harry Hudson.

"--"

"Things are gonna get uglier. You just watch, you don't think so. You think your California's all about beach parties and feelin' groovy."

Harry Hudson was confused. Had Holcomb forgotten he came from Oregon?

"I mean, look at the history. Fuckin' Indians killed just for sport, women and kids.... Bunch of acorn-eaters, couldn't even fight a real battle. The Chinese exclusion, once they'd got done building' the railroads. L.A. cops standin' out on the Arizona border drivin' the Okies back. Not to mention the zoot suiters, the farm workers...."

"J-japanese," Harry Hudson said.

"There you are. The feelin'-groovy part, that just lasted as long as aerospace did. No more. Now, sooner or later your Latinos are gonna be the majority here and take over the place and maybe give it all back to Mexico. Way to go, *I* say. I'm all for 'em. But until then, the Sick 'n' Tireds are comin' up to bat, top of the ninth. Ugly ain't even the word for it. That's the story I wish we could be coverin' from now on, but even if this hadn't happened to me, there's no way we could."

"Will S-singletary k--" *Keep you from doing it?* he wanted to say.

This only exasperated Holcomb more. "I ain't talkin' about them tellin' us to cover stuff or keep hands off something else. But we won't have the money or the people to do a decent job of it. Same thing, in the end."

Holcomb had half raised himself on his elbows; now he fell back. Judy wouldn't like to see him worked up like this, Harry Hudson thought. But he admired Holcomb for caring so much, even now. If he had seen ghosts of Riker on the freeway and Anderson in the Low Fox, Holcomb was Vance Foster--here at the Clarion after all.

"But what am I tellin' *you* this for? You ran out on us. Twice. Judy said they fired your ass."

"--"

"I'm sorry about that, Harry. I mean, I don't know what was goin' on. Maybe you had a reason." Holcomb's voice rose again. "But, frankly, I don't care *what* it was. Story like this, I'd've dragged myself to work with two broken legs. This is what it's *about*, don't you know? But I guess you don't. What was I thinkin' of? Shit."

It was almost as if Harry Hudson were still the one under the green blanket and Holcomb were still standing in the doorway and saying: *Anybody ever tell you you're a fucking idiot?*

"Yes," Harry Hudson whispered.

#　#　#　#

A single white postcard in his mailbox in Belmont Shore. Two messages on the machine.

The first was from Castle: "I don't even know why I'm doing this. I guess I just hate not knowing the answers. Was there anything we did ... could have done? Any miscommunication? I like to think I'm a pretty up-front kind of supervisor. But I don't suppose you'd tell us, Harry, would you?"

The second, no nonsense, was from Springer: "When we make a mistake around this place, it's a lulu. Well, no more. You're gone. You can pick up your check anytime, as of now."

The card was from the AIDS clinic. Now that it no longer mattered, Harry Hudson didn't even have to look at it to know the results were OK.

# # # #

Time now was moving fast. There was barely enough left for him to go to Payroll, the bank and the post office before they closed.

Payroll, thank God, was on the ground floor, not up near the newsroom, so he didn't have to face anybody he knew.

Altogether, he had about four thousand dollars.

A thousand to Deborah--a couple of months' worth, whether she wanted it or not.

Three thousand cash in an envelope that he took back to the hospital for Kelly.

Quickly, before he could change his mind.

# # # #

Pin a ooh-wee button on me.

Harry come back and give me all this money, and say he mean it: He still want to marry me.

'Set down,' I tell him. 'No need for you to go runnin' off so fast, like last time. You hear me?'

I got Melissa with me now. She nursin'. Little jaws just a-workin'. Took no time at all for her to get *that* right. She got Sidney's forehead--I be sure of that now--and maybe my mouth and chin. Little tiny feet she got on her, and the littlest fingernails you ever saw.

It feel so nice, though I still be all worn out and sore.

Sidney ought to see her. That's the main thing on my mind, even while I'm thankin' Harry. Shit, he give me a envelope so full of money I don't know *where* to put it so it be safe. My purse? I ain't even sure where that is now. Back in that first room, maybe. So I raise my head up real slow so it don't throw Melissa off her rhythm none, and I hide it under my pillow.

Gotta *call* Sidney out there in Chino, soon as I get to a phone. Call Miss Crenshaw, too. And my mama.

Harry look at me. Like if I don't answer him all over again, right now, he gonna disappear again, go *poof.*

Shit.

'Set *down*, Harry,' I tell him. 'Don't think I ain't grateful. I am. For *real.* But you gonna make me nervous, fidgetin' like that. The baby, too.'

So he set down and take hold of my hand again and watch Melissa go at it. I figure it ain't nothin' he ain't seen before.

What can I say?

I remember once he asked me what I meant--sayin' I had to teach this child, once she growed up, how to be black. What's *that* all about? he ask. Bein' black? And I tell him, 'Ain't nothin' I can explain, lessen you know it already. Just *bein',* ' I tell him. 'Learnin' *how* to be, cause this baby ain't got no choice.' And ol' Harry nod, like he do, like he understand me--or he tryin' his best to. But it make me *tired,* you hear what I'm sayin'? Havin' to explain all the time. Harry don't know *what* he askin' to get into, even if he think he do.

So I switch Melissa over from my right titty to my left, so I can see Harry better, and I tell him about the time them polices run Sidney naked.

Harry, I know, don't think the same as me. He say the cops done saved his ass when he got shot. And I guess they did. Shit, when they come and pulled Darnell off me that time, I loved 'em too.

But what happened to Sidney ... Sidney never even told me about it till we been married a while, even after he told me all kinds of other shit--*worse* shit, most people'd think.

This was maybe ten, twelve years ago, and he been runnin' a string of girls out of them motels off of Willow. It was foggy, he said, when they done swooped down and busted him--early mornin', but they was plenty of people drivin' to work, over that Willow Street bridge. Rubberneckin' at him while them polices made him strip off all his clothes, get buck-naked, and run all the way across that bridge. And then run *back.* You understand what I'm sayin'? Sidney wasn't up to no good, then--he'll tell you that now. Ol' One Time had a right to bust him. But makin' him run that bridge ... so cold, he said, that his dick flappin' out in the wind shriveled up into a little goosebump, and them people in the cars and the cops laughin' at him. It was worse than gettin' shot, he told me--and Sidney *been* shot, and cut, too. All that evil catchin' up with him. And I know why he feel that way. Cause they wouldn't never have treated a white man like that, no matter *what* he done. I know this. There just be so much Sidney and me don't have to say.

Harry don't say anything for a while.

Then he say, 'I'm not t--,' stutterin' *real* bad. When he can't say the rest of it, he look away, and then he look at where I hid that money, under the pillow. And I know he tryin' to let me know he wasn't tryin' to buy me.

Shit, all this time he ain't said a *word* about Junior. Not one word.

'I know you ain't, Harry,' I say. 'You my *friend*. Always was. Always will be.'

Melissa, she asleep now. Lyin' right there in between 'em, breathin' in time with my breathin'.

She my heart.

'I l-love you,' Harry say.

And I squeeze his hand and say, 'I love you, too, Harry. In my own special way.'

#   #   #   #

Are you insane?

Deborah was right, he thought, back outside, shivering in the evening breeze. It had been a kind of insanity, feeling so sure that he had AIDS when the chances of it, really, were slim. Harry Hudson had left the blur behind, and already he couldn't quite remember what it had been like to be in it, certain of his guilt and punishment. It was better not to be crazy, he knew, but he couldn't help feeling that he had lost something rather than gained. A clarity, a view of the truth that only craziness made possible.

#   #   #   #

Just before curfew, he drove up to Anaheim Street, past the Chieu Hoi and back down the Boulevard. Fog had come in to mix with the blowing trash in the streets, the flakes of ash in the air. The bar was still OK. *They knew*, he thought with satisfaction. Knew Mama Thuy was a good person and spared the place. It was only right. Guardsmen were patrolling the sidewalks now, and except for the camouflage colors of their uniforms and the change in rifles--M-1s to M-16s--they looked like the Guardsmen in a famous photo of Watts in 1965 that hung in many newspaper offices, like the U.S. ON MOON! page in Finnegan's: the fog and the ruined buildings, the bayonets gleaming in the eerie half-light, the empty, receding street. None of that had changed.

#   #   #   #

What you really *want to do in life,* Finnegan had said.

#   #   #   #

Daddy?

#   #   #   #

Harry Hudson dreamed. He was driving north on Interstate 5 when the answer came to him, shockingly simple: He should go to Nancy Ishida. He turned west on I-580 over Altamont Pass, where rows of windmills twirled on the hills, generating electricity (he had seen wire photos of them), then around the southern lobe of San Francisco Bay. She had been waiting for him all these years--strange that he hadn't known it before. The ease and rightness of it were like the sunlight that made the water of the bay sparkle. And he could see her, even as he drove, in a high house where the same sunlight came in the windows and shone on her long black hair. For her hair was long again, as it had been in the English classroom in Beattie; and wasn't that proof? All he needed to do was get there, to Palo Alto. But on the far shore of the bay he slipped into fog, and wandered through endless streets of long, low buildings that he knew had to be the computer factories of Silicon Valley. Everything became flat and grey. Harry Hudson despaired. He had almost forgotten where he wanted to go when he finally climbed up among expensive homes, eucalyptus trees, thick green hedges. Fog eddied around pastel siding, dripped off the leaves. His car made no sound. The streets here were curved, and he went round and round them, looking at mailboxes. He squinted until his eyes hurt, but her name, he realized, wasn't Ishida anymore; and without her name, how could he ever find her?

# # # #

In the morning, he hauled his mattress out to a dumpster. Back up in the apartment, he saw dustballs drifting on the bare floor, the stacks of old Clarions, and knew he had wasted his money. *The Reef. That would have been plenty good enough for me.*

And when he had packed the Nissan, turned in his keys, collected no deposit because he had given no notice, the morning air in Belmont Shore was so bright and clear that nothing could hide the truth. He might not be gay, but he was ... what? Bisexual? No word seemed to fit. He might still be carrying disease. He had enough money to get to Garbersville, but no more. Even if Owsley would hire him--which was far from certain--he couldn't imagine working for a newspaper again. Nor could a middle-aged cripple get a lumber-mill job, even if the mills were still open. Harry Hudson had no other trade. He couldn't cook, fix cars, sell appliances, drive a bulldozer. And where would he live? All the Clarion's travel section showed of the area now were four-star resorts along the Deschutes River and gated golf-course communities. Maybe there was no longer a cabin in the woods, an ex-company house, a cheap room over a grocery store where he could hole up to be near his son. Maybe things had changed too much. Maybe people, even back home, would see him as screwy, even dangerous. *And would they be wrong?* he thought. *Would I be doing the kid any good?*

Fear expanded in him, as pure and sharp as the seaside light, so that his mind winced and he thought of other things--proof of his strangeness in their way, but not so threatening.

In a year and a half in Greater L.A., Harry Hudson had never been to Disneyland. Or Knott's Berry Farm or Universal Studios. Or the Getty Museum. He hadn't seen the Dodgers or the Angels play. He hadn't been to Malibu or Beverly Hills or Catalina. He hadn't walked on the sidewalk stars in Hollywood or heard a Philharmonic concert, or even the Long Beach Civic Light Opera. The one time in his life he'd had money to burn, he'd spent it all in dives.

It was almost funny.

The fear was so great that it would have stopped him right then; but, as when he'd first come back from Vietnam, he had no other plan.

# # # #

Ransom wrote in an appendix to his diary:

My good old friend Battese, I regret to say, I have never seen or heard of since he last visited me in the Marine Hospital at Savannah.... I don't know of a man in the world I would rather see today than him, and I hope some day when I have got rich out of this book (if that time should ever come) to go to Minnesota and look him up.

Surely, Harry Hudson thought, *he must have tried.*

#   #   #   #

Mama Thuy was throwing a bucketful of water on the sidewalk in front of the Anaheim Street door when Harry Hudson came up. "Look like it's over, you think?" she said, squinting past him in the direction of Compton and L.A. "No more smoke."

"Maybe so. I'm g-glad they l--" He licked his lips. "L-left *you* alone."

"Oh, no, Harry. They get me. They get me *good*. You see. Come on in. I got coffee on. You want some chili?"

Stanley and Black Jimmy and two young Guardsmen were sitting at the bar. "See?" Mama Thuy said, pointing. And although they had been talking about it all morning, everyone looked up again.

A hole--just like the one Ron's truck had once made in the wall--had been punched through the ceiling, littering the pool table with chips of plaster. The upper floor had been unrented for months, she explained. "Somebody get up there, Harry. Maybe the Chinaman leave a door open. Maybe they break a window. I don't know. They jump down here, break the cash register open, take all my money. Then they leave."

Harry Hudson sat down. He gazed at the mug of coffee she poured as if he'd never seen any before.

"I don't know anything till I open up today. I think everything still locked up, still OK.... And wine. No beer. They just want wine. Heavy duty, huh?"

Swede came through the curtain with a package of trash bags. He had backed *his* truck into the alley next to the bar. Once they swept up all the wreckage, he could haul it away.

"Look like you been rode hard there, Harry," Black Jimmy said. "Got *too much* news for a change."

Jimmy had looked uncertain, almost scared, sticking his head in just after she opened; she had never seen him that way. Not that she blamed *him*. She was glad to see that Stanley and Harry were treating him the same as usual--though the Guardsmen kept their distance.

"N-no more," Harry Hudson said. "Leavin' town."

He put his mug down and looked at Mama Thuy strangely--not so different from the way Jimmy had looked.

"Where you goin', Harry?" she said. "You never told *me*."

"Oregon. W-where I come from." He wouldn't quite meet her eyes. "Got a s--" He licked his lips. "Boy there to raise."

"I didn't know you had a kid, Harry," Stanley said.

See? I always knew you married, Mama Thuy wanted to say, but Harry didn't seem in the mood to joke. Swede was raising a cloud of plaster dust; the Guardsmen--barely drinking age--ordered more beer. She already had too much on her mind these days. Like Billy. The rioting had frightened him--maybe he would settle down now, go to school. And Ron and Loan! Ron had knocked Loan up, the night of the party. Crazy! The very first time they did it. Now they were living together. Good thing he was taking care of her and the boy, Mama Thuy supposed. But having Ron as a brother-in-law would just be too weird.

Like if he can't get me, he get my sister. And he look at me like he say it's my fault. What kind of bullshit is that?

"T-three years old," Harry Hudson said.

"Well, we miss you, Harry. No lie. Just wish we have time to give *you* a party. Have some chili, anyway."

"C-can I use your phone?"

"Local call?"

"S-st. Mary's."

"OK. Go ahead." Maybe somebody he knew had gotten hurt, Mama Thuy thought as she ladled chili into a bowl and set it on the counter.

"Them young bucks just went *off*," Jimmy was saying. "Ain't got nothin' against you, Mom."

"They think I'm Korean," Mama Thuy said. "Shoot some black girl in a store, think she steal something."

"No way, babe. You gotta stop thinkin' *that* way."

"What I supposed to think? Look at *that*," she said, and they all gazed at the ceiling again.

321

What to do now? Her friend Kim Lee in San Diego was thinking of selling out there and moving to Vegas. *Not the Strip*, she'd told Mama Thuy. *Too expensive there. But maybe North Las Vegas, up by Nellis Air Force Base. Still lots of military there.*

Maybe Kim was right. Vegas was the one city that was still booming. Mama Thuy liked her own idea better--Hawaii. But that was *beaucoup* expensive too, people told her.

And who would buy the Chieu Hoi Saloon now, after it had been in a war zone? Scared the living shit out of her family. What had they left Vietnam for, to have America turn out like this? This morning her father had tried to keep her home--told her to wait another week, at least, to reopen the bar. Not that he was so worried about *her*, she thought, but he didn't want to be left alone.

If I don't open up, what do we do for money? she had told him. *You think the bank will let us take a vacation? The beer companies? Edison?*

Now look at the place. Six customers, counting Swede. Who didn't count.

"What I don't understand," Stanley was saying in his new, wavery, old-man's voice, "is how come they burned down their own neighborhood. Makes no sense to me."

Jimmy glanced up, as if he might answer, then changed his mind. The two Guardsmen--blond, skinny kids who might have been twins, with hair cut as short as Marines'--didn't say anything either.

Harry came back from the phone. "Gone home already," he said, shaking his head.

"Eat your chili, Harry," Mama Thuy said as the Budweiser truck pulled up outside.

Rick came in with his clipboard of invoices, cheerful as ever. "Workin' hard or hardly workin'?" he said--stealing her line.

"Workin' *hard*," she said, showing him the hole in the ceiling, the plastic bags Swede was getting ready to load.

"Holy shit," Rick said. She got him coffee and told him all about it before he went back out for the dolly. Five cases of Bud, two of Bud Light. Not like the old days.

"You aren't in a hurry, are you?" she told him. "Stick around. Take a load off."

What was Harry doing? He had shoved up his left sleeve, absently rubbed the inside of his forearm, then pulled the sleeve back down and buttoned it. Now he caught her watching him; he looked shamefaced. But still he stared, and Mama Thuy began to understand: *He wants his hug.* More than that. He thought he deserved something special, just because he was leaving and wouldn't bother her again. A lot of men, leaving town over the years, had looked at her the same way.

Just in one year, Mama Thuy thought. Pop dead. Charlene gone to Vegas with Les, going to have *some* kind of baby. Randy pissed. Ron smirking, claiming he'd quit drinking--beer, anyway--and just wanted to stay home with Loan. Rita gone. Walt hardly ever around anymore. Wade, maybe, finally giving up.

Things went along the same for a long time and then, suddenly, they changed.

Now Harry. Maybe it *was* time to move on.

"Hey, somebody play music," she said. "Too quiet around here."

The taller of the Guardsmen got up, leaving the two rifles with his partner, their helmets on the bar. He bent over the jukebox and scanned the play list. "Nothin' but oldies here," he complained. "Country."

"Got rap, too, man," Black Jimmy said, but the Guardsman gave him a sour look and went back to his stool.

"Nothin' *wrong* with rap," Jimmy said loudly, more like himself. "It's just music. Ain't got nothin' to do with that--" He was gobbling his words again, cheeks puffed out-- "all that shit happened out there."

"Yeah. Cop-killin' music," the Guardsman said.

He was afraid of Jimmy, Mama Thuy could tell--the heavy shoulders, the big scarred fists--but he had his gun. *Oh, my God,* she thought. Her nerves weren't so good anymore. Swede had gone out to the truck with the last of the bags. Fortunately, Rick put up a hand and said, "Not here, guys. This is a peaceful place, OK? Let it ride," and they did. She smiled at Rick, opened a fresh beer for Stanley.

"Anything on TV?" Rick said. "How about the Dodgers? Aren't they playin' back East? Oughta be some early game."

The old TV set--why hadn't the burglars taken *that?*--was high in a corner over the pool table. Mama Thuy had to stand on a chair to turn it on. It was Saturday. May already. Time for ball games, all right. But the first channel that came on was the news. Right here in Long Beach, a few blocks away, the cameras showed police searching apartment buildings, finding looted stuff

323

piled inside, some of it in unopened boxes, dragging it out onto the balconies while the people who lived there shook their fists and yelled that the stuff was theirs. Mama Thuy paused with her hand on the dial. She didn't know whether to laugh or feel sorry for them. Imagine living in places so small there was no room to hide anything. Pitiful. Her family had lived like that in Vietnam ... and even after she had switched to the baseball game, she didn't see the players spaced out on their green carpet so much as Billy and a couple of his no-good friends crouching beside the safe in her bedroom two weeks ago and jerking up when she burst in on them, having forgotten her keys and driven straight back home from the Chieu Hoi: the safe with her $16,000 gold bar in it. What were they trying to do? Pick the lock? No way they could break into it otherwise, she thought. They tried to laugh it off and slunk out, but the thought of it--Billy robbing his own mother!--haunted her still. Climbing down from the chair, she saw his round, smug face, heard his excuses. Had the rioting scared him *enough?* She glanced at the gold statue of the Buddha and prayed silently that it had. Then she went to the storeroom for rags and cleanser, and had her back turned when she heard the shorter Guardsman--who had said hardly a word until now--tell Harry Hudson shyly: "She's a beautiful lady, isn't she?"

"You got *that* right," Harry said without stuttering at all.

#   #   #   #

Sitting on his stool, eating chili, he had been filled with gratitude for Mama Thuy, for all these women who held him at arm's length for his own good, and theirs. Mama Thuy was a friend. It was all she had ever wanted to be. Was it her fault that he hadn't ever been able to talk to her easily; that he couldn't imagine living with her, as he could with Kelly? Even now, when her hair was undone, her face smudged and her plain grey sweatsuit grimy from sweeping, all he wanted to do was grab her and bury his face between those breasts. He had tried to apologize, then signal his regret to her silently with his eyes. After that, there had seemed nothing left to do but go.

Outside, though, in the sun, Harry Hudson felt his fear swirl up again like a gust of scraps from the gutter. *I should go back in,* he thought for an instant. *Where all the people are.* Only the faintest inertia kept him moving down the sidewalk past the Budweiser truck. The orange paint job on the Nissan had already faded. *I should have traded it in when I had the chance.* The interior of the car was hot enough to make him sweat, and he rolled down the driver's-side window, which balked in its groove. The engine stumbled, caught. *Too late now.* He put his left arm out on the ledge, but that made his shoulder ache. The armrest on the door, his lap--no place else seemed comfortable either. Yet he had seven or eight hundred miles to go. The windshield was dirty-- speckled with bugs from that night going back and forth on the 91. He might stop in Bakersfield or somewhere and get it washed. But as he turned out into Anaheim Street and tried to imagine what he would be doing when he finally got to Garbersville, he very nearly drew a blank.

I ought to get a dog, Harry Hudson thought.

# # # #

Mama Thuy was fishing beers for Rick and Jimmy out of the cooler, popping the caps, sliding them over the bar when she noticed that Harry Hudson was gone. "Where he go?" she asked.

"Who?" Rick said.

"Harry."

Jimmy, swallowing chili, shrugged in the direction of the door.

"Why he do *that?*" Mama Thuy was indignant. That wasn't any kind of proper goodbye. Why did men have to act that way? She could have given him his hug--he just had to wait. She pushed through the curtain, a bar rag still in her hand. "Harry?"

She was just in time to see the orange Nissan, suitcases piled behind the hatchback window, turn north onto Long Beach Boulevard. The engine sputtered; the tailpipe puffed thick, black smoke. Her years with Wade had taught her what that meant. *Burning oil.* Would Harry make it all the way to Oregon, or wherever he was going? Mama Thuy realized that she couldn't do anything to help him. He was on his own now. She waved the rag over her head, flapping it back and forth, but she wasn't sure he saw.

About the Author

Michael Harris grew up in Dunsmuir, Calif., served as an information officer with the 1st Air Cavalry Divison in Vietnam and received master's degrees from Harvard and the University of Iowa Writers' Workshop. For 30 years, he has worked on West Coast newspapers, including the Los Angeles Times, for which he is a regular book reviewer. He lives in Long Beach with his wife and son. This is his first novel.

Printed in the United States
21042LVS00005B/46-153